Inside

Notting
Hill

This 2nd edition published May 2007
by Umbrella Books (1st edition 2001)
13 Blenheim Crescent London W11 2EE
www.umbrellabooks.com

Editorial

Supplementary listings (2001 edition) by Andrew Baldwin,
Caroline Bretherton, Fernanda Hanson, Leigh Diamond,
Jessica Morris, Katrina Phillips, Peter Ridley and Polly Thomas.

Pictures

Inside: 22, 164, 230, 233, 234 illustrations and photos courtesy of RBK&C;
23 Stephen Wiltshire; 20, 39, 106, 108, 138, 175, 177 Lucia Reed; 39,45,
215, 254 Michael Woods; 56, 216, 244, 279 Charlie Phillips; 95, 143
(barge), 145 Chris Wade-Evans; 134, 312 courtesy Wilf Walker; 137 Leon
Morris; 139 Charlie Murphy; 143 (Trellick) Peter Ridley; 163 courtesy NH
Methodist church; 167, 293, 297 Tony Sleep; 179 from Sandy Sanderson
collection; 209 Keith Morris © Redfern's; 213 UrbanImage.tv Adrian Boot;

Other photos throughout text Sarah Anderson

Front cover photo Sarah Anderson

Back cover photos

UrbanImage.tv Adrian Boot (Aswad) & Sarah Anderson

First map based on a map supplied by Royal Borough
of Kensington & Chelsea Council

© Crown Copyright and/or database right. All rights reserved.
Licence number 100047185.

Design Georgia Vaux

Printed in the UK by CPI Bookmarque, Croydon, CR0 4TD

ISBN 978-0-9542624-1-9

Inside

Notting
Hill

Miranda Davies and Sarah Anderson
with Annabel Hendry

Umbrella Books
London 2007

CONTENTS

Foreword

PART 1
THE GUIDE

1 Notting Hill Gate 11

In and around
Hillgate Village 12

Along the Gate 13

Kensington Park Road 17

Ladbroke Grove south 21

Listings 27

2 Portobello Road 41

Pembridge Road to Elgin Crescent 42

Elgin Crescent to the Westway 45

Beyond the Westway 57

Listings 59

3 Westbourne Park &
Westbourne Grove 93

Westbourne Park Road 94

All Saints Road 94

In and around Powis Square 97

Westbourne Grove 102

Listings 110

4 Ladbroke Grove, Golborne Road &
Kensal Green Cemetery 131

In and around the Grove 131

Golborne Road 136

Kensal Green Cemetery 143

Listings 149

5 Notting Dale &
Holland Park 161

Lancaster Road 161

Latimer Road via the 165
St Quintin's Estate

Bramley Road and Frestonia 166

The Parish of St Clement 168

and St James

In and around Treadgold Street 170

Walmer Road to Pottery Lane 172

Clarendon Cross and Princedale Road 176

Holland Park Avenue
and the Park 180

Aubrey Road, Campden Hill Square &

Aubrey Walk 182

Listings 187

Directory 201

PART 2
MUSIC & FILM

Getting it Straight in Notting Hill Gate
Tom Vague 206

Growing up with Carnival
Polly Thomas 216

Notting Hill in Film
Adam Moon and Harry Fogg 222

PART 3
HISTORY

A Brief History of Notting Hill **230**
Annabel Hendry

PART 4
WRITINGS 1767–2007

Days in the Life of Lady
Mary Coke 1767-69 256

Clarendon Road circa 1883
Arthur Machen 259

The Napoleon of Notting Hill
GK Chesterton 262

All Done from Memory
Osbert Lancaster 264

Notting Hill in Wartime
Vere Hodgson 266

Sunny Napoli
Colin MacInnes 270

Anna Kavan
Virginia Ironside 273

Michael X:
Views from the Grove
John Michell 277

Carnival Poem
Michael Horovitz 281

The Magical City
Jonathan Raban 282

Rocking under the Westway
Michael Moorcock 287

The Free Independent
Republic of Frestonia
Nicholas Albery 291

Working at North Kensington Law Centre
Elisa Segrave 297

Metropolitan Myth
Glenys Roberts 301

Londoners
Nicholas Shakespeare 305

My London
Mustapha Matura 309

A Taste of the Action
Duncan Fallowell 312

The Real Notting Hill
Tim Lott 315

A Pashmina Incident
Justine Hardy 319

But then Notting Hill
Nikki Gemmell 321

Fresh & Wild Rendezvous
Rachel Johnson 328

Sources and Further Reading **332**
Copyright Acknowledgements **334**
Index **336**

Acknowledgements

Together with the previous edition, the making of this book has relied on the goodwill and support of many different people. Among those who so kindly shared their knowledge, contacts and Notting Hill stories, special thanks go to: Eddie Adams, Richard Adams, Liz Anderson, Clarice Armatrading, Ruth Atkins, Liz Bartlett, Joe Boyd, Kevin Brownlow, Tim Burke, Henry Clive, Siobhan Cross, Andrew Fergusson-Cuninghame, Bridget Davies, Rich Deakin, Iain Finlayson, Paul Fogelman, Jeremy Franks, Mary Gaine, Mark Girouard, Gertrude Goode, Andrew Hewson, Michael Horovitz, Angus Hyland, Pansy Jeffrey, Marie Jelley, Jane John, Anthony Juckes, Carol Kane, Keith at Smile, Linda Kelly, Isabel Kenrick, Father Mark Langham, John Michell, Michael Moorcock, Clive & Matthew Phillip, Charlie Phillips, Katrina Phillips, Colin Prescod, Susana Raby, Lucia Reed, Jean Ross-Russell, David Stern, Henry Vivian-Neal, Liz Walker, Wilf Walker, Beelie Williams and Robert Winder.

Thanks also to the helpful staff of the London Library and Kensington & Chelsea Libraries, especially Richard Marshall in the Kensington Local Studies section and those working at the Ladbroke Grove and Pembridge Road branches.

Finally, a huge thank you to Annabel Hendry, who has not only contributed an excellent history and written with equal authority on several of Notting Hill's churches, but also provided support, humour and a much needed critical eye all along the way.

About the authors

Miranda Davies is an editor, writer and translator. She has lived in Notting Hill since 1973.

Sarah Anderson is the founder of the Travel Bookshop, which she started in 1979. She moved to Notting Hill in 1981 and has lived and worked in the area ever since.

FOREWORD

We are delighted to be publishing this fully revised edition of *Inside Notting Hill*. Our new guide includes detailed information on recent developments, updated listings, an extra Music & Film section and more writings. We've also reorganised the listings, which we hope makes the book easier to use.

Much has changed in Notting Hill since we published the first edition in 2001. Escalating rents, the extension of the Congestion Charge and the prospect of a gigantic shopping mall at White City have given local residents and business people plenty to worry about. Speculators and high-street chains have tightened their hold. Yet the spirit of the place lives on: Carnival has resisted attempts take it off the streets and remains as vibrant as ever; the market is still the area's hub; the Electric Cinema is flourishing; the Portobello Film Festival is gaining international recognition; and Notting Dale is finally on the map.

Inside Notting Hill is a practical guide that reflects the rich history and diversity of this elusive neighbourhood. We hope you find it useful, illuminating and, above all, an enjoyable read.

Miranda Davies and **Sarah Anderson**
May 2007

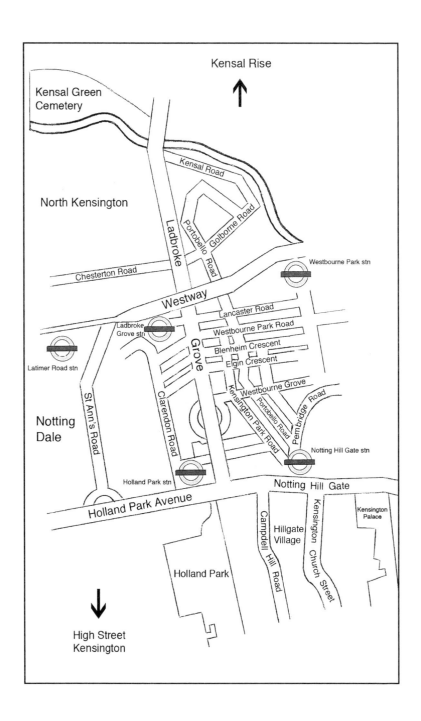

THE GUIDE

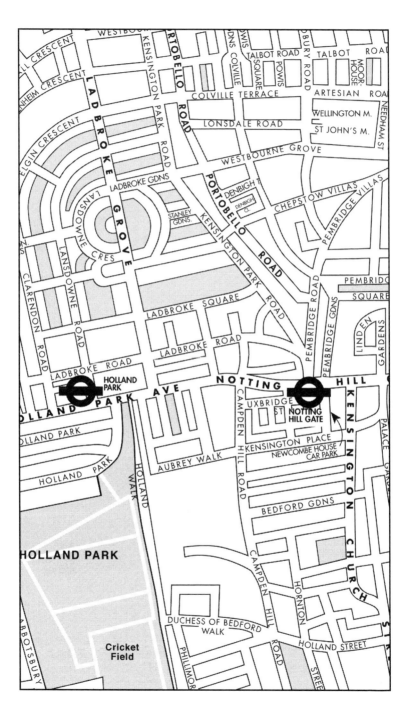

1. NOTTING HILL GATE

Tube: Notting Hill Gate
Highlights: Farmers' Market, Clarke's, Notting Hill Coronet, Video City, Gate Theatre, Notting Hill Arts Club

The appeal of Notting Hill Gate is not immediately obvious. Much of this once quaint Victorian high street was destroyed and redeveloped from the late 1950s to the early 1960s, and the immediate impression is of a busy thoroughfare choked with traffic and bordered by feature-less concrete. In fact the Gate still has its points of interest, although most of the attractions lie in the streets which lead off from it, among the small, pastel-coloured houses of Hillgate Village to the south, and north along Pembridge and Kensington Park Roads – two of the main routes into the heart of Notting Hill.

Notting Hill Tollgate looking east c. 1835

ORIGINS OF NOTTING HILL GATE

'The Gate' has long been an important thoroughfare, from Roman times, when it formed part of the Great West Road running from London to Silchester (near Basingstoke in Hampshire), up to the 18th century, when the allure of its proximity to glamorous Kensington Palace was boosted by the spread of roadside inns. But even in these early days, the rough sometimes rubbed uneasily against the smooth, and the road became a notorious target for aggressive highway robberies, as well as thefts from the gardens, orchards and poultry-yards of the still rural Notting Hill.

It was the attempt to control highway theft through the Turnpike Acts of 1769 that gave the Gate its name. The idea was for tolls to be issued to road users, controlled by tollgates, with the funds vested in trustees made responsible for lighting, protection and upkeep. One of three such gates was located at the junction that now marks the exit from the underground station. The tollgates were never popular, provoking decades of public protest and campaigns that finally put an end to the system in 1864 – a foretaste of the kind of hard-fought community action for which the area is still renowned.

In and around Hillgate Village

Bordered by Kensington Church Street and Campden Hill Road, Hillgate Village has two pretty pubs – the Hillgate and the Uxbridge Arms, both miraculously festooned with flowers all year round – and some good, reasonably priced restaurants. Otherwise, apart from the odd media office, this network of pretty flat-fronted terraced houses is strictly residential. Teresa Waugh offers an apt description in her novel *The Gossips* (1995):

Annie's house, tucked away in HillgateVillage, behind Notting Hill tube station, was in a quiet street of brightly painted, early nineteenth-century workmen's cottages, a bit jerry-built, but somehow resistant to the passage of time despite insidious rising damp and somewhat insecure foundations. Sometimes, when she walked down her street, it reminded her of nothing so much as the set for a musical comedy.Whenever a house changed hands, it was always a matter of concern what colour the newcomers would paint it. There were a few nasty years when number fourteen, on which Annie looked out, was painted a hideous shade of purple, but it had lately been changed to a more tasteful mushroom with an olive-green door. Annie's house was always painted grey and her door was always white, but, whilst never wishing to choose them herself, she rejoiced in the cheerful blues and pinks and yellows of her neighbours.

Hillgate Village is also the home of Fox, one of the best and certainly the grooviest primary schools in West London. If you're around on the third Saturday in June, it's worth visiting Fox for its annual Summer Fair. As well as games stalls, bric-à-brac and a superior auction, there is a mouth-watering barbecue by local chefs Alastair Little and Rowley Leigh. While Little and his wife Sharon run an Italian delicatessen in Westbourne Grove, Leigh's inspired dishes lie behind the long-lasting success of Kensington Place, just around the corner in Kensington Church Street.

Leading out of Notting Hill, the top end of Church Street has more recommended restaurants, plus a scattering of specialist antique shops. In Newcombe House car park, at the back of Kensington Place restaurant, there is a Saturday morning market where farmers and other producers sell an impressive range of fruit, vegetables, meat, cheeses, bread and pastries.

Along the Gate

Facing west outside the underground station, two very different cinemas, The Gate and the Notting Hill Coronet, offer a choice between arthouse films and more mainstream productions. Only once have their programmes coincided, in May 1999, when both featured *Notting Hill*. Being the location where Hugh Grant gazes wistfully at Julia Roberts on screen, the Coronet clearly won hands down. With its silver dome and wedding-cake façade, this former music hall theatre stands as a delightfully frivolous antidote to the unremarkable buildings all around.

THE GATE CINEMA

This small independent cinema started life as the Electric Palace and was converted from a restaurant in 1911. Nothing much to look at on the outside, you'll be surprised by the fabulous plasterwork walls and ceiling which helped establish architect William Hancock as an early cinema specialist.

THE NOTTING HILL CORONET

A Grade II-listed building, the Coronet was originally built as an opera house in 1898 to a design by WGR Sprague for the theatre impresario Edward George Sanders. Inside, the theatre boasted six gilt boxes upholstered in red plush, seating for 1,100 and a 'crush bar' where the foyer is today. Of its initial splendour only the distinctive dome and the ornate auditorium of Screen One, with its huge proscenium arch, curved balcony and red velvet seats, remain. During the 18 years or so before it was converted into a cinema, many stars graced the stage, among them Henry Irving, Sarah Bernhardt, Lillie Langtry and Mrs Patrick Campbell.

Less well known from that time is the theatre's resident ghost, as described in Richard Jones's **Walking Haunted London** (1999):

One Christmas in the early 1900s a cashier was caught stealing from the till and, confronted by the manager, ran up to the Gods and threw herself from the balcony. Thereafter, when staff meetings were held in the upper section of the cinema her ghost caused so much disturbance that such meetings were transferred to offices lower down in the building. Footsteps have often been heard climbing the stairs that lead to the Gods, and on one occasion pots of paint were moved by an unseen hand from a room that was awaiting decoration. Staff have more or less come to accept the inconvenience that their resident spectre causes. The ghost is most active in Christmas week, the anniversary of the cashier's suicide.

The Coronet has come under threat from other powerful sources, including an ominous bid from McDonalds, but the cinema's future now seems secure. Since 2004, it has been under the bizarre ownership of the Kensington Temple (p18), but any fears of it becoming a vehicle for the church appear unfounded. It continues to show popular and occasional arthouse films, with the added attraction of half-price tickets on Tuesdays

Between the cinemas, in among the rash of estate agents, No. 99 used to be a showcase for the Notting Hill Improvements Group. Formed by the sponsors of the award-winning Turquoise Island in Westbourne Grove, over the last 20 years or so the group has been behind many, if not all, of the street's improvements, from new litter bins and pedestrian railings to tree planting, the building of a 'Haiku' sculpture garden (on the corner of the Czech Embassy at No. 25 Kensington Palace Gardens) and Barney McMahon's multicoloured mural (alongside the alley just east of Marks & Spencer). Further plans include two solar-powered neon haloes (at the intersection of Pembridge Road and Kensington Park Road) and fresh colour schemes for the drab Sixties façades, one of which (above Boots) could become the capital's first hairy building, accomplished by planting the walls with thousands of fibre-optic cables that would glow and quiver like a 'vertical meadow'. For up-to-date information, visit the project's website at www.nhig.co.uk.

At the end of this block, past the excellent Video City and a couple of pizza restaurants, is the junction with Campden Hill Road, popular with drivers for its quick access to Kensington High Street. It's hard to imagine but Campden Hill was once the site of a reservoir, replaced in the 1850s by the grey brick water tower famously championed by the writer GK Chesterton in *The Napoleon of Notting Hill* (see Writings, p 262). The reservoir was covered over to become tennis courts, still very much in use but, to the anguish of conservationists, obsolescence led to the tower's demolition in 1970. Thirty years on, the Campden Hill Residents' Association lost another battle, this time against the building of 19 houses and 48 apartments by property company St

James Homes. As well as the loss of trees and open space, this entailed the destruction of the Victorian pumping station and part of the old tennis club. The novelist and critic Ford Madox Ford (1873–1939), author of *The Good Soldier* and *Parade's End*, lived at No. 80.

Directly across from the junction with Campden Hill, Marks & Spencer is a dull substitute for Pharmacy, the wackily themed bar and restaurant that briefly put this site on the map. The brainchild of artist Damien Hirst and PR man Matthew Freud, Pharmacy opened on New Year's Eve 1997 and became instantly famous as the showpiece for Damien Hirst's pharmaceutical installations and the gastronomy of Marco Pierre White. Driven by the venture's celebrity status, people came in droves to perch on aspirin-topped stools and to sip 'strong pre-scriptions' among walls of glass cases stacked with the neatly arranged contents of a chemist's shop. Upstairs in the restaurant the pharmaceu-tical theme continued, dominated by a giant molecule allegedly repre-senting Hirst's own DNA. But the food was erratic and success was short-lived. By the turn of the millennium the business had been sold off and Pharmacy, together with Outpatients, its adjoining deli-catessen, closed three years later, returning only briefly to the limelight when the entire contents were sold at auction for a cool £11 million.

Heading back east, the north side of Notting Hill Gate takes you past the concrete high-rise apartment block of Campden Hill Towers and across Pembridge Road and Pembridge Gardens, home of two good hotels. The next block is the only terrace to have escaped Sixties rede-velopment and leads to the entrance into Linden Gardens, once pro-tected from the unruly high street by ornamental gates. Known in Victorian times as Linden Grove, this oval-shaped cul-de-sac stands on one of the first of James Ladbroke's plots ever to be built upon (see History, p 230). The largest of these early two-storey houses was Linden Lodge, designed in 1826 by Thomas Allason, who also lived there for a time. Contemporary records describe the house as having two acres of gardens, including a lake, stables and a gardener's cottage, all of which were demolished within less than 50 years for the making of the railway. Other prominent residents of Linden Gardens were the artist Thomas Creswick (No. 42), William Mulready, who designed the first penny postage envelope depicting Britannia, and Ossie Clark, one of the most influential fashion designers of the 1960s and 70s.

After the turning into Linden Gardens, the old high street quickly becomes the Bayswater Road, leaving Notting Hill to skirt Kensington Gardens and its main children's attraction – the Princess of Wales Memorial Playground (see Listings, p 33).

THE GATE THEATRE

As you climb the narrow stairs up to the box office, it may be hard to imagine that this tiny chamber theatre has been a springboard for so many talented actors, writers, translators and directors, the most famous perhaps being Stephen Daldry, film and stage director of **Billy Elliot**. Since starting up in 1979, the theatre has achieved international recognition and a loyal audience for its productions of classical and contemporary work from overseas. It has helped to revive interest in major dramatists, including Euripides, Goldoni and Strindberg, as well as discovering lesser known names through its partnership with the International Centre for Drama in Europe (an online database of European plays translated since 2000). Boosted by Arts Council funding since 2003, the theatre is run by a small number of paid staff, plus a team of volunteers, all of whom are full of enthusiasm for their work. Often they'll stay on to help facilitate post-show discussions where members of the audience can meet the artists, either in the auditorium or in the Prince Albert pub downstairs. In London, where you can easily pay a small fortune to see mediocre productions in the West End, the Gate is a gem.

Kensington Park Road

Back at the underground station, turning north near the site of the old tollgate and the courageously innovative Gate Theatre, Pembridge Road forks, offering alternative paths into the hub of Notting Hill. Visitors tend to be drawn to the right, down the cramped commercial strip of Pembridge Road that leads directly to the top of Portobello. Since the market doesn't start till further down, it's pleasanter to follow the wide and far more peaceful Kensington Park Road, with its two immediate landmarks: Kensington Temple and the green Cabbies' Shelter.

Theatre and ballet fans may also be interested in the stone-built Mercury Theatre around the corner in Ladbroke Road. Having started life in 1851 as a Congregational Sunday School, the building was transformed into a theatre in 1931 by the playwright Ashley Dukes, husband of Marie Rambert. Within five years Dukes had gained national recognition for the Mercury by staging the first ever production of TS Eliot's *Murder in the Cathedral*. Around this time it also became the headquarters of Marie Rambert's School of Russian Dancing, precursor to the world-famous Ballet Rambert. It was here that Madame Rambert ran her Ballet Club company, showcased in a series of Sunday evening performances that featured such budding stars as Robert Helpmann and Frederick Ashton. The Mercury was also a musical venue of some importance. Several of Benjamin Britten's early works were performed here, attended by Britten, and both Vaughan Williams and Holst conducted. Other performers included Iris Lemare and Anne Macnaghten, who gave a series of highly regarded concerts in the early to mid-Thirties. No longer a theatre, the building retains a ballet connection as the premises used by the West London School of Dance.

KENSINGTON TEMPLE

This hugely popular evangelical church on the corner of Kensington Park Road was built in 1846 as an Independent Presbyterian Chapel with an adjoining Sunday School, which later became the Mercury Theatre (see above). Originally Horbury Chapel, it was renamed the Kensington Temple (KT to its contemporary followers) in 1935, when it was used by George Jeffreys, founder of the Elim Pentecostal movement, which now has over 500 congregations throughout the UK. The current minister, Colin Dye, draws a packed international congregation every Sunday, with a live TV link nearby to cater for the overflow at the 11 o'clock service. In an era when less than nine per cent of London's seven million population attends church of any kind, this has to be quite an achievement. For more information, telephone 020 7908 1700.

THE CABBIES' SHELTER

In the middle of Kensington Park Road, beside the Temple, stands a bright green hut serving tea and sandwiches to taxi drivers from the adjoining rank. This is one of London's last remaining cabbies' shelters still in use. As described in Andrew Duncan's **Walking London** (1997), the origin of these refreshment rooms for cab drivers dates back to 1874, when Captain George Armstrong, managing editor of the *Globe* newspaper, was looking for a hansom cab in bad weather. On reaching the stand, he found plenty of vehicles but not a driver in sight. He was determined to get a ride and eventually tracked the men down to a nearby pub, where they were enjoying a drink out of the way of the weather. Convinced that they'd be better off hiding from the elements in a less tempting environment – many cabbies were notorious drunkards – Armstrong came up with the idea of building special shelters, complete with tables, benches and cooking facilities, so that they could take a break and enjoy reasonably priced refreshment protected from the influences of alcohol. By the following year, the Cabmen's Shelter Fund had been formed and 61 shelters had been built by 1914. The hut in the middle of Kensington Park Road is one of only 13 left, five of which can be found in Kensington & Chelsea. It was restored in 1988.

Carrying on, Kensington Park Road will soon take you alongside Ladbroke Square. Covering seven acres, this is the largest of Notting Hill's communal gardens and, like all of them, officially only open to resident keyholders, who pay an annual fee for the privilege.

THE LADBROKE ASSOCIATION

Ladbroke Square lies at the heart of the Ladbroke Conservation Area designated by the Ladbroke Association, a membership organisation of local residents devoted to promoting and encouraging high standards of architecture and town planning within the area's boundaries. (These are bounded by Holland Park Avenue to the south, Clarendon Road to the west, Blenheim Crescent and Elgin Crescent to the north and Portobello Road and Pembridge Road to the east.) Among the association's stated aims are the stimulation of 'public interest in and care for the beauty, history and character of the neighbourhood' and 'the preservation, development and improvement of features of general public amenity and interest'. Present concerns include excessive or inadequate tree pruning, mobile phone and TV aerials, the preservation of shop fronts and the re-designation of Portobello Road as a local shopping area (see also Friends of Portobello, p 251). The association, which publishes a comprehensive newsletter, is always looking to extend its membership; for information on the group's work and how to join, see www.ladbrokeassociation.org.

Alan Hollinghurst captures the square's quality of seclusion in his award-winning novel *The Line of Beauty* (2004):

The communal gardens were as much a part of Nick's romance of London as the house itself: big as the central park of some old European city, but private, and densely hedged on three sides with holly and shrubbery behind high Victorian railings. There were one or two places, in the surrounding streets, where someone who wasn't a keyholder could see through to a glade among the planes and tall horse chestnuts — across which perhaps a couple would saunter or an old lady wait for her even slower dog. And sometimes in these summer evenings, with thrush and blackbird song among the leaves, Nick would glimpse a boy walking past on the outside and feel a surprising envy of him, though it was hard to know how a smile would be received, coming from the inside. There were hidden places,

Cherry blossom in Stanley Crescent

even on the inside, the path that curled, as if to a discreet convenience, to the gardeners' hut behind a larch-lap fence; the enclosure with the sandpit and the children's slide, where genuine uniformed nannies still met and gossiped with a faint air of truancy; and at the far end the tennis courts, whose overlapping rhythms of serves and rallies and calls lent a calming reminder of other people's exertions to the August dusk.

After crossing Chepstow Villas the road slopes downhill, past St Peter's Church, which stands opposite the turning for Stanley Gardens. White and cream stucco mansions line this elegant street, which has the added cachet of housing the Portobello Hotel, discreetly situated halfway down on the left. The hotel has always been associated with musicians, models and film stars, from Mick Jagger to Kate Moss and Johnny Depp. Less is known about its appeal to literary figures, such as the late Jean Rhys, who enjoyed several winter holidays here towards the end of her life. In the memoir *Stet* (2000), Diana Athill, her editor and friend, recalls visiting Rhys at the Portobello, which she soon realised provided a lively antidote to the writer's bungalow home in a sleepy West Country village:

The first time I visited Jean there I was greeted at the reception desk by a faun-like being in a pink T-shirt trimmed with swansdown which had little zipped slits over each breast, both of them unzipped so that his nipples peeped out. This seemed such a far cry from Cheriton Fitzpaine that I wondered whether Jean, much as she longed for a change, would find it upsetting; but she loved it, was fussed over charmingly by both the manageress and the saucy faun, and would have been happy to spend the rest of her days at the Portobello.

Continuing downhill, Kensington Park Road leads to the intersection with Westbourne Grove. Even if you can't afford the prices (or feel nostalgic for the raucous cry of parrots outside L'Artiste Assoiffé, the charmingly eccentric restaurant which occupied this site for nearly 30 years) it's worth entering Paul Smith's corner emporium for the impeccable style of everything, from natty tailored suits to clockwork toys and other hand-picked curios, not to mention the beautifully restored interior.

Further on down, past a line of narrow villas with pretty wrought-iron balconies, you arrive at the nucleus of restaurants and shops which, along with greedy landlords and the rise of Westbourne Grove, have been a key factor in Notting Hill's recent history.

If eating and shopping aren't immediate priorities, instead of heading down to the crossing with Westbourne Grove, a left turn opposite Chepstow Villas will take you along the lofty residential splendour of Kensington Park Gardens. The scientist Sir William Crookes (1832–1919), who made significant contributions to both physics and chemistry, lived at No.7, which was the first London house ever to receive electricity. Around the same period, the real-life 'Darling' family, immortalised in JM Barrie's *Peter Pan*, occupied No.31. They were actually Arthur and Sylvia Llewelyn Davies, and sons George, Jack and Peter. Sylvia's brother was George du Maurier, the original Captain Hook and father of writer Daphne.

Ladbroke Grove south

Kensington Park Gardens leads to the upmarket end of Ladbroke Grove and St John's Church on the brow of the hill. Erected in 1845, on a site that once offered a grandstand view of the Hippodrome Racecourse, this was the first Kensington church to be built north of

THE HIPPODROME RACECOURSE

During the building slump of the late 1820s and 30s (see History, p 235) the developer John Whyte attempted to establish a huge Hippodrome racecourse on the crown of Notting Hill. The project stands out as not only one of the most spectacular failures in the history of development in Notting Hill, but also provides an early example of just how effective community action can be.

Bounded by Portobello Lane to the east and on the west side by the 'public way' from Notting Barns, the racecourse covered nearly 200 acres, with an entrance at Notting Hill Gate. As well as three courses, this vast racing emporium was to provide all manner of recreational activities: a saddling paddock for 75 horses; training and riding facilities; ponies and donkeys for the use of children and invalids; and provisions for 'revels and amusements', including archery and cricket on non-racing days.

There was local opposition to the enterprise from the start. The opening of the Hippodrome in 1837 was marred by a huge invasion of protesting locals, boosted by a healthy injection of spirited support from the Potteries. Local feeling ran very high because the racecourse closed off a footpath that crossed the hill from north to south. For decades this path had been used by local inhabitants anxious to bypass Pottery Lane (long nicknamed 'cut-throat lane'), which intersected the Potteries of Notting Dale. The racecourse was replanned and the contentious footpath reopened but to no avail: the track was on heavy clay and the jockeys hated it. Riff-raff continued to lower the tone and as Barbara Denny put it in **Notting Hill and Holland Park Past** (1993), 'a growth of sleazy betting booths and gin shops added to the deterioration'. The course never caught the imagination of the racing public. It failed, and closed in 1841.

The Hippodrome racecourse 1837–1841

THE CHURCH OF ST JOHN THE EVANGELIST

This church remains the centrepiece of the Ladbroke Estate. Constructed of ragstone in the 'Early English Gothic' style, it is a typical example of grandiose 19th-century Anglican architecture. Its grand scale attracted criticism, and even **The Ecclesiologist** thought it looked too much like a cathedral. The architects John Hargrave Stevens and George Alexander designed a basic cruciform shape with a central tower and broach spire, the top 26 feet of which was rebuilt in 1957 after damage during the Second World War. Of the remaining stained glass, notable are the Charles Eamer Kempe windows at the east end, and a little rose window in the west gable and small panel in the south aisle, both by William Warrington. Added in 1890, the panelling, reredos and sedilia are of terracotta in a neo-Perpendicular style. Art Nouveau-influenced sculptures of the Crucifixion, the Revelation and the Commission are by Emmeline Halse, as, possibly, are standing angels on either side of the reredos.

St John's has an active congregation that organises several popular events, among them a carol service for children and the May Fair, a fundraising event that draws people from all over the area. The church also has a Sacred Space Gallery showing contemporary sacred art (www.sacredspacegallery.com). For general information, telephone 020 7727 4262

St John's Church

THE CHURCH OF ST PETER

This elegant and welcoming church was designed by Thomas Allom, the architect responsible for many of Notting Hill's large Italianate houses. It was one of the last Church of England churches to be built in London in the classical style after 1837 and is the focal point for the view looking east down Stanley Gardens, its design in harmony with Allom's overall scheme for the estate. The stucco façade has a pediment and entablature on six Corinthian columns, and the central square clock-tower is topped by an octagonal copper-roofed belfry. Inside, immediately to the right is the tiny baptistry (soon to be converted into a space for quiet prayer). Mounted on its south wall is a charming Florentine low-relief plaque of the Madonna and Child, a replica of a relief by Antonio Rossellino (1427–c.1479). The gallery fronts are decorated with floral swags, winged **putti** and panels containing the Keys of St Peter. The mosaic version of Leonardo da Vinci's **Last Supper** in the apse was executed in 1880. The marble altar in the 16th-century Florentine manner and the marble dado behind it were carved in Italy. The 1889 pulpit is of alabaster and marble and the font has bronze acanthus-leaf rings. The recently restored stained-glass windows are a joy; the earliest, on the top of the balcony northside, date from the foundation of the church and are very finely crafted. The splendid organ was made by JW Walker and Sons, the Rolls-Royce of organ makers, in 1908.

St Peter's was consecrated on 7 January 1857 and assigned a district chapelry in the same year, but its most interesting history is far more recent. When the merger with St John's took place in 1983, St Peter's had been virtually abandoned by its congregation and the building left to deteriorate. It took the inspiration of one curate, Bruce Collins, to rescue it from ruin. Collins came to the parish in 1984 with a vision of St Peter's once again filled with worshippers. His vision was so powerful that 10 members of the congregation of St John's came over and every Wednesday night for nine months prayed on their knees for the revival of this crumbling church. Their numbers gradually increased and on Whit Sunday 1986 the doors were finally reopened to a congregation of 30, all aged under 35. St Peter's has since grown into a vibrant Christian community, so much so that in 2003 it was able to re-establish itself as a parish independent from St John's and these days in a normal week more than 1,000 people come through its doors. Funds are currently being raised for a refurbishment scheme.

In addition to regular services, the church is used as a venue for concerts and plays, as well as a flourishing crèche. The church hall in Portobello Road houses a nursery school and is hired out for a plethora of activities from drama classes to Narcotics Anonymous meetings. For more information, telephone 020 7792 8227.

Holland Park Avenue. Until 2003, it shared its parish with the less gloomy-looking St Peter's in Kensington Park Road.

Two less salubrious landmarks lie a three-minute walk in either direction. To the south, at No. 7 Ladbroke Grove, stood the house where the distinguished biographer James Pope-Hennessy was murdered on 25 January 1974. At the time, he was working on a biography of Oscar Wilde. Apparently, the house was already haunted by two ghosts: according to Pope-Hennessy, 'a little man who was always smiling and friendly' used to hang about on the stairs where a local ostler who looked after horses for a nearby inn had been stabbed; a second more evil presence roamed the upper floors. Pope-Hennessy even called in a Catholic priest to exorcise them. The house was subsequently demolished and replaced by a mock-Georgian building that is occupied today by a charity, the Tudor Trust. One can't help wondering if the biographer now haunts the site on which he was choked with his own hairnet by an 'associate' of the dodgy young men with whom he liked to mix.

Back up the hill is the location of another untimely death. Bear right past the front of St John's into Lansdowne Crescent and you come to Nos. 21–22, the Samarkand Hotel, where, on 17 September 1970, electric guitar virtuoso Jimi Hendrix died from a drug misadventure in the basement rented by his girlfriend, Monika Danneneden. US writer and agony aunt Irma Kurtz was living next door at the time, where she once sheltered two of the era's leading young revolutionaries in her attic. She describes their brief stay in *Dear London* (1997):

Hans Werner Henze, the German composer whom I had interviewed in Italy, came over for tea when he was visiting London, and he left behind two handsome young protégés who needed a place to stay for a while. One of them was Dani Cohn-Bendit who I hear is a plump green politico in Germany these days. At the time 'Dani the Red' was admired everywhere in the world where young people were planning revolution; he was not all that well known in London. The other boy was the German firebrand, Rudi Dutschke. Rudi was intelligent and fierce, and apparently he meant every word he said for he did not make old bones. My goodness, could those boys talk! With the volume of Paris in the old days, though what they had to say was more cynical than our arty palaver, and they were much more apprised of evil than café philosophers at the end of the Fifties and into the early Sixties. While the boys talked and talked, and ate, smoked, drank and talked, and slept in my upstairs study, men in raincoats watched the house from the front seats of a series of cars that would have looked ordinary enough except they had too many aerials. The presence of 'fuzz' didn't suit Lansdowne Crescent, especially when they got out to stretch their legs and marched around like extras on the set of Oliver. *From my window I watched one of them grind a cigarette out on his gloved hand, rather than drop it on the pavement. Policemen were a lot more ill at ease in the crescent than the revolutionaries who seemed perfectly at home and were in no great hurry to leave.*

Across Lansdowne Crescent, on the opposite side of Ladbroke Grove, several large Victorian houses stand set back from the road. One of these, No. 46, has a strong Russian connection and until 2005 provided the meeting place for the Pushkin Club, now based in Bloomsbury. Founded in 1955 by eminent Russian émigrés, the club hosts a regular programme of readings and lectures in both Russian and English, concentrating on Russian poetry from Pushkin's time to the present.

Carrying on north along Ladbroke Grove, a few minutes' walk down the hill leads you past the junctions with Lansdowne Road and Elgin and Blenheim Crescents, with their rows of pretty coloured houses backing onto communal gardens. Several well-known figures have lived in Elgin Crescent, including the artist Osbert Lancaster at No. 79 (see *All Done from Memory*, p 264), actor Laurence Olivier at No. 86, the writers Katherine Mansfield and John Middleton Murry at No. 95 and Jawaharlal Nehru, the first prime minister of India, at No. 60. The Russian artist Lazar Berson started the Ben Uri art gallery (which is now in St John's Wood) at 67 Blenheim Crescent.

After these turnings the buildings in Ladbroke Grove become noticeably shabbier and the atmosphere distinctly less rarefied. Maybe it is only here, in and around the streets close to Portobello Road, that you can still detect the true beating pulse of Notting Hill.

PLACES TO STAY

The Abbey Court

20 Pembridge Gardens W2

020 7221 7518/www.abbeycourthotel.co.uk

Comfortable Victorian townhouse hotel, conveniently placed in a quiet street midway between Notting Hill Gate and the top of Portobello Road. Each of the 22 rooms (all with jacuzzi) is individually designed using antique furniture to create a traditional, cosy feel. Rates from £99 for a standard single to £195 for a deluxe double; continental breakfast included. Like almost every hotel in this book, it's interesting to note that it has altered its prices little since the first edition came out in 2001.

The Lennox Hotel

34 Pembridge Gardens W2

0870 850 3317/www.thelennox.com

Replacing the less formal Pembridge Court that used to occupy this site, the Lennox (transferred from Knightsbridge) goes in for cool, minimalist décor. Facilities include in-room beauty treatments, complimentary newspapers and discounted dance classes in the adjoining dance school in the basement. Room rates from £100 for a small single to £220 for a junior suite. Breakfast not included.

The Portobello Hotel

22 Stanley Gardens W11

020 7727 2777

www.portobello-hotel.co.uk

Discreetly situated in an elegant white Victorian terrace, the Portobello's interior is serene yet delightfully eccentric. Potted palms, travellers' curios and squishy sofas scattered with richly embroidered cushions set the scene downstairs, while each of the 24 rooms has its own style, from colonial to Japanese or Moroccan. Facilities include a restaurant and 24-hour bar where, in 1990, you might have been served by Damon Albarn before Blur hit the big time and he could afford to buy his own house around the corner. For almost 40 years, the Portobello has attracted an impressive list of music celebrities, actors and writers among its guests. A single will set you back £135, a double £180 but this can rise to £300 for a 'Special Room', all with 'complimentary' continental breakfast.

EATING & DRINKING

CAFÉS & TAKEAWAYS

Arancina
19 Pembridge Road W11
020 7221 7776
Daily 7.30am–11.30pm

This charming, welcoming place with a takeaway at street level and a small dining area upstairs is clearly devoted to its orange theme, including the brightly coloured 'Topolino' (the old Fiat 500) which fills the window. The reason for the café's name and décor is quintessentially Italian: their speciality is *arancine*, a traditional Sicilian dish: small risotto balls, stuffed with a variety of ingredients, shaped to the size of small oranges (*arancine*) and fried. Focaccia and pizza are included on the menu, plus a daily selection of hearty, often Sicilian, *tavola calda* dishes, with prices starting at £3.

Costas Fish Restaurant
18 Hillgate Street W8
020 7727 4310
Tues–Sat 12 noon–2.30pm & 5.30–10.30pm

This much-lauded takeaway has been serving consistently high-quality fish and chips for longer than this writer can remember. The small licensed restaurant at the back offers a slightly extended menu including kalamari, Greek salads, hummus, pastries and retsina. Reasonably priced.

Rotisserie Jules
133a Notting Hill Gate W11
020 7221 3331/www.rotisseriejules.com
Mon–Sat 12 noon–11.30pm;
Sun 12 noon–10.30pm. Delivery Mon–Sat
12 noon–3pm, 6pm–10.30pm (last order);
Sun 12 noon–10.30pm

Jules specialises in free-range chicken, flame-roasted at the entrance of this plain restaurant, more popular as a takeaway. A whole chicken costs around £12, and there is a limited choice of side dishes – roasted vegetables, gratin dauphinois, fries and salads. Delivery free on orders over £10.

FOOD SHOPS

Clarke's Shop & Café
124 Kensington Church Street W8
020 7221 7196/7229 2190
www.sallyclarke.com
Mon–Fri 8am–8pm; Sat 9am–4pm

Next door to Sally Clarke's excellent restaurant, this tiny shop sells a mouth-watering selection of cheeses, homemade preserves, quiches, cakes and pastries, but it's mainly the freshly baked breads that have earned it such a high reputation. The café at the back serves pastries, sweet and savoury tarts and delicious coffee and organic teas, plus light meals (12.30–2pm).

The Farmers' Market
Newcombe House car park
Kensington Place W8
www.lfm.org.uk
Saturdays only 9am–1pm

This enticing market sells fruit and vegetables, meat, cheese, fish, flowers and a dazzling array of home-baked bread and cakes – all direct from the producers. Best value are the free-range eggs (especially if you pick out your own 'misshapes'), plants and freshly picked flowers. Also highly recommended are the seasonal fruit, juices and pots of compote sold by David Deme and family from their orchards near Chegworth in Kent (www.chegworthvalley.com).

The Fish Shop at Kensington Place
201 Kensington Church Street W8
020 7243 6626
Tues–Fri 9am–7pm;
Sat 9am–5pm

Linked to the restaurant next door, this shop sells high-quality fresh fish as well as ready-cooked dishes such as monkfish stew and bream with spring onions and ginger.

PUBS & BARS

The Champion
1 Bayswater Road W2
020 7243 9531
Mon–Sat 12 noon–11pm;
Sun 12 noon–10.30pm

Notting Hill's only overtly gay venue – pretty much men only – has always had a mixed reputation (see Duncan Fallowell, p 312).

The Churchill Arms
119 Kensington Church Street W8
020 7792 1246
Food: Mon–Sat 12 noon–10pm;
Sun 12 noon–9.30pm

The Thai food served in the conservatory of this hugely popular pub is way above average and reasonably priced. Also serves real beer.

The Hillgate
24 Hillgate Street W8
020 7727 8543
Food: Mon–Fri 12 noon–3pm, 6pm–9pm;
Sat 12 noon–8pm; Sun 12 noon–7pm

It's tucked away on a corner of the Village, but you can't miss this unpretentious pub because of the hanging baskets that decorate the walls all year round. Recommended for lunch as an excellent antidote to the traffic and bustle of Notting Hill Gate.

The Ladbroke Arms
54 Ladbroke Road W11
020 7727 6648
Food: Sun–Fri 12 noon–2.30pm;
Sat 12.30pm–3pm; daily 7pm–9.45pm

Popular owner-managed pub conveniently situated opposite the police station, should any customers get out of order. Outside there's a pleasant seating area and inside is reminiscent of a lounge bar in an out-of-town hotel. A short menu of the day offers straightforward, well-prepared dishes for lunch and dinner at reasonable prices. It gets busy in the evenings and tables can only be reserved up to 7.30pm.

The Uxbridge Arms
13 Uxbridge Street W8
020 7727 7326
Mon–Sat 11am–11pm;
Sun 12 noon–10.30pm

This traditional English pub has changed very little over the years.

Real ales, a cosy ambience, no music and a prime position behind the Gate draw a mixed crowd of cinema-goers and regular locals, some of whom feel clearly at home. Standard pub fare is served at lunchtime, only snacks in the evening.

The Windsor Castle
114 Campden Hill Road W8
020 7243 9551
Mon–Sat 12 noon–11.30pm;
Sun 12 noon–11pm

Close your eyes and ears to the traffic outside and this could be an old pub in the country. Don't be surprised to find a few hunting and fishing types here too. Standard pub food is supplemented by treats such as oysters in season, and there's a pretty back garden for summer drinking.

RESTAURANTS

Clarke's
122 Kensington Church Street W8
020 7229 2190
www.sallyclarke.com
Brunch Sat only 11am–2pm;
lunch Mon–Fri 12.30–2pm;
dinner Tues–Sat 7–10pm

Almost as soon as it opened in the

1980s, Sally Clarke's restaurant, with its legendary no-choice menu, became a Notting Hill institution. Renowned for high standards, Clarke's sources only first-class seasonal ingredients including specialist meat and fish supplies, and salads and vegetables from small organic growers, largely in the south of England. As a recent concession three choices are currently featured on the lunch and dinner menus: winter starters might include smoked haddock, leek and potato 'chowder' or salad of blood oranges with shaved fennel, pea leaves and *pecorino sardo*; pan-roasted fillet of Cornish plaice with mustard and lemon mayonnaise and chips, and chargrilled calf's liver with onion glaze and sweet potato mash might figure among the mains. Desserts are equally delicious. Not surprisingly, this level of quality doesn't come cheap but it's worth it.

Geales

2 Farmer Street W8
020 7727 7528/www.geales.co.uk
Mon–Sat 12 noon–3pm & 6–11pm;
Sun evenings only 6–10.30pm

Opened in 1939, this must surely be the oldest restaurant in Notting Hill. Traditional fish and

chips have always been the mainstay, but the major refurbishment instigated by new owners Mark Fuller and Garry Hollihead includes a brand-new menu. Fish will still be a strong feature but prices remain to be seen. A takeaway and home delivery service are also planned.

Kensington Place

201–205 Kensington Church Street W8
020 7727 3184/www.egami.co.uk
Mon–Sat 12 noon–3.30pm & 6.30–11.45pm;
Sun 12 noon–3.30pm & 6.30–10.15pm

You'll almost certainly need to book for a table at this hugely successful glass-fronted restaurant renowned for its din, for people-spotting and above all for excellent food. Over nearly two decades head chef Rowley Leigh built up an impressive reputation with his dexterous handling of seasonal ingredients using original combinations – for instance, the autumn menu might include a starter of pappardelle with girolles, followed by grilled partridge with hazelnut piccata. Leigh has moved on. Let's hope that his successor will maintain (or even surpass) the standard of cooking that has been a feature of Kensington Place for so long.

Malabar
27 Uxbridge Street W8
020 7727 8800
Mon–Sat 12 noon–2.30pm & 6.30–11pm
(Sun 10.30pm)

A sophisticated but friendly Indian restaurant that never lets you down – except when you can't get a table. Sizzling hot and well-spiced food. Average prices.

New Culture Revolution
157–59 Notting Hill Gate W11
020 7313 9688
Daily 12 noon–11pm

The home cooking of northern China provides the inspiration for this canteen-style restaurant, serving lightly cooked food, with an emphasis on freshly made dumplings and noodles and plenty of choice for vegetarians. The prices – from around £5 for a main course – make it good value, and you leave feeling healthy too. It feels a bit stranded at the end of the Gate, but this is the longest-surviving restaurant on this site, so the formula must be working.

Pizza Express
137 Notting Hill Gate W11
020 7229 6000
Daily 11.30am– midnight

We're not a fan of chains but this branch of Pizza Express is friendly and reliable and achieves the difficult feat of appealing to parents and children. Pizzas are thin and crispy; salads feature increasingly on the menu but they need to go easy on the dressing. Eat in or take away from around £6.

The Twelfth House
35 Pembridge Road W11
020 7727 9620/www.twelfth-house.co.uk
Mon–Fri 12 noon–11pm;
Sat & Sun 10am–11pm with brunch
10am–4pm; Happy Hour for cocktails
Mon–Thurs 6–8pm

This astrology bar/café/restaurant offers everything from coffee to a three-course meal, plus a 15-minute chart reading for a fiver. Much of the food is traditional English, but there are quite a few vegetarian options and lighter snacks are available in the downstairs bar. Customers are given restaurant cards inscribed with flattering notes related to their birth sign and you can phone in advance for a full chart reading (£30). Food and drink prices are reasonable, with a set menu for two courses or three courses.

For food also see **Pubs & bars**

ENTERTAINMENT

CHILDREN

The Princess of Wales Memorial Playground
Kensington Gardens W2
020 7298 2000
Daily summer 10am–6.45pm; winter 10am–3.45pm. Children must be accompanied by an adult (one adult per five children) and adults can only enter in the company of a child except between 9.30 and 10am.

Much thought went into the planning of this enclosed play area and it shows. Conceived as a lasting tribute to Princess Diana, it was built on the site of an existing playground just north of her home in Kensington Palace. The designers have used the park's long association with another local resident, JM Barrie, author of *Peter Pan*, to link different areas of play. These include a beach cove complete with a magnificently rigged pirate ship, a tree house encampment, and a movement and musical garden where children can create melodic tunes on various interactive instruments, from wooden xylophones to metal dance chimes, or swivel and spin on turning discs and saucers. Near the cove there's even a ticking crocodile half submerged in a rivulet of water. Care has been taken to appeal to a range of ages up to 12, with special attention to the needs of children with disabilities. There's also a café, toilets and baby-changing facilities.

Extensive planting and landscaping using only natural materials ensure that the playground blends harmoniously into the surrounding parkland.

A more energetic antidote to the consumer pressures of Notting Hill is the circular Memorial Walk, which can be picked up from here. This second tribute to Diana covers seven miles across Kensington Gardens and three more parks – Hyde Park, Green Park and St James's. The way is charted by 90 plaques set into the ground by sculptor Alec Peever.

FILM & THEATRE

The Gate Cinema
87 Notting Hill Gate W8
020 7727 4043
www.picturehouses.co.uk

The Gate shows some of the more arty or cultish current releases in rapid turnover, as well as Sunday afternoon one-off screenings of classics such as *Les Enfants du Paradis, Casablanca* and *The Passenger*, chosen in conjunction with Video City (p 35). Membership entitles you to screenings and discounted tickets.

The Gate Theatre
11 Pembridge Road W11
Box office 020 7229 0706/Disabled access and administration 020 722 5387
www.gatetheatre.co.uk

Over the 28 years since its inception at these same tiny premises above the Prince Albert, the Gate Theatre (no relation to the cinema) has built up a strong reputation for staging high-quality, innovative productions, mainly from abroad. The front door, to the left of the pub, is easily spotted by the notice-board with posters for the current season of plays. On Monday nights you pay whatever you can afford; otherwise tickets cost up to £15. Book early to avoid disappointment.

The Notting Hill Coronet
103 Notting Hill Gate W8
020 7727 6705

With two screens, the Coronet shows popular current releases in an irreverent atmosphere left over from its former status as the last smoking cinema in London.

MUSIC & CLUBBING

The Gate
87 Notting Hill Gate W11
020 7727 9007
www.gaterestaurant.co.uk
Daily 6pm–1.30am

DJs play seven nights a week, mixing a diverse selection of music; the pace picks up at 10.30pm and the party continues until 1.30am. Check website for resident DJ listings and their genre of music, ranging from Brazilian drum & bass to funky house and R&B.

The Notting Hill Arts Club
21 Notting Hill Gate W11
020 7460 4459
www.nottinghillartsclub.com
Mon–Sat 7pm–2am; Sun 7pm–midnight

Expect to find a good range of ages and people at this basement club, which, though undoubtedly trendy, somehow manages to represent the more genuine aspects of Notting Hill. The music varies from live jazz to Brazilian funk, punk rock and French disco – the small dance floor soon fills up, whatever the style. Comfortable leather armchairs and sofas are provided for the less actively inclined. Arrive early, especially on Friday and Saturday, when the queues extend quite a way along the Gate. Thursday hip-hop, R&B and funk night YOYO (You're Only Young Once) is also very popular. Entrance fee around £7 – free before 8pm.

STAYING IN

Video City
117 Notting Hill Gate W11
020 7221 7029
Mon–Thurs 9am–10pm; Fri & Sat 9am–10.30pm; Sun 11am–10pm

With its huge selection, including hundreds of foreign and arthouse films, managed by unfailingly friendly, efficient and knowledge-able staff, Video City easily lives up to the claim of being the best small video shop in London. Prices – to rent or buy – are reasonable too. An added bonus is the presence of **Midpoint Services** (Mon–Sat 9am–6pm), selling TVs, DVDs, hi-fis and other equipment. Ever helpful, Gary behind the counter will install your new purchases as part of the deal.

HEALTH, BEAUTY & FITNESS

Bladerunners
158 Notting Hill Gate W11
020 7229 2255
Mon, Tues & Fri 10am–7pm;
Wed & Thurs 10am–8.30pm;
Sat 10am–6pm; Sun 10am–5pm

Bladerunners specialises in extensions and treatments for African-type hair, but caters for everyone, with a range of treatments such as 'glossing', 'body boosting' and 'deluxe reconstruction' (for limp hair), as well as the usual cut and blow-dry.

Calders Pharmacy
55–57 Notting Hill Gate W11
020 7727 3185
Mon-Fri 9am-7pm;
Sat 9am-6.30pm

This friendly chemist offers a good selection of necessities, an outstanding line in beauty products (including Clarins, Vichy, Roc, Caudalie, Nuxe and Avène) and a wide range of homeopathic and other alternative remedies. Staff are on hand to provide advice. They also sell pretty hair ornaments.

The Life Centre

15 Edge Street W8
020 7221 4602
www.thelifecentre.org
Mon–Fri 8am–10pm;
Sat 8.30am–7.30pm;
Sun 9am–7pm

Dedicated to natural health and fitness, the Life Centre offers a variety of alternative therapies and exercise, the latter with an emphasis on 'dynamic yoga'. Other classes include tai chi and pilates, and all take place in the building's main space – a large, airy studio with a glass roof through which you can watch the clouds scudding by from your relaxation mat. Prices range from £10 to £12 for exercise classes (depending on length), while natural therapies and treatments start at £20 for a half-hour Indian head massage and go up to £80 or so for healing and homeopathy.

SHOPPING

ART MATERIALS

The Print Gallery

22 Pembridge Road W11
020 7221 8885
Mon–Fri 9am–6pm;
Sat 10am–7pm

All you need in the way of photocopying, laminating, binding and offset-printing services is combined with a reliable selection of graphic and fine-art supplies. Staff are friendly, helpful and admirably unflustered in the face of a seemingly constant demand for instant photocopying.

BOOKS

Notting Hill Books

132 Palace Gardens Terrace W8
020 7727 5988
Mon–Sat 10.30am–6pm;
early closing Thurs 1pm

Sheila Ramage fulfilled her dream of starting a bookshop in 1969, making this now the oldest bookshop in the area. She sells good-quality remainders and review copies, with the emphasis on art, literature and history. There's also

NOTTING HILL GATE 37

a table of reduced-price paper-backs by the bus stop outside.

CHARITY SHOPS

The Charity Shop
Notting Hill Housing Trust
59 Notting Hill Gate W11
020 7229 1476
Mon–Sat 10am–7pm;
Sun 1–6pm

Notting Hill Housing Trust has developed its own range of house-hold goods – mainly cushions, bedcovers, candles and ceramics – to sell alongside the usual second-hand clothes, books and bric-à-brac. Prices are very reasonable and some of the special items such as animal-print cushion covers and spotty china are as stylish as any you'll find in many of the popular high-street stores.

Oxfam
144 Notting Hill W11
020 7792 0037
Mon–Sat 10am–6pm; Sun 12 noon– 6pm

Clothes and accessories are the main draw here, with a high turnover that often includes designer items for both women and men. Also good for books.

Trinity Hospice
20a Notting Hill Gate W11
020 7792 2582
Mon & Thurs–Sun 10.30am–8pm;
Tues & Wed 10.30am–7pm

This rather shabby establishment has had none of the style-con-scious treatment bestowed on some of the other charity shops. The result is lower prices and an even better chance of finding a good bargain.

FASHION & HOME

Dolly Diamond
51 Pembridge Road W11
020 7727 2479
www.dollydiamond.com
Mon–Fri 10.30am–6.30pm;
Sat 9.30am–6.30pm; Sun 12 noon–6pm

Dolly Diamond has trawled high and low, including the West Coast of America, for the rich combina-tion of Twenties to Eighties clothes that make up her unique collection. A popular hunting ground with designers, among them Galliano, who enthused about an exquisite black top edged with layers of petals in a recent book. Dolly also sells shoes, bags and jewellery and will hunt out special items if needed.

Frontiers

37–39 Pembridge Road W11
020 7727 6132
Mon–Sat 11am–6.30pm;
Sun 12 noon–4pm

This attractive shop sells a combination of jewellery, ceramics and furniture, with a special line in Lloyd Loom chairs, mostly displayed in the basement. Pots and jewellery, mainly from Asia and North Africa, include both new and ancient pieces, with some wonderful amber necklaces.

John Oliver

33 Pembridge Road W11
020 7221 6466/www.johnoliver.co.uk
Mon–Fri 9am–5.30pm; Sat 9am–5pm

One of several old and established shops in this road, John Oliver specialises in high-quality paints in a range of beautiful shades of his own invention. They also stock a huge selection of wallpapers and will give advice on mixing and matching colours, patterns and textures. Expensive but worth it.

Paul Smith

Westbourne House
122 Kensington Park Road W11
020 7727 3553/www.paulsmith.co.uk
Mon–Thurs 10.30am–6.30pm;
Fri & Sat 10am–6.30pm

Paul Smith has sympathetically renovated a large Victorian house to create probably the most elegant retail space in Notting Hill. A beautiful glass staircase connects three floors on which you will find his complete ready-to-wear and made-to-measure lines for men, women and children, as well as a tasteful range of lifestyle objects, from the more usual cushions and vases to original posters from the Sixties. The clothing is smart and sophisticated and if you find nothing to your liking on the shop floor, a bespoke suit can be ordered from a master tailor upstairs. Most of the clothes are made in Italy, all with the finest fabrics and craftsmanship. Well worth a visit even if you can't afford to buy. Another shop on the opposite corner sells miscellaneous items.

Sebastiano Barbagallo

15–17 Pembridge Road W11
020 7792 3320
Mon–Fri 10.30am–6.30pm;
Sat 10am–7pm; Sun 10.30am–6pm

Heading along the well-beaten tourist path to Portobello Road, you might easily miss this treasure trove selling antiques, crafts, furniture, textiles and clothing from India, South East Asia, Tibet and

China. Barbagallo specialises in statues of Buddha and in textiles and clothing. The shop is popular with textile and fashion designers, who come here looking for inspiration, from pre-revolutionary Chinese garments to cute pyjamas for children. The garments hung in the wooden cupboard may look haphazard but are worth checking out.

Teaze
47 Pembridge Road W11
020 7727 8358
Mon–Sat 10.30am–6.30;
Sun 12 noon–5pm

Suitable for shoppers in the 15–25 age group, Teaze offers affordable T-shirts sporting just about every trendy, ironic or controversial logo or slogan. Worth looking out or is the cute and sexy Ave Maria

lingerie with a Jesus and Mary theme. The shop also stocks a large selection of Paul Frank bags and wallets.

Vessel
114 Kensington Park Road W11
020 7727 8001/www.vesselgallery.com
Mon–Fri 10am–6pm; Sat 10am–6.30pm

Upstairs houses a range of beautiful yet functional glass and ceramic tableware; downstairs showcases more experimental work by the likes of Tom Dixon, Tord Boontje, Nigel Coates and Anish Kapoor. Nothing is cheap, but smaller items such as bottle openers, bowls and coffee cups are affordable for anyone prepared to invest in lasting quality and style.

Mural, Codrington Mews W11

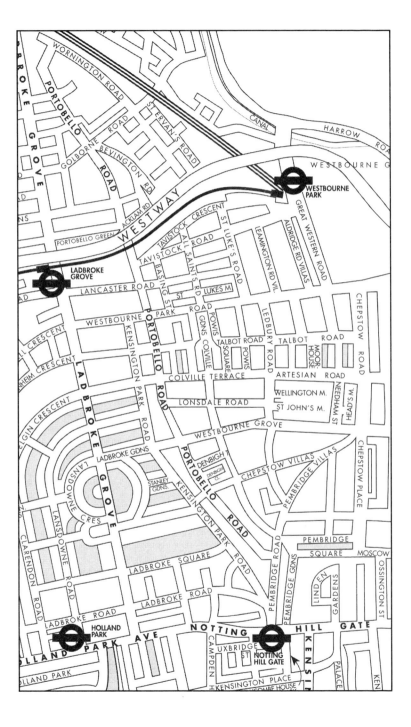

2. PORTOBELLO ROAD

Tube: Notting Hill Gate, Ladbroke Grove
Highlights: Portobello Market, Travel Bookshop, Electric Cinema, eating and drinking, music shops, vintage fashion, Portobello Green Arcade

Notting Hill's popularity has always owed a lot to Portobello, from the road's 18th-century beginnings as a pleasant green lane, winding north from the Kensington Gravel Pits (now Notting Hill Gate) towards the

Shop in Portobello market

village of Kensal Green, to its development as a thriving commercial centre. By 1880 the Lane, as it was known then, was already lined with shops, augmented by regular fruit and vegetable stalls. After the Second World War its appeal was increased by growing interest in the bric-à-brac that had long been sold in the market on Saturdays, later joined by antiques. Novelist Monica Dickens, who grew up around the corner at 52 Chepstow Villas (also once home to a cousin of Napoleon Bonaparte), recalls visiting the market as a child in the 1920s in *An Open Book* (1938):

Ever since memory the Portobello Road market has happened on Saturday mornings. In those early days when we ran down for a packet of sherbet, or walked in kilts and tams to the grocers with Fanny, it was still literally a flea market. All along the gutter rickety stalls and barrows were piled high with rags, torn jerseys, mismatched shoes, chipped china, bent tin trays, three-legged furniture and unfunctioning appliances from the early days of electricity.

Now, of course, thousands of visitors flock here every Saturday in search of antiques and collectibles. Yet despite its international reputation as a number-one tourist attraction and the escalating impact of ruthless developers, Portobello Road, inseparable from the market, has managed to retain its own very special character.

Pembridge Road to Elgin Crescent

ORIGINS OF PORTOBELLO

Portobello Road was named after Portobello Farm, itself named after Admiral Sir Edward Vernon's capture of Puerto Bello from the Spanish in the Gulf of Mexico. The battle took place in November 1739 at a time when the farm – all of 170 acres – was owned by a builder called Adams. When news of the victory finally reached England the following March, there was widespread rejoicing, with many streets and even a town in Scotland named after the event. Vernon's triumph is also commemorated in Vernon Mews, off Portobello, as well as at Admiral Vernon's Antiques Market at Nos. 139–51.

The first landmark on Portobello Road is the Sun in Splendour, Notting Hill's oldest surviving pub, built in 1850 and still serving traditional ale and basic pub food in rather spartan surroundings. With the exception of Giselle Menhenett's fabulous Portobello Gallery, the shops along this stretch tend to cater for the cheap end of the tourist market. Walking on between the gallery and the Gate Hotel, you soon come to a long terrace of two-storey Victorian cottages much in the style of Hillgate Village, though with tiny gardens at the front. At least two writers are known to have lived here: novelist and political essayist George Orwell at No. 22, and the poet Roger McGough a little further down. On the other side of the road, it's worth stopping at the Lazy Daisy Café, both for its peaceful court-yard setting and for the food, which manages to be wholesome, delicious and fairly cheap. This was once the premises of Petersberg Press, printers of fine art whose regular clients included David Hockney, Jim Dine and Henry Moore. It became a café in 1991, soon after the press went into liquidation. The current café owner rents the galleried space from St Peter's Church on Kensington Park

The Sun in Splendour pub

George Orwell's plaque, Portobello Road

Road, which also runs the nursery school next door.

Across Chepstow Villas, the first mansion on the right was a location for some of the filming of Hanif Kureishi's *London Kills Me* (1991). Kureishi's foray into directing was intended as an authentic look at the seedy underbelly of Notting Hill. He employed the services of various dubious characters who smartly repaid him by squatting the building as soon as filming was over. It took a while to get them out, after which the building spent months boarded up and the film was panned by the critics. Although films of Kureishi's work have often been a success, he has yet to have another go at directing.

MARKET DAYS

Until recently many visitors headed for the market on weekdays and especially Sundays, only to feel let down by the dormant antiques arcades and slightly tatty air of Portobello without the crowds. But in the last few years the situation has changed: with Sunday trading an accepted fact of London life, more and more Sunday street stalls have joined the shops that are already trading seven days a week. That said, to avoid disappointment it's still important to know that the market divides into three main sections, each with its own location, trade and approximate opening hours:

• The antiques market, mostly between Chepstow Villas and Elgin Crescent, is mainly on Saturdays, at least for the arcades (approx 6am–5pm), but now attracts a variety of Sunday traders.
• The fruit and vegetable market occupies the middle blocks of Portobello up to the junction with Lancaster Road. It is open daily except Sundays – around 9.30am–6pm, closing 1pm Thurs. There is also a small organic market on Thursdays, 9.30am–6pm, under the canopy beneath the Westway.
• The flea market, starting from beneath the Westway, is most extensive on Saturdays but in many ways is best on Fridays (around 8am–5pm) and Sundays, starting a little later.

After Chepstow Villas, the next section of Portobello marks the beginning of the antique shops, many of which, including Alice's on the corner of Denbigh Close, have been here since the 1960s. Poet and writer Christopher Logue lived in the close in those days and refers to this corner in his tale *Prince Charming* (1999):

By 1965, the stall holders of Denbigh Close had begun to arrive each Saturday morning at 5am, for the Portobello Road street market was becoming the rage it remains. The bargain hunters of old were replaced by Italian dealers. Furniture conversion became antique restoration. Mad John was dead. Harry Dust had a council flat. Middle-class people had bought the cottages that they had lived in. Having introduced decorative mirrors, Kenny put a number of art-school students to work painting furniture, turning out pictures to resemble naïve art. HMS Victorys and Battles of Portobello sold well. I borrowed money to raise the roof of No. 18.

Living at the blind end of the mews was Mr Eric Jones. Since 1934 he and his mother had occupied a cottage with a third floor the height of my planned extension. Eric was a cross-dresser with dyed, orange-blond hair. On summer Saturdays before the road boomed, he would tie on an apron over his pink dress and sweep the mews from end to end when the marketeers had left.

Denbigh Terrace, next on the right, has been home to two more colourful characters, comedian Peter Cook and tycoon Richard Branson, both of whom resided at different times at No. 19. The other side of the terrace suffered badly from wartime bombing and was replaced by council flats.

Alice's, Portobello Road

Past the Earl of Lonsdale pub and Italian wine shop Negozio Classica, on the corner of Westbourne Grove, antique shops and arcades continue down to the crossroads with Elgin Crescent and Colville Terrace. The arcades are open only on Saturdays, when they're joined by a medley of stalls set up on either side of the road. Gong, at No. 182, provided the location for the Travel Bookshop scenes in the film *Notting Hill*. (The real bookshop on which it was modelled is in Blenheim Crescent, just a few minutes' walk away, see pp 52 & 79).

Elgin Crescent to the Westway

Elgin Crescent, with its upmarket food and home shops, has long been something of a battleground as a cluster of business-es struggles to keep up with escalating

Dolls for sale, Portobello market

rents. Among the main survivors is Mr Christian's delicatessen, opened in 1974 and still much loved by locals for its affable staff and delicious homemade food. Since 2002 the shop has been the focus of a September street party in support of the Octopus Challenge, a charity set up by former owner Greg Scott as a tribute to his son Sam, who tragically died from cancer at the age of 17. Just nine weeks before he died, Sam cycled 26 miles through London for charity. In his memory, a regular highlight of the party is the arrival of up to 100 jubilant cyclists, who pedal from France to Notting Hill in just one of many events that raise money for Octopus, in conjunction with Cancerbackup, thoughout the year (see www.octopuschallenge.org.uk).

Another survivor from the 1970s is Graham & Green, which started off selling attractive household goods and ethnic items such as baskets, kilims, beaded curtains and pottery from Morocco. Antonia Graham still imports from India, Africa and the East but also has a skilled eye for European designer objects such as lighting and kitchen-ware. Less resilient was Tom the florist, who pioneered the trend for creating unusual flower combinations wrapped in raffia and brown paper. Like the much-lauded Elgin Books, Tom was forced out of his shop premises by rent increases and now just has a stall on the corner with Kensington Park Road, with a tiny shop on Clarendon Road (p 197).

A longstanding critic of the changes imposed by Notting Hill land-lords is writer and musician Michael Moorcock, whose rollercoaster novel *King of the City* (2000) includes a reference to the time when

Annie Lennox, later of Eurythmics fame, served behind the counter at
Mr Christian's:

*I loved and admired Annie Lennox. She was a pro, like Rosie. She didn't mind
working. I'd known her when she was with the Tourists, grafting days behind the
counter at Mr Christian's the grocer in 1977 when I lived in Colville Terrace, off
Portobello Road, married to Barbican's alleged half-sister Julie May.*

*By then the area was getting iffy. The Grove was filling up with liberal pro-
fessionals – writers, TV producers, models, literary agents, bohemian aristos, film
directors, lefty columnists, barristers – the entire fucking fancy. So many wankers
that if you went out to the pub your feet stuck to the pavement. The pubs
remained, in the main, our own. Speed in the Alex. Dope in the Blenheim. Junk
in Finch's. They kept tarting up Finch's and Heneky's and we kept tarting them
down again. As my friend DikMik put it late one evening: you could take the
needles out of the toilets but you couldn't take the toilets out of the needles.*

Annie Lennox has since moved into her own house up on the hill, while
Moorcock lives in Texas. As for drugs and pubs, illegal substances
remain an indelible part of Notting Hill but most of the pubs have been
more or less straightened out, with the introduction of better ameni-

Mr Christian's delicatessen

Tom at Harper & Tom's

ties, fancy food and a ubiquitous change of name: Finch's on Elgin Crescent is now the Duke of Wellington, the Alex, a former bikers' hangout, became the Portobello Gold and Heneky's the Earl of Lonsdale.

Few of the old businesses in Kensington Park Road have survived the rent increases. The Special Photographers Company (now Reunion) has moved to Westbourne Park Road and the family-run Crystal Cleaners (which took over from the dolls' hospital that occupied this site until 1977) has been replaced by the sleek Scin Beauty Boutique. Otherwise the street is now almost entirely given over to clothes shops and restaurants, among which the Peniel Chapel, an example of Victorian Gothic revival, squats rather awkwardly, as if half waiting to be put to similar use. In fact, the chapel has an active congregation, drawn mainly from the Caribbean community. A further escapee from fashion is the Notting Hill Synagogue at Nos. 206–208, which houses a Montessori nursery school.

THE NOTTING HILL SYNAGOGUE

From the 1880s until the beginning of the 20th century, pogroms drove thousands of Jewish people from their homes in Russia and Poland. Of the many who fled to England, a number settled in and around Portobello Road. By 1883 there was already a synagogue in St Petersburg Place, Bayswater, and by the turn of the century enough Jewish people lived in Notting Hill to merit the opening of another. Moses David, a wealthy businessman who lived at 40 Ladbroke Grove, found a suitable site in a former church hall in Kensington Park Road and, on 27 May 1900, Notting Hill Synagogue was consecrated.

The synagogue was given a **Sefer Torah** from Moscow and silver ornaments were donated from various sources. In 1904, a Jewish Lads' Club was opened next door, followed by a club for Jewish girls that later moved to near Westbourne Park. The Jewish community increased dramatically during the First World War and by the early 1920s there were well over 600 Jewish families living in Notting Hill. Sarah Soremekun recalls the extent of the community in **Portobello: Its People, its Past, its Present** (1996):

Portobello Road was our family's shopping street. There were lots of kosher butchers, eight or nine quite close, and Jewish delicatessens where you could get lovely bagels and kosher bread ... We attended Saturday worship at the synagogue in Kensington Park Road. It was nothing to go there in the Twenties and Thirties and have to stand, there were so many people.

The Notting Hill Synagogue was one of the first to be affiliated to the Zionist Federation and over the years it attracted several famous cantors and scholars, including Rabbi Judah Newman, appointed in 1922. Among his pupils was Abe Herman, who went on to become Israeli Ambassador to the US. Also in the 1920s, a group of local Yiddish writers – Leo Koenig, Shlomo Goldenberg, AM Kaizer, L Credito, Asher Balin, Shamai Pinaky and Alexander Myerovitz – met frequently in the area. But 10 years on, the community was dwindling and by the end of the Second World War the vitality had gone, as people moved out of the area, often to North London. On 8 June 1997 there was a service of commemoration to mark the centenary of the first Notting Hill service, after which a dedicated few kept the synagogue going until its final closure in September 2000. The building is now occupied by Dr Rolfe's Montessori School

Of the restaurants in Kensington Park Road, 192 (now Luna Rossa) was the trendsetter in the early 1980s and a popular hangout for artists and musicians, among them the legendary Joe Strummer of the Clash. As Chris Salewicz writes in *Redemption Song* (2006), Strummer enjoyed the relative privacy of 192 compared to the rowdier atmosphere of the Warwick Castle pub around the corner:

By contrast with the slumming element of himself that enjoyed the down-at-heel Warwick and illegal drinking dens, Joe Strummer – who moved with ease through different social worlds – was also very partial to visits to 192, an

award-winning wine bar and restaurant, on Kensington Park Road, a block west of Portobello Road. In the Warwick Joe would be public property and it would be hard to hold an in-depth conversation with him; at 192 he loved to perch on a stool at the bar and talk intimately for hours about matters of the soul; lubricated by bottles of 'shampoo', as he would archly refer to champagne, Joe's attention was only distracted by the beautiful girls who frequented this watering hole (part of the attraction he admitted to me) favoured by local participants in the film and literary worlds.

Before then several establishments came and went, most notably on the site of Osteria Basilico, which, after nearly 20 years, is firmly entrenched. The most successful previous occupant was Monsieur Thompsons, another favourite of Notting Hill's literati. They included Emma Tennant, a prolific writer and founder of the ground-breaking literary magazine *Bananas*. Edited by Tennant and designed by Julian Rothenstein (who went on to form Redstone Press), the magazine was based at 2 Blenheim Crescent. It attracted some of the most talented creative figures of the 1970s, among them Angela Carter, Bruce Chatwin, Ted Hughes, Alberto Moravia and Yevtushenko. Tennant, who still lives in the area, would quite often lunch or dine with authors at Monsieur Thompsons, referred to in the summer 1976 entry of her *Burnt Diaries* as the 'Ruff Tuff Saloon':

Someone waved a hand over the dreary dog-dinner-on-tin-plate restaurant around the corner from the Bananas *office and it has become Monsieur Thompsons, le patron mange ici joint with a palm tree, a feeling of authentic French provençal, with faded ochre walls and pine tables where you can sit as long as you like. 'Shall we share a starter?' says Ian Hamilton, poet and editor of the* New Review, *who has become a friend despite his kick-off review of* Bananas' *first issue as a 'literary magazine like any other, but raunchy'. Dominique Rocher, proprietor and maître d' of Thompsons – as this modest establishment on the corner of Portobello Mews and next to a new dry-cleaners soon becomes known – doesn't mind if all you do is share a starter. The food is on the whole excellent, however, even if some of the dishes, like 'skirt of beef', are weirdly translated, or have clearly been stewing in translation for some time. The waiters are so French it's impossible to imagine them even knowing where England is – and indeed this corner of Notting Hill would be hard to define in a travel guide. It's possible to think of it as Albion, when Michael Horovitz walks past, or as Boadicea's city, when John Michell, decoder of ancient runes and druidic circles, breezes along the pavement outside.*

Linda Wakeling unloading vegetables

Back along Portobello Road, the fruit and vegetable stalls begin at the corner with Colville Terrace – how many traders depends on the day of the week. Fridays and Saturdays will always find the first pitch occupied by the Caines selling fruit, not the cheapest but always of high quality. A few stalls along, next to the flowers, Linda and Alan Wakeling have been selling vegetables on various sites in Portobello since 1983, with six stalls currently in the family. Like every trader, they lament the changes: the lack of weekday trade since the rise of supermarkets, the dwindling numbers of family customers, the unwillingness of youngsters to carry on the trade and the rise of stalls selling everything but food. But the Wakelings are survivors. They soon picked up on people's growing taste for Mediterranean fare and now sell some of the best aubergines, rocket and baby plum tomatoes to be found. A few stalls along, Cheryl Devlin (born Collins) unusually has two children, Sonny and Arabella, working with her, making them the fourth generation of stallholders in 90 years. The market's heyday may be over but it's still a great place to do your food shopping.

Heading north on Portobello takes you past the famous Electric Cinema, with its distinctive blue neon sign. A Grade II*-listed building, the Electric has strong claims to be the oldest surviving purpose-built cinema in England, almost unchanged since its construction in 1910. A fine example of movie-house design, the façade is covered in cream faience tiles and swags of fruit and flowers, with more ornate fruit, gilded plasterwork and pink art deco glass lightshades inside the now fashionable interior. Throughout most of its history the Electric has been used as a cinema, apart from a short spell as a music hall, the

Imperial Playhouse. Towards the end of the 1990s, after a period of steady decline, it stood empty for a while until it was bought by Peter Simon, founder of the Monsoon Group, who started his fashion empire from a stall outside and now has his headquarters in Notting Dale. The building has since been taken over by Nick Jones of the Soho House Group, which runs it as a private members' club (Electric House) and a popular restaurant (Electric Brasserie), as well as the cinema (see p 66 for more details).

Sonny, Cheryl and Arabella Devlin in Portobello market

Almost opposite the Electric Cinema, like many of the most enduring businesses, the excellent Tea & Coffee Plant started life as a market stall. The Caines have another fruit stall on the corner of Talbot Road, sadly depleted by the death of Nelly Caine. Although she never seemed old, she must have been well into her 70s as she stood out in all weathers, her immaculate blonde hair tucked

A vegetable stall on the move

under a beret against the cold. In keeping with market tradition, Nelly's flower-covered funeral cortège passed along Portobello Road as stallholders ceased trading to pay their respects.

The next turning on the left is Blenheim Crescent, known mostly for its trio of specialist bookshops: Books for Cooks, Blenheim Books and the Travel Bookshop. But for the presence of Minus Zero Records, with its devotion to psychedelia, it's difficult to imagine this patch

Tourists outside the Travel Bookshop,

dominated as it was by the alternative culture of the Sixties: Marc Bolan lived at No. 57 in 1967 when he was forming his band T Rex, while Minus Zero used to be the Dog Shop, selling hippy paraphernelia. Aquarius Waterbeds was above, later to become the premises of the Frestonian Embassy (see Writings, p 291). Even harder to picture is the time, only a few years earlier, when Totobags, the 'most important West Indian café' in the neighbourhood, occupied No. 9. As Tom Vague writes in *Psychogeography* (1998), for the mostly Jamaican regulars 'dominoes, cards and smoking were the order of the day'. Writer Colin MacInnes and wealthy aristocrats such as Sarah Churchill used to come here regularly to savour a bit of low life.

THE TRAVEL BOOKSHOP

The Travel Bookshop, founded by Sarah Anderson in 1979, transcends the division between guides and other forms of writing by including every kind of book about a country on the same shelf. Books are arranged geographically, but with fiction, history, biography, natural history and out-of-print books alongside the more obvious maps and guides. It's an inspiring place: one visit will change the way you travel. Over the past 28 years the Travel Bookshop has developed an enthusiastic following among travellers, writers and dreamers alike, but no one could have predicted the extraordinary flood of interest sparked by the film Notting Hill. In the mid-Nineties, Richard Curtis, a neighbour, asked if he could sit in the shop and take notes as he was thinking of writing a film set in a bookshop. This was followed a while later by a photographer taking stills which were used to help build the film set of both the interior and the exterior of the shop (see p 53). During filming the area buzzed with camera crews and stars. Julia Roberts and Hugh Grant visited the Travel Bookshop as part of their research. **Notting Hill** opened in 1999 and the shop is still a 'must-see' for the film's aficionados.

Site of the original blue door

The next junction with Portobello is Westbourne Park Road, a busy bus route dominated on one side by Nuline, the ever-expanding builders' merchants, while opposite lies No. 280, the location of the original blue door of Notting Hill fame. This was removed after the film, when the property changed hands and the new owners installed a substitute, firmly painted black.

After Lancaster Road, even during the week, it's usually busy outside

RICHARD CURTIS ON THE DREAM THAT BECAME NOTTING HILL

I suppose I started writing this film about 34 years ago. I was seven years old, and every night, to lull myself to sleep with a smile, I would have the same fantasy. It was my sister's birthday. Presents were unwrapped – and there didn't seem to be one from me. She would be unhappy, and then I'd say, 'Oh yes, well, actually, I did get you one little thing,' then walk to a big cupboard and swing the doors open and there inside would be the four Beatles. They'd come out, chat, sing, 'And I Love Her' and leave. And then I'd be asleep.

Twenty-five years later, I was still having the same dream. The personnel had changed but the basic plot was still the same. Now, when I couldn't get to sleep, I would imagine going to dinner with my friends Piers and Paula in Battersea, as I did most weeks. I'd casually say I was bringing a girl and then turn up unexpectedly with Madonna – usually Madonna, sometimes Isabella Rossellini – but usually Madonna. Piers would open the door and be very cool about it, though secretly thrilled. His wife Paula would have no idea who Madonna was and behave accordingly, and my friend Helen would arrive late and explode with excitement. By which time, I'd have dozed off again.

Five years later, we were doing the first week's filming of **Four Weddings** and I was sitting in a cold room in Luton Hoo, beside James Fleet, asleep, trying to work out what I should write next. I remembered these dreams and thought it's not a bad idea for films to be about dreamy situations, and so I decided I'd have a bash at writing a film about someone very ordinary going out with someone very famous. This script is the result of that. (From **Notting Hill**, 1999)

Tesco's supermarket, where the Price family runs one of the last traditional vegetable stalls. They also own the last surviving greengrocer in Golborne Road. You'll find a lot more stalls selling food here on Fridays and Saturdays, including fish, fruit and veg and olive oil. Two shops are also worth noting – the Grain Shop, renowned for delicious vegetarian takeaways, and the Spanish supermarket and café Garcia & Sons. Beyond here the merchandise gives way to feather boas, cheap trinkets, cut-price make-up, CDs and new clothes, soon to blend into the glorious mix of junk, unexpected treasures and cutting-edge design under the Westway.

THE WESTWAY

The devastation caused by redevelopment plans to build the Western Avenue Extension (as it was then called) provoked one of the longest and most successful series of community-action campaigns in Notting Hill's history.

Until the building of the extension, the fast entry into London from the West of England stopped at White City. By the 1950s this had led to tremendous bottlenecks and accidents as frustrated motorists tried to find back routes for the final three miles into London via Notting Hill. The answer was to construct a new urban motorway linking the existing road to the Marylebone Road in Central London. The project was designed in the late 1950s, site clearance began in 1964 and the road was officially opened by Conservative minister Michael Heseltine in July 1970. Erected on concrete pylons just above roof height, it was an engineering triumph but a disaster in terms of social planning. Huge swathes of North Kensington became a building site; streets were chopped in two and around 700 houses were demolished to make way for the project.

Protesters caused total confusion on the day the road was opened and it took another two years of community action before all those immediately affected were rehoused. Local activists moved in again when it came to deciding what to do with the 23 acres that lay immediately beneath the Westway. Indecision and disagreements among local politicians had left this area derelict and abandoned. An alliance of residents (see Frestonia, pp 291) had successfully campaigned for the building of co-operative low-rent housing in Notting Dale, but the travellers and totters who had been displaced to make way for the road were given nothing. Eventually, the independent North Kensington Amenity Trust was set up to organise the use of this land and to compensate the community for the destruction caused. In time, the trust proved successful, filling much of the site with a mixture of amenities and private enterprises.

The area under the Westway stands out as one of the most potent symbols of social change and community action in Notting Hill. And it's not just about local politics. In recognition of the many Spanish people who fled here from Franco's dictatorship, a mosaic was recently unveiled under the bridge (on the left heading north), commemorating those

Spanish civil war mural under the Westway

who died fighting against Fascism in the Spanish Civil War.

More than any other local landmark this concrete elevation and the life beneath it have captured the imagination of artists and writers – Will Self, Michael Moorcock, Martin Amis and JG Ballard, to name a few. In 'This revolution is for display purposes only' (*Wall and Piece*, 2005) graffiti artist Banksy tells how he used the iron bridge over Portobello as a canvas for a series of Che Guevara posters. One night at about 4am he was painting on the bridge when two cars arrived below him, reversed onto the pavement and crashed into a doorway. He peered over the bridge and saw six people in hoods running into a mobile phone shop and filling their bags with everything they could. Rushing back into their cars they sped off down Portobello Road leaving Banksy with his 'mouth hanging open'. Realising that he would be a likely suspect he also then fled. On a different occasion, he stencilled a monkey on the same spot (succeeding the brilliant 'Nuclear waste fades your genes'), since tiled over by the Council.

Westway has even been used as the title of an award-winning radio soap, broadcast for eight years by the BBC World Service until October 2005. Set in an inner-city health practice, the soap had its gritty moments, but it takes Martin Amis, who lived for many years off Ladbroke Grove, to convey the truly sinister side of the Westway, as he does in *The Information* (1984):

If anything was going to happen, it would surely happen under Westway. That black cavity, where the very walls and pillars were drenched in eel juice and snake's hiss, and tattooed with graffiti. If something was going to happen, it would surely happen under Westway.

JG Ballard used the overhead motorway as the crash setting for his novel *Concrete Island* (1974), and a totally different aspect is evoked in Michael Moorcock's *King of the City* (2000). The description of a free rock concert under the Westway, on the ground now occupied by Portobello Green, is based on one of many such events that used to happen here during the 1970s (see Music & Writings). Nowadays this space is rarely used for music outside Carnival, though it did rock again one summer evening in 2000 when the local Moroccan and Arabic-speaking women's centre Al-Hasaniya hosted an electrifying concert of Moroccan and Somali music. It has also been a venue for Saturday screenings during the Portobello Film Festival.

Thanks to the Amenity Trust and all the planners, community architects and local campaigners who fought so hard for the Portobello Green development, the mix of commercial and community enterprises that now fill the motorway bays on either side of Portobello Road is an impressive achievement. There can't be many places where refugee

Portobello Road north of the Westway, early 1970s

groups, youth projects, a Citizens' Advice Bureau, a skate park and an adventure playground share space with market traders, a nightclub and some of London's hottest fashion designers.

Beyond the Westway

Past the overhead bridge, up to the junction with Oxford Gardens, the north end of Portobello Road has several popular café-restaurants, as well as an eclectic mix of shops, from Honest Jon's for lovers of jazz and world music to Sandie Stagg's Antique Clothing Shop, the wonderful Cloth Shop and Dave's cavernous Last Place on Earth, selling antiques, clothes and bric-à-brac.

The road then follows the brick wall that used to enclose a Franciscan convent, later turned into the Spanish school that thrives here now. On the other side of the road, council housing occupies the site of the farmhouse that, until 1864, belonged to Portobello Farm. This block represents the grottier end of the Friday and Saturday market, dominated by junk but not devoid of bargains for those dedicated enough to rummage through boxes of cracked china, or dig deep into the mounds of old shirts, jumpers and other second-hand clothes that gradually take over the battered trestle tables up to the crossing with Golborne Road. Although stalls peter out at the northernmost end of Portobello, the market carries on to the right, past the Victorian bulk of the Fat Badger gastropub and along Golborne Road.

THE SPANISH CONVENT AND SCHOOL

In 1857 Father (later Cardinal) Henry Manning asked a nun, Mother Elizabeth Lockhart, to move from Greenwich into three adjoining houses at 34 Elgin Crescent. From this base she and her small community of sisters taught in the school for poor girls attached to St Mary of the Angels (see p 107) and within a year they were instructing about a hundred pupils as well as looking after several orphans. Father Manning encouraged them to become Franciscans and by the time the community moved to the convent at 317 Portobello Road in 1862, they were the first group of Franciscan Third Order women to live in England since the Reformation. The convent, designed by Henry Clutton (1819–1893), was a large building with sufficient grounds to provide a triangular grass cemetery for the burial of nuns who died there. In 1897 the Franciscans left and were replaced by a Dominican order, who set up an orphanage and home for young girls convicted of minor offences. This lasted until the 1970s, when the convent was bought by the Spanish government and transformed into the **Colegio Español,**

England's first and only Spanish school. Clutton's vaulted chapel, with its two banners designed in 1866 by Francis Bentley, serves as the school's assembly hall. Further information from 020 8969 2664.

You're now on the final stretch of Portobello Road and the last section to have received the kind of makeover treatment that still sits rather uncomfortably in Golborne Road. George's Portobello Fish Bar looks positively jazzy these days, but Cockney's Pie & Mash over the road has a determinedly timeless air, as does Valerie's Flowers and the aptly named Temptation Alley – a wonderfully old-fashioned haberdashery stuffed with buttons, ribbons and trimmings of every description. Apart from Galicia, few restaurants have made a go of it up here. The juxtaposition of extreme wealth and some of the poorest housing in London makes for an explosive cocktail, and burglary is common.

A Portobello Road busker,

PLACES TO STAY

The Gate Hotel
6 Portobello Road W11
020 7221 0707/bookings@gatehotel.com

More bed and breakfast than hotel, The Gate has only six rooms, all simple, clean and equipped with refrigerator and tea- and coffee-making facilities. Probably the cheapest option, with prices ranging from £55–£75 single to £110 for a triple en suite in high season, including continental breakfast.

Portobello Gold Hotel
95 Portobello Road W11
020 7460 4910/www.portobellogold.com

This five-room hotel is renowned for several reasons, from its origins as a notorious bikers' pub, the Princess Alexandra (affectionately known as the Alex), to its present status as having, in the Buzz Bar, one of the first licensed cybercafés. It was also, in 1995, the first UK hotel to offer internet access in every room, now free to guests. The recently refurbished accommodation is comfortable and reasonably priced – from £70 for a double room to £170 for a two-floor maisonette

apartment that sleeps up to six. Dogs are welcome in the apartment (they are even offered a free dinner on the first night), which comes with a pretty roof terrace also available for hire separately. Continental breakfast is included in room prices, and there's a lively downstairs bar, plus a conservatory restaurant offering global-style dishes at reasonable prices.

Also see the **Earl Percy Hotel** (p 149)

EATING AND DRINKING

CAFÉS & TAKEAWAYS

Babes 'n' Burgers
275 Portobello Road W11
020 7229 2704
Daily 10am–11pm

The place for 'healthy fast food' in a child-friendly atmosphere. Service is a bit erratic but the organic burgers, smoothies and salads are good value and delicious. Vegetarian options are available, as is alcohol. A far cry from its predecessor, the greasy Mountain Grill of Hawkwind fame.

Bossa Nova Café

339 Portobello Road W10
020 8968 3050
Mon–Sat 8am–8pm; Sun 10.30am–8pm

Brazilian food and hospitality are the main themes of this pretty café just north of Golborne Road. Customers are often drawn in by the tempting array of cakes and pastries that adorn the window, but this is also a good place for lunch or early dinner: traditional fish and meat dishes are served with rice or potatoes, while salads are accompanied by *pan de queijo*, Brazilian cheese bread baked on the premises.

Caravaggio

7 Blenheim Crescent W11
020 7792 0888
Mon–Sat 10am–11pm

This longstanding independent café also supports artists, with a rotating exhibition of works by the owner, Lebanese cartoonist Nabil Abu Hamad. Formerly Argile, it has undergone a makeover, with a new bar, an Italian chef and the introduction of 'proper dinners'.

Eve's Market Café

222 Portobello Road W11
Mon & Tues 7.30am–5.30pm;
Wed 7.20am–5.30pm; Thurs 7.30am–3pm;
Fri & Sat 7.30am–5.25pm

Formerly the Anglo-Yugoslav, Eve's is one of the few workers' cafés to survive. It's a typical English greasy spoon, popular with market traders, which may have something to do with the odd precision of the opening times. The curious (or desperate) may like to try a late-night visit to Tesco Disco in the adjoining basement.

Makan

270 Portobello Road W10
020 8960 5169
Daily 11.30am–7pm

This friendly café-restaurant and takeaway specialises in Malaysian food: spring rolls and samosas, fish, chicken or squid sambal and green chicken curry. The many vegetarian dishes include several with tofu, spicy pineapple curry and delicious chickpeas, spinach and dates. Deservedly popular, especially at lunchtime.

Progreso

156 Portobello Road W11
020 7985 0304
Mon–Thurs 7am–6.30pm; Fri & Sat
7am–7pm; Sun 8.30am–7pm

An excellent antidote to Starbucks *et al,* Progreso is the UK's first high-street chain of Fairtrade coffee bars created to benefit coffee growers. Under the auspices of Oxfam, the first branch opened in Covent Garden in 2004 and this one followed in 2006. The aim is for farmers in Ethiopia, Honduras and Indonesia to trade their way out of poverty by selling their produce through co-operatives that own 25 per cent of the chain. Enjoy excellent coffee in a friendly, laid-back atmosphere. Cakes, soup and light meals also served. Internet access.

Also see **Gail's Bakery** and **Tea & Coffee Plant**

FOOD SHOPS

The Breadstall
Opposite Tea & Coffee Plant
Portobello Road
Daily except Thurs & Sun

One of the most welcome additions to the area, the stall has an enormous range of breads, including baguettes made with proper French flour and delicious olive focaccia. Bagels and rye bread are delivered daily by taxi from the Brick Lane bakery and

the Cornish pasties come from Bodmin. They also offer a choice of sandwiches and patisserie. Try the wonderful lemon tart or chocolate brioche (which makes a great version of bread and butter pudding).

Mr Christian's
11 Elgin Crescent W11
020 7229 0501
Mon–Thurs 7am–7pm; Fri & Sat 5.30am–6.30pm; Sun 7am–5pm

Friendly, knowledgeable staff, delicious homemade dishes and quality goods from small suppliers have ensured this deli's popularity for more than 25 years. A team of six work full-time in the downstairs kitchen to produce a mouthwatering array of food, from pastries, tarts and flapjacks to soups, stews, salad dishes and sandwiches. The chocolate brownies are a dream. A huge choice of cheeses, pâtés, olives and sauces grace the delicatessen counter, while oils, vinegars and packaged goods spill over into the small room at the back.

Corney & Barrow
194 Kensington Park Road W11
020 7221 5122
www.corneyandbarrow.com
Mon–Fri 10.30am–9pm; Sat 10.30am–8pm

An Aladdin's cave of wine, with the emphasis on traditional, fine and rare older vintages, which often come in tempting bin-ends. House wines start at under £5 and, although prices can be as high as £895 a bottle, the qualified and friendly staff will help find something for everyone. It stocks the best local selection of Cuban cigars, as well as specialist whiskies and wine accessories. Tastings and discounts can be organised through the company's wine society and although much of its trade is local (they deliver), wine is despatched all over the world.

The French Cheese Stall

Opposite Oxfam Books
Portobello Road W11
Fridays & Saturdays only

Yann Leblais used to have a cheese shop in Normandy and now brings a fantastic assortment of really good-quality French cheeses, pâtés, rillettes, honey, and saucissons over on the ferry every week. The choice of goat's-milk cheese is especially impressive. Prices are reasonable, and there are always good deals of the day starting at £1.50.

P De La Fuente

288 Portobello Road W10
020 8960 5657
Mon–Sat 9am–6pm

Smaller and less well known than Garcia & Sons (below), this friendly Spanish grocers offers a similar range of food and wine, from *chorizo* and whole hams to cakes, biscuits, sugared almonds and reasonably priced traditional wines. One of the best buys is Serrano ham, which is astonishingly cheap. Let's hope that rumours of the shop's imminent closure are unfounded.

Gail's Bakery

138 Portobello Road W11
020 7460 0766/www.gailsbread.co.uk
Mon–Fri 7am–9pm; Sat & Sun 8am–9pm

Gail's specialises in freshly baked bread, pastries and cakes from the Bread Factory, which already supplies Mr Christian's and the Grocer on Elgin around the corner, as well as some of London's best restaurants. There are 25 types of bread to choose from, including several sourdough loaves and a blue cheese campagne, plus sandwiches, quiches, muffins and soups to eat in or take away.

R Garcia & Sons

248–250 Portobello Road W10
020 7221 6119
Tues–Sat 8.30am–6pm

This traditional Spanish super-market sells an impressive selection of wines, oils, olives and cheeses as well as a wide choice of tinned foodstuffs, cakes and preserves. Earthenware pots are another good buy, and Christmas always brings a wide variety of Italian *panettone*. Their adjacent café is especially recommended for *churros* and brandy – perfect on a cold winter's day.

The Grain Shop

269a Portobello Road W11
020 7229 5571
Mon–Sat 9.30am–6pm

The Grain Shop lost some of its character in the refit in 2005, but lunch-time queues testify to the enduring success of this whole-food takeaway, which started life as Ceres in the early Seventies. Vegan and vegetarian food are the main draw, with a choice of about ten hot dishes, and salads in small, medium or large portions. Everything is cooked on the premises, including the pastries, cakes and bread – at once whole-some and delicious. The shop has

an arrangement with Mau Mau, just a few doors along, where you can eat your takeaway as long as you buy a drink.

The Grocer on Elgin

6 Elgin Crescent W11
020 7221 3844/www.thegroceron.com
Mon–Fri 8am–8pm; Sat & Sun 8am–6pm

This sophisticated shop sells delicious bread, pizzas and pastries as well as the pouches of gourmet meals like chicken and tarragon or *boeuf bourguignon* for which it is renowned. All meals come freshly cooked in the Grocer's kitchen in the former Bali Sugar restaurant (under the same owner) on All Saints Road. Prices are steep but quality pretty much guaranteed. There's a small café hidden away at the back.

The Hummingbird Bakery

133 Portobello Road W11
020 7229 6446/www.hummingbirdbakery.com
Tues–Sat 10am–5.30pm; Sun 11am–5pm

London magazine *Time Out's* runner-up for the best patisserie, this American cornucopia of sweetness has pecan, pumpkin and Mississippi mud pies as well as blueberry cake, lemon pie and pretty cup cakes. A few seats inside, and two tables outside.

Kingsland, the Edwardian Butchers
140 Portobello Road W11
020 7727 6067
Mon–Sat 7.30am–6pm

Wood panelling, striped aprons and bowler hats provide the Edwardian element of this traditional English butcher's, which offers free-range eggs, chutneys and cheeses, in addition to organic and non-organic meat. Expect to queue on Saturdays and especially at Christmas, when Kingsland provides an excellent and far cheaper alternative to the famous Lidgate on Holland Park Avenue (see p 189).

Portobello Wholefoods
266 Portobello Road W10
020 8968 9133
Mon–Sat 9.30am–6pm; Sun 11am–5pm

Allied to Neal's Yard Bakery, this longstanding business is a perfect complement to the Grain Shop. Cereals, dried fruit, nuts, pulses, honey, jam, eco-friendly cleaning materials, soaps and potions are the mainstay, with a limited selection of organic bread, fresh fruit and vegetables.

The Spice Shop
1 Blenheim Crescent W11
020 7221 4448
www.thespiceshop.co.uk
Mon–Sat 9.30am–6pm; Sun 11am–5pm

Starting from a market stall, Birgit Erath has built up an impressive business round her passion for spices of all kinds. Opened in 1995, her tiny, welcoming shop is crammed with more than 1500 herbs, spices and blends, plus nuts, beans, grains and dried fruit, each of which she will happily discuss in great detail. Weather permitting, pots of fresh herbs, nuts and ropes of garlic adorn the bright yellow façade.

Tea & Coffee Plant
180 Portobello Road W11
020 7221 8137/020 7655 4574
www.coffee.uk.com
Mon–Sat 8am–6.30pm; Sun 9.30am–5pm

The Tea & Coffee Plant started as a stall on Portobello. The shop is dedicated to importing Fairtrade coffee beans, freshly roasted in its premises in North Acton. Bestsellers include Italian roast, organic Mexican and House blends, plus chocolate ginger biscuits and organic 70 per cent cooking chocolate. They also sell everything needed for making coffee. Approved by the Soil Association.

PUBS & BARS

The Duke of Wellington

179 Portobello Road W11
020 7727 6727
Mon–Sat 11am–11pm; Sun 12
noon–10.30pm

A free house, this was once owned by the brewer Finch's (spot the moniker on the clock above the wonderful round bar). It's a large, sprawling, noisy place, serving standard pub drinks but above-average food, and spilling its customers out onto the pavements most Friday and Saturday nights. Enjoy the feel of a village local, which is essentially what it is.

The Market Bar

240 Portobello Road W11
020 7229 6472
Mon–Fri 12 noon–11pm; Sat 11am–11pm
(Sun till 10.30pm)

One of those few remaining haunts where there still lingers a reputation for dodgy doings, the Market has a surprisingly sumptuous urban rococo interior, complete with Miss Havisham's front parlour curtains and dripping candles. There's no better place to be on a busy Saturday afternoon when the funk, reggae or soul is blasting out.

Mau Mau

265 Portobello Road W11
020 7229 8528
Mon–Sat 11am–11pm; Sun 11am–10.30pm

Laid-back, friendly bar offering drinks at fair prices, good food and a strong selection of DJ nights, with a small stage at the back for live bands. Great for a night out with friends in an unpretentious atmosphere.

Portobello Gold

95/7 Portobello Road W11
020 7460 4906/www.portobellogold.com
Bar 10am–11pm; restaurant Mon–Fri
7.30pm–midnight, Sat 12.30pm–5.50pm,
7pm–11.30pm, Sun 1pm–8pm

Friendly staff, comfortable benches, newspapers on a stick and an open fire serve to make this one of the most congenial bars in the area. It even has the seal of approval of President Clinton, who astounded local drinkers by dropping in with his entourage for a lunch-time half-pint of organic lager in December 2000. Also good for live music (see website for up-to-date listings). As well as bar food, the restaurant at the back (with a conservatory roof which opens in summer) offers an impressive menu with a Pacific-rim feel, specialising in vegetarian and seafood dishes including Irish oysters.

Trailer Happiness
177 Portobello Road W11
020 7727 2700
Tues–Fri 5pm–midnight; Sat 6pm–midnight;
Sun 6pm–10.30pm

This is described on its website as a 'retro-sexual haven of cosmopolitan kitsch and faded trailer park glamour – cork tiles and shag pile, love songs and vol au vents' You'll either love or hate the over-the-top décor, but the bar serves great cocktails. DJs play an eclectic mix of music most nights from 8pm.

RESTAURANTS

The Electric Brasserie
191 Portobello Road W11
020 7908 9696/www.the-electric.co.uk
Mon–Wed 8am–12.30am; Thurs–Sat
8am–1am; Sun 8am–11.30pm. Meals served
Mon–Fri 8am–11pm; Sat 8am–5pm,
6pm–11pm; Sun 8am–5pm, 6pm–10pm

This hugely popular restaurant next to the cinema serves meals all day, from sandwiches and American-style breakfasts to hearty salads, grilled fish and suckling pig. Service can be off-hand and you may well struggle to get a table, especially outside and at weekends, but it's a great place to eat in the heart of the action. Expensive.

E&O
14 Blenheim Crescent W11
020 7229 5454/www.eando.nu
Dim sum Mon–Sat 12 noon–midnight; Sun
till 11.30pm; lunch Mon–Sat 12 noon–3pm,
Sun 12.30pm–3.30pm; dinner Mon–Sat
6pm–10.30pm; Sun till 10pm

E&O's pan-Asian fusion cooking receives regular rave reviews, as do the cocktails served in the elegant bar – lychee and watermelon martinis strongly recommended. In the restaurant popular food dishes, beautifully presented, include the black cod with sweet miso paste, rock shrimp tempura, lamb curry and stem ginger tiramisù. Cheaper than you might expect given its trendy reputation.

Essenza
210 Kensington Park Road W11
020 7792 1066/www.essenza.co.uk
Daily 12.30pm –11.30pm

This rather cramped upmarket Italian serves very good food including pastas, risotto and excellent fish. Best for lunch:

evening service can be brusque as waiters favour the well heeled regulars who treat it as their neighbourhood local. Expensive.

The Fat Badger

310 Portobello Road W10
020 8969 4500
Mon–Fri 12 noon–11pm; Sat 11am–11pm;
Sun 12 noon–10.30pm

This relatively new gastropub has earned almost consistently good reviews, both for its friendly atmosphere and the high standard of the food. Pigs' trotters and lambs' tongues feature on the largely traditional British menu, alongside roast beef and Yorkshire pudding plus various fish dishes – spicy octopus and mussel stew is especially recommended. Urban-themed wallpaper by Glasgow design group Timorous Beasties adds a surreal touch to the cosy bar.

First Floor

186 Portobello Road W11
020 7243 0072
Mon–Sun 12 noon–3pm;
Mon–Sat 7pm–11pm

It's the spacious dining room with its atmosphere of faded grandeur that makes this restaurant special. White linen tablecloths add to the elegance, and in the evening clusters of candles soften the dim light given off by a huge crystal chandelier. It's not easy to assess the quality of the cooking as chefs tend to come and go, but standards are generally high and prices reasonable, especially for the set lunch.

Galicia

323 Portobello Road W10
020 8969 3539
Tues–Sun 12 noon–3pm & 7pm –11.30pm

Authentic Spanish food, beer and wine are accompanied by a healthy disregard for the vagaries of fashion is this homely restaurant cum tapas bar. The cooking is plain and filling, with some good fish dishes such as *merluza a la gallega* and, especially recommended, *gambas al ajillo* – six fat prawns sizzling in garlic butter. There's rarely a time when you won't find a group of local Spaniards (usually men) propping up the bar at the front. Shut your eyes and you could be in Northern Spain.

Notting Hill Brasserie

92 Kensington Park Road W11
020 7229 4481
Lunch daily 12 noon–3pm;
dinner Mon–Sat 7pm–11pm

Excellent modern European food characterises this restaurant, discreetly situated near the corner with Westbourne Grove. Perfectly executed dishes such as wild mushroom risotto, chateaubriand steak served with chips and béarnaise sauce, roasted fillet of monkfish and a mouthwatering choice of desserts ensure a loyal clientele. Live jazz in the evenings. Expensive.

Osteria Basilico

29 Kensington Park Road W11
020 7727 9957/www.osteriabasilico.co.uk
Lunch Mon–Fri 12.30pm–3pm, Sat
12.30pm–4pm, Sun 12.30pm–3.15pm;
dinner Mon–Sat 6.30pm–11pm,
Sun 6.30pm–10.30pm

Osteria Basilico took off from the moment it opened on this prime site in 1992. It's not the place for a relaxing evening – booking is essential, scheduling tight and the waiters can get frantic to the point of being rude. But the food is reliable and any long delays are alleviated by the usually swift arrival of delicious warm bread for dipping into olive oil. The self-service antipasti are especially recommended. Tables upstairs are good for people-watching and there is also pavement seating.

Also see **Portobello Gold** and **Books for Cooks**

ENTERTAINMENT

FILM

The Electric Cinema

191 Portobello Road W11
020 7908 9696/www.the–electric.co.uk
Box office Mon–Sat 9am–8.30pm; Sun
10am–8.30pm

Billed as a luxury cinema, the Electric is extremely comfortable, with leather seating (including two-seater sofas), footstools and tables for the drinks and snacks you can purchase at the well-stocked bar – open half an hour before screening. Films vary from regular blockbusters to art-house favourites, plus occasional film-school productions and private screenings for the film industry. Prices range from £5 for the front three rows (Mon only) to £12.50 for regular seats and £30 for a sofa. A Saturday Kids' Club and Sunday-morning screenings are open only to members of the Electric House club.

See also **Portobello Film Festival** (Notting Hill in Film, p 228)

MUSIC & CLUBBING

Inn on the Green
3–5 Thorpe Close W10
020 8962 5757
Mon 2pm–12midnight; Tues–Thurs 10am–12
midnight; Fri & Sat 10am–1am; Sun
10am–11pm

Long-term locals Tina and Dave
run this friendly bar tucked away
under the Westway. Not a bad
place for a quiet drink, but it
comes alive on music nights –
sporadic and likely to feature die-
hard performers such as Gaz
Mayall and survivors from
Hawkwind. Also used as a venue
for events during the Portobello
Film Festival (see p 228).

Also see **Mau Mau, Portobello Gold**
and **Trailer Happiness** above, plus
Neighbourhood (Chapter 4)

HEALTH, BEAUTY & FITNESS

Base Cuts
252 Portobello Road W11
020 7727 7068/basecuts@lineone.net
Mon–Sat 10am–6pm;
Thurs 10am–7.30pm; Sun 11m–4pm

Wrought-iron mirrors give a
Gothic touch to this friendly salon

right in the heart of Portobello.
Prices are fair, while its position,
on a corner site beside the plaza,
means plenty of outside action to
keep you entertained.

Bliss
333 Portobello Road W10
020 8969 3331/www.bliss.me.uk
Clinic: Mon–Fri 9am–9pm; Sat 9am–7pm;
Sun 11am–7pm

A combination of 'creative' health
centre, café, clinic and shop, Bliss
offers a range of complementary
health treatments including aromatherapy, reflexology, acupunc-
ture, Reiki, Alexander technique
and massage. The company was
founded by acupuncturist Aliza
Baron-Cohen and nutritionist
Helen Thorp with the aim of making such treatments available to a
wider public. Prices are reasonable, with concessions at certain
times (phone for details). Books,
tapes, herbs, homeopathic remedies and essential oils are sold.

Children of Vision
195 Portobello Road W11
020 7792 2494
www.thegallery.childrenofvision.co.uk
Mon–Sat 10am–7pm;
gallery Tues–Sat 10.30am–6pm

This wacky hairdresser with its

slightly sinister title specialises in dreadlocks, extensions, plaits and colour – the wilder the better. The basement gallery opened by Italian artist Anna Laurini is a relatively new venture – for details see the website.

DR Evans
15 Elgin Crescent W11
020 7727 6882
Mon–Sat 9am–6pm

This friendly pharmacy stocks the usual chemist's items, plus an impressive selection of skincare products: Clarins, Darphin, Dr Hauschka, Caudalie, Avène, Vichy and Roc, to name a few. Solgar and Health Aid supplements are stocked, and Biocare and Lamberts can be ordered. A Health Point terminal on site covers 3000 topics. The owner takes good passport photographs; Evans also prints photographs from digital cards at competitive prices. Along with Calders in Notting Hill Gate (p 35), the best chemist in the area.

Portobello Green Fitness Club
3–5 Thorpe Close W10
020 8960 2221/www.pgfc.org.uk
Mon–Fri 6.30am–10pm;
Sat & Sun 9am–7pm

Run by the Westway Development Trust, PGFC is a non-profit-making organisation dedicated to encouraging fitness in the community through a wide range of exercise, from gym workouts to pilates, aerobics and boxing, as well as physiotherapy and seminars on nutrition. Beauty treatments also available. Membership, including free classes, starts at £48 a month.

Portobello Green Room
The Body Shop
194 Portobello Road W11
020 7243 8211
www.thegreen-room.co.uk
Wed–Sat 10am–6pm

The first-ever London Body Shop started around the corner at 23 Blenheim Crescent. So too began the Green Room, a separate but complementary enterprise offering natural face and body treatments using only Body Shop products. Soothing New Age music is played as you wait for your luxury hydrating facial to take effect, interrupted only by the cries of the market traders below. A relaxed and friendly atmosphere and fair prices, especially if you can pay for a course, are guaranteed to keep the regulars coming.

Saint's Tattoo Studio

201 Portobello Road W11
020 7727 8211
Wed–Sun 1pm–6pm; no appointment
necessary

Marc Saint started here in 1983,
and ever since the demand for tat-
toos and body piercing has esca-
lated beyond his wildest dreams.
Today he sees around 20 customers on a quiet day, 30 on
Saturdays – most of them women.
The slightly dodgy air of the
place, with its two-way mirror
and cubby-hole doorway into the
back studio, belies its official cer-
tification. Saint has his own rules
too: no one under 18 or over 80
and nothing on the face.

Scin

27 Kensington Park Road W11
0203 2200 121/www.scin.uk.com
Mon–Wed, Fri & Sat 9am–7pm;
Thurs 9am–8pm; Sun 12 noon–5pm

When sisters Anna and Nicky
Noble opened Scin in 2005, the
aim was to create a business that
combines boutique charm with
the practical philosophy of 'providing simple, quality treatments
that work'. And they more than
succeed. From the moment you
enter this light, airy space lined
with high-quality products you
know you're in good hands. New
customers are asked to fill out a
form detailing everything from
their daily water intake to
whether they suffer from claus-
trophobia (downstairs treatment
rooms are small but perfectly
relaxing). Customised facials,
aromatherapy massage, hydrother-
apy, organic body treatments,
manicures and pedicures are just
some of what's on offer. A
standard facial left my skin feeling, and looking, cleaner and
brighter than it had for a long
time. Highly recommended.

Zarvis

Unit 4, Portobello Green
281 Portobello Road W10
020 8968 5435/www.zarvis.com
Wed–Sat 12 noon–6pm;
Mon–Tues by appointment

Vivian Zarvis already mixes
medicinal and cosmetic herbs in
her tiny but enticing shop, but she
dreams of being able to have a
large space in which she could use
a giant pestle and mortar to blend
her concoctions. Way ahead of her
time, Vivian has been using simple
glass bottles and aluminium tins
with hand-written labels for her
brews for years. She studied
Ayurvedic medicine in India but,
rather than treating people who

are ill, encourages people to be good to themselves. She sources her ultra-pure ingredients from all over the world and sells tempting tins with names such as Dreamtime and Redemption. It would be easy to spend a fortune.

SHOPPING

Portobello antiques market

Portobello antiques market is a world in itself, a place where dealers trade with each other and visitors wander, some in search of a chance bargain, others hunting for specific curiosities. You'll find almost anything here, from 20th-century costume jewellery to antique prints and maps, enamel boxes, Georgian silver, oriental art and old teddy bears.

Below is only a tiny selection, mostly in order of specialisation and attempting to pick out some of the quirkier or more specifically British antiques that make the market unique. Unless otherwise stated, all are Saturday traders only.

The dealers themselves say that the strength of the pound, the difficulty of finding stock and rising rents are making life tough for those who trade in Portobello, and rumours abound that this arcade or that is about to be sold to some high-street retail chain. Despite the prevailing pessimism, there's a certain family atmosphere here and everyone knows everyone else; if you're looking for a particular treasure, ask around and you'll be directed to the right person.

A guide to the market can be found on many stalls and is also available from the Portobello Road Antique Dealers Association (PADA) at 223a Portobello Road, London W11 1LU (020 7229 8354; info@portobelloroad.co.uk; www.portobelloroad.co.uk; office open Tues & Fri 9.30am–2.30pm). There is also a Saturday information booth at the junction of Portobello Road and Westbourne Grove. PADA members subscribe to a code of practice printed on the back of the guide.

Trading begins at around 5.30am and most stallholders are in place by 8am. The old-timers tend to slope off home by about 2pm, some do antiques fairs at certain times of the year, and not all come in every week, so if you're intending to see a specific person, it's always worth checking they'll be there first.

PORTOBELLO MARKET STALLS & ARCADES

Battersea Pen Home
John Mckenzie
Admiral Vernon Arcade
141–49 Portobello Road W11
0870 900 1888/www.penhome.com

Vintage fountain pens
(Parker, Waterman, Swan and others) bought and sold, with all repairs and servicing by the Pen Home.

The Beatles Stall
Good Fairy Arcade
100 Portobello Road W11
020 8446 2886/07836 264336
beatlesyeahyeahyeah@hotmail.com

A range of **Beatles memorabilia** including original singles, picture discs, albums, magazines, photographs and some of the merchandise produced for their fans. Great fun.

Charles Vernon-Hunt
Geoffrey Van's Arcade
107 Portobello Road W11
020 8854 1588
c.vernonhunt@btinternet.com
Sat 8.30am–3.30pm

Specialises in **non-Western art and material-culture reference books** – new books, quality remainders and exhibition and auction catalogues. All books listed on ABE books, where they can be browsed under cultural area. Mail order and book search.

Delehar
146 Portobello Road W11
020 7727 9860 (Sat)/Sat 9.30am–4pm

This family-run business was established in 1911. The third generation now offers an eclectic selection of some of the best-quality antiques you will find anywhere. Flora Offord (020 8950 1474) specialises in **costume jewellery from the 1880s to 1960s,** chosen for wearability and style rather than just designer signatures. Her sister Marion Gettleson displays exquisite 18th- and early 19th-century English paste. Marion's main area of expertise is, well, indefinable; let's say **esoteric decorative objects, games** and **curiosities.** Peter Delehar (020 8423 8600) is an expert on **scientific and medical instruments.** The back of the shop is the domain of third sister Valerie Jackson-Harris (01923 829079). One of Britain's top dealers in **ephemera**, a term covering a wide range of marginalia from valentines to royal commemoratives, she has particularly fine material relating to London. The entire family are passionate about what they do and generous with their time and knowledge.

Erna Hiscock
Chelsea Galleries
69 Portobello Road W11
01233 661407

Samplers are **needlework** panels made from the 17th to the 19th centuries by young girls in order to show their skills with a needle. They would also embroider maps of the British Isles to learn the counties. Erna Hiscock has a large collection of these hugely decorative pieces of English social history, with prices ranging from £60 to £10,000. You will also find children's ceramics on this stand, as this is the field of Erna's partner John Shepherd (see below).

Eureka Antiques
Geoffrey Van Arcade
105 Portobello Road W11
020 7229 5577 (Sat)
0161 941 5453 (weekdays)

Tartanware was the product of a prolific cottage industry between 1830 and 1870 in and around the village of Mauchline, Ayrshire. A host of objects were produced, such as boxes and cotton reels for the souvenir market. Made from sycamore, they were covered in hand-printed or, more rarely, painted paper in every clan tartan going. Noel Gibson has been dealing for 40 years, 15 in Portobello, and his clients range from the Scottish aristocracy to North Americans looking for their family tartan. Some pieces have hand-painted miniatures with local views on them, and others are decorated with ferns (known as 'fernware').

Hilary Kashden
Stall 21, Admiral Vernon Arcade
141–49 Portobello Road W11
020 8455 3697/07712 532111 (mobile)

Hilary has been doing Portobello on and off for over 40 years, dealing in **pewter**, a material consisting of 90 per cent tin, which fulfilled the role of plastic from the 14th to the 19th centuries. Although produced all over Europe, British pewter is often reckoned to be of the best quality. It was used to make all manner of affordable domestic and tavern ware, enjoying its finest moment in the 17th century, until porcelain came along as a cheaper alternative. Designs copied those used for silverware, and Hilary has some splendidly decorative pieces, especially flagons, plates, candlesticks and spoons. She also has a small display cabinet of curios including pilgrim badges. Also vellum documents from the 13th to 19th centuries.

John Carnie Antiques
First Floor, Red Teapot Arcade
020 7221 6710 (Sat)/
07973 197974 (mobile)

After spending 20 years at Bermondsey market, John Carnie moved to Portobello in the mid-1990s. Although he only advertises as a specialist in **clocks, watches** and **barometers**, he also has a number of delightful **music boxes**, live **steam trains** (the biggest of which could pull 14 children) and various mechanical eccentricities. As he put it himself, these are 'toys for old boys'.

John Shepherd
Chelsea Galleries
69 Portobello Road W11
01233 661407

John Shepherd started his career as an archaeologist specialising in medieval pottery, before dealing in **English ceramics** dating from the Middle Ages up to the 1840s. His stock is mainly blue-and-white and creamware, with a growing collection of children's ware to complement the needle-work displayed by his partner Erna Hiscock.

Kleanthous Antiques Ltd
144 Portobello Road W11
020 7727 3649/antiques@kleanthous.com

Costas Kleanthous is the chairman of the Portobello Road Antiques Dealers Association, which has been trading since 1969. Kleanthous has a wide range of stock and specialises in **period jewellery** from the Georgian period through to Art Deco. Also a good selection of **vintage wrist** and **pocket watches**.

Lawrence Gould
Stand 29–30, Dolphin Arcade
157 Portobello Road W11
020 8459 7957

The only word for polyglot Lawrence Gould and his daughter Nicky is boisterous. Lawrence started as a keen collector who had to sell to make space; Nicky joined him 17 years ago. Trading insults and jokes at the top of their voices, it's quite a double act, but they really know their stuff.

Eighteenth- and 19-century English and continental **perfume bottles** and **Bilston enamel patch boxes** (a British speciality) make up the bulk of their stock, and they have the kind of pieces you'd expect to see in the V&A (and some of them have indeed ended up there). With their international client base, you can catch them at Olympia and Miami Beach antiques fairs as well as at Portobello.

Wynyard RT Wilkinson
Red Lion Arcade
165–169 Portobello Road
01787 237372

The unanimous word on the street is that if you're looking for **good-quality silver** at sensible prices, then this is your man. Extremely knowledgeable and highly respected in the trade, he has produced two books on Indian silver, as well as a history of hallmarks. Areas of specialisation include flatware (spoons and forks to you and me); cutlery, which apparently should only mean knives; full sets of 12 times everything, known as 'canteens'; and an array of collectibles from port labels to a novelty shot measure shaped like a top hat. Pieces date from 1650 to 1980 and come from England, Ireland, Scotland, North America, the Commonwealth and India.

ANTIQUES & VINTAGE CLOTHING

Alice's
86 Portobello Road
020 7792 2456
Tues–Sat 9am–5pm

Unmissable with its bright red façade, Alice's has been here for ever. In the Sixties this was the place for Edwardian policeman's cloaks and military costumes of the type worn by the Beatles on the cover of *Sgt Pepper's Lonely Hearts Club Band*. Nowadays the shop sells a cheerful selection of painted furniture, painted advertising boards, pine, toys and other pieces – both reproduction and antique.

The Antique Clothing Shop
282 Portobello Road W10
020 8964 4830
Fri & Sat 9am–6pm

Several vintage clothes shops have been squeezed out by trendy streetwear boutiques, but this rich resource, much favoured by models and stylists, at least appears to be surviving. Clothes and accessories span many eras, from Victorian bustle dresses, pantaloons and bonnets to Sixties flares and bright satin shirts – all at surprisingly reasonable prices.

Katrina Phillips
99 Portobello Road W11
020 7229 2113
Mon–Sat 9am–5pm; Sun 12 noon–6pm

Katrina has a wonderful eye for style. Born into the antiques trade (her father, Eddie Phillips, originally opened a shop here in 1963), she sources furniture, lighting, ceramics, vintage handbags – whatever catches her fancy – from all over the UK. Some items she customises, like a beautifully shaped armchair upholstered in plain linen but with its outline bordered in metal studs. She also sells lighting, jewellery and silverware by contemporary artists and has a growing line in imported furniture from Sri Lanka, where she goes often.

Last Place on Earth
307 Portobello Road W10
Mon–Thurs 11am–6pm; Fri & Sat 8.30am–6pm; Sun 11am–6pm

The mix of second-hand books, DVDs and bric-à-brac on the pavement outside belies the discoveries to be made in this shop's cavernous interior. Chandeliers, hand-embroidered cushions, Fifties lighting, cowboy boots, leather furniture, Victorian china, stuffed animals, gilt mirrors are just some of the items you might find, with clothes and accessories in the space at the back. Look out for the smaller, equally enticing branch of this Portobello institution now open on Bramley Road (p 200).

Mensah
291 Portobello Road W10
020 8960 8520
www.mensah.uk.com
Tues–Sat 10am–6pm
Sun 11am–5am
(closed Mon except by appointment)

Herbie Mensah's passion for fashion stems from his Ghanaian childhood, when he absorbed a great deal from observing people dressed up in their Sunday best, as well as from hours spent watching his seamstress mother at work. Herbie started collecting clothes while modelling for Vivienne Westwood, Jean Paul Gaultier and others in the Eighties, later selling them on a stall in Camden Market, followed by Portobello. The next logical step was this small but perfect boutique that he opened with his wife Sarah in 2005. Mensah specialises in wearable vintage clothes and accessories from the 1920s to the 1980s, but especially items from Mary Quant, Biba, Ossie Clarke and other well-known labels from the Sixties and Seventies. The couple also run a personal finding service and stock a limited selection of items by cutting-edge designers such as KIND, Mrs Jones and Louis de Gama.

Portobello Gallery
11 Portobello Road W11
020 7727 6739
Giselle_menhenett@btinternet.com
Wed, Thurs, Fri & Sat – afternoons

Vintage jewellery, objets d'art and crystal chandeliers. A treasure trove.

Sheila Cook Textiles
105–7 Portobello Road W11
020 7792 8001
www.sheilacook.co.uk
Open by appointment only

Sheila Cook has had shops in the area for the past 30 years. Her unique collection of textiles, costume and accessories dates from the late 18th century to the 1970s and cuts across the fashion and antique worlds, appealing as much to the public as to the film and television designers who hire from her. Rummage around for wonderful woven paisley shawls, or that little Forties garden-party dress, or ask for help from the bevy of young and friendly assistants.

ART MATERIALS

Lyndon's
216 Kensington Park Road W11
020 7727 5192
lyndons@artgraphics.fsnet.co.uk
Mon–Sat 9.30am–6pm

The move from Portobello into a bigger shop has enabled Lyndon's the stationers to expand its range of art materials, cards, stationery and office supplies. Competitive rates for colour photocopying.

Lyndon's Stitch & Beads
197 Portobello Road W11
020 7727 4357
www.beads-online.co.uk
Mon–Sat 9.30am–6pm

The corner branch now focuses more on crafts, with all you could possibly need in the way of beads, wools, buttons and dyes. A bead-stringing service is available, as well as a large range of haberdashery items and the increasingly popular Swarovski crystals.

BOOKS

Books for Cooks
4 Blenheim Crescent W11
020 7221 1992/www.booksforcooks.com
Bookshop Tues–Sat 10am–6pm; lunch
Tues–Fri 12 noon–3pm; Sat 11am–5pm

Like the Travel Bookshop opposite, Books for Cooks is something of a mecca for pilgrims – in this case serious foodies. Heidi Lascelles founded the shop in 1983, largely in response to the meagre stock of cookery books available in even the biggest London bookshops. Despite housing around 8000 cookery books – including many foreign-language editions – the real secret of its success lies in the idea of testing recipes from the books on the shelves and serving the resulting dishes at lunch time.

Blenheim Books
11 Blenheim Crescent W11
020 7727 0777
Mon–Sat 9am–6pm; Sun 12 noon–5pm

Originally Garden Books, opened in 1996 by Valerie Scriven and Rob Cassy, this attractive shop now stocks a wider range with the accent on interior and exterior design.

Oxfam Bookshop
170 Portobello Road W11
020 7727 2907
oxfamshop4753@btconnect.com
Mon–Thurs 10am–5.20pm; Fri & Sat
10am–6pm; Sun 12 noon–6pm

One of the growing number of Oxfam charity shops dedicated to books (at the last count there were 110 branches in the UK, the first of which opened in Oxford in 1987). It's also worth visiting for old records and CDs. Donations of the latter are particularly welcome.

The Travel Bookshop
13 Blenheim Crescent W11
020 7229 5260
www.thetravelbookshop.com
Mon–Sat 10am–6pm;
Sun 12 noon–5pm

Blenheim Crescent's first bookshop has a distinguished reputation with travellers and would-be travellers all over the world. Since 1999, it's also become a curious source of pilgrimage for the countless fans of Richard Curtis's film *Notting Hill* (see pp 52– 53).

CHILDREN'S CLOTHES & TOYS

Cheeky Monkeys

202 Kensington Park Road W11
020 7792 9022
Mon–Fri 9.30am–5.30pm; Sat
10am–5.30pm

The first of five in the Cheeky Monkeys chain, this is an old-fashioned toyshop, without a video game in sight. Adults enjoy themselves here as much as children, oohing over the beautiful traditional toys, including doll's-houses, fancy-dress costumes and an enormous range of those little gizmos you always longed to buy with your pocket money. There are also games, many of them with an educational bent, and a small range of clothes. Bookshop downstairs.

Honeyjam

267 Portobello Road W11
020 7243 0449
www.honeyjam.co.uk
Mon–Sat 10am–6pm;
Sun 12 noon–4pm

Lifelong friends Jasmine Guinness and Honey Bowdrey opened this delightful toyshop partly in response to the closure of Barnetts, the highly popular toyshop that for many years dominated the corner of Elgin Crescent and Kensington Park Road. Carefully designed to allow room for manoeuvring buggies, Honeyjam has a spacious, airy feel but with plenty to choose from: wooden toys and ride-ons, classic board games, vintage doll's-houses plus a good range of smaller items with presents in mind. The dressing-up outfits – from pirates to angels – are especially imaginative; like most of the toys, the few clothes on display, including cashmere babies' outfits and pretty nightdresses, tend towards the traditional.

One Small Step One Giant Leap

3 Blenheim Crescent W11
0207 243 0535
www.onesmallsteponegiantleap.com
Mon–Fri 10am–6pm; Sat 9am–6pm;
Sun 11am–5pm

Good for a wide range of children's footwear – many French shoes as well as the traditional Start-rites. Special fitting service on child-sized chairs.

Sasti

Unit 8, Portobello Green
281 Portobello Road W10
020 8960 1125/www.sasti.co.uk
Mon–Sat 10.30am–6pm; Sun 11am–4pm

Exciting children's wear and accessories (age range is 0–6 years) for those who want something trendy and different to the high street without paying designer prices. Labels include Squirt knitwear, Our Life and Ten Fingers Ten Toes. The shop includes a lovely play area with toys to keep non-shoppers happy. Comprehensive mail order service available on website.

Their Nibs
214 Kensington Park Road W11
020 7221 4263/www.theirnibs.com
Mon–Fri 9.30am–6pm;
Sat 10am–6pm; Sun 12 noon–5pm

Here the accent is on designer children's wear with a retro feel, inspired by the kinds of fabrics and prints you might well find on a trawl through the market – there's even a vintage rail. Cowboys and pirates are popular themes for boys, and girls' dresses and blouses are predictably flowery, but designs are original and clothes well made, with lots of attention to detail.

FASHION

Beatrice von Tresckow
9 Portobello Road W11
020 7243 8747/ww.beatricevontresckow.com
Mon–Sat 10am–6pm

If you're after a sparkly or glittery outfit for a special occasion – this is the shop for you. They also do hats and a made-to-order service.

The Dispensary
200 Kensington Park Road W11
020 7727 8797
Mon–Sat 10.30am–6.30pm;
Sun 12 noon–5pm

A popular place for offbeat streetwear, trainers and accessories for men, women and children, the Dispensary has a large cult following among Japanese tourists and media and advertising types. Its own label consists of denim, unusual T-shirts, bags, belts and a good collection of leather jackets and trousers.

Euforia
61b Lancaster Road W11
020 7243 1808/www.euphoria.uk.com
Mon–Sat 10.30am–6.30pm

Avant-garde creations and an eclectic mix of footwear and accessories share space with carefully selected pop-culture books, collectors' fashion and lifestyle magazines. Owner Annette Olivieri is a leather expert; among the clothes she designs and makes herself are some gorgeous ruched jackets and coats with delicate string-tie fastenings and necklines. Popular with the fashion in-crowd.

The London Beach Store

23 Kensington Park Road W11
020 7243 2772
www.londonbeachstore.co.uk
Mon, Wed & Fri 10am–6.30pm;
Tues 10am–5.30pm; Thurs 10am–7.30pm;
Sat 9.30am–6.30pm; Sun 12 noon–5.30pm

This friendly shop has successfully cornered the Notting Hill market in sports and travel clothing and accessories – not just stylish and wearable swimwear but clothes and equipment for mountaineering, snowboarding, kite-surfing and a whole lot more.

Nancy Pop

19 Kensington Park Road W11
020 7221 9797/www.nancy.pop.com
Mon–Sat 10.30am–6.30pm; Sun
11.30am–6pm

This fabulous boutique has a distinctly European feel, from architect Joel Degermark's angular mauve interior to the rails of cutting-edge clothes that line the walls – a far cry from the floral patterns and bohemian chic that tend to dominate this street. Buyer Helen Roysdotter describes the shop as 'directional', with an emphasis on clothes and accessories by Scandinavian labels like Lizette Snorgaard and 10 Swedish Designers, as well as the more affordable Nancy Pop label. Look out for shoes by Strutt Couture.

Olivia Morris

355 Portobello Road W10
020 8962 0353
Open by appointment only

One of the UK's top shoe designers, in the six years or so since she moved from Portobello Green to this shop at the far northern end of Portobello (look out for the pink neon stiletto sign), Morris's business has gone from strength to strength. Very much a designer's designer, her beautifully crafted shoes (made in Italy) are distinctively quirky, with Frida Kahlo, Diane Arbus, Pop Art and the 1950s quoted as inspirations.

The Portobello Road Cashmere Shop
166 Portobello Road W11
020 7792 2571
www.portobellocashmere.com
Mon, Thurs & Fri 10am–6pm;
Sat 9am–6pm;
Sun 11am–5pm (times vary slightly according to season)

Devoted to the best-feeling wool in the world, this shop sells great-value cashmere in a range of good colours. Using only Scottish wool, owner Annemarie Beatty designs many of the gloves, scarves, sweaters and cardigans herself – many of them are made in Hawick. European *Vogue* has described it as 'the kind of shop you have to keep popping into'. Many locals would agree.

Also look out for second–hand cashmere on **market stalls** under the Westway (Fri & Sat) and on Fridays between the junctions of Cambridge Gardens and Oxford Gardens.

Preen
Unit 5, Portobello Green Arcade
281 Portobello Road W10
020 8968 1542
Thurs & Fri 11am–6pm;
Sat 10am–6pm

Popular for its hybrid style of clothes, fusing antique with modern, masculine with feminine, Preen is immediately recognisable by signature touches of small but significant detailing, such as puffs and tucks, as well as the imaginative use of recycled pieces. A favourite with celebrities such as Kate Moss, Liv Tyler and Kylie Minogue, the company has had phenomenal success in Britain, New York and Tokyo, and is much sought after by buyers and press during London Fashion Week.

Still
61d Lancaster Road W11
020 7243 2932
info@.still-shop.uk
Mon–Sat 11am–6pm;
Sun 12 noon–4pm

In this lovely calm space, just around the corner from the bustle of Portobello Road, owner Sophie Mason has graduated from stocking only vintage clothes to also selling her own designs. As ever, the emphasis is on beautiful textiles. Sophie's collections are sometimes made from vintage fabrics but increasingly she uses ethically produced organic cotton or wool, such as Donegal tweed and felt bought direct from nomadic sheep herders in Asia.

Sub Couture

204 Kensington Park Road W11
020 7229 5434
subcouture@x-stream.co.uk
Mon–Sat 10.30am–6.30pm;
Sun 12 noon–5pm

Nestling quietly among the restaurants and wine bars, Sub Couture offers a selection of contemporary designer wear from bohemian to classic, including accessories and shoes by 32 labels, from Christian Lacroix, Amaya Azaruga, Bruns Bazaar, Kenzo and Missoni to Cutler & Gross. The shop's look changes almost weekly to coincide with the arrival of new collections. The clientele's ages range from 25 to 45 and everyone is treated with the personal touch and honest advice. Tailoring service available.

Supra Girls/Supra Boys

249 Portobello Road W11
info@suprafly.com
Mon–Thurs 11am–6pm; Fri & Sat
10.30am–6pm; Sun 12 noon–5pm

This shop is a favourite of Natalie Imbruglia and rock chicks who still like to wear their Levi's but teamed with some seriously fashionable T-shirts and accessories. Labels include Tatty Devine, Mr Friendly, Zakee Shariff and PPQ.

A small selection of trainers and shoes is also available.

For contemporary designers also see **Mensah.**

FLOWERS & PLANTS

Toms

Corner Elgin Crescent & Kensington Park Rd
020 7792 8510
Mon, Thurs, Fri & Sat 9am–6.30pm;
Tues & Wed 9am–6pm; Sun 10am–5pm

High rent increases forced Tom out of his Elgin Crescent shop but he kept a stall on this corner site and now also works out of a tiny studio in Clarendon Road (see p 197).

Valerie's Flowers

337 Portobello Road W10
020 8969 2927
Mon–Sat 8.30am–6pm

Being at the 'wrong' end of Portobello Road, Valerie Pile is able to offer very competitive prices. With its tiled floor, the shop has an old-fashioned feeling, but Valerie, who did her apprenticeship with Moyses Stevens, does contemporary arrangements for all occasions and will also deliver locally.

GALLERIES

East West
8 Blenheim Crescent W11
0207 229 7981
www.eastwestgallery.co.uk
Wed–Sat 10am–6pm and by appointment

David Solomon and Jill Morgan travelled around Eastern Europe in a camper van, meeting painters, before opening in 1990 with a show by an artist from Belgrade. Their appearance on the art scene was a baptism by fire, for within a short time 24 galleries in the neighbourhood (briefly known as the second Cork Street) closed. David had trained as an accountant, Jill as a painter, but neither had any experience running a gallery. However, they survived and now organise 12 exhibitions a year featuring interesting work from around the world. Both are great believers in drawing, and most of the paintings exhibited are figurative. They do not consider themselves leading-edge but rather show painters who have an intelligence behind what they do and who they believe will endure.

Portobello Auctions
07950 647 485
portobelloauctions@tiscali.co.uk

Situated at the junction of Portobello Road and Elgin Crescent, the auctions of paintings, watercolours and drawings take place fortnightly on summer Saturdays – viewing from 11am and the auction starts at 2pm. Most are in the £50–£250 price range.

The Portobello Print and Map Shop
109 Portobello Road W11
020 7792 9673 or 020 8852 2717
portobelloprint@v21net.co.uk
Tues–Fri 11am–4pm; Sat 8am–5pm

The biggest selection of original maps, prints and engravings in Portobello: classified by subject, every possible category is covered, from furniture design to birds. If you're looking for something particularly British there are maps starting from the 17th century, views of London and the rest of England, charming song sheets (the forerunners of hit singles), sporting and coaching prints, and the crude satire of 18th- and 19th-century political cartoons. All pictures have new mounts and prices are surprisingly reasonable, starting at around £15.

GIFTS & HOME

Bellhouse & Company
33 Kensington Park Road W11
020 7221 0187/bimbi@bellhouseco.com
Opening times by appointment

If your place needs a facelift, Bimbi Bellhouse's basement fabric library, also featuring wall coverings and specialist flooring, is a great place to go for inspiration and friendly advice. For those seeking more help, Bimbi and her team offer a professional interior design and project management.

Ceramica Blue
10 Blenheim Crescent W11
020 7727 0288
www.ceramicablue.co.uk
Mon–Sat 10am–6.30pm;
 Sun 12 noon–4pm

New Zealander Lindy Whiffen opened her first small shop in Clarendon Road in 1987, moving to Blenheim Crescent, 'the best street in the area', two years later. Ceramica Blue stocks the best of international tableware and table linen from Italy, Spain, France, Tunisia, Colombia, South Africa, New Zealand, England, Wales, Holland and Thailand. Lindy travels widely, always on the lookout for new stock.

Chloe Alberry
84 Portobello Road W11
0207 727 0707/www.chloealberry.com
Mon–Sat 9am–6pm; Sun 10am–5pm

With its blue façade and striped blue and white awnings, this pretty doorknob shop matches the seaside feel that characterises this end of Portobello. Door fittings come in a range of materials including wood, iron, ceramics and coloured glass.

The Cloth Shop
290 Portobello Road W10
020 7968 6001
www.clothshop.co.uk
Mon–Sat 10am–6pm

An original combination of antique linen sheets, Welsh blankets, saris and dyed muslin pack the shelves of this likeable shop, which also stocks a large range of cotton furnishing-fabric in strong pinks, reds, greens and other good plain colours.

Gong
182 Portobello Road W11
020 7565 4162
Mon–Sun 10am–6pm

Eastern style permeates this shop, though Belgian owner Jo Plismy has introduced an increasing number of well-chosen objects from Africa and the Mediterranean since opening in 1999. Crackle-glazed vases and bowls, plain bamboo lamp-stands, finely made Chinese mats and leather shopping bags from Mali are just some of the items you might find. Gong is also the place to buy bamboo curtain poles, reasonably priced and tastefully stained in various shades of brown.

Graham & Green

4 & 7 Elgin Crescent W11
020 7727 4594
www.grahamandgreen.co.uk
Mon–Fri 10am–6pm; Sat 9.30am–6pm;
Sun 11.30am–5pm

Each of these shops is a great source of presents (especially if you're feeling generous), as well as an inspiration for ideas on how to embellish your home. No. 4 is cluttered with sumptuous embroidered cushions and throws, kelims, mirrors, wooden candlesticks, hats and hand-painted furniture, while No. 7 has a more modern, cutting-edge feel. Here mock-leather bags, baskets, ceramics and chrome gadgets jostle for space with the latest in Italian lighting. Rent increases make it hard for any independent business on this patch, but origi-

nality and a knack for keeping up with the times will surely enhance G & G's chances of survival.

Temptation Alley

361 Portobello Road
020 8964 2004
Mon–Sat 10am–5.30pm

This treasure trove of trimmings is indeed a dress or soft-furnishing maker's heaven. A good old-fashioned haberdashery (probably the only one for miles around), it's packed with a chaotic collection of ribbons, lace and braid – in boxes, on the counter, hanging from the ceiling – and all manner of catches and cottons and buttons.

Verandah

15b Blenheim Crescent W11
020 7792 9289
Mon–Sat 10am–6pm; Sun 12 noon–5pm

Happily, when textile designer Simone Russell took over this long-established treasure house of ceramics, lanterns, colourful baskets, Mexican mirrors, painted trays from Thailand, flying teddies and other knick-knacks, she inherited many of her predecessor's stockists. She also cut down on the clutter, but this is still a great place for original presents, especially at Christmas, when the shop shimmers with brilliantly coloured decorations from different parts of the world. A clothes range designed by Simone and produced in India is also proving to be popular.

Yaya
263 Portobello Road W11
020 7243 0733
Mon–Sat 10am–6pm;
Sun 11am–5pm

No. 263 is essentially a clothes shop selling basic items like men's shirts and women's jackets and coats, but West African owner Yaya has a small collection of brightly coloured papier mâché bowls that he sells to raise funds for the charity Wola Nani. The bowls are inexpensive – they come in three sizes, the largest costing £9.99. They make great presents and a proportion of every one sold goes towards supporting women living with HIV/AIDS.

JEWELLERY

Andea Jewellery
203 Portobello Road W11
020 7221 5690
Mon–Sat 10am–6pm;
Sun 11am–5pm

Long-established wholesalers in the area, Andea specialises in silverwork designed and made in Mexico – not just rings, bracelets and necklaces, but gift items such as babies' rattles, paper knives and key rings. Prices can vary from around £3 for plain hoop earrings to £400 for a heavy silver necklace. It's also a good place for Chinese pottery, silk cushions and ancient stoneware for the house or garden.

Horace
312 Portobello Road W10
(corner of Golborne Road)
020 8968 1188
www.horacedesign.com
Tues–Sat 10am–5.30pm

With its mixture of bling and more low-key pieces, this purple-fronted jewellery shop has a huge selection of modern rings, bracelets, cufflinks, pendants and other necklaces aimed at the well-heeled urban market.

Isis
Unit 3, Portobello Green
281 Portobello Road W10
020 8968 5055
Mon–Sat 9.30am–5.30pm

Isis has been selling modern silver jewellery in Portobello Green since its inception. As for most designers in the arcade, the combination of workspace and shop means that Linda Atkinson can design and make her jewellery as well as sell it on the spot. She also displays the work of other contemporary jewellers that complements her own pieces.

Jessie Western
82b Portobello Road W11
020 7229 2544
www.jessie.western.com
Mon–Sat 10am–6pm; Sun 12 noon–5.30pm

This tiny shop is crammed with Western-inspired goods, from authentic cowboy hats and Texas-made boots (for women and men) to Native American arts and crafts (as opposed to artefacts, which are illegal) bought directly from makers on the reservations. Genuine turquoise jewellery is a strong feature, as are turquoise-studded leather bags and belts.

Sarah Bunting
Unit 22, Portobello Green
281 Portobello Road W10
020 8968 2253
sarahbunting@enterprise.net
Mon–Sat 10am–6pm (or later by appointment)

Sarah Bunting does many jew-ellery commissions for engagements and weddings, which she designs and makes in her studio-cum-shop. She loves working alone and produces pieces in gold, silver and platinum using precious and semi-precious stones.

Also see **Supra Girls** for jewellery by, among others, Tatty Devine

MUSIC

Honest Jons
278 Portobello Road W10
020 8969 9822
www.honestjons.com
Mon–Sat 10am–6pm;
Sun 11am–5pm

One of the best-known music haunts in London, Honest Jons began trading in the early 1970s, moving to its present position in 1979. Roots music with passion is the order of the day and careful sifting is guaranteed to unearth some gems. In partnership with local musician Damon Albarn, co-owners Alan and Mark have produced a great series of compilations on their own label, among them *London Is the Place for Me*, celebrating the music of black Londoners from the 1950s onwards.

Intoxica

231 Portobello Road W11
020 7229 8010/www.intoxica.co.uk
Mon–Fri 10.30am–6.30pm;
Sat 10am–6.30pm;
Sun 12 noon–5pm

Founded in 1975, this collectors' paradise changed in the mid-Nineties from a specialist Sixties-only shop to one selling across-the-board specialist records. Nowadays you'll find as many records by Yusef Lateef as by the Yardbirds. Through the street-level shop containing Sixties vinyl, some with the rarity value of a Ming vase, steps lead down to a cellar where jazz buffs will be amazed and delighted to find a huge selection of jazz esoterica. This space also doubles as an art gallery, with some wonderful jazz and pop memorabilia for sale.

Minus Zero Records & Stand Out Collectibles

2 Blenheim Crescent W11
020 7229 5424/020 7727 8406
www.minuszerorecords.com
Fri & Sat 10.30am–6.30pm;
mail order in operation for the rest of the week

As co-proprietor Bill (1) explains, the arched wooden door of No. 2 Blenheim Crescent leads into two separate, yet oddly similar, shops: to your left, Minus Zero takes its name from a well-known Dylan song and specialises in highly collectible pop, rock and folk, mainly from the mid to late Sixties, while in Stand Out Collectibles on the right, the equally affable Bill (2) sells much the same. A glance through the catalogue will render the most avid enthusiast speechless as undreamed-of Jethro Tull albums and ancient recordings by the Incredible String Band nestle alongside bands even more obscure than the 13th Floor Elevators.

Rough Trade

130 Talbot Road W11
020 7229 8541
www.roughtrade.com
Mon–Sat 10am–6.30pm;
Sun 12 noon–5pm

A spearhead organisation at the start of the punk era, Rough Trade continues to thrive into the 21st century thanks to its ongoing policy of promoting some of the most obscure and vibrant music of the day. Prospective purchasers can check out the panoramic range of vinyl on the decks provided or trawl through the racks of fliers advertising forthcoming events throughout London. The shop also stocks a wide variety of fanzines and mags.

Sounds

236 Portobello Road W11
020 7467 0708
Mon–Sat 12 noon–7pm; Sun 1pm–6pm

This intimate shop caters to a younger clientele and has an excellent range of soul, R&B and dance music. Judging by the Friday and Saturday crowd, the music on offer, plus a nicely chilled vibe, make it a popular choice with cutting-edge youth. Sifting through the wide-ranging music revealed some intriguing Seventies remixes and, somewhat incongruously, albums by the Corrs.

NEWSAGENTS

Rococo

12 Elgin Crescent W11
020 7727 5209
Mon–Sat 5am–7pm; Wed & Sat till 7.30pm;
Sun 5am–5pm

With nearly 2000 magazine titles jammed into its shelves, this has to be one of the best-stocked newsagents in town. It has a good selection of foreign journals and newspapers, and will order anything that is not in stock.

Stationery, cards, sweets and lottery tickets also sold. However, it is under new ownership and it remains to be seen if the high standards will continue.

Portobello Gold, Portobello Road

Mural of Samuel Beckett, Blenheim Crescent

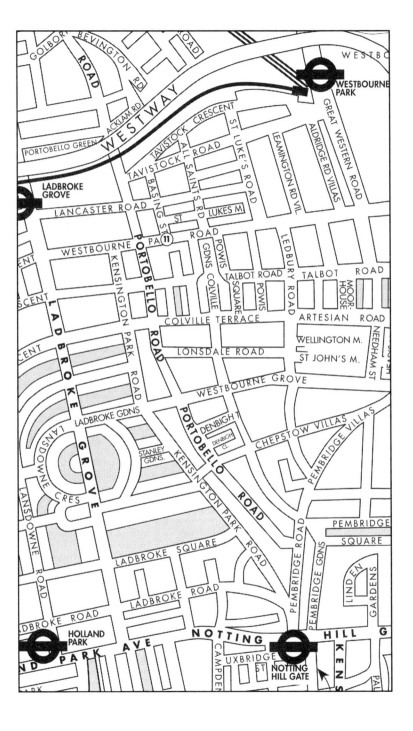

3 WESTBOURNE PARK AND WESTBOURNE GROVE

Tube: Westbourne Park, Notting Hill Gate
Highlights: 20th Century Theatre, music legends, shopping, galleries, eating and drinking

*One vivid contrast hung in his mind symbolical. On the one hand were the
coalies of the Westbourne Park yards, on strike and gaunt and hungry, children
begging in the black slush, and starving loungers outside a soup kitchen; and on
the other, Westbourne Grove, two streets further, a blazing array of crowded
shops, a stirring traffic of cabs and carriages, and such a spate of spending that
a tired student in leaky boots and graceless clothes hurrying home was continu-
ally impeded in the whirl of skirts and parcels and sweetly pretty womanliness.*
(HG Wells, *Love and Mr Lewisham*, 1900)

This still applies today: the scale of municipal housing, from
Westbourne Park station on Great Western Road, in and around All
Saints Road and Powis Square to Westbourne Grove, remains in stark
contrast to the wave of Parisian-style boutiques that has invaded this
modern version of the Grove
since the early 1990s. After
English, often with a North
American twang, French and
Italian are the languages spoken
here. All Saints Road and Powis
Square, with their heady memories from the 1960s and 70s, are
equally cosmopolitan but in a
quite different way. A large number of West Indian families occupied the tenement buildings of
that time, and though many may
have died or since moved on,
many remain. It was no accident
that this was one of the main

Turquoise Island, Westbourne Grove

hotspots of the 1958 race riots that so shook the fabric of Notting Hill.

Westbourne Park Road

Coming out of Westbourne Park tube station, a right turn takes you down the busy Great Western Road, past blocks of council flats to Westbourne Park Road. To the left, this unremarkable road soon shifts tone with the presence of the Cow 'Saloon Bar and Dining Rooms', followed by the equally popular Westbourne on the corner where the road takes on the grander name of Westbourne Park Villas. Owned by Tom Conran of the Conran dynasty (also with his own nearby diner and deli, see pp 110 & 112), the Cow is a down-to-earth pub with a comfortable atmosphere and good food. The Westbourne, opposite a curve of interesting shops, tends to draw a younger crowd. Situated in the borough of Westminster (as opposed to Kensington & Chelsea), this is very much the outer edge of Notting Hill. The poet and novelist Thomas Hardy (1840–1928) lived at No. 16.

The main expanse of Westbourne Park Road lies in the other direction, westwards towards Portobello Road. Apart from the transformation of the grotty pub on the corner of Ledbury Road into the Liquid Lounge (now Bumpkin), the appearance of this stretch, past the junctions with Aldridge Road Villas, Leamington Road Villas and St Luke's Road, has changed relatively little in the past 20 years. The naturalist and novelist WH Hudson (1841–1922) died at No. 40; best known for *Green Mansions* and *Far Away and Long Ago*, the autobiography of his childhood in Argentina, the memorial to him in Hyde Park is a Jacob Epstein statue of Rima (the mysterious girl/spirit in *Green Mansions*).

All Saints Road

Walking down this street of classy shops and restaurants, it's hard to believe that for nearly three decades – from the late 1960s to the early 1990s – All Saints Road epitomised the so-called 'frontline', and it wasn't simply a no-go area controlled by drug dealers. With the Mangrove restaurant at its centre, this short road represented an important focal point for many black people, both inside and outside Notting Hill. A popular West Indian takeaway, Philsen's Phil-Inn Station, occupied the site on the corner of St Luke's Mews West now taken up by the Ripe Tomato restaurant. Shops displayed the Rastafarian colours, crowds chatted on the pavement, reggae music wafted or boomed from every other parked car, and, much to the frustration of some residents, there was usually a shebeen close by. Chris Salewicz gives a great description of these illegal drinking dens in *Redemption Song* (2006), his biography of Joe Strummer:

Joe introduced Sean to the Ladbroke Grove world of Jamaican shebeens, illegal basement drinking-dens with roughly constructed bars, the staff protected from hold-ups by chicken-wire in which a small slot had been cut to accept money and dispense cans of Tennant's and Special Brew, the super-strength beers that guaranteed hangovers; in these barely lit dives, like the one run by reggae legend Alton Ellis at the top of Ladbroke Grove, the pair would stand and sway in the corners as the spine-jerking bass rumbled out of enormous sound system speakers; invariably they would be the only white people present.

The Mangrove Steel Band, based at the Tabernacle, sometimes plays for carnival out on All Saints Road, but apart from this seasonal burst of live music, only the presence of People's Sounds reggae music shop and the activism of its owner, Daddy VGo, give any hint of the street as it used to be. As well as seeing to it that strings of red, green and gold carnival bunting are put up every year, VGo organises a free family day for local children in July.

The Mangrove, All Saints Road

THE MANGROVE

The Mangrove restaurant was opened in the late 1960s by Frank Critchlow, who originally came from Trinidad. His previous venture, the Rio Café on Westbourne Park Road, had already combined being a black community centre and a slightly risqué meeting place for white adventurers such as Colin MacInnes and, later, Christine Keeler and friends (see History, p 242). As Courtney Tulloch, a black activist at the time, put it, 'All kinds of people in high places used to go for their quaint cup of coffee down in the ghetto. Slumming.' But the Mangrove was a more ambitious project. Critchlow's aim was to create a smarter place, tastefully decorated, where a mixed crowd could meet over drinks and Caribbean and English food. And it worked. By day it was a popular hang-out for locals; by night it was packed with people from all over, among them academics, politicians, actors, musicians and other performers, black and white. In the words of Frank Critchlow, quoted in *Windrush* (1998),

We had Sammy Davis there, we had a lot of stars there. Nina Simone, Vanessa Redgrave, Maurice Bishop, Walter Rodney, Darcus Howe. CLR James used to have a lot of people; he used to take over one side of the restaurant and talking to people because everybody wants to hear ... very, very in-crowd.

But the police were never far away. Notting Hill was becoming an increasingly popular haunt of musicians, hippies and bohemian types, many of whom scored their dope in All Saints Road. The police response was to target the Mangrove and other Caribbean venues, raiding them again and again in a manner quite disproportionate to the level of crime at that time. Eventually, in exasperation, Critchlow led a protest march in 1970. When hordes of police tried to alter the direction of the march, trouble broke out and many were arrested, resulting in nine coming to trial in the 'Mangrove Nine' case. All were found innocent by the jury. Conflict continued well into the 1980s as drugs became an increasingly serious problem on the frontline, culminating in 1987 with the arrest of Frank Critchlow. Despite testimony against him from 36 police officers, it was proven to be a trumped-up drug charge and he was released. Within three years he was awarded compensation, but felt defeated. Unable to restrain the continuing conflict between youth and the law that would often escalate around Carnival, he decided to sell the restaurant. In no time the building reopened as the Portobello Dining Rooms, the street's first trendy restaurant, later replaced by the bar Ruby & Sequoia.

All Saints Road has other claims to fame besides its turbulent history and its current reputation for cutting-edge food and design. It was here, in August 1992, that Shaznay Lewis first met Mel Blatt, leading to the formation of the band All Saints, recently revived in 2006. They were introduced in Metamorphosis recording studios (No. 18, on the site of the old Apollo pub) where, joined by sisters Natalie and Nicole

Appleton, they went on to record their first big hit *Never, Ever*. St Luke's Mews West, just around the corner from the Jackson sisters' colourful shop, The Jacksons, also has strong musical associations. In the early 1970s, No. 35 was squatted by members of heavy metal rock band Motörhead. Ten years later, in Sarm West studios at the other end of the mews, Band Aid recorded the famous hit *Do They Know It's Christmas*, raising millions of pounds for charity. Sarm West continues to record a host of big names including Madonna, Blur, Radiohead, Boyzone, George Michael and M People, whose singer Heather Small was born and brought up off the Portobello Road.

Musicians also visit All Saints Road for its guitar and fiddle shop, run by a trio of enthusiasts at No. 13. On the next block running north, bicycle enthusiasts will find another specialist haven – Ninon Asuni's Bicycle Workshop. As well as doing repairs, Ninon carries a huge quantity of spares, plus publications and accessories, and will even order unusual new bikes.

In and around Powis Square

Back on Westbourne Park Road, almost directly opposite the junction with All Saints Road, is Powis Gardens, leading to Powis Square. The square, with the handsome red-brick Tabernacle at one end, has an interesting history, as does All Saints Church and the old church hall that was demolished in the 1970s.

Towards the end of the 19th century, the large Victorian houses in and around Powis Square had become seriously dilapidated as investors such as the ill-fated Reverend Walker (see History, p 235) were unable to fund the building work necessary for their upkeep. Many houses were divided into flats and single rooms, often used as boarding houses for students. One particular block on Powis Square provided the premises for Wren College, a coaching establishment run by Walter Wren, who specialised in preparing young men for the Indian Civil Service. So many of these men took lodgings in the vicinity that according to Florence Gladstone, author of *Notting Hill in Bygone Days*, 'the neighbourhood acquired the name of "Little India"'. Unfortunately, this did little to halt its decline, which continued well into the 1950s, when Peter Rachman came on the scene to make this the heart of his shady empire, later emulated, at least in part, by the highly controversial and erratic Michael X, who lived at various times in Colville Terrace, Powis Terrace and Powis Square. This area was also a focus for some of the three days of violence that constituted the Notting Hill race riots in 1958, referred to by Peter Ackroyd in *London: The Biography* (2000):

... the worst rioting took place on Monday 1 September, in the central area of Notting Hill Gate. Mobs congregated in Colville Road, Powis Square and Portobello Road before going on a 'smashing rampage, chanting "Kill niggers!" ... ' One observer noted that 'Notting Hill had become like a looking-glass world, for all the most mundane objects which everyone takes for granted had suddenly assumed the most profound importance. Milk bottles were turned into missiles, dustbin lids into primitive shields.'

In the wake of the riots, Powis Square remained in and out of the news throughout the 1960s, chiefly as a significant focus of community action. Among local people's many grievances was the lack of anywhere safe for children to play. In their midst, behind metal fencing and firmly locked gates, lay a tantalising patch of green grass – the abandoned square. According to the late André Shervington, who lived nearby, it was so overgrown that at one point a goat was thrown in, presumably to fatten up for a good West Indian curry. Public protest came to a head with two separate occupations of the square, the second of which led to its permanent liberation when the Council was finally persuaded to capitulate and take the land out of private ownership to create a public play space for children. It took further years of campaigning by, among others, Rhaune Laslett, a great champion of children and a key figure in the history of Carnival (p 216), to obtain a play hut and equipment of the kind you see today.

In 1968, the year in which it was liberated, Powis Square attracted public attention of a very different kind with the filming of Nicolas Roeg and Donald Cammell's *Performance* at No. 25. Only the exterior of the house was used, together with the square garden, which Cammell considered to be the ideal location for conveying 'kaleidoscopic moods in a strange and faded area of London'(also see p 225). Nicolas Roeg now lives nearby.

Many of the meetings held to plan community action took place in All Saints Church Hall, which was also used for socials and benefits

Emily Young in her Free School days

connected to the London Free School, based at No. 26 Powis Terrace, opposite the former studio of David Hockney. In Jonathon Green's *Days in the Life: Voices from the English Underground 1961–1971* (1998), Emily Young, a recruit from Holland Park Comprehensive, recalls the 'very curious double life' she led between home, Holland Park and the Free School:

Nothing was really taught but it was great fun. Local people could come in and play their instruments and it was a place for them to rehearse. John Michell had an interesting influence. He was knowledgeable, he did have these odd books – there were a lot of books, great enthusiasm for interesting old arcane knowledge, and much about flying saucers, the measurements of Jerusalem and all this stuff.

The School lasted about two years, its precarious funding aided by several benefit concerts at All Saints Church Hall, the most memorable of which featured Pink Floyd in 1966 and virtually launched their career (see Music, p 206). The hall was also used for children's playgroups and a number of theatrical events, including a production of Langston Hughes's *Shakespeare in Harlem*. Along with all the church's ancillary buildings, it was eventually redeveloped in the 1970s, in co-operation with the Notting Hill Housing Trust, to provide the flats now bordering Powis Gardens, as well as a new church hall, sacristy and vestry.

The following story was published in the London Free School newsletter, **The Grove**, 23 May, 1966:

MUHAMMED ALI VISITS W11

World Heavyweight Champion Muhammed Ali paid what was supposed to be a private visit to the Play Group of the London Free School at 3pm last Sunday.

But for the entire neighbourhood it was one of those days when there was something in the air from first thing in the morning. Maybe it was the steady flow of well-washed children into 34 Tavistock Crescent, maybe it was the dozen or so determined looking helpers who dutifully gathered to make sure that no harm came to the great man.

Whatever it was, Muhammed Ali had been in the house for only ten minutes and the street was blocked with expectant people. What a Sunday afternoon! The newspapers, bless them, had also heard and the cameramen waited patiently.

Inside, Muhammed gently sat down on the floor and talked with the children, signing countless autographs. Half an hour passed quickly, and party dresses got crumpled, carefully brushed hair wildly ruffled. But no one minded, least of all Muhammed himself. It's not often you have the chance to climb all over the World Heavyweight Champion!

After a short word with the grown-ups, Muhammed went out and stood in the porch, shaking hands and talking to anyone who could hear enough. The crowd went wild and he just grinned. 'Are you happy?' a voice shouted. 'Yes, I'm happy here,' he replied, almost in a whisper.

Then it was time to go. After some time a path was cleared through the cheering crowd, and our visitor was gone. The street full of people, sun shining, warm day.

MUHAMMED ALI VISITS W11

ALL SAINTS CHURCH

All Saints Church was the project of the Reverend Walker, who planned it as the centrepiece of his housing development in and around what are now Powis and Colville Squares. It was also intended as a memorial to his parents, so it must have been doubly disappointing when, in 1855, building work had to be abandoned due to lack of funds. The structure, designed by William White, was complete, but having no glass or furniture, the church couldn't be used. It remained abandoned for another six years, when it was popularly known as 'Walker's Folly' or 'All Sinners in the Mud'. Walker eventually managed to fund the remaining work, though in a more modest style than his original dream, and in 1861 the church was opened up to the community.

The church was badly bombed in the Second World War and was again unused until 1951, when it reopened, resplendent with new shrines in honour of the saints, and gold-leaf altarpieces by Sir Ninian Comper. These were symbols of the kind of ultra-High Church worship for which All Saints had become renowned under its flamboyant vicar, Father John Twisaday (1931–1961). Entering All Saints, one is struck by the wide, open sanctuary with its centrally placed stone altar, above which hangs the newly restored hanging rood, first installed in 1934. This was designed by Cecil Hare, as was the reredos beneath the east window. To the south, the small chapel dedicated to Our Lady of Walsingham reflects Father Twisaday's involvement in the restoration of pilgrimages to Walsingham in the 1930s. Halfway along the south side, the statue of St Mary Magdalene was designed and executed by Monsieur Dupon of Bruges, who also made the figures of St Joseph (on the north side) and St Anthony of Padua. These, together with other items, were brought back from Bruges bit by bit in the boot of Father Twisaday's car. In the south transept is the altar of St George, designed by Martin Travers as a memorial to the men of All Saints who gave their lives in the First World War. As with all the stained glass, the window above it was installed as part of the post-war restoration of the 1950s. It depicts, among others, the patron saints of the four nations – England, Ireland, Scotland and Wales – and the Celtic missionary St Columba, marking the link with Reverend Walker's hometown of St Columb Major in Cornwall. On the north side, the church also has a chapel of St Columb with an altarpiece by Sir Ninian Comper, who designed the two stained-glass windows and altarpiece in the Lady Chapel.

All Saints has a very active congregation, with as many as 300 people attending Mass on high days and holidays. The church has developed a strong musical tradition and supports Carnival and, in particular, the Mangrove Steel Band. For more information, telephone 020 7727 5919

Leaving Powis Square, with all its radical associations, a right turn into Colville Terrace, followed by a left into Colville Road will soon lead you to the glamorous world of Westbourne Grove. On the way, there is a worthwhile detour: turn left into Lonsdale Road and another left leads into pretty Colville Mews, home of a handful of designer spaces and boutiques, which sadly tend to sink rather than swim in the face of rising rents and the damage to business caused by the congestion charge. On the corner, good for family entertainment, though maybe not for escaping the consumerism surrounding you on all fronts,

Objects from the Museum of Brands, Packaging and Advertising

is the **Museum of Brands, Packaging and Advertising.** The brainchild of the social historian Robert Opie, this display of 10,000 consumer goods and promotional images is the result of 25 years' collecting which all began with a Munchies packet when he was 16. Organised as a time tunnel, the museum documents our consumer history over the last 200 years. The display cases are stacked with ephemera encompassing everything from corsetry to cocktail cabinets. Fads and fashions are documented, such as the Edwardian craze for ping-pong, and the 1970s passion for platform shoes. Along with thousands of food packages and items of everyday need, many toys are displayed, as well as clothing from each period. Some cases are devoted to historical events such as the Festival of Britain (1951) and the whole museum provides insights into social history. A final section displays how a selection of brand packages has changed through the ages. (Also see listings, p 116)

Westbourne Grove

Coming from the direction of Powis Square, the first Westbourne Grove landmark is the famous Turquoise Island. Fifteen years on from its opening, this space-age temple must still be London's poshest public lavatory. Commissioned by the Notting Hill Improvements Group and designed by Piers Gough, the building was opened in 1992 by Lucinda Lambton, author of *Temples of Convenience* (an illustrated history of the water closet). Following a ripple of outrage from local residents, most of whom were objecting to its failure to blend in with the surrounding architecture, it went on to win several awards and now, of course, seems a perfect match for the trendy outlets all around.

Horse trough, Turquoise Island

ORIGINS OF WESTBOURNE GROVE

The development of Westbourne Grove began in the 1840s. Until then it had been a real 'grove', a lane flanked by tall trees and banks of wild flowers. To the east, around what is now Ossington Street, it was cut across by the River Westbourne (or Bays Water), running south towards the Thames and long since diverted underground.

The first building work was carried out by William Henry Jenkins, who in 1844 leased 28 acres from James Ladbroke on the agreement that all houses would be of good quality, with none worth less than £300. These were constructed at the far western end of Westbourne Grove, in and around what are now Pembridge and Chepstow Villas. Louis Kossuth (1802–1894), the Hungarian patriot remembered as one of the great national heroes of Hungary, stayed at 39 Chepstow Villas while William Powell Frith (1819–1909), the popular painter lived at both Nos. 7 and 10 Pembridge Villas and kept a mistress, Mary Alford, by whom he had seven children, less than a mile away.

The Jenkins family also owned estates in Wales and Herefordshire, hence the naming of both these streets and others, such as Denbigh Road and Ledbury Road. The building on this section of Westbourne Grove, then known as Archer Street, consisted mainly of shops which, though popular, were not in the same league as the fashionable businesses about to spring up further east. In 1863, the combined influences of the inauguration of the underground railway at Bishops Road (near Queensway) and the opening of William Whiteley's first shop, at No. 31 Westbourne Grove, led to the stretch towards Paddington rivalling Oxford Street as London's most fashionable shopping centre. This lasted nearly half a century, until around the time of the Second World War, when people's priorities changed and bomb damage left its scars. Always the poorer end, Archer Street (renamed Westbourne Grove in 1938) became more run-down. Certainly, no one could have predicted that it would ever attain its current status as West London's answer to Parisian chic or that Whiteley's former patch of Westbourne Grove would be struggling to catch up

Taking a short detour west towards Ladbroke Grove, the road leads you past brick council flats up to the junction with Portobello Road. This area was badly damaged in the Second World War. Among the casualties was Denbigh Road Methodist Church, which was rebuilt in 1957. Under a trilogy of ministers, assembled in the wake of the 1958 riots (see Notting Hill Methodist Church, p 163), the church and its subsequent ecumenical centre became an important focus for the cohesion

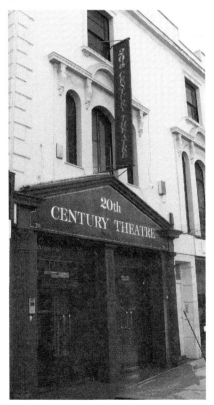

of the community. This was the case right up until the 1990s, when the site was sold to the Westway Housing Association to provide accommodation to Caribbean families.

Along the next block are several antique shops and arcades, EJ Barnes's cycle shop (established in 1951 at No. 285) and, just a few doors down, the 20th Century Theatre. Originally the Bijou Theatre, this building had performances by many famous names, from the early days of Marie Lloyd and Albert Chevalier to Laurence Olivier, who made his London stage debut here in 1924. Soon afterwards, Westbourne Grove ends at the junction with Kensington Park Road and the route it follows becomes Ladbroke Gardens.

THE 20TH CENTURY THEATRE

The 20th Century Theatre started life as the Bijou Theatre in 1863. Since then it has had a varied and often illustrious history, as an auction house, a cinema, a theatre, a furniture showroom, a meeting place for amateur dramatic societies and, most recently, a venue for publishers' parties and launches for events such as London Fashion Week.

While Charles Dickens is only rumoured to have read from the stage of the Bijou, it is certain that Henry Irving, Henry Beerbohm Tree and Marie Lloyd all appeared here. In 1893, the building was being used as an auction house and was badly damaged by fire. Alterations were made to the interior, and in 1911 it became a cinema before reverting to a theatre in 1918 under the stewardship of Lena Ashwell, who called it the Century Theatre. She had made her stage debut at the original Bijou, appearing in a play called **Young Mrs Winthrop** alongside the celebrated character actor and stage manager Sir Herbert Beerbohm Tree. Returning with her own repertory company, the Lena Ashwell Players, she performed in Archer Street as part of a special arrangement with several London boroughs, to produce entertainment affordable to the poor. At one time the Players were joined by Laurence Olivier as the Suliot Officer in Alice Law's play **Byron.** His family had lived nearby, as his father, the Reverend Olivier, had been appointed to the slum district of Notting Hill in 1910. (The Reverend was attached to St James but dismissed after two years for being too High Church, having swung incense in the tin-roofed mission hut.)

From 1929, the theatre was used by amateur theatrical societies from Harrods, the department store DH Evans and the BBC. It also provided an overflow for the local synagogue, as well as being a place for political meetings. The present name of 20th Century Theatre was bestowed by the Rudolph Steiner Association, which took over in 1936 and started to stage performances of Eurythmy, the Steiner art form which uses colour and movement to convey music and speech. Around this time, right up to its closure as a theatre in 1963, it continued to be used by local amateur groups, including the Guild of Friendship and the Notting Hill Players. There followed several decades as a furniture showroom and warehouse. It is only recently, under owner Sandra Kamen, that it has once again become a serious theatre for plays, ballet and other performances. The building can also be hired for parties, provided these are relatively peaceful, although they do now have a licence for live music until 11pm. For more information telephone 020 7229 4179.

Heading back towards Queensway, marking the other end of Westbourne Grove, the atmosphere is decidedly cosmopolitan. Hidden behind the bus stop opposite the Turquoise Island, Tom's café and deli provides delicious sandwiches, pastries and cappuccinos to take away, as well as groceries and a regularly changing menu. Above the shop are the offices of Karma Kars, a taxi service with the ethos that 'it's the journey that counts, not the destination'. Inspired by his extensive travels in the Indian subcontinent, owner Tobias Moss runs a fleet of Indian-built Ambassador cars, decked out in brightly coloured silk, with ragga music playing and incense burning on the dashboard. The cars, based on the design of the 40-year-old Morris Oxford, can be spotted by the garlands of plastic flowers wound around the bumpers.

A few doors along from Tom's, organic supermarket Fresh & Wild has just closed as this book goes to press. It is not yet known what will take its place. Virtually every other building is occupied by galleries, boutiques and designer furnishing shops, often European-owned and invariably selling beautiful objects for beautiful people. An exception is the Oxfam shop, across the road from Tom's, where there's always a chance of finding a bargain. Beyond Nicole Farhi, the next junction is Ledbury Road, another shoppers' mecca, much featured in our listings below. On the corner is an unusual development of flats built behind the façade of the old Westbourne Grove Baptist Church and retaining its twin spires. Then comes Needham Road, home to a couple of galleries – Flow and the more traditional Wolseley Fine Arts – and the famous Pentagram Design group, tucked away in a huge converted dairy. Also look out for Banky's rat stencil outside. Since 1972, when it had premises in Latimer Road, Pentagram has built up an international reputation for architecture, graphic and product design. This building, at No. 11 Needham Road, was designed by the late Theo Crosby,

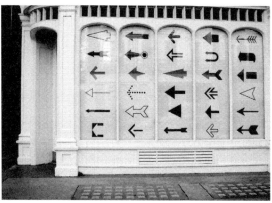

Signs to Pentagram, Needham Road

one of the company's five original partners. It's a magnificent space, filled with light, with a glass atrium to one side planted with a single tree. Outside, across from the Pentagram Gallery (currently put to other use), Crosby retained the wooden ramp up which the horses walked to their stalls after a day's work delivering milk from the dairy; the stalls were transformed into individual offices for the partners. The building is not strictly open to the public but it's a friendly place and it's worth asking at the reception desk for a quick glimpse of the interior.

At the end of Needham Road (entrance in Moorhouse Road), lies the interesting church of St Mary of the Angels. After a faltering start, the building was constructed to the designs of John Francis Bentley, best known for designing Westminster Cathedral. (see also the Church of St Francis of Assisi p.174).

THE CHURCH OF ST MARY OF THE ANGELS

The construction of St Mary of the Angels began in the mid-19th century with plans by the architect Thomas Meyer, but like so many projects of the time it foundered when the money ran out. The building remained unfinished and derelict for several years until Cardinal Wiseman began looking for a church in which to set up a community of the Oblates of St Charles Borromeo (an order of priests founded in Milan in the 16th century). The challenge was finally taken up by Father (later Cardinal) Henry Edward Manning. The church was consecrated and opened for worship in 1857, to be served by Oblates of St Charles until the 1970s, when Cardinal Heenan dissolved the order.

In keeping with his firm belief that 'you should build a school before you build a church', St Mary's already had an adjoining school, for which he recruited Mother Elizabeth Lockhart, who later moved with her community of sisters to the Franciscan Convent in Portobello Road (see p 57). Manning wrote that the eight years he was at St Mary's were the happiest in his life, and while there he preached a famous course of sermons to packed congregations. After he was made second Archbishop of Westminster in 1865, he still followed the work of the Oblates and frequently returned to the church.

The building was completed in early French Gothic style by Francis Bentley, who later added a second aisle in 1869. He also designed several stained-glass windows, including those in the Lady Chapel. Bentley later became a Catholic and was married in another church of his own design – St Francis of Assisi in Pottery Lane. Manning showed his disdain for Gothic architecture by doing his best to transform the interior of St Mary's into a semblance of an Italian church. He hung thick curtains over the tracery of the Gothic windows and covered the stained glass with paintings, all of which were removed when he left the parish. The High Altar in alabaster is in late Gothic style and was made by Messrs Jones and Willis. Manning brought back many relics of St Charles Borromeo from Italy, including a green chasuble. The Oblates' motto, HUMILITAS, can be seen around the church.

In 1978 Father Michael Hollings became the parish priest. He was much loved by the local community, ran the parish as an 'open house', never turning away a stranger, and would often give up his bed for 'men of the road'. After he died in 1997 it was decided to open a centre for the homeless in his name in what had originally been the school building in Artesian Road.

Originally the parish served the Irish immigrants who were building Paddington Station. Later, their numbers were swelled by members of the Caribbean and Hispanic communities, and today the church hosts a large Portuguese congregation. The services have a weekly attendance of over a thousand people. Parish office telephone: 020 7229 0487.

Banksy rat, Needham Road

Our final stretch of Westbourne Grove leads to Chepstow Road, on the fringes of Bayswater. The south side of the street has row of fashionable shops and restaurants, culminating in the ultimate chic of Solange Azagury-Partridge and Guesthouse West. The first is a jeweller's, whose secretive entrance and plush interior have had it mistaken for a high-class brothel, while the second, which only opened in 2004, aims to provide 'elegant luxury' in 'familiar and comfortable' surroundings. Beyond the Guesthouse, the buildings become scruffier up until Alastair Little's delicatessen, Tavola, and the Mexican restaurant Taquería, opened in 2005 by Dodie Miller, founder of the Cool Chile Company, who used to have a stall on Portobello Road.

The modern block opposite, on the corner of Chepstow Road, was once the site of Arthurs Stores, a high-class department store which at one time occupied the whole of Nos. 114–20 Westbourne Grove. Writing in *Westbourne Grove in Wealth, Work and Welfare* (2000), Eddie Adams describes how some people considered it to be a small equivalent of Fortnum & Mason. Besides having 'many departments including provisions, flowers, furnishings and ironmongery', it was noted for its 'attractive window displays and the big clock over the main entrance which used to be a meeting place for friends and lovers'. Upstairs, uniformed waiters served tea, coffee or meals on the balcony while a small orchestra played in the restaurant. As the prosperity of Westbourne Grove declined, so did Arthurs Stores, and it closed in 1937, to be replaced eventually by the Odeon Cinema, which opened in 1955. Unable to sustain enough custom despite the addition of three screens, this in turn closed its doors in the early 1980s. The poet John Heath-Stubbs, though blind, was among those who mourned its destruction, in his poem *On the Demolition of the Odeon Cinema*:

> *Never one for the flicks, I did not frequent the place:*
> *Though I recall the Voyage of the Argonauts,*
> *And a second feature – some twaddle about*
> *A daughter of King Arthur, otherwise unrecorded*
> *By history or tradition. Now, each day,*
> *I pass it, and I hear the brutal noise*
> *Of demolition: clatter of falling masonry,*
> *Machines that seem to grit and grind their teeth,*
> *And munch in gluttony of destruction.*
>
> *Its soft innards, I guess, are gone already:*
> *The screen, the lighting, the plush seats; the ghosts likewise –*
> *Shadows of shadows, phantoms of phantoms,*
> *The love goddesses, the butcher boy heroes,*
> *The squawking cartoon-animals.*
>
> *This Odeon – I should regret it? –*
> *In which no ode has ever been recited.*
> *Yet there's a pang – for I've lived long enough*
> *To know that every house of dreams*
> *Must be torn down at last.*

One of Notting Hill's great eccentrics, Heath-Stubbs was not only an outstanding poet but also a much respected editor, translator and critic. He was still based in the area, in Artesian Road, when he died, aged 88, on 26 December 2006.

PLACES TO STAY

Astors Leinster Hostel
7–12 Leinster Square W2
0870 042 9290/9292

This former hotel is off the map for this book but only 20 minutes' walk from Portobello Road and a good option for budget travellers. Prices start at £16 per person for the cheapest room sharing with eight others, rising to £30 for a twin-bedded room with shower.

Guesthouse West
163–65 Westbourne Grove W11
020 7792 9800
www.guesthousewest.com

At the other end of the scale, this boutique hotel (or re-invention of the B & B) has 20 en-suite rooms. Elegance, comfort and understatement are the keynotes. At ground level there is the Parlour Bar (hung with paintings by local artists donated by the Notting Hill Improvements Group), a small conservatory and a pretty heated terrace. All can be hired for parties or meetings. All rooms have flat-panel TVs, air-con, broadband internet access, DVDs and CD libraries, and skincare and toiletries by Molton Brown. Prices from £150 + VAT including breakfast. Check the website for special deals.

EATING & DRINKING

CAFÉS

202
202–4 Westbourne Grove W11
020 7727 2722/020 7792 6888
Mon 10am–6pm; Tues–Sat 8.30am–6pm; Sun 10am–5pm

Part of the Nicole Farhi shop, where the clothes and homewares take second place to eating and drinking. Breakfast till 11.30 – the porridge is popular – and after 4pm drinks only. Most of the customers are well-heeled women (often with babies) who favour starters for lunch. A few tables outside. No bookings taken.

Lucky 7 & Crazy Homies
127 Westbourne Park Road W2
020 7727 6771
Mon–Thurs 10am–11pm; Fri, Sat 9am–11pm; Sun 9am–10.30pm

Tom Conran's American diner can get very crowded (no bookings taken) but if you don't mind the prospect of sharing with strangers, it is worth squashing into a booth for a burger and shake. Next door and equally cramped, Crazy Homies serves tasty Tex Mex food and cocktails from south of the border: freshly made tacos and enchiladas with a range of fillings, such as baja shrimp, spiced chicken and smoky black beans, and excellent margaritas. Both places are reasonably priced.

Tea Palace
175 Westbourne Grove W11
020 7727 2600
www.teapalace.co.uk
Daily 10am–7pm;
tea served daily 3pm–7pm

This tall, smart shop sells 168 varieties of tea, all stylishly presented, plus a small range of teapots and other accoutrements. The tables are generously sized and spaced, and you can enjoy breakfast (including Eggs Benedict and Florentine) or lunch, though by far the best option is a slap-up tea of freshly baked scones, cakes and dainty sandwiches. The excellent website is full of gift ideas.

Also see **Negozio Classica, Tom's** and **Ruby & Sequoia**

FOOD SHOPS

Melt
59 Ledbury Road W11
020 7727 5030/www.meltchocolates.com
Mon–Sat 9am–6pm; Sun 11am–4pm

The smell that greets you as you enter this pretty all-white shop is irresistible for chocolate lovers. Chocolates are made by hand on the premises, using subtle flavours such as jasmine tea and cocoa from single plantations.

Negozio Classica
283 Westbourne Grove W11
020 7034 0005/www.negozioclassica.co.uk
Mon–Thurs & Sun 11am–11pm; Fri 11am–midnight; Sat 9am–midnight

First and foremost a wine shop, this attractive store also serves excellent, if expensive, snacks and light meals to accompany a glass of wine or cup of coffee. Sicilian wine and produce a speciality.

Ottolenghi
63 Ledbury Road W11
020 7727 1121/ledbury@ottolenghi.co.uk
Mon–Fri 8am–8pm; Sat 8am–7pm; Sun 8.30am–6pm

Eat at the large communal table downstairs or take away delicious home-made food from a mouthwatering, exquisitly presented selection. Not cheap, but one of the best takeaways in the area.

Tavola
155 Westbourne Grove W2
020 7229 0571
Mon–Fri 10am–7.30pm; Sat 10am–6.00pm

Run by Alastair and Sharon Little, this delightful delicatessen stocks a range of Italian groceries, including specially imported olive oil. They also have many preserves and jams and a fridge stocked with good soups and cooked dishes to heat up at home. The menu of takeaway food prepared on the premises changes daily and includes a wide range of antipasti, mains and puddings. Or for £5.50 you might want to choose a lunch box containing, for instance, *porchetta* with roasted fennel and *caponata Siciliana* with rocket, with a piece of focaccia included. Friendly and impeccable in every way, Tavola is justifiably very popular with the locals. The shop also sells a small selection of kitchenware, including Deruta pottery, at a fair price.

Tawana Thai Supermarket
18 Chepstow Road
020 7221 6316/www.tawana.co.uk
Daily 9.30am–8pm

All you need for cooking your own Thai specials: fresh vegetables, herbs and fruit (flown in by air twice a week), curry pastes, fish sauce and a huge variety of canned goods from Thailand and beyond.

Tom's
226 Westbourne Grove W11
020 7221 8818
Daily 8am (Sat 9am)–6.30pm

The ground floor of this friendly upmarket deli displays mainly bread, sandwiches and patisserie, with an excellent café serving fresh food at the back. Downstairs, you'll find an even more tempting array: the best of French, English and Italian cheeses; meats, salads, cooked dishes and a small range of good wines. The homemade pesto (rocket or basil) is especially hard to beat. Tom's also stocks staples such as pasta, rice, oil and various preserves – usually of high quality, though you may find the same item much cheaper elsewhere.

PUBS & BARS

The Cow
89 Westbourne Park Road W2
020 7221 0021
Daily: bar 12.30pm–3pm &
6.30pm–10.30pm;
restaurant 12.30pm–3pm & 7pm–11pm

Eating on this corner has become something of a battle of the gastropubs, for, like the Westbourne across the road, the Cow has its own style, which it does extremely well. Downstairs serves a variety of seafood from a Parisian-style seafood bar, as well as daily specials such as ham and white-bean stew or linguine with squid, chilli and flat-leaf parsley. Upstairs, with its own entrance, is the more formal Cow Dining Room. Great chefs have passed through here on their way to larger venues, and a visit will rarely disappoint.

Earl of Lonsdale
277–81 Westbourne Grove W11
020 7727 6335
Mon–Fri 12 noon–11pm; Sat
10.30am–11pm; Sun 12 noon–10.30pm

Twenty years ago this was Heneky's and definitely not the place to be on a Friday night, with fights breaking out regularly at closing time. Now it's been redone, with a decent terrace (parading as a 'garden' in summer) and, in spite of its location in the middle of the tourist market, you'll still see the same barflies year in year out. The dartboard is popular and the back room pleasant enough, especially in winter. Also a Monday-night knitting venue: www.stitchnbitch.co.uk.

Prince Bonaparte
80 Chepstow Road W2
020 7313 9491
Daily 12 noon–11pm;
food served 12.30pm–3pm, 6.30pm–10pm

A fashionable pub to be seen in, the Bonaparte is nearly always packed with a youngish crowd of local residents and destination drinkers. Hard to imagine that only a decade or so ago, when it was still the Artesian, this was a sleazy dive notorious for its Friday-afternoon striptease. Nowadays you're more likely to frequent it for the Friday and Saturday night DJs or one of the rocking carnival parties. The food isn't bad either.

Ruby & Sequoia
6–8 All Saints Road W11
020 7243 6363/www.ruby.uk.com
Bar: Mon–Thurs 6pm–12.30am;

Fri 6pm–2am; Sat 11am–2am;
Sun 11am–12.30am; Restaurant: brunch Sat
& Sun 11am–4pm; dinner daily 6pm–11pm

DJs are the big draw here – expect the basement bar to be packed out at weekends. With its funky décor and friendly staff, this trendy joint on the site of the legendary Mangrove is also recommended for cocktails, dinner or brunch. The food is better than average and reasonably priced.

The Walmer Castle

58 Ledbury Road W2
020 7229 4620
Mon–Sat 12 noon–11pm;
Sun 12 noon–10.30pm

Everyone panicked when scaffolding went up a few years ago, but the Walmer emerged unscathed – still a good old pub, only cleaner. On a summer's evening the pavement outside is thronged with drinkers, mainly locals, many of whom seem to know each other at least by sight. In fact, you wouldn't realise that it's owned by a chain, Dragon Inns, which specialises in pubs downstairs and Thai restaurants above. Generous bar snacks with a Thai slant are on offer. The restaurant upstairs is also good, with a familiar Thai menu and pleasant service.

The Westbourne

101 Westbourne Park Villas W2
020 7221 1332
Tues–Sun 12.30pm–3.30pm; Mon–Sun
7pm–10.30pm

Increasingly popular since opening in 1996, the Westbourne has become one of the premier gastropubs in Notting Hill. A table on a Friday or Saturday evening is virtually impossible to find or enjoy, due to the heaving mass of fashionable drinkers. Return at lunchtime, or on a week night, and the scene will be different. Dark wood floors, a mish-mash of old furniture and a relaxed atmosphere make this an easy place to be. The menu changes daily and is reasonably priced, imaginative and well executed.

RESTAURANTS

Assagi

39 Chepstow Place W2
020 7792 5501
Mon–Sat 12.30–2.30pm; 7.30–11pm

Assagi offers Tuscan simplicity at its best. This large, airy room above the Chepstow pub makes a delightful setting for lunch, especially when the sun is out. Although pricey, the food is very good and served with impressive understatement in true Italian style. Good wine list. Book well in advance (up to six weeks), particularly for dinner.

Bumpkin
209 Westbourne Park Road W11
020 7243 9818/www.bumpkinuk.com
Mon 5.30pm–midnight; Tues–Fri 12 noon–3pm & 5.30pm–midnight; Sat & Sun 11am–midnight (10.30pm Sun)

Aimed at 'city folks who like a little country living', this rustic-style successor to the Liquid Lounge combines a ground-floor brasserie with an upstairs restaurant as well as private dining rooms and whisky rooms. An immediate hit with 'yummy mummies', downstairs is especially good for well-cooked Sunday roasts in a relaxed, child-friendly atmosphere. Average prices.

Centonove
109 Westbourne Park Road W11
020 7221 1746/www.centonove.com
Mon–Fri 7pm–11pm; Sat & Sun till midnight

Subdued lighting, an open-plan kitchen and a great downstairs area with open fires and deep red walls make you feel instantly at home, as does the gregarious head waiter. The food is good and robust: huge portions, fresh ingredients and reasonable prices. Starters include *bruschetta al pomodoro*, large (almost too large) slabs of grilled country bread smothered with ripe vine tomatoes, basil and olive oil. *Linguine alla scoglio* turns out to be a gargantuan dish of pasta with a tomato and garlic sauce stuffed with squid, clams and mussels. The salt-crusted seabass is presented with a flourish. A full menu is displayed on the restaurant's website.

The Ledbury
127 Ledbury Road W11
020 7792 9090/www.theledbury.com
Mon–Fri 12 noon – 2.30pm & 6.30pm–10.15pm; Sat dinner till 10.45pm

Excellent French food served in elegant surroundings makes the Ledbury probably the outstanding restaurant in the area – it's certainly the only one to boast a Michelin star. Australian chef Brett Graham uses prime ingredients to produce delicious, complex and highly original dishes. Local diners and critics alike wax lyrical over the lasagna of rabbit with wild mushrooms, celery and thyme, loin of monkfish with white beans, chorizo, squid and rosemary – and these are only starters. Pricey but well worth it.

The Ripe Tomato
7 All Saints Road W11
020 7565 0525
Daily 7pm–midnight
No credit cards

On the corner of St Luke's Mews and All Saints Road, this small, friendly neighbourhood restaurant delivers generous portions of pizza, pasta and other Italian staples in a delightfully unpretentious atmosphere. Prices reasonable.

Rosa's Dining Rooms
69 Westbourne Park Road W2
020 7221 5329
Mon–Thurs 7pm–10.30pm; Fri, Sat 7pm–11pm; Sun 12.30pm–4.30pm

The cosiness of this neighbourhood restaurant, with its tea lights and floral oilskin tablecloths, is well matched by the comforting food: pumpkin soup, goose rillettes, fish pie, braised lamb shank with carrots and mash are typical choices.

Taquería
139–42 Westbourne Grove W11
020 7229 4734/www.coolchiletaqueria.com
Daily 12 noon–3.30pm & 5.30–11pm

Deservedly popular Mexican restaurant offering a wide range of dishes, including stuffed chiles, ceviche, tacos and tostadas, all at the cheap end of the scale. Another great business that started life as a market stall.

See under **Pubs & bars** for **The Cow, The Walmer Castle** and **The Westbourne**

ENTERTAINMENT

MUSEUM

The Museum of Brands, Packaging and Advertising
2 Colville Mews, Lonsdale Road W11
020 7908 0880
www.museum of brands.com
Tues–Sat 10am–6pm;
Sun 11am–5pm;
closed Mon except bank holidays
Admission: adults £8.50; children (7–16) £2.00; family £14.00; concessions £3.50

The 10,000 consumer goods and promotional images contained in this nostalgic museum represent 25 years' collecting by social historian Robert Opie – see p 102 for details.

MUSIC & CLUBBING

Woody's

41–43 Woodfield Road W9
020 7226 3030/www.woodysclub.com
Open until 3am (last orders 2am).
Mon–Wed £5, Thurs–Sun £10

Woody's is, strictly speaking, not in Notting Hill but is so much part of the scene that it can't be left out. Each of the four floors is dedicated to a different activity, from the dark sweaty dance cave in the basement, where a catholic range of music is played, to the airy restaurant upstairs overlooking the canal. The chill-out rooms up top, like a Seventies glam-rock star's pad, offer a chance to collapse and gossip on comfy cushions (this is the only club in London where you can hear yourself think). Available for private hire, it also has facilities for screenings.

HEALTH, BEAUTY & FITNESS

Beauty Works West

8–9 Lambton Place W11
020 7221 2248/www.beautyworkswest.com
Mon–Fri 10am–8pm; Sat & Sun 10am–6pm

Tucked away in this mews off Westbourne Grove, a calming atmosphere greets you as you climb the stairs into Beauty Works West. The spa offers a range of treatments, many with the emphasis on anti-ageing, and consultations with the famous Dr Daniel Sister are available.

Lambton Place Health Club

Lambton Place W11
020 7229 2291
www.lambton.co.uk
Mon–Fri 6.15am–11pm;
Sat & Sun 8.30am–9pm

Hidden away in a mews, the Lambton Place Health Club opened in its present guise in 1988, having previously been a squash club. It has a fully equipped gym (and is constantly upgrading its machines), an exercise studio and a small but pretty swimming pool. A range of therapies, including aromatherapy, physiotherapy, shiatsu, osteopathy, beauty treatments and reflexology, are open to non-members as well as members. The pool area incorporates a steam room and jacuzzi, and there are separate saunas for men and women.

Miller Harris

14 Needham Road W11
020 7221 1545
www.millerharris.com
Mon–Sat 10.30am–6.30pm

Since she opened this beautiful perfumery shop in 2000 with her partner, Christophe Michel, Lyn Harris's business has become something of a legend. Harris studied in France for five years, so is well qualified to launch her unique, ever-expanding range of soaps, scents, candles, eau de toilette and eau de parfum. She will even spend time with you to create your very own scent – for around £4,000.

Nail 2000

215 Westbourne Park Road W11
020 7727 2704
Mon–Sat 10am–10pm; Sun 1–4pm

Florentine Ruks offers an infinite variety of nail treatments, from sculpted acrylic extensions to manicures, pedicures and natural nail repair, all done with her friendly personal touch. Prices depend on the exact procedure and the state of your nails, but are generally mid-range.

Screen Face

20 & 24 Powis Terrace W11
020 7221 8289/www.screenface.com
Mon–Sat 9am–6pm

Using products developed by make-up artists for make-up artists, Screenface has been supplying the entertainment industry for well over 20 years. Of these two shops (there's a third outlet in Covent Garden), No. 20 focuses on natural glamour while No. 24 is more geared to the needs of film and theatre professionals. Both places are stacked with a staggering collection of pencils, mascaras, false eyelashes, foundations, concealers, powders and lipsticks, plus every imaginable kind of applicator, at well below big-name prices. In case you find so much choice bemusing, the friendly assistants are full of helpful advice.

SPACE.NK

127–131 Westbourne Grove W2
Shop: 020 7727 8063 /Spa: 020 7727
8002/www.spacenk.com
Shop: Mon–Sat 9.30am–7pm (Thurs to
8.30pm); Sun 12 noon–6pm/Spa: Mon–Fri
9am–9pm; Sat 9am–8pm; Sun 10am–7pm

Rows of enticingly labelled pots and jars of cream for skin and hair from all over the world are arranged on stylish shelves in this spacious shop, once the site of Bradley's Silk Mercers and Furriers. Its own label (which includes a fragrance, SPACE.NK. WOMAN) concentrates on bath products. This is the only branch of Nicky Kinnaird's ever-expanding empire to have a spa attached, offering very pricey holistic treatments. It is hard to vouch for the therapy rooms when you are neither allowed to know how many there are nor see any of them.

SHOPPING

BIKES

Bicycle Workshop
27 All Saint's Road, W11
020 7229 4850
Tues–Sat 10am–6.00pm
(closed 2pm–3pm)

Ninon Asuni has been running her bicycle workshop for 27 years and has a large loyal and local following. She carries a huge quantity of spares and is therefore able to have very quick turnaround – but booking is advisable especially in the summer. She also sells bicycle books and accessories and will order unusual new bikes.

CHARITY SHOPS

Oxfam
245 Westbourne Grove W11
020 7229 5000
Mon–Sat 9.30am–5.30pm;
Thurs 9.30am–7pm

This branch of the charity chain is well worth visiting. Bargain clothes can often be found; items from Ghost, Agnes B and Joseph are not unusual. Most of the proceeds go directly to Oxfam projects in the developing world, so at least any rash purchase funds a good cause.

FASHION

Aimé
32 Ledbury Road W11
020 7221 7070/www.aimelondon.com
Mon–Sat 10.30am–7pm

Owned by French-Cambodian sisters Val and Vanda Heng, Aimé introduces London to the cutting edge of Parisian creativity. Designer wear and home accessories represent high-quality French contemporary design, with established names such as Isabelle Marant and Christophe Lemaire sitting comfortably next to lesser-known up-and-coming talent from French fashion and art colleges. Revolving exhibitions of paintings and photography regularly transform the delightfully simple yet sophisticated décor.

Bill Amberg

21–22 Chepstow Corner, W2
020 7727 3560/www.billamberg.com
Mon–Sat 10am–6pm; Wed till 7pm

Bill Amberg's name is synonymous with beautiful leather bags, wallets, briefcases and other simple but inventively styled accessories, even baby pouches. You will also find a selection of luxurious leather homeware, from waste-paper bins, place mats and cowhide rugs to a zebra-skin ottoman. Everything exudes fine craftsmanship and an eye for detail, with prices to match.

Celia Birtwell

71 Westbourne Park Road W2
020 7221 0877/www.celiabirtwell.com
Mon–Fri 10am–1pm & 2pm–5pm; Thurs 11am–1pm & 2pm–6pm

When Celia Birtwell opened her fabric shop more than 20 years ago, this corner of Westbourne Park Road was just a backwater. Sandwiched between two well-known gastropubs and a host of other designer shops, she's in just the right spot for selling her fine printed textiles, even if the bulk of sales still comes from trade. Sheers, silk, cotton and linen are designed mainly for use in curtains or upholstery. Ever since her brief marriage to the late fashion designer Ossie Clark, Birtwell has been associated with his world and that of her close friend, the painter David Hockney. However, she has long proved herself as a strong creative spirit in her own right and prefers to leave the past behind her. A recent sell-out collection for Top Shop marks her return to high-street fashion.

Duchamp

75 Ledbury Road W11
020 7243 3970/ww.duchamp.co.uk
Tues–Sat 10am–6pm

The black storefront offsets the riot of colour that characterises Mitchell Jacobs's inspired range of shirts, ties and accessories for men. Everything is immaculately displayed, including silk ties, Egyptian cotton dress-shirts and the cufflinks for which he is renowned.

Emma Hope

207 Westbourne Grove W11
020 7313 7490
www.emmahope.co.uk
Mon–Sat 10am–6pm; Thurs 10am–7pm

Unlike her busy shop in Sloane Square, Emma Hope's outlet on the corner of Ledbury Road provides the perfect calm space in which to contemplate her elegant creations. Beautiful soft ankle-boots in red and turquoise, brocade slippers and classy stilettos all carry her hallmark of exquisite detailing and style.

Ghost

36 Ledbury Road W11
020 7229 1057/www.ghost.co.uk
Mon–Fri 10.30am–6.30pm;
Sat 10am–6pm

In nearly 25 years Tanya Sarne's Ghost label seems to have gone from strength to strength. What's more, she has barely wavered from the original flowing silhouette that made her name, winning support from such celebrity customers as Nicole Kidman and Madonna. The hallmark of the clothing is an exclusive fabric woven from viscose yarns, derived from specially grown soft woods. The result is a collection of sensuous garments in mouthwatering colours that are flattering to the figure, with the added bonus of being easy to wash and unnecessary to iron.

Issues

181 Westbourne Grove W11
020 7727 1122
Mon–Fri 10am–6.00pm; Sat 10am–6.30pm

This branch of the Natural Shoe Store sells the usual comfortable range for women, men and children, plus a few extra styles for fashion-conscious Notting Hillbillies. These include cowboy boots and cosy slip-ons in bright pink and purple suede.

J&M Davidson

42 Ledbury Road W11
020 7313 9532
www.jandmdavidson.com
Mon–Sat 10am–6pm; Sun 12 noon–5pm

Famous originally for their canvas bags and leather belts, husband and wife team John and Monique now have a worldwide following, especially in the fashion capitals of New York and Tokyo. The look is understated elegance and luxury. Specialities include cardigans and sweaters in mixes of cashmere, merino wool and silk, with the trademark belts. While the wood-panelled upstairs is devoted to clothes and accessories, downstairs houses the growing homeware line with bedlinen, throws, quilts and pyjamas in 100 per cent linen.

The Jacksons

5 All Saints Road W11
020 7792 8336/www.thejacksons.co.uk
Mon–Fri 10am–6pm; Sat 11am–6.30pm

The two Jackson sisters have come a long away since they started, selling trend-setting accessories from their studio. Today their creative spirit is evident in the wide range of fun, fashionable merchandise that fills this colourful shop on the corner of St Luke's Mews. Signature pieces include flower-bedecked flip-flops and hair clips, unusual throws and wraps, wacky T-shirts and roomy leather bags with beaded handles.

Laundry Industry

186 Westbourne Grove W11
020 7792 7967/Uklon@laundryind.com
Mon–Sat 10.30am–6.30pm; Sun 12 noon–5pm

More like a tunnel than a shop, this Dutch company's European flagship store is certainly unusual. Subtle lighting, which changes colour during the day, softens the concrete interior, and the clothes are simply displayed in two parallel lines – women's on one side and men's on the other. Well-priced trousers, jackets and tops in eclectic fabrics. A lot of consideration is given to creative merchandising. Definitely worth checking out.

Paul & Joe

39–41 Ledbury Road W11
020 7243 5510
www.paulandjoe.com
Mon–Fri 10am–6pm; Sat till 7pm

Following its runaway success in Selfridges department store, this Paris-based shop opened to great acclaim in 1999. This is chic power-dressing at its best. Clothing is beautifully cut and presented, with the emphasis on contrasting styles of ladylike glamour and glitz. A great place for that different item that will set off your wardrobe for years to come.

Pistol Panties

75 Westbourne Park Road W2
020 7229 5286
www.pistolpanties.com
Tues–Sat 12 noon–6pm

Frilly lingerie and Fifties-style swimwear are the mainstay of Deborah Fleming's successful label, for which this is the flagship boutique. A former figure-skater, born and raised in Paris, Deborah cites her mother as one of the main inspirations for her glamorous collections.

Ray Harris

73 Westbourne Park Road W2
020 7221 8052
Tues–Fri 11am–6pm; Sat 11am–6pm;
private fittings by request

On the quiet eastern stretch of Westbourne Park Road, this studio-shop caters for independent-spirited women who won't be dictated to by trends and figure-hugging garments. Clothes flow around the body in luscious colours, using natural fabrics with tribal designs in mind. Everything is designed and produced in-house, and Harris prides himself on his ethical approach, paying seamstresses well for their skill.

Sweaty Betty

110 Westbourne Grove W2
020 7727 8646
www.sweatybetty.com
Mon–Fri 10am–6pm; Sat 10am–6pm; Sun
12 noon–5pm

Just across Chepstow Road, Tamara Hill Norton stocks women's athletic and casual sportswear and trainers for every activity, from tennis to pilates. Labels include Nike, Adidas, Danskin and Us Pro, but it's the smaller names such as Cassal of Spain and Australian Metalicus that make the shop special.

Summer brings an impressive range of beachwear, while in winter there's all the kit you're likely to need for skiing.

Wall

1 Denbigh Road W11
020 7243 4623/www.wall-london.com
Mon–Fri 10.30am–6.30pm; Sat 10am–6pm;
Sun 12 noon–5pm

Wall specialises in plain, understated sweaters, jackets, long skirts and dresses in sombre colours. The emphasis on wearability and luxurious fabrics, such as alpaca and hand-picked pima cotton (owner Hernán Balcázar is from Peru), makes for a winning combination of comfort and style. Smaller items include wonderfully soft socks and furry alpaca slippers. Mail order service.

FLOWERS

Wild at Heart

49a Ledbury Road W11
020 7727 3095
www.wildatheart.com
Mon–Sat 8.30am–7pm
And at the Turquoise Island
Mon–Sat 8am–6.30pm

Nikki Tibbles's designer flower stall is a perfect complement to

Piers Gough's turquoise creation on the triangle in Westbourne Grove. Having started at the Turquoise Island, she now has headquarters and a shop in Ledbury Road, as well as a further outlet in Liverpool Street's Great Eastern Hotel. Among local places supplied by Wild at Heart is the London Lighthouse (p 133), which receives a complimentary bouquet every Monday in memory of Diana, Princess of Wales and her support for the charity and all people affected by HIV/AIDS.

GALLERIES

Axia
21 Ledbury Road W11
020 7727 9724
Mon–Fri 10am–6pm; Sat by appointment

A sense of tranquillity descends as you walk through the immense dark red door into Axia, which specialises in Eastern Christian and Islamic art. The few well-chosen objects on display lend this gallery an air of great sophistication and taste.

England & Co
216 Westbourne Grove W11
020 7221 0417
Mon–Sat 11am–6pm

Jane England was born and grew up in Australia, coming to England via Italy. An art historian who had worked as a photographer, she opened her first gallery in nearby Needham Road in 1987. The gallery began with a programme of retrospective and contemporary exhibitions. Having outgrown that space, England & Co moved to this large purpose-built gallery designed by Will White in 1999. It has sold works to many museums, public galleries and institutions and holds regular exhibitions.

Flow
1–5 Needham Road W11
020 7243 0782
gallery.flow@ukgateway.net
Mon–Sat 11am–6pm

Yvonna Demczynska started selling contemporary applied arts in 1999. The wonderful space has a selection of craftwork in glass, felt, leather, wood and metal, ceramics and jewellery. The emphasis is on young UK-based artists – Yvonna is always visiting studios in search of new talent.

Gallery Maya
28 Chepstow Corner, Chepstow Place W2
020 7229 6279/www.gallerymaya.co.uk
Wed–Sat 12 noon–6pm

Carole Arumainayagam, a banker by profession, opened this white-washed gallery with its stone floor in September 2006. She deals exclusively in contemporary Asian art and at the moment only shows artists who are already established in their own countries. Each show is on for about a month, accompanied by a lavish catalogue.

Hanina Fine Art

180 Westbourne Grove W11
020 7243 8877/www.hanina-gallery.com
Mon–Sat 10am–6pm

After 15 years in New York, Hanina came to London in 1995 to set up this gallery specialising in the Paris School 1900–1975. Every three months, it shows exhibitions of oils and sculptures on different themes, encouraged by a growing volume of passing trade.

Richard Morant

27 Chepstow Corner, Chepstow Place W2
020 7727 25866/www.richardmorant.com
Mon–Fri 10am–6pm; Sat 11am–5pm

A successor to David Black, Richard Morant displays antique alongside contemporary carpets and textiles and can help you design your own from modern or classical images. Regular exhibitions showcase exquisite weaving and embroidery from countries such as Turkey, Nepal and Uzbekistan. Richard also makes frequent visits to his weavers in Central and Western Anatolia in Turkey, with similar projects under way in Rajasthan.

Stern Art Dealers

46 Ledbury Road W11
020 7229 6187
www.pissarro.net
Mon–Sat 10am–6pm

David Stern is the world's leading dealer in Camille Pissarro and his descendants, and holds regular exhibitions of their work. He has been in the area for 37 years and in his present premises, originally a café and restaurant, for 20.

Turf Gallery

81 Westbourne Park Road W2
020 7221 5215
www.turfgallery.tk
Wed–Sat 10am–5pm or by appointment

Royal College of Art graduates Stephanie Carlton Smith and Gaea Todd conceived their gallery as a space to exhibit the work of fellow painters and sculpture by artists in an informal atmosphere. Each has her own workshop in the basement.

Wolseley Fine Arts

12 Needham Road W11
020 7792 2788
www.wolseleyfinearts.com
During exhibitions, Tues–Fri 11am–6pm;
Sat till 5pm; otherwise by appointment

Founded in 1990 by Rupert Otten, Wolseley Fine Arts opened this gallery off Westbourne Grove in 1995. Otten and his partner, Hanneke van der Werf, now specialise in the works of Eric Gill, Edgar Holloway and David Jones. They have also held exhibitions by Edward Ardizzone and John Buckland Wright, and every June they organise an exhibition of French art.

HOME

B&T Antiques

47 Ledbury Road W11
020 7229 7001
www.bntantiques.co.uk
Mon–Sat 10am–6pm

Lovely shop specialising in French Art Deco mirrors and mirrored furniture. The owner, Bernadette Lewis, has a pied-à-terre in Paris, from which she also sources carefully selected pieces of furniture, mostly from the same period. Her joy in what she does, from finding pieces to visiting clients at home to help place them, is reflected in her showroom here.

Big Table Furniture

56 Great Western Road W9
020 7221 5058
www.bigtable.co.uk
Mon–Sat 10am–6pm (Thurs till 10pm);
Sun 12 noon–5pm

No one can remember exactly how Big Table came to specialise in beds, but if you want a good, solid wooden frame, plus custom-made mattress, this is the place. There are five styles to choose from, including bunk beds and a plain four-poster, all handmade in Scandinavian pine. Care is taken to preserve the forest by replacing every mature tree felled with four saplings. Run by a furniture co-operative established here in 1984, the company has earned a strong reputation for friendly, efficient service, top quality and affordable prices.

Brissi

196 Westbourne Grove W11
020 7727 2159
Mon–Sat 10am–6.30pm; Sun 12 noon–6pm

Almost everything in this shop is tempting. Downstairs there are things for the kitchen, bathroom and for babies, upstairs for the living room – all in muted colours. Also a range of their own paints, and a small selection of clothes.

Jenny-Lyn
25 All Saints Road W11
020 7792 4957/jenny-lyn@btconnect.com
Mon–Fri 10.30am–6pm; Sat 12 noon–5pm

Stylist Jenny-Lyn has created a treasure trove of chandeliers, sensuous throws, Sixties glass furniture, table lamps, French Art Deco mirrors, all firmly based on what she likes. Most items are sourced from the States, France and Italy but she has recently started to design her own pieces of bespoke furniture, which customers can order to their specification. A selection of vintage clothes is also in the pipeline.

Jones Lighting
196 Westbourne Grove W11
020 77229 6866
www.jonesantiquelighting.com
Tues–Sat 10.30am–5pm

Jammed with every kind of light-fitting you can imagine, and some you wouldn't even begin to think of, all the pieces here are original and chosen with an eye for the decorative and fantastic. Prices reflect the shop's location and

clientèle but are not too unreasonable. French Art Deco a speciality.

Lanna
3 Denbigh Road W11
020 7229 6765
Mon & Tues 10am–4pm;
Wed–Sat 10am–6pm

This recently renovated shop, painted in glorious lacquer red, sources 90 per cent of its stock of silk jackets, jewellery, belts, bags and flip-flops from Thailand. Quilts and teddy bears from Pakistan and the whole range of River Book titles make up the rest.

Revival Upholstery
22 All Saints Road W11
020 7727 9843
Mon–Sat 9am–6pm and by appointment

Revival Upholstery makes, restores and sells antique and contemporary upholstered furniture. The best upholsterers in the area, attracting big-name interior designers who would prefer not to be mentioned, this is the place for re-covering all those chairs and sofas you've bought on the Golborne Road and don't know where to take. They also make properly sprung – not foam –

sofas. The proprietor may seem a little grumpy, but persistence and a knowledge of Samuel Beckett are worth their weight in azure velvet, Mongolian sheepskin and tempered leather.

Themes & Variations
231 Westbourne Grove W11
020 727 5531
www.themesandvariations.com
Mon–Fri 10am–1pm, 2–6pm;
Sat 10am–6pm

Liliane Fawcett's spacious gallery cum shop specialises in 20th-century decorative arts and contemporary, mainly European, design. Artists represented include Gio Ponti and Fornasetti from the Fifties, and contemporary names Tom Dixon and Mark Brazier-Jones. The epitome of chic.

For stalls and arcades in Westbourne Grove see **Portobello Antiques Market**

JEWELLERY

Dinny Hall
200 Westbourne Grove W11
020 7792 3913/www.dinnyhall.com
Mon–Wed 10am–6pm; Thurs 11am–7pm;
Fri & Sat 10am–6pm; Sun 12 noon–5pm

Dinny Hall designs her own jewellery in simple forms with a timeless style that does not depend on fashion. She uses both precious and semi-precious stones, with many affordable prices.

Solange Azagury-Partridge
187 Westbourne Grove W11
020 7792 0197
www.solangeazagurypartridge.com
Mon–Sat 11am–6pm

Described by *Elle* magazine as 'the girl who made rocks hot again' and with work on display in the Louvre, Azagury-Partridge is one of the top designers of precious jewellery around. Her sumptuous shop is a delight.

MUSIC

People's Sounds Record Shop
12 All Saints Road W11
020 7792 9321
Mon–Sat 10am–8pm

Specialising in reggae, ska and raga, People's Sounds was founded in 1988 and has survived thanks to the energies of VGo, the proprietor, who sees music as essential to the well-being of the community. His catalogue is an education in the past, present and future worlds of African-Caribbean music, of which he himself has an encyclopaedic knowledge.

Portobello Music
13 All Saints Road W11
020 7221 4040
Neil@fiddles.demon.co.uk
Mon–Sat 10.30am–6pm

Taking a break, Notting Hill, late 1960s

This is a music shop run by musicians for musicians. With an excellent range of guitars and basses, including some lovely vintage models, it's the picker's Aladdin's cave. Unusually, owners Neil, Andrew and Gervis also deal in violins, cellos and double basses. Even more unusually, they understand them, too. The shop has existed in its present form for four years and brings a welcome hands-on approach in a business that grows more corporate by the second. Offering an expert and comprehensive repair service, plus hire schemes, PM is also a networking resource for local musos.

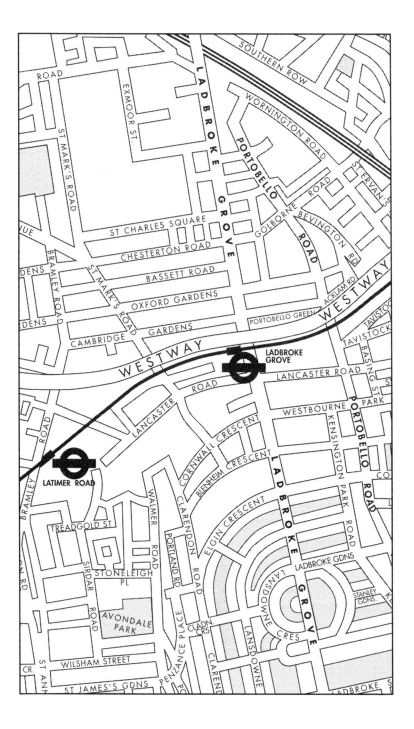

4 LADBROKE GROVE, GOLBORNE ROAD AND KENSAL GREEN CEMETERY

Tube: Ladbroke Grove, Kensal Green
Highlights: The Lighthouse café and scented garden, antiques and collectibles, flea market, Moroccan produce and garden, Portuguese patisseries, Trellick Tower, the Cemetery

This chapter concentrates on the northern section of Ladbroke Grove, from just before the Westway, past the right turning into Chesterton Road leading to Golborne Road, and over the Grand Union Canal to Harrow Road and Kensal Green Cemetery. Though officially North Kensington, Ladbroke Grove and Golborne Road are still wrapped up in both the history and the current life and character of Notting Hill. The cemetery, too, has strong links with the district as a whole.

Even with creeping gentrification, the Grove, as this end of Ladbroke Grove became known in the Fifties, stands a world apart from the lofty houses and communal gardens that border the southern stretch. Its main focus of interest is the Westway. Otherwise this shab-

Trellick Tower, Golborne Road

by road is not much more than another busy thoroughfare, west towards Notting Dale and east in the direction of Paddington via Portobello market and Westbourne Park. It's also the place from which to take the No. 52 bus up to Harrow Road and the unexpected delights of Kensal Green Cemetery.

In and around the Grove

The northern strip of Ladbroke Grove has virtually none of the early Victorian grandeur bestowed on the southern slopes of Notting

Hill. This is largely due to its location, downhill and away from the royal cachet of Kensington, and the relatively late development of housing, which only began after 1864 and the inauguration of the Hammersmith and City railway at Ladbroke Grove Station (formerly Notting Hill). Today, looking south, the blue metal railway bridge is almost totally eclipsed by the concrete swathe of the Westway. Martin Fizpatrick, writing for the local website, www.mynottinghill.co.uk, sums up its impact (with embellishment from Will Self):

Today the Westway is part of the furniture and quite a few have come to appreciate and even admire it. Writing in the Evening Standard a few years back, the novelist Will Self described the Westway as 'a monument to the best that architectural modernism has to offer. A road sweeping across the city's cubist scape depositing you, dazed by the hubbub after the cool heights, in the bebop beat of central London'. Groovy! And there's no doubt the Westway has indeed become a potent symbol of modernity.

Coming up to the Westway, one of the few notable buildings is North Kensington Library on the corner of Lancaster Road. Opened in 1891, it was the first purpose-built library in the borough and the architect Henry Wilson won a prize for its design. Other close landmarks are the Church of St Sava, next door at No. 89 Lancaster Road, which is owned by the Serbian Orthodox Church, and the London Lighthouse at Nos. 111–17. Once famous for being Europe's first hospice for people suffering from HIV/AIDS, supported by the late Diana, Princess of Wales, the building is now a counselling and drop-in centre, and HIV testing clinic, under the auspices of the Terrence Higgins Trust. The Lighthouse also has a great café, best visited in summer when you can eat outside in the beautiful scented garden.

THE CHURCH OF ST SAVA

Walking into the unprepossessing-looking converted Church of St Sava is enough to take your breath away: nothing prepares you for the candles, chanting, icons and incense or the vast brick dome towering above the carpeted floor. The building was originally constructed in 1901 as the Anglican church of St Columb, and was renowned for its High Church liturgy before its sale to the Serbian Orthodox Church in 1951. Six years later, St Sava's was decorated with copies of frescoes from monasteries in Serbia; the iconostasis is new and from Macedonia.

The Serbs and the British were allies in the Second World War, and in the early Fifties many soldiers who had belonged to the Royal Serbian army fled to England, forming the core of what is now a large local community. The church was consecrated by the theologian Bishop Nikolai Velimirovic, who, having survived Dachau concentration camp, settled in London. It is run by Father Milun Kostic, who has been here for nearly 30 years, and Father Radomir Acimovic. The adjoining community centre is open on Saturdays and Sundays. Services are held on Sundays and feast days at 10.30am; vespers on Thursdays at 8.30pm and Saturdays at 6pm. Everyone is welcome at the services, but the church is not open at other times except by special request. For further information telephone 020 7727 8367.

THE LONDON LIGHTHOUSE

The London Lighthouse opened its doors in 1988 as one of the first organisations dedicated to the provision of high-quality community care to people affected by HIV and AIDS. It has since gone through numerous changes, and financial pressures have forced it to shrink in size. Government funding has dried up, and the lack of publicity now given to HIV and AIDS (despite a trebling in the number of people affected in London), coupled with the loss of such a high-profile sponsor as Diana, Princess of Wales, has taken its toll. In order for the Lighthouse to survive, in 1999 part of the original building was sold off to the Notting Hill Housing Trust for use as sheltered housing. Fortunately, it has managed to retain most of the big airy space downstairs, along with its tall palms, comfortable seating and café (p 149). As part of its policy to break down barriers and prejudice, the Lighthouse has always been open to the public, and visitors are welcome (weekdays only 9am–9pm). For more information telephone 020 7313 2900 or check out the website at www.tht.org.uk.

Under the Westway, attempts at installing trendy bars and eateries have largely failed, and Martin Amis's menacing image of a black cavity tattooed with graffiti (see p 56) somehow sticks. Not that there haven't been improvements: the Westway Project has applied a new coat of paint and introduced better lighting to brighten up the pedestrian stretch leading to Portobello Road and Acklam Road beyond. Saturdays see this walkway crammed with market stalls, mainly selling music, jewellery and clothes. On other days it's quiet, especially at night, when any action tends to be concentrated underground at Neighbourhood. Formerly Bay 63, then Subteranea, this club was built on the spot once occupied by Acklam Hall, itself a focus of musical innovation in the Seventies.

PUNK MEETS REGGAE IN THE GROVE

Talk to anyone about music in the Grove and they invariably come up with the name of Wilf Walker. The following is as much Wilf's story as it is a glimpse of the ways in which music evolved in and around Acklam Hall in the 1970s.

Ladbroke Grove has a rich musical history, from the early days of West Indian clubs and shebeens, to the germination of home-grown steel bands, through to the development of reggae and its unexpected alliance with punk in the mid-1970s. A key venue during the Seventies was Acklam Hall in Acklam Road. Like many developments in Notting Hill, the use of Acklam Hall as a regular music venue was a direct result of communi-ty action, this time in the form of a project called Public Pictures that was dedicated to painting murals

Wilf Walker, Stanley Gardens 1977

on the concrete walls under the Westway. Money was needed for paint, so John Tabieri, then manager of local pub band The 101'ers (later to lose Joe Strummer to The Clash), organised a string of benefit concerts in Acklam Hall. He was supported by aspiring music promoter Wilf Walker, also a community activist, who went on to become a key figure in Notting Hill's music scene.

Wilf had arrived in Notting Hill from Trinidad via Shepherd's Bush in 1961. Unusually for a West Indian, he began his career by putting on white rock performers such as Hawkwind, the Pink Fairies, Quintessence and John Otway in 1974, some of whom had supported the mural project. But after the Carnival riots of 1976, knowing of his previous involvement in benefits, members of the black community approached Wilf to raise funds for Carnival defen-dants. Only then did he start to connect with the growing number of London reggae bands. A benefit took place, headed by Aswad from Westbourne Grove, but it was a decision by US band The Last Poets to play their first-ever UK gig at Acklam Hall that gave Wilf his big break-through. Born out of Harlem and inspired by the South African black consciousness move-ment, these fathers of rap and hip-hop excelled in the poetry of outrage and rebellion, to the accompaniment of African rhythms. Jimi Hendrix was among their admirers, and their arrival in Ladbroke Grove created a storm of media interest that launched Wilf's career as a full-time promoter. From then on, riding on the wave of the British Rock Against Racism movement, he was able to set up an office under the Westway and transform Acklam Hall into a regular performance place. This was the era of punk, and every Friday night Wilf put on two punk bands and one reggae act. Unlike mainstream promoters, he recognised the links between these two very different types of music. In the words of Anthony Marks, writing in Paul Oliver's anthology **Black Music in Britain** (1990):

Like Rastafaris, punks viewed the musical and political establishment as an enemy; unlike the Rastafaris, punks were prepared to fight the system on a very basic level. The alliance of punk and reggae groups in the late 1970s for Rock Against Racism concerts prompted a surge in interest in reggae, as well as a heady optimism engendered by the sense of working for a common aim.

So it was that bands like The Slits, The Raincoats and The Members shared a stage with Aswad, Merger, Sons of Jah, Barry Ford and King Sounds. In addition, two other elements favoured the rise of reggae here: the presence of Chris Blackwell's Island Recording Studio in Basing Street (now Sarm West, p 97) and the occasional visits of Bob Marley, who used to hang out with young bands when visiting his wife Rita's family in the Grove.

Wilf's Friday-night concerts went on for 18 months, until petty theft and attacks by skinheads drove him to concentrate his energies elsewhere. Among other things, he went on to join the Notting Hill Carnival Committee and initiate the staging of live acts during Carnival, first under the flyover, then in Meanwhile Gardens and Powis Square. In true community spirit, a mix of big names – Courtney Pine, Carol Grimes, The Passions, Sugar Minnott – were featured alongside local unknowns who were picked from a mountain of tapes sent in to a central office. But this too changed and with the new corporate face of the Carnival from 1992, Wilf abandoned his efforts in favour of schemes he could more easily believe in. Today he is still promoting black music, but also spends as much time as he can in his native island of Tobago. (For more on the music scene, see Tom Vague, p 206).

Moving up Ladbroke Grove takes you past several well-kept residential streets on the left, all of which eventually cut through the St Quintin's Estate on the fringes of Notting Dale. One of these, Cambridge Gardens, is said to have had a ghost in the form of a phantom No. 7 bus which, in the 1930s, haunted the junction with St Mark's Road. The story goes that a young motorist was killed here in June 1934 when, for no apparent reason, his car swerved off the road, hit a lamp-post and burst into flames. Witnesses reported having seen a London Transport bus tearing down the road towards them and 'how they desperately swung their vehicles off the road to avoid it'. When they looked back, no bus was ever seen. The No. 7 still takes this same route down Cambridge Gardens.

Most of the Victorian houses off Ladbroke Grove have been divided into flats, either by private landlords or by one of the many housing trusts that provide accommodation for people on low incomes. This may insure against the total gentrification of Notting Hill, but it has not prevented the mushrooming of cars that every night sit double-parked along Oxford Gardens or Bassett Road. Amis, who once lived in Chesterton Road, hits the nail on the head again in *Money* (1984):

The car and I crawled cursing up the streets to my flat. You just cannot park around here any more. Even on a Sunday afternoon you just cannot park around here any more. You can double-park on people: people can double-park on you. Cars are doubling while houses are halving. Houses divide, into two, into four, into sixteen. If a landlord or developer comes across a decent-sized room he turns it into a labyrinth, a Chinese puzzle. The bellbutton grilles in the flaky porches look like the dashboards of ancient space ships. Rooms divide, rooms multiply. Houses split — houses are triple parked. People are doubling also, dividing, splitting. In double trouble we split our losses. No wonder we're bouncing off the walls.

Running west off Ladbroke Grove, Chesterton Road is one of the prettiest streets around here, especially in spring when clouds of cherry blossom briefly transform it into an impressionist painting. These days some house is always being renovated, not just by private occupiers but by the housing trusts, which began buying up properties here in the 1970s and now own probably half of the street. Before then, the buildings were nearly all inhabited by poor Irish and West Indian tenants, some of whom, like Mary Gaine, have stayed on. Mary came over from Tipperary in the late 1950s and with her husband Tom moved into a two-room flat at No. 48 in 1962. With no bathroom and only one toilet shared between four floors, they raised four children. Sixteen years later the landlord died and the building was bought by the Notting Hill Housing Trust. Mary still remembers the day in 1978 when the family was rehoused in a three-bedroom flat over the road, and the feeling of excitement at turning on the tap and seeing hot water gush out. A widow now, she still lives in the same flat with two of her sons and maintains that 'I'd die a slow death if I moved out of this road'. Not so Martin Amis, who no longer lives next door.

Golborne Road

On the other side of Ladbroke Grove, the eastern end of Chesterton Road becomes Golborne Road as houses give way to commercial premises. By turn blighted and revered for its position in the shadow of

Trellick Tower, Golborne Road is packed with contradictions. In the first half of the last century Golborne ward contained some of London's most notorious slums – especially the area around Southam Street, so famously captured in the 1950s photographs of Roger Mayne. Today it's a magnet for shops, galleries, hairdressers and restaurants cashing in on the wave of well-to-do residents who have moved here in the past decade. These, together with the Friday and Saturday flea market, are the main attractions. But more than any other part of Notting Hill, it's the different communities that have settled here over the years that have shaped the neighbourhood's character. The Moroccan foodstores, Portuguese patisseries, restaurants and shops selling furniture, bric-à-brac and exotic fabrics all stamp their own impression on the traditional Victorian façades.

Clover, Priscilla, Susan and friends

Moroccans, Portuguese and Spanish were among the many nationalities who settled here in the 1960s, drawn to North Kensington by its proximity to the West End of London, where they came to work in schools, the National Health Service and in the service industries. A number of refugees from Franco's Spain had also come during the Spanish Civil War, hence the mosaic under the Westway on Portobello Road which depicts some of those who perished, among them Lewis Clive, a local Communist councillor who died fighting with the International Brigade (see p 55).

People continue to arrive from overseas, most recently refugees from Somalia, Sudan and Ethiopia, but in the last few years it is the Moroccan community that has most made its mark on Golborne Road. The street has Moroccan cafés, restaurants, stalls and shops selling

Golborne Fisheries, Golborne Road

Fez, Golborne Road

pottery, slippers, carpets, music, halal meat and other foods. Less visible are the community organisations providing services and facilities, both to Moroccans and to the wider Arabic-speaking community, predominantly refugees and asylum seekers.

THE MOROCCAN COMMUNITY OF NORTH KENSINGTON

Souad Talsi, founder of Al-Hasaniya Moroccan Women's Centre, writes:
North Kensington's Moroccan community dates back to the 1960s when migrant workers directly recruited in Morocco by British employment agencies arrived in West London. Single men and women were later joined by their families, who now have children themselves, and the community today numbers between 8,000 and 12,000, some 80 per cent of whom originate from Larache, a small town on Morocco's northern coast.

The outcomes of this immigration have been mixed. On the one hand, in the words of one Moroccan community worker 40 years on: 'The generation gap is bigger than ever ... most of our immigrants came to alleviate their economic situation, but in the process they lost much more.' At the same time, the Council and non-governmental organisations working with the Moroccan community have risen to the challenge with a range of cultural, social and educational initiatives. The second and third generation are doing much better in terms of educational attainment and employment; it is no longer a matter of getting a job for some young people but a case of choosing a career and making a success of it.

Today identity for some has become much more of a complex issue. Recent world events have had a formidable impact on how Moroccans see themselves: some identify themselves as Moroccan and then Muslim, others see themselves as British-Moroccans, with another group seeing themselves as Muslims full stop. The latter group, I fear, is having a negative impact on community integration, cohesion and achievements. For example, a Moroccan woman wearing nikab has become a common sight in Golborne Road although it is not traditionally worn by women in Morocco.

That said, Golborne Road is a marvellous area to live in and be a part of. Moroccan shops, mint tea vendors, fruit & veg stalls, café, street food and the newly opened garden by the canal all add up to a very special atmosphere for Moroccans and non-Moroccans alike.

Moroccan women and children, Horniman's Pleasance playground, off Kensal Road

By all accounts, Golborne Road in the 1960s was a friendly shopping street not dissimilar to Portobello Road. Both have retained their markets but lost all but a few of the original family-owned butchers, bakers, grocers, confectioners and other shops that used to serve more or less all the needs of local people. The chief difference is that while Portobello catered for many different classes, including some left over from the grand old days of Chepstow Villas and Ladbroke Square, the absolute slum conditions of the surrounding housing meant that Golborne Road served mainly the very poor. This also meant that far fewer buildings survived the massive redevelopment of the 1960s and 70s, as symbolised by the fearsome presence of Trellick Tower.

Walk east along Golborne Road and you can't fail to notice the famous high-rise with its separate lift shaft; from Blur's *The Great Escape* to Nick Barlay's novel *Crumple Zone* (2000), it has triggered nearly as much creativity as the Westway. Writing in *Crumple Zone*, the second in his 'urban trilogy', Barlay's narrator takes an uncompromising look out of his window in the sky:

One minute I'm standing in the middle of my place, the next face up to the corner window. Nothing's moved on. Below, far below, the alleys and narrow walkways that knot round Trellick suggest a million directions property could disappear. On one side the Grand Union Canal flows west towards Willesden Junction, away from yuppie balconies on the opposite bank laden with Ikea bullshit, window boxes, Japanese lanterns. On another side there's a scarred up chicken-wired basketball court like something out of West Side Story. Which I guess it is, only without the fake knives. Inside, it's graffiti stand-off between Stanky Fly, Honk Fonk and some lone Nubian activist: My Bredrin, them that got beaten by police has got Staying Power.

Going the other way is Golborne Road. You can see right along it to where it hooks on to Portobello. Same crowd shifting. Or not. Slumming trustafarians in their Goa chic and blonde dreds. Slumming trustafarians in Gucci slingbacks and Versace wraps. Arab men, Portuguese men, drinking black coffee, smoking Marlboros. Ootie smoking and haggling in front of his store with his cousin Amil. Bicycle bobby O'Hara, the laughing lawman, squeaking his way through toytown till his batteries run out or till the last crime is solved. Whichever comes first. And shadows, the dark fugitive shadows of Burston and his crew that seem to fall everywhere, get in everywhere.

High above in the electric blue red sky is a Philips airship, glowing with its message: 'Let's make things better'. One day Stanky'll tag that too.

It's hard to say how much Trellick has influenced the rather bizarre transformation of this neighbourhood from urban ghetto to semi-chic hang-out for Notting Hillbillies. Outstanding views across London and its proximity to Notting Hill have certainly made it ripe for exploitation as a luxury apartment block. Similarly, the Cobden Club in Kensal

TRELLICK TOWER
Love it or hate it, Trellick Tower has become a symbol of the area for those who live here. Visible from the London Eye, it is the most easily recognisable landmark for miles around,

dominating the skyline in the way that St John's Church once did for Ladbroke Grove. The tower is the pivotal element of Ernö Goldfinger's design for the Edenham Street housing scheme, one of two large projects he undertook for the Greater London Council which replaced dilapidated Victorian terraces close to the Grand Union Canal. At the time, its 31 storeys made it the tallest high-rise in Britain and certainly the most uncompromising, with its bush-hammered external concrete and cantilevered boiler-house on top of the lift and stair tower.

It was begun in 1966 at a time of severe housing shortages when the government was keen on high-rise developments and on using industrial-type building systems. The estate was organised as an integrated living unit, incorporating a central laundry, a nursery school, old people's clubs, doctor's surgery and so on. This was in keeping with Goldfinger's theories of urbanism and his belief in the notion of the concentrated city; communal facilities were intended to eliminate the need for individual domestic arrangements. If it had been up to him, London would have become a beautiful skyscraper city.

By the time the estate was finished in 1972, the tide had already turned against this school of urban planning in favour of low-rise schemes. However, Goldfinger's work was always exceptionally well built, using the best materials and meticulous in detail. In the secondary dwellings he designed for the estate (which ranged from two-room flats to five-room, three-storey houses) he used marble in the entrance halls, provided high ceilings, ensured that the balconies faced south-west to catch as much sun as possible, and planned generously, often exceeding the minimum areas required by housing law.

The inhabitants of Trellick Tower are always quick to defend it against criticism, and recent articles have appeared in the press suggesting that what started life as an emergency response to a lack of housing has become one of the most sought-after addresses in the neighbourhood.

Wild West 11, magazine cover, Tom Vague

Road has metamorphosed from working men's club into the sumptuous Gothic-style watering hole frequented by Duncan Fallowell (see Writings, p 312).

Beneath Trellick, the Moroccan garden initiated by Al-Hasaniya Moroccan Women's Centre offers a quiet refuge for contemplation by the canal. The garden is part of Meanwhile Gardens: established by a local sculptor in 1976 on a piece of council wasteland, this stretch of green bordering the water houses London's first community skate bowl as well as environmental projects and numerous community-led activities and festivals. Thanks to the fundraising efforts of its Community Association around the time of the millennium, the gardens underwent massive refurbishment, including the rebuilding of the skate bowl and introduction of new pathways, lighting and disabled access.

Returning to Golborne Road, you'll find some of the best opportunities for eating and shopping in all of Notting Hill. The sea of junk that is the Friday and Saturday market can still yield a genuine bargain, be it wrought-iron garden furniture, double-lined velvet curtains or the perfect butler's sink. The shops, too, offer an eclectic mix of furniture, fabric, fireplaces and smaller household goods: Eighty-eight Antiques (at No. 88) sells a reasonably priced selection of old pine chests of drawers, cupboards and tables; at No. 82, Bazar stocks old kitchen and garden furniture, vases, door plaques and other knick-knacks, mainly from France; while both Ollies at No. 69 and Les Couilles du Chien at No. 65 sell a combination of antique leather chairs, animal skins, lighting and potted palms.

Market days are when the Moroccan community comes into its own – the Rai music of Cheb Khaled or more traditional Andalusian and Moroccan artists plays in shops and on stalls, and Berber rugs are hung out on the pavement. In between the shops and community advice and information centres, there are plenty of eating places to choose from. Coffee and cakes in the Portuguese Lisboa Patisserie are amazing value, equalled only by those at the similar but younger Oporto Patisserie over the road at No. 62a. For more substantial fare, the main options are Lebanese at Baalbak, North African at Moroccan Tagine, Caribbean at Rachel's, Palestinian at Maramia and British at the Fat Badger.

Food shops reflect the area's Moroccan, Portuguese and African-Caribbean mix. As Moses Aloetta proclaims in *The Lonely Londoners* (1956), Sam Selvon's vivid novel of immigrant life in London in the 1950s, commercial interests rarely waste time before setting up shop to exploit new custom:

The grocery it had at the bottom of the street was like a shop in the West Indies. It had Brasso to shine brass, and you could get Blue for when you washing clothes, and the fellar selling pitchoil. He have the pitchoil in some big drum, in the back of the shop in the yard, and you carry your tin and ask for a gallon, to put in the cheap oil burner. The shop also have wick, in case the wick in your burner go bad, and it have wood cut up in little bundles to start coal fire. Before Jamaicans start to invade Brit'n, it was a hell of a thing to pick up a piece of saltfish anywhere, or to get thing like pepper sauce or dasheen or even garlic. It had a continental shop in one of the back streets in Soho, and that was the only place in the whole of London that you could have pick up a piece of fish. But now, papa! Shop all about start to take in stocks of foodstuffs what West Indians like, and today is no trouble at all to get saltfish and rice. This test who had the grocery, from the time spades start to settle in the district, he find out what sort of things they like to eat, and he stock up with a lot of things like blackeye peas and red beans and pepper sauce, and tinned breadfruit and ochro and smoke herring, and as long as the spades spending money he don't care, in fact is big encouragement, 'Good morning sir,' and 'What can I do for you today, sir,' and 'Do come again.'

At the time of writing, the Council has contentious plans to make Golborne Road less haphazard; to smarten it up as part of its programme of 'strategic public realm enhancements'. Among other things, it is keen to improve the management of the market to make the road a 'high quality public space that is valued by people who use it and pass through it'. What this will mean in practice remains to be seen. It was meant to have had a makeover once before, in 1900, when it was going to be renamed Portobello Park, but second-rate developers moved in and nothing came of the idea.

Kensal Green Cemetery

Back on Ladbroke Grove, heading north across two roundabouts and over the canal will soon take you to Kensal Green Cemetery at the junction with Harrow Road. The canal towpath just beyond Kensal

Canal barge by Kensal Green Cemetery

Trellick Tower, the Grand Union Canal and the Westway

Road offers miles of peaceful walking in either direction. Otherwise, the way here is fairly bleak and best made by bus. Kensal Green station on the Bakerloo line is also nearby.

Kensal Green may not have been typical in terms of its grand pretensions, fashionable associations or its wealthy clientele, and its creation certainly did not solve the problems associated with the overcrowding of city burial grounds. But therein lies its singular fascination and its unique atmosphere. Furthermore, the Victorian cemetery ideal was that of 'sweet breathing places, set aside for contemplative recreation and the moral improvement, spiritual enlightenment and general education of the living'. This is a role that Kensal Green Cemetery can fulfil even – and perhaps especially – in the present age. (Friends of Kensal Green Cemetery, 1994)

Pyramids and stone mansions whose original pomposity has been weathered by long indifference into something more democratic: a sanctuary for wild nature, a trysting place for work-experience vampires. Irrelevant memory doses. Boasts and titles and meaningless dates. (Iain Sinclair, *Lights Out for the Territory*, 1998)

Kensal Green Cemetery is an extraordinary place – not only a vast walled burial ground peopled by stone sphinxes, angels and the ghosts of hundreds of remarkable characters, but a nature reserve where foxes prowl among the graves and bats are allocated special boxes attached to the trees. In addition, the monuments, many vandalised, robbed of their busts and decorations or simply demolished by time, provide a fascinating record of Victorian taste.

History

The population of London increased so rapidly in the early 19th century that churchyards became dangerously overcrowded and there was soon a shortage of places to bury the dead. Commercial cemetery companies were set up in response, and it was the first of these, the General Cemetery Company, that established Kensal Green Cemetery as the city's biggest and in many ways greatest necropolis.

The General Cemetery Company was founded in 1830 by George Frederick Carden, a barrister. On a visit to Paris in 1821, he was so impressed by Père-Lachaise that he began to dream of creating a similar burial ground in London. The opportunity came over a decade later when Royal Assent was given to a Bill 'for establishing a general cemetery for the interment of the dead in the neighbourhood of the metropolis'. Carden spotted an ideal site in the expanse of fields just north of the Grand Junction Canal and, with the financial backing of Sir John Dean Paul, a governor of the Bank of England, 55 acres of land in Kensal Green were purchased in 1832 for £9,000; a further 22 acres were added in the 1860s.

Having established the site, Carden's company launched an architectural competition for the design of cemetery buildings. This was won

Angels, Kensal Green Cemetery

by Henry Edward Kendall, but his florid Gothic plans were disliked by Dean Paul, who preferred Greek Revival styles and saw to it that the commission was given to his protégé, the architect John Griffith of Finsbury. By June 1837, Griffith had completed the Main Gate with its triumphal arch, the Dissenters' Chapel, the Anglican Chapel and the North Terrace Colonnade. The two chapels were constructed in Doric and Ionic styles over catacombs, a third set of which lies sealed beneath the Colonnade. The terrain was landscaped in the manner of a country park with thousands of specimen trees, creating an ideal habitat for the foxes, voles, kestrels, jays and many species of butterfly (half of those found in the British Isles) that now enjoy its protection.

In 1833, 48 acres were consecrated by the Bishop of London, the remaining seven acres being set aside for Dissenters. All kinds of burial – in catacombs, brick-lined vaults, earth graves or mausoleums – were possible at Kensal Green. From the beginning, plots of land were sold in perpetual freehold, a system retained by the General Cemetery Company, which still owns and manages the site. Although 18,000 funerals took place in the first 19 years, the cemetery's success was only guaranteed when a plot was bought by Augustus Frederick, Duke of Sussex and sixth son of King George III. The guide records that the

Duke was 'a notable eccentric – his house was full of singing birds and chiming clocks, and during his final illness he subsisted on a diet of turtle soup and orange ices'. He also held progressive views, and it was a wish to be buried with his wife, whom he married in contravention of the Royal Marriage Act, that led him to select a plot at Kensal Green.

In the early days there was a view over London to the Surrey hills, and people could choose their vistas, buying plots wherever they wanted. It is said that you can still see the hills on a clear day, but, although there are still plots for sale, the choice of view is now strictly limited. The variety and scope of the tombs are remarkable – Gothic fantasies, Graeco-Egyptian mausolea and classical-style monuments jostle with simpler structures. Among the graves of the famous are touching epitaphs of the lesser known: 'He burnt the candle at both ends – but oh what a lovely light'.

Notable names and monuments

Many legendary figures are buried here; more than 800 are listed in the *Dictionary of National Biography*, among them its first editor, Leslie Stephen, father of Vanessa Bell and Virginia Woolf. His wife, Harriet Stephen (1840–1875), was the daughter of William Makepeace Thackeray (1811–1863). She lies next to her husband's distinguished family, while Thackeray's grave occupies another plot marked by a Yorkstone slab. Other novelists include Wilkie Collins (1824–1889), author of *The Woman in White*, said to be the first-ever work of detective fiction, who is interred with both his wife and his mistress; and Anthony Trollope (1815–1882), whose remains rest beneath a red granite ledger with a cross in relief. The poems of poet and humorist Thomas Hood (1798–1845) were stolen from his monument, as were the bronze bust and decorations which once adorned the red granite stele designed by Matthew Noble. More recently, the ashes of playwright Terence Rattigan (1911–1977) were brought here from Bermuda to be placed in the family grave.

Although he is not buried here, the great poet Byron (1788–1824) has enough connections with Kensal Green to have warranted the inauguration of a Byron Day on 2 September 2006, when some 30 visitors gathered for a glass of madeira, followed by a Byron tour and a poetry reading in the Dissenters' Chapel. Among the resting places visited were those of Byron's half-sister, the Hon. Augusta Leigh, Anne Isabella Noel to whom he was married for 14 months, his publisher John Samuel Murray and the fellow poet, critic and essayist James Henry Leigh Hunt.

Two performers, Emile Blondin (1824–1897) and Andrew Ducrow (1793–1842), are well worth seeking out, as much for their eccentric pursuits as for the statuary that distinguishes their graves. Few can match the daring of Blondin, 'the most famous tightrope walker of all time', who not only crossed Niagara Falls on a rope but once paused halfway to cook and eat an omelette. He and his wife share a pink granite monument surmounted by a large angel. The flamboyant Ducrow was a circus performer and owner renowned for his equestrian stunts, hence the extravagant Egyptian sarcophagus complete with sphinxes, horses, angels, shells and other assorted ornaments which shield his remains. He even composed his own epitaph, beginning 'Within this tomb erected by genius for the reception of its own remains … '. Another extrovert performer, Freddy Mercury of Queen, was cremated at Kensal Green but his ashes were scattered in Bombay.

Others are distinguished for their achievements in design and engineering. Thomas Allom (1804–1872) lies in a marble-pillared chest tomb. Isambard Kingdom Brunel (1806–1859), chief engineer of the Great Western Railway, shares a plain rectangular block of marble with many members of his family. The clothes designer Ossie Clark (1942–1996) is commemorated by a simple upright slab of Welsh slate, engraved 'with love from his two sons Albert and George'.

At least three notable doctors are buried here, the first of whom, James Barry (circa 1795–1865), Inspector General of the Army Medical Department, was revealed on 'his' death to be a woman. Dr George Birkbeck (1776–1841), the philanthropist and educationalist who founded Birkbeck College, is commemorated by a handsome mausoleum in Portland stone. The tomb of Dr John Elliotson (1791–1868), friend and doctor of Dickens and Thackeray and the first person to use a stethoscope for diagnosis, has partially collapsed. Less damaged are the monuments to William Whiteley (1831–1907), the tycoon who was shot in his own department store, in white Carrara marble, and to William Henry Smith (1792–1865), whose mother founded the successful stationery chain. A book adorns the pink and grey granite chest that serves as his tomb.

Among those of noble birth, the Duke of Portland (1800–1879) has the largest plot in the cemetery, where yuccas compete with English greenery. Princess Sophia, sister of the Duke of Sussex, also bought a plot here. Repressed by her father and blighted by scandal (she gave birth after a chance evening alone with a court equerry who turned out to be a rogue), she led a lonely life and eventually went blind. Her monument – a *quattrocento* sarcophagus in Carrara marble – was erected by public subscription and faces her brother's tomb across the way.

Marble cannot withstand the English climate, and many such monuments are on the verge of collapse and would cost thousands of pounds to repair. On the other hand, the fanciful canopied tomb to Captain Charles Spencer Ricketts (1788–1867), which is made of artificial stone and granite designed by William Burges, will probably last hundreds of years.

The cemetery is open daily April–Sept 9am (Sun 10am) to 6pm; Oct–March 9am (Sun 10am) to 5pm; Bank Holidays 10am to 1pm. Walking round on your own turns up serendipitous discoveries but there is also an excellent tour every Sunday. This starts at 2pm at the Anglican Chapel and on the first and third Sundays of the month includes a highly recommended visit to the catacombs. The Dissenters' Chapel is also open to visitors and has a small exhibition space (accessible from Ladbroke Grove) where artists and photographers show their work. For more information, including how to join the Friends of Kensal Green Cemetery and obtain their highly informative guide and magazines, see www.kensalgreen.co.uk.

PLACES TO STAY

The Earl Percy
225 Ladbroke Grove W10
020 8960 3522
www.earlpercyhotel.co.uk

For reasonably priced, no-frills accommodation, you could do a lot worse than stay in this pub on the corner of Chesterton Road. All rooms have been refurbished and are clean and comfortable. Prices range from £50 for a twin-bedded room with bathroom across the way to £85 for a double with en-suite.

EATING & DRINKING

CAFÉS & TAKEAWAYS

Baalbak
91 Golborne Road W10
Daily 12 noon–10pm

This plain Lebanese café offers good value as well as reliable, freshly cooked food. A plate of mixed *mezze* is a meal in itself; main dishes include shawarma (marinaded lamb or chicken on the spit), *shish tark* (spicy boneless chicken) and a vegetarian moussaka. Baalbak also does great sandwiches, a range of coffees, including Turkish, and mint tea.

The Garden Café
London Lighthouse
111–17 Lancaster Road W11
020 7792 1200
Mon–Fri 9am–2.30pm

The café sells a limited range of inexpensive sandwiches, salads and hot food, but it's more the setting that you come for. Built as a pioneering support centre for people affected by HIV and AIDS (see p 133), the Lighthouse has won awards for its building but more specifically for its secluded garden, which is open to the public all year round. This wonderfully peaceful space incorporates a Tudor scented garden set around a small square camomile lawn, a healing garden and a fountain, as well as a paved area for sitting out next to the café. A perfect retreat from the noise and pollution of Ladbroke Grove.

Lisboa
57 Golborne Road W10
020 8968 5242
Daily 8am–8pm;
no credit cards

This hugely popular café/patisserie has long been one of the highlights of Golborne Road, and deservedly so. The *pasteis de nata* (custard tarts), macaroons, apricot pastries and millefeuilles-type concoctions all melt in the mouth, and the coffee and savouries, such as croissants filled with ham and cheese, are pretty good, too. Add the astoundingly cheap prices, a great atmosphere and incredibly hard-working staff, and it's easy to see why Lisboa is such a success story. The only problem is trying to get a table.

Moroccan Tagine
95 Golborne Road W10
020 8968 8055
Daily 12 noon–11pm

People come from far and wide to sample the wide variety of tagines, soups, couscous and other North African dishes prepared by the friendly Hassan, mostly from his own family recipes. With so many Morroccan food shops plus the excellent Golborne Fisheries on his doorstep, fresh ingredients are more or less guaranteed.

Taste of Punjab
Kerrington Courts
316b Ladbroke Grove W10
020 8960 9925/Tues–Sat 11.30am–11pm;
Sun 1pm–11pm

Right on the roundabout where Barlby Road meets Ladbroke Grove, the family-run Taste of Punjab offers some of the best Indian food this side of Westbourne Grove. The straightforward menu includes a familiar range of dishes, baltis and biryanis, chicken tikka massala and sag king prawn, and a wide choice for vegetarians, all freshly cooked in the tiny open kitchen at the back.

Tea's Me
129 Ladbroke Grove W10
07830 021 391
Mon-Sat 7am–7pm
(entrance Ladbroke Crescent)

Tucked away in a cul-de-sac close to the junction with Westbourne Park Road, this tiny café is a hidden gem. Whether you fancy an omelette, patisseries or simply tea or coffee, it's the perfect place for a quiet breakfast. Portuguese owner Carla also runs her own catering business, not only producing food but organising staff, music and flowers and helping to find a suitable venue.

Yum Yum

312 Ladbroke Grove W11
020 8968 1497
Mon–Thurs 10am–10pm; Fri & Sat till 11pm

This great Caribbean takeaway is tucked away on the same roundabout as Taste of Punjab. Choose from curried goat, chicken, steak or oxtail, plus several fish and vegetarian dishes, including a mouth-watering bean and dumpling stew – all served with rice, boiled yam, dumpling or plantain. Owner Oakland Foster also makes some of the best patties in West London.

Also see **Pubs & bars** for the **Earl Percy**, the **William IV**, and Portobello Road chapter for **Bossa Nova Café** and the **Fat Badger**.

FOOD SHOPS

L'Etoile

79 Golborne Road W10
020 8960 9769
Mon–Sat 8am–6pm
No credit cards

A mouth-watering array of North African pastries, packed with dates, almonds and honey, are sold alongside French baguettes, croissants and creamy concoctions. This friendly Moroccan bakery is enough to make anyone nostalgic for the Maghreb (or France).

Golborne Fisheries

75 Golborne Road
020 8969 3100
Mon–Sat 8am–6pm

Golborne Fisheries has long been renowned for its impressive range of seafood, but a change of management in 2006 has lifted it to a new level. The variety of produce on offer (clams, lobster, king fish, wild halibut, mackerel, grouper, crab, swordfish, salmon, sea trout, to name a few) is greater. And labels now indicate whether fish is organic, farmed or wild, with helpful staff often able to tell you where it has come from.

Lisboa Delicatessen

54 Golborne Road W10
020 8969 1052
Mon–Sat 9.30am–7.30pm;
Sun 10am–1pm

Almost directly opposite the famous patisserie/café of the same name, Lisboa stocks a comprehensive selection of Portuguese and Brazilian groceries. Packets of almond biscuits and tins of olives, anchovies, tuna, beans and vegetables fill the shelves, while the bread is displayed in wooden bins. Hams, sausages and cheeses are sold behind the gleaming counter at the back, where you will also find salt cod, pigs' trotters and other pork delicacies, as well as beer and wine.

Le Maroc
94 Golborne Road W10
020 8968
Mon–Sat 9am–7pm

The most alluring of Golborne Road's Moroccan groceries combines household goods such as colourful tagines, ceramics, trays and wall hangings with traditional Moroccan food. Halal meat and delicious home-made merguez sausages are sold at the counter, surrounded by stacks of couscous, nuts, olives, oil, honey as well as bundles of fresh mint, ladies' fingers, other vegetables and fruit – in short, everything you need to conjure a genuine taste of Morocco.

PUBS & BARS

The Earl Percy
225 Ladbroke Grove W10
020 8960 3522
Bar: Mon–Thurs 12 noon–11pm;
Fri & Sat 12 noon–midnight;
Thai food served daily 12 noon–10pm

After a bad patch when even long-term regulars were giving it a wide berth, the Earl Percy has had a makeover, with mainly positive results. Some find the cream interior a bit sterile but staff are friendly and the Thai food is above average. Also a hotel (see p 149).

The Elgin
96 Ladbroke Grove W11
020 7229 5663
Mon–Thurs 12 noon–11pm;
Fri 12 noon–11.30pm;
Sat 11am–11.30pm;
Sun 12 noon–10.30pm

On the corner of Westbourne Park Road, the Elgin is a large, no-frills pub that comes into its own during the football season. Each of its three rooms has a huge TV screen, tables and comfortable seating where it's easy to settle in with the crowd for a long afternoon or evening's viewing. Traditional pub food is served from 12 noon to 9pm.

Golborne Grove
36 Golborne Road W10
020 8960 6260
www.groverestaurants.co.uk
Daily 10.15am–11.30ish

Good food, unpretentious style and quality service are the mainstays of this increasingly popular gastropub on the corner of Golborne Road and Southam Street. The furniture is plain wood, while the menu features an appetising list of Mediterranean dishes. Be sure to leave a gap for the sticky toffee pudding.

The William IV
786 Harrow Road NW10
0208 969 5944
www.williamivlondon.com
Tues–Thurs 12 noon–midnight;
Fri & Sat 12 noon–1am;
Sun 12 noon–10.30pm

Frequented by music and media types (there's a lot of music industry business around Kensal Green), this pub with a trad name isn't trad at all; big-name DJs and late opening hours ensure it's always packed, so come early if you want to be sure to get in. Equally good for tapas or Sunday lunch, when the menu features a combination of traditional English and Mediterranean dishes, well

cooked and reasonably priced. This pub is conveniently placed for a stroll or organised tour in the cemetery across the road.

ENTERTAINMENT

CHILDREN

Skate Bowl
Meanwhile Gardens W10
020 8960 4600
Open 24 hours

Colourful graffiti decorate this bowl, which reopened after major refurbishment in the spring of 2000. Free access and its position, amid landscaped gardens beside the canal, make it a popular meeting place for young spectators, as well as those honing their skateboarding skills, especially in summer. The gardens also have a One O'clock Club for the under-fives. *Currently open Mon–Fri 12.30pm–5pm, but due for extension.*

Playstation Skatepark
Bay 65–66
Acklam Road W10
0795 7124 465/www.pssp.co.uk
Mon, Thurs & Fri 12 noon–4pm; 5pm–9pm;
Tues & Wed 12 noon–4pm; 5pm–10pm;

Sat & Sun 10am–12 noon (beginners);
12 noon–4pm; 5pm–9pm

Children – mainly boys – of all ages flock to this skateboarding park, which opened under the Westway in 1997, with input from the team who designed the original bowl at Meanwhile Gardens. Users pay a £10 yearly membership fee, plus £4 for a four-hour session; non-members simply pay £6. Sponsored by Sony – hence the name.

MUSIC & CLUBBING

Neighbourhood
12 Acklam Road (under the Westway) W10
0208 960 9331
www.myspace.com/neighbourhoodclub
Daily 9pm–2.30am

Deep under the Westway just off Portobello Road, Subteranea's successor hosts an eclectic range of music nights, from Norman Jay, reggae and dub (especially around Carnival) to house, funk, disco and live broadcasts by the likes of Choice FM. Free before 10pm.

STAYING IN

Channel Video Films
142 Ladbroke Grove W10
020 8960 2148
Daily 10am–10pm

The place to go if you can't get what you want at Notting Hill Gate's Video City. Higher prices and inflexibility over late returns are compensated for by the multiple copies they have of all the latest releases. A large selection of old films is stocked in the basement.

HEALTH, BEAUTY & FITNESS

Kell Skött Haircare
93 Golborne Road W10
020 8964 3004
www.kellskotthaircare.com
Mon 10am–6pm; Tues 9am–6pm;
Wed & Thurs 9am–8pm;
Fri 9am–7pm; Sat 8am–6pm

Arguably the best salon in the area, this small, friendly business cuts and colours with flair. Prices are reasonable and irresistible brownies accompany the wide range of complimentary teas and coffees on offer. Kell is a keen photographer and his atmospheric land- and seascapes adorn the walls.

Virgin Active
119–31 Lancaster Road W11
020 7243 4141
www.virginactive.co.uk
Mon–Thurs 6.30am–10.30pm;
Fri 6.30am–10pm;
Sat & Sun 8.30am–9pm

Converted from a school, this health club (formerly Holmes Place) has managed to create a feeling of light and space on every floor, topped by a lovely swimming pool, at the same time keeping the original Victorian façade. Tai chi, pilates, chi ball and several variations of yoga, as well as less holistic body-conditioning classes, are complemented by a range of beauty treatments, from facials to nail and hair repair. Crèche.

See Portobello chapter for **Bliss**

SHOPPING

ANTIQUES

Arbon Interiors
80 Golborne Road W10
020 8960 9787/www.arboninteriors.com
Mon–Sat 9am–5pm

Here you'll find everything to do with beautiful fireplaces, but also decorative antiques, great big chandeliers, crystal wall-lights, mirrors, pretty fabrics, curtains and bistro tables. Fireplace surrounds range from £70 to £16,500 (for a 19th-century Surina marble fireplace) and include antiques and reproductions in stone, wood and marble. Gas-effect fires are also in stock. Arbon has its own fitters for the installation of surrounds, hearths and grates. Valuations can be arranged for insurance purposes. Also offers prop hire.

Bazar
82 Golborne Road W10
020 8969 6262
Tues–Sat 10am–5.30pm

For more than 30 years, Bazar has been selling a range of French furniture and items: painted armoires, lovely made-to-order pine tables, sewing tables, country-kitchen shelves, and bamboo and wood coat racks. The shop has a light, sparkly feel about it and, as well as selling items in wood, stocks stylish armchairs, chandeliers, glasses, ceramics and properly made baskets.

Les Couilles du Chien

65 Golborne Road W10
020 8968 0099
www.lescouillesduchien.co.uk
Mon–Thurs & Sat 9.30am–5.30pm;
Fri 8am–5pm

Unless you're a dealer or stylist and can identify an Eames or a Mies van der Rohe with mercurial speed in the presence of stuffed water buffalo, skeletons and looming arc lights, you had best take your time in Jerome Dodd's emporium. This is where to go to buy the most fantastic lighting at affordable prices. The ubiquitous arc light comes in various sizes and starts at £125, but more interesting is Jerome's stock of glass, metal and wooden chandeliers and wall-lights, which range from the arborial to the celestial, including beautiful ferns, floral bouquets and crystal waterfalls. Stuffed animals, framed entomological specimens and hide rugs peep out from between the unfaltering leather chairs. You'll find many buried treasures, from the stylishly practical to the ravishingly impractical, which rather describes Jerome and his eccentric assistant Oscar Darling. The 'dog's bollocks' also does prop hire.

Eighty-eight Antiques

88 Golborne Road W10
0208 960 0827
Mon–Sat 9am–5pm

Eighty-eight specialises in Victorian stripped pine and quality reproduction shelves and chests of drawers, tables, blanket boxes and other storage pieces for those who are tired of trying to arrange their linen and paperwork into piles of boxes and baskets. Also available are one-off hand-crafted kitchens. No wood-stripping service.

Mac's

86 Golborne Road W10
020 8960 3736
Mon–Sat 9am–5pm (though erratic, so phone)

This is the place for grand architectural pieces; the term decorative antiques is not palatial enough to describe Mac's taste. Opulent gilded mirrors, unusual painted enamel sinks, vast gates, lead urns, and soaring horticulturally inspired light fittings are just a few of the objects on offer. Stately, elegant and mysterious.

Ollies

69 Golborne Road W10
07768 790725
Mon–Sat 9am–5pm

Ollies is colonial cowboy hip – a mix of zebra-skin rugs, leather sofas, bamboo etc, changing with current fashions. Good buys are a pair of leather club chairs, glamorous Venetian mirrors, Twenties and Thirties furniture, antique textiles, and lamps (especially arc lamps) designed with a meeting of James Dean and Lawrence of Arabia in mind. The shop, visited by the likes of Damon Albarn and Richard E Grant, also stocks seasonal tropical plants, such as orange and lemon trees. It also does prop rental.

BIKES

Halfpipe

40 Golborne Road W10
020 8969 2999/www.half-pipe.co.uk
Mon–Sat 10am–6pm; Sun 12 noon–4pm

On the site of one of his Dad's fish and chip shops, Johnny Perricos has opened a bike shop that sells BMX, standard bikes, clothes, snowboards and skateboards. Also bike repairs.

FASHION & VINTAGE

The Crazy Clothes Connection

134 Lancaster Road W11
020 7221 3989
Tues–Sat 11am–7pm

Derrick and his daughter Esther are said to have the best selection of 1920s–70s vintage clothes in London. They also offer costume hire. Rave reviews in the press won't prepare you for the rather dingy appearance of the overcrowded shop, full of bulging clothes racks reminiscent of a run-down charity shop, or the prices: £75–£100 or so for evening dresses, £50 upwards for men's coats, and so on. Fashion editors love it, so who are we to argue?

Jane Bourvis

89 Golborne Road W10
020 8964 5603/www.janebourvis.co.uk
Mon 1pm–5pm; Tues–Sat 11am–5pm

Jane Bourvis's shop represents a pleasantly haphazard version of the lifestyle concept that dominates so many retail outlets, especially in Notting Hill. Prettily wrapped soaps, whimsical ornaments and flower-bedecked tea cosies mingle with exotic fabrics, throws, cushions, cashmere cardigans, silk wraparound skirts and wonderfully soft leather slippers and shoes for adults and children. The focus is more and more on unique dresses for special occasions.

Rellik
8 Golborne Road W10
020 8962 0089
www.relliklondon.co.uk
Tues–Sat 10am–6pm

Notting Hill chic still sits rather incongruously at the bottom of Trellick Tower. Rellik offers a diverse selection of one-off designs, from vintage Vivienne Westwood to designer wear customised with antique lace and fabric.

See Portobello chapter for **Horace** (jewellery) and **Olivia Morris** (shoes)

FLOWERS

The Flowered Corner
110 Ladbroke Grove W11
020 7221 3320
Daily 8am–8pm

Grandfather Perring started up as a flower-seller more than 20 years ago, after giving up work as a tot-

ter. He went on to build a thriving business, with another flower stall on Portobello Road (corner of Talbot Road), all still run by his extended family. Prices are very fair and the flowers always fresh, creating a welcome splash of colour at the busy junction with Lancaster Road.

GIFTS & HOME

Buyers & Sellers
120–1 Ladbroke Grove W10
0845 080 2201
Mon–Fri 9.30am–5.30pm
(Thurs 10am–6.30pm); Sat 9.30am–6.30pm

A wide range of upmarket domestic appliances which claim to be the cheapest in the UK. Free delivery nationwide.

Fez
71 Golborne Road W10
020 8964 5573
Mon–Sat 10am–7pm

Tea glasses are one of the best buys in this authentic Moroccan houseware shop, which also sells teapots, ceramics, rugs, rush mats, wall hangings, slippers and other items, with little if any concession to fashion. The main aim is to serve the local community.

Portfolio

105 Golborne Road W10
020 8960 3051
Mon–Fri 9.30am–5.30pm; Sat 10am–5pm

A great place for greetings cards and posters, as well as odd gifts, Portfolio has the added prestige of having been transformed into a restaurant for a scene in *Notting Hill*. This is where Hugh Grant and friends mull over his decision to reject the beautiful Julia Roberts, before setting off on a wild car chase to her hotel. Curious locals watched for hours as the actors repeatedly dashed out into the waiting vehicle, which merely shot down Bevington Road and back again.

Warris Vianni & Co

85 Golborne Road W10
020 8964 0069
www.warrisvianni.com
Mon–Sat 10am–6pm

A combination of quality, originality and style make this one of the best fabric shops in London, but, of course, it doesn't come cheap. Rolls of organza, muslin, silk, cotton, linen, chenille and other hand-loomed materials originate from all over the world, with prices ranging from £10 to more than £50 a metre.

MUSIC

Dub Vendor Records

150 Ladbroke Grove W10
020 8969 3375
Mon–Sat 10.30am–7.30pm; Sun 11am–5.30pm

An enduring landmark that started out as a small shack beside Ladbroke Grove station, Dub Vendor specialises in reggae, soca, soul and the full panoply of remixes. Typical customers are a dense gaggle of 15-year-olds checking the latest beats, proving that, like all the music shops in this book, Dub Vendor is not just a place to buy CDs but a positive meeting point for local youth. Sweatshirts, t-shirts and baseball caps and other clothes also for sale.

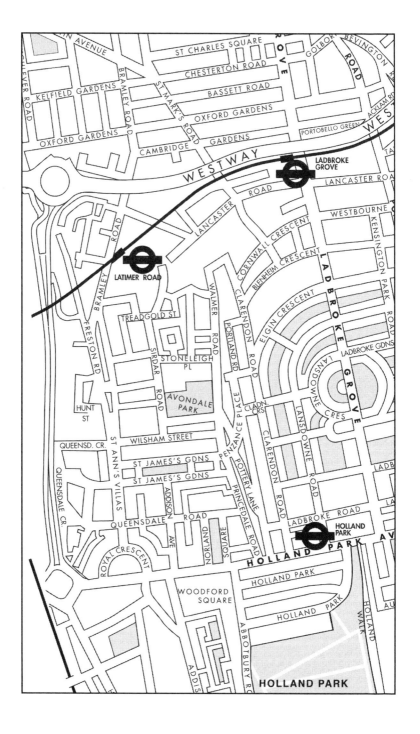

5 NOTTING DALE & HOLLAND PARK

Tube: Holland Park, Latimer Road
Highlights: St Helen's Gardens, delis and pubs, Redfern's Music Picture Gallery, Clarendon Cross, Church of St Francis of Assisi, Holland Park

This chapter, more than any other, encapsulates the contrasts of extreme poverty and wealth that make up the history and fabric of Notting Hill: on the one side Notting Dale, with its 19th-century colonies of gypsies, brick-makers and pig-keepers, and on the other, Holland Park and its grand society, centred around Holland House.

At first glance, Notting Dale today presents a confusing network of recently built streets and public housing, swathed by the Westway. But look closer and you'll discover, scattered among the tower blocks, quiet corners of terraced cottages, a historic park and three magnificent churches. This may not be the place for shopping, though it is beginning to gain its share of trendy eateries, but it's well worth exploring for its historical interest and as a less-trodden route to the fashionable reaches of Clarendon Cross and beyond. Many residents consider that Holland Park, even the north side of the Avenue, is simply not Notting Hill. In the past, however, the two areas were inextricably intertwined.

Lancaster Road

The boundaries of Notting Dale have never been totally clear, but for the purposes of this chapter we begin at the western end of Lancaster Road, after the London Lighthouse at the junction with St Mark's Road. It was near this intersection, at 10 Rillington Place, that, in 1943, John Christie carried out the first of a horrific spate of murder that was to shake Notting Hill for many years to come. An upstairs neighbour, Timothy Evans, was wrongfully hanged for the murders in 1950, after which the real killer went on to strangle his wife and three more women. Christie was finally caught, convicted and hanged in 1953. Evans was pardoned in 1966, largely thanks to the efforts of Ludovic Kennedy, whose book *10 Rillington Place* (1961) indirectly led to the abolition of the death penalty. The book opens with a description of this section of Notting Dale as it looked in the 1940s, before it was replaced by the neat private houses of Wesley and St Andrew's Squares:

You will not find Rillington Place in any street map of London now, for it has long been demolished. It was a mean shabby cul-de-sac of ten houses on either side. Although the houses had three floors, they were small, almost miniature houses, and their most striking characteristic was peeling paint and rotting stucco. The street was bounded at one end by St Mark's Road and at the other by the wall of Rickard's

Transport Depot for Coaches and Vans. Originally Rickard's was Bartlett's Iron Foundry, and the foundry chimney still stands. It rises, as it were from the centre of the boundary wall; and its squat pear-shaped form seemed to dominate the street.

Just beyond the houses on the north side lay the Metropolitan Railway Line, and the sounds of the trains coming and going were part of the lives of the people who lived there. Many of them lived two and three to a room. On summer evenings the children played in the street and on the pavements, and the parents sat at the open windows watching the world go by. No. 10 was the last house on the south side.

Ruth Rendell paints a more contemporary picture in the thriller *Thirteen Steps Down* (2004), whose main character, Mix Cellini, is drawn to the area by an obsession with Christie:

It was a funny part of the world altogether. Mix hadn't got used to it yet, the Westway to the north and Wormwood Scrubs and its prison not far away, a tangle of little winding streets, big houses, purpose-built blocks, ugly Victorian terraces, Gothic places more like churches than like homes, cottages cunningly designed on different levels to look as if they had been there for two hundred years, corner shops, MOT testing centres, garages, meeting halls, real churches for Holy Catholic Apostolics or Latter Day Saints and convents for Oblates and Carmelites.

Past the junction with St Mark's Road, just before the corner where Lancaster becomes Silchester Road, stands Notting Hill Methodist Church. As well as providing a beautifully simple and serene place of worship, the church has a strong tradition of working towards peace in the neighbourhood, in particular the inclusion of the African-Caribbean community. Part of the basement is used by the Kensington & Chelsea Community History Group, whose publications have provided much valuable material for this book.

NOTTING HILL METHODIST CHURCH

The site where the church now stands was originally occupied by the Anglican Church of St Andrew, which was destroyed by fire in 1865. The current church was built in 1878–79 by Jesse Chessure of Shoreditch as a two-storey structure with a hall in the semi-basement beneath.

Over the years, extensive alterations have been made to the building's interior to accommodate the congregation's changing needs, and today few of the original furnishings remain. Historically important as a social centre and as the site for a Sunday school, the church played an important role during the years following the riots of 1958 (see pp 97 & 241). Feeling the need for a stronger Methodist presence and for more inter-congregational activity, to try to unite the different communities of Notting Dale, Donald (later Lord) Soper (1903–1998) invited three young priests to work at the church in a Team Ministry, which

would welcome all and attempt to break down barriers in a friendly multi-racial atmosphere. Drawing on their experiences in other inner cities, and in Jamaica and East Harlem, these three priests helped to bring the community together through informal meetings, and they became a key driving force in the formation of the Notting Hill Social Council in 1962.

The church has remained very active, and today the building is arranged over three floors: the area for worship at the top is also used for a range of classes, meetings and activities; the middle floor is devoted to meeting rooms and administrative offices, and the lower section is in constant use as a meeting place for various community and church groups. In addition to the Kensington

& Chelsea Community History Group, a Day Project operates from here. The project invites people who have been recently rehoused to use the space for classes and activities and as a centre to seek and be directed to practical advice. The church also owns a hall on part of the site in Denbigh Road once occupied by another Methodist church as well as several other premises, including the Oxfam shop on Westbourne Grove. Typical of the area, this church combines the secular and the sacred in a way that both welcomes and serves the mixed community in which it is rooted. It is open to visitors during the day. For information on services and other activities, telephone 020 7229 7728.

Around the corner on the left was once the site of the Lancaster Road Baths and Wash House, opened in 1888 and later renamed Silchester Baths. As well as providing a desperately needed facility for the hundreds of families who lived without running water the buildings served as an important social meeting point for local women, 60,000 of whom did their washing there in 1897. The threat of closure in the early 1970s sparked a vigorous campaign which led to the provision of a public launderette under the Westway. The baths were demolished in 1975 to make way for the public housing you see now.

At this point, the sudden transformation of Lancaster into Silchester Road illustrates the extent to which Notting Dale has been demolished, dissected and redesigned. Streets stop and start all over the place, making it hard to negotiate on foot, let alone by car. Beginning with a brief diversion to Latimer Road, the following route is a circuit taking in some key landmarks on the way to Holland Park.

Silchester baths, Notting Dale 1898

Latimer Road via the St Quintin's Estate

Silchester Road passes under a railway bridge before reaching Bramley Road, where a left turn leads into the heart of Notting Dale and Holland Park beyond. A right deviation beneath the Westway and up to St Helen's Gardens takes in the Edwardian streets of the St Quintin's Estate. The area is named after Colonel St Quintin. who owned much of this land, which remained largely undeveloped until early last century.

In recent years the estate has graduated from its reputation as a sub-urban wasteland to being celebrated in *Tatler* magazine for its prime position in 'London's hottest postcode' – W10. Conservative Party leader David Cameron lives there, and estate agents are not shy about mentioning the 'Cameron effect'. Nor is the man himself. On being challenged by *Time Out* journalist Michael Hodges about his member-ship of the Notting Hill set, the would-be prime minister retorted (28 November 2006): 'You've just been to my house. It's not Notting Hill. I've done all my neighbours a huge favour because it's been rebranded as Notting Hill! Everyone's house is worth more.'

Someone else who spotted a local opportunity is architect Alex Michaelis, who allegedly paid £750,000 for a plot of land in nearby Oxford Gardens despite the constraint that he would not be able to build above the surrounding six-foot wall. The result is a highly innova-tive eco-house complete with a vast timber-floored living room, a swimming pool, solar panels, underfloor heating, water supplied directly from the property's own borehole and a grass-covered roof, the only feature visible from the pavement. This changing demograph-ic has been accompanied by a spate of new businesses, notably along the stretch of shops at St Helen's Gardens, where an expensive flower shop, upmarket café-delicatessen, two dry cleaners and the Big Tomato ceramics company have all moved in the last few years.

Heading west (on the other side of St Helen's Gardens), the road passes Oxford Gardens Primary School, alongside a low white building that was the studio of society photographer Patrick Lichfield until his death in November 2005, then rows of mainly two-storey red-brick houses up to the desolate reaches of Latimer Road. Though primarily an industrial estate, Latimer Road has two attractions – ponies and Thai food.

Facing the flyover, a lane on the right is marked Stable Way. This leads to one of North Kensington's most surprising finds – Westway Stables. As long ago as 1860, the patch of ground that now lies in the shadow of the A40 was a well-known site for gypsies, many of whom were gradually rehoused in the terraced cottages south of Latimer Road. Those who kept their horses and carts became totters or 'rag-and-bone-men', collecting scrap metal, old clothes and household implements from door to door. Their base was this yard, since transformed into a curiously picturesque oasis where brightly feathered cockerels pick among the dung, and pretty-faced ponies peer over wooden stable doors. For the last 12 years or so Westway Stables has been run as a riding school for inner-city children and the odd keen adult. Supported by the Westway Development Trust, owner Sarah Tuvey has managed to build up a loyal following, including a of voluntary helpers, who come regularly to ride in the sandpit ring under the flyover or further afield on Wormwood Scrubs Common. Travellers still have a site nearby.

Back on Latimer Road, a few blocks north is the delightful Thai River café & restaurant. Eating in the cosy, candlelit space or in the leafy garden, it's easy to forget you're in London.

The St Quintin's Estate is built on a grid system, so it is quite easy to find your way back to St Helen's Gardens, which, running south, soon turns back into Bramley Road.

Bramley Road and Frestonia

Bramley Road unexpectedly branches off, while the route it was following takes on another name. After the junction with Silchester Road, a short walk takes you past the Irish Pig & Whistle pub, under the railway bridge at Latimer Road tube station, and alongside the Lancaster West Estate, a huge and notoriously deprived housing estate dating from the 1970s. Behind lies Treadgold Street, home to the Church of St Clement (see p 170). Soon afterwards, Bramley Road appears to become St Ann's Road. In fact, it veers off to the right. Right again at the Armadillo Café lies a turning into Freston Road, birthplace of one of the most imaginative, spirited and successful projects to have come out of the 1970s: the Free Independent Republic of Frestonia (see p 291).

Formerly Latimer Road, the street was renamed after the construction of the Westway effectively cut it in two. This disruption,

exacerbated by the political squabbling and indecision that allowed the now-derelict area around the flyover to lie abandoned, sparked an upsurge in community action.

From the early 1970s, squatters had begun to occupy houses in and around the old Latimer Road. Many were artists, writers and musicians, and by the middle of the decade they had created a lively community, incorporating a communal garden, the Car Breakers' Art Gallery and the Apocalypse Hotel. In 1977, the Greater London Council announced that the whole area was to be leased out for industrial development, and it was then that an alliance of locals was formed, declaring themselves 'the Free and Independent Republic of Frestonia'. They organised a series of protests, both provocative and crazy in spirit, and were successful: the original plans were ditched and the Bramley Housing Co-operative was formed. Working with the Notting Hill Housing Trust, the co-op organised the building of homes on a human scale and managed on a co-operative basis, some of which border St Ann's Road. This movement marked a significant change, since when, it is hoped, harsh developments such as the Lancaster West Estate have become a thing of the past. (A first-hand account is provided by the late Nicholas Albery, who was Frestonia's 'Minister of State for the Environment', see p 291.)

Today this corner of Notting Dale is better known as the headquarters of Chrysalis Music (publisher of local musicians Damon Albarn and Paul Simonon's project 'The Good, the Bad and the Queen') and the radio station Heart FM. There's also a chance it will enter the guidebooks as the location of the Louise T Blouin Institute on Olaf Street, just past the People's Hall. The project of Canadian millionairess Louise T Blouin, the institute, opened in 2006, is a vast and beautiful exhibition space converted from a former coachworks. As well as showcasing the work of contemporary artists, the building is a base for Blouin's Foundation dedicated to exploring the 'crossover between art and science'.

The Parish of St Clement and St James

Returning to the main highway, St Ann's Road continues past Henry Dickens Court, a municipal housing development attributed to the good work of Henry, grandson of Charles Dickens. In her memoirs, *An Open Book*, the writer's great-granddaughter, Monica Dickens (herself a novelist), recalls her father's achievements as a councillor with the Royal Borough of Kensington in the 1950s:

In the desperate need for housing after the war, he caused some good blocks of council flats to be built on the far side of the curving Lansdowne streets that once were a racecourse. The estate is called Henry Dickens Court. The buildings are named after characters from Charles Dickens, but they stand as a memorial to the industry of his grandson, hammering against the fearful odds of bureaucracy. When the Queen Mother came for the official dedication of the estate, Henry was on the platform with her in his fur-lined Alderman's robe. And afterwards they had tea together in 4 Dombey House, with Mrs Langham pouring.

Soon after Henry Dickens Court, as St Ann's Road becomes St Ann's Villas, the architecture takes on a sudden grandeur, albeit in the shadow of tower blocks, and continues east and south to Royal Crescent and Holland Park Avenue. Albert Chevalier (1861–1923), the music hall comedian was born at No. 17.

One of the most attractive landmarks here is St James's Gardens, with its majestic church of St James Norlands. St James's and its sister church, St Clement Notting Dale, provide vivid illustrations of the two disparate worlds that existed side by side throughout the second half of the 19th century, and, to some extent, continue in their equivalent forms today.

Although united into the same parish since 1985, these two churches and their congregations could not be more contrasting. St James's stands imposingly at the centre of its elegant square, looking down Addison Avenue, one of the most exclusive stretches of housing in the area, while St Clement's merges into its humble surroundings – the artisan dwellings of Treadgold Street, directly next to the grim blocks of the Lancaster West Estate. Both churches are of architectural merit, listed Grade II by the Department of National Heritage, and the stroll through the streets between them provides a social history lesson in itself.

In true Notting Hill spirit, every effort is made to unite the two congregations, and the parish runs a plethora of community activities, including English classes, a study support group to help children with their homework, a steel-band workshop, and dance, yoga, painting and drawing workshops. The parish also runs a community shop providing low-cost clothes, toys and household goods to people on benefits, as well as refugees and asylum seekers.

THE CHURCH OF ST JAMES NORLANDS

St James's was designed as the centrepiece for the surrounding domestic development of the Norland Estate. The architect was Lewis Vulliamy, son of the famous clock maker Benjamin Vulliamy, a previous owner of the estate. It was built between 1844 and 1850 in the Gothic revival style. Lack of funds hindered the project's progress and Vulliamy's plans were never fully realised. The chancel was added in 1876 to a design by Robert Jewell Withers.

The church is built in white Suffolk brick, and its exterior is notable for its fine tower, positioned so as to mark the north-south axis of the estate. Had the money not run out, the tower would have been topped with a spire. Until 1948, most of the interior was coloured or decorated, and the columns and arcades (up to the stringcourse) embellished with printed patterns. Murals decorating the north and south aisles were removed in 1950. Today the effect is austere: the tall, wide arcades standing on their elegant monochrome quatrefoil iron piers are whitewashed and there is no flamboyance in the decoration, except for a recent candy-stripe detail on the west gallery underneath the organ. But the fine stained-glass windows (1880) remain **in situ**, along with a number of striking features. The wooden reredos of the main altar is finely and extravagantly carved with polychrome decoration depicting the Last Supper (made in 1880). The Lady Chapel contains a pleasing copy of a Raphael Madonna and child. The sturdy font features green marble and glazed tiles, and a fine brass eagle lectern is dated 1893. Perhaps most impressive is the wonderful organ, located since 1921 in the west gallery. A three-manual and pedal instrument, with prettily stencilled front pipes, it was made by Auguste Gern in 1878, then rebuilt by JJ Binns of Leeds in 1895. It was restored in 1996 and is put to very good use: the church has excellent acoustics and is the site of many musical events, including the highly rated W11 Children's Opera, which takes place every year in early December (www.w11opera.org). For further information, telephone 020 7221 3548.

Leaving the Church of St James, it is simple to wend your way through pretty, affluent streets to Princedale Road and Clarendon Cross. The route described below takes in both these landmarks, only backtracking slightly via St Clement's, before moving on to Walmer Road and the heart of Notting Dale's poverty-stricken past.

In and around Treadgold Street
Back along St Anne's Road, past Henry Dickens Court, a right turn takes you into Stoneleigh Place. The next left, Stoneleigh Street, leads directly into Treadgold Street and the church of St Clement – unprepossessing on the outside but well worth entering for its wonderfully harmonious decoration.

THE CHURCH OF ST CLEMENT NOTTING DALE

It would be easy to pass this church without noticing it – small, squat and made of yellow brick with little embellishment. Yet it stands as an important memorial to its founder, the Reverend Arthur Dalgarno Robinson. An energetic humanitarian, Robinson came to Notting Dale in 1860 and founded one of the earliest schools for the children of the Potteries. He bought the land for the site of the church out of his own pocket and, prior to its completion in 1867, worked for seven years without pay. The church was designed by JP St Aubyn, was inexpensively built and consecrated in 1867 to provide 900 seats.

As with St James's and so many other Victorian churches, the original richness of the decoration inside has been almost totally obliterated by later monochromatic over-painting. Yet the interior is still astonishing: here Victorian high-tech meets traditional timber craftsmanship to very happy effect. A series of finely crafted cast-iron pillars rise to a vast wooden roof of oversized rafters supported by scissor-blades. The impression is of an airy, unified space with no interruption between the nave and the aisles. Its treasures include the highly decorative painted wooden Renaissance-style reredos of the main altar, an elaborate crucifix made and signed by Omar Ramsden in 1833, and a set of copper candlesticks made by Robe in 1855. The tessellated pradella incorporates **fleur de lis** motifs and the anchor of St Clement. The simple open benches are by St Aubyn and the south-east chapel contains an altar with a charming **repoussé** copper front. On the west wall there is a commemorative plaque to the Reverend Robinson. Standing here, you can readily believe that his spirit still lingers in this cheerful, busy, well-used space.

While St James's hosts the rather grand W11 Opera, St Clement's has become very much associated with the Carnival. Each year, the congregations help to organise a float and costumes, and all are invited to attend a special Carnival mass. St Clement and St James Norlands are in the same parish. For further information, telephone the parish office 020 7221 3548.

The surrounding buildings are a mixture of relatively new housing developments and a few rows of terraced cottages that escaped war damage and have been allowed to remain. Compared to the East End of London, Notting Dale was relatively unscathed by the Second World War. The housing problems that made it such a troubled area in the 1950s and early 60s stemmed more from neglect than bomb damage. Those who could afford it moved out to the suburbs, leaving poor-quality accommodation for the less fortunate, who were joined by a growing number of incomers from overseas.

In a seminal study into housing conditions and how to improve them, *A Troubled Area: Notes on Notting Hill* (1964), Pearl Jephcott provided a vivid snapshot of the local population in 1962:

The racial and social characteristics of Notting Dale are as heterogeneous as its housing. Saris and sandals, the Sikh's white turban and black beard, the carefully careless headscarf of the Nigerian, and the goffered guimp of the Italian nun lend a (slightly seedy) exoticism to the area ... Habits and ménages are as bizarre as costumes and accents. Teddy boys hail taxis with assurance; a dignitary of some Eastern Church, purple cassocked, conducts his daily services in his council flat; and an elderly refugee landlady from Shanghai fights a losing battle with her smooth-tongued tenants from Cork. Cosmopolitanism on this scale means that even the officials whom it causes so much extra labour and anxiety agree that the place is oddly stimulating.

Jephcott's report was commissioned in the wake of the 1958 race riots, which marked a turning point in Notting Hill's history (see pp 97 & 241). They lasted over three days and were fuelled in large part by the Union Movement of Sir Oswald Mosley. A self-proclaimed fascist, Mosley was given to bringing out his soapbox on street corners throughout Notting Hill, where his small, but for a time influential, party was based. Although he was reputed to be a charismatic speaker, film-maker Kevin Brownlow had a very different impression. He went to hear Mosley speak only a few months before the riots, as part of his research for the film *It Happened Here*:

In April 1958 my co-director, Andrew Mollo, and I visited Porchester Hall in Westbourne Grove to attend one of Sir Oswald Mosley's meetings. We had always been told that however much of a villain he may have been, Mosley was a superb orator. We were disappointed. The speech he delivered was long-winded and absurd. He advocated the removal of blacks from the coasts of Africa – nobody would be forced to move – and their replacement by whites. This would simultaneously prevent Communist incursion and black emigration. Andrew stood up and asked him what would happen if Africans refused to move. Mosley said they would be given incentives. I stood up to make another point; Mosley denied being anti-Semitic but the current issue of his paper, Action, *had an anti-Semitic headline. Mosley snapped, 'You've already asked a question', and turned to someone else.*

Mosley took advantage of people's insecurities over jobs and housing. In the months preceding the riots, he deliberately whipped up the tension, and gangs of white youths paraded the streets of Notting Dale, threatening black people and smashing up their property. When the tension finally erupted, the majority of people were determined that such an explosion of racism and violence should never happen again.

Among several positive initiatives to emerge after the riots were Pearl Jephcott's recommendations that people be given the opportunity to take control of their own living conditions. This new, enlightened attitude helped inspire many subsequent campaigns, including the laundry protests of 1973 (see p 164).

Walmer Road to Pottery Lane

Not far from the Church of St Clement, Treadgold Street becomes Grenfell Road. Follow the next right into Bomore Road and you'll come to Kensington Sports Centre. Another right turn takes you into Walmer Road, leading directly to Avondale Park, Pottery Lane, with its beautiful Church of St Francis of Assisi, and Clarendon Cross.

A short way into Walmer Road, one of the first buildings on the left is the Rugby Club, established in the late 19th century by Arthur Walrond, a former pupil of Rugby School. In 1889, with the support of the school, he managed to purchase an old bus yard in Walmer Road, and built a club for boys in search of warmth, light, amusement and comradeship. A fair amount of preaching went on here, but the centre was also noted for its swimming pool (one of the first private pools) and its many sporting activities, especially boxing. Theatrical productions were staged here too, providing funding for the club and activities such as summer camps every July and August.

Walmer Road continues between a mix of old terraced housing and modern developments up to Avondale Park, opposite which the old bottle kiln provides a reminder of the time when Potteries & Piggeries dominated Notting Dale (see History, p 236). Wandering around Avondale Park, with its well-tended flowerbeds and children's playground, it's hard to imagine the treacherous ocean of clay sludge and pig's swill that lay over this site in the late 1840s right up to the time it was filled in to create the park in 1892. Living conditions and sanitation in the surrounding houses were so poor that when London's cholera epidemic of 1849 spread to Notting Dale, Charles Dickens was prompted to publish a piece about the area in the first issue of his journal *Household Words*. The article by WH Wills began:

In a neighbourhood studded thickly with elegant villas and mansions, viz Baywater and Notting Hill, in the parish of Kensington, is a plague-spot, scarcely equalled for its insalubrity by any other in London; it is called the Potteries. It comprises some seven or eight acres with about 260 houses, if the term can be applied to such hovels, and a population of 900 to 1,000. The occupation of the inhabitants is principally pig-fattening; many hundreds of pigs, ducks and fowls are kept in an incredible state of filth. Dogs abound for the purpose of guarding the swine. The atmosphere is still further polluted by fat boiling. In these hovels discontent, dirt, filth and misery are unsurpassed by anything known even in Ireland. Water is supplied to only a small proportion of houses. There are foul ditches, open sewers, and defective drains, smelling most offensively and generating large quantities of poisonous gases; stagnant water is found at every turn.

After the park, Walmer Road curves leftwards into Hippodrome Place (named after the racecourse, see p 22), while straight ahead lie Pottery Lane and the Roman Catholic Church of St Francis of Assisi. When it opened in 1860, the church provided a great source of comfort and celebration to the largely Irish community who first attended, and it continues to be hugely active today.

THE CHURCH OF ST FRANCIS OF ASSISI

St Francis was built at the personal expense of the Reverend Henry Augustus Rawes. A member of the priestly community of the Oblates of St Charles Borromeo, he arrived at a time when the Potteries were described as suffering from a pestilent moral atmosphere. Rawes commissioned Henry Clutton (an associate of William Burges) to design the church on an awkwardly shaped plot of land situated on a north-south axis. The original building work was supervised in 1859–60 by Clutton's then assistant John Bentley. Very soon, enlargements were needed and Bentley, now in independent practice, was responsible for adding a baptistry, porch, presbytery and school to the original structure between 1861 and 1863.

The church's austere exterior is of stock brick relieved by bands of black bricks, and is entered via a small courtyard. The simple interior in French provincial style is notable for the graceful eastward curve of the Lady Chapel, a device to accommodate the awkward shape of the plot. This uncluttered architecture provides the perfect setting for a treasure chest of spectacular, exquisitely crafted church furniture, all made from the finest materials available. Bentley was particularly interested in metalwork and the decorative arts, and St Francis contains fine examples of his early work.

The alabaster altar of St John on the north wall of the Lady Chapel contains many elements of Bentley's creative genius, with its miniature columns, huge capitals, delicately inlaid marble and small painted panels by Nathaniel Hubert John Westlake. Bentley also designed the intricately made main altar and piscina for this chapel and the charming offertory box at its entrance. The chapel contains paintings by Westlake depicting the Seven Dolours of Our Lady.

The high altar and reredos, made in 1863 with inlays of marble and glass mosaics, are masterpieces of Victorian craftsmanship. The brass door of the tabernacle, set with enamels and precious stones, is particularly notable. Also superb are the first and second superaltars, the latter ornamented by circular recessed panels, divided vertically by inlays of black foliate pattern with a distinctly Art Nouveau appearance. The reredos is set beneath a strongly carved leaf cornice. Above this a corbel projects and carries a throne on high. All of which is topped by a gilded canopy surmounted by a Pelican in Piety.

The paintings showing the Stations of the Cross are by Westlake, who claimed that these were the first Stations ever to be depicted in Britain. The bracket for the statue of St Francis by the west door was made by Bentley, as was the canopied niche for the statue of Our Lady, in 1870. The statue itself is by Theodore Phyffers, who had been brought from Antwerp by AWN Pugin to work on the Palace of Westminster.

Some of the objects that Bentley made for St Francis (including a monstrance) are no longer on display, but the church still contains a final small masterpiece intact and in all its glory: the baptistry. At the west end of the aisle, built in 1863, it was declared by **Building News** as having the promise to be one of the 'most complete little chapels in England'. It has two bays supported on marble columns with elaborately carved capitals. The huge font, of highly polished red granite on a marble and alabaster pedestal with an elaborately carved oak canopy, is integral to the design. Whether you love or hate all this ornamentation, there is no denying that this chapel stands as a magnificent expression of exuberant Victorian spirituality. While building the extensions to the church, Bentley converted to Catholicism. He took Francis as his baptismal name, was the first to be baptised here (by Cardinal Wiseman in 1862), and donated parts of the font to the church in thanksgiving for his conversion.

The church has been redecorated and restored several times, but has lost none of its charm. Together with the courtyard and cluster of small buildings containing the community centre (all built in the same French provincial style), it is a welcoming and tranquil corner of Notting Dale. A new stained-glass rose window was commissioned in 2005 with 'The People of God' as its theme recognising the spiritual journey that both the parish and individuals were making. The artist, Benjamin Finn, has completed works for both Ely and Southwark cathedrals – consent from the Historic Churches Commission is still pending but it is hoped that it will be installed in late 2007. The community centre acts as the base for meetings of the local Eritrean and Filipino communities and a Gheez rite mass is celebrated weekly. For further information, telephone 020 7727 7968.

Clarendon Cross and Princedale Road

Hippodrome Place leads directly to Clarendon Cross, a picturesque corner devoted to classy shopping. There is only a small cluster of shops but each is special in its own way. Of the 'old school', Myriad Antiques offers a labyrinth of rooms filled with furniture, old textiles and quirky objects for the home and garden, while Virginia stocks an exquisite collection of vintage clothes. Equally tempting is The Cross, a girlie treasure trove of embroidered cashmere, saris, exquisite shoes, toys and accessories, much frequented by the stars. On a more down-to-earth note, Summerill & Bishop across the way sells an inspired mix of kitchen equipment from around the world, including some serious tools for professionals. When you've had enough of shopping, Julie's Wine Bar is the perfect place for refreshment. Opened circa 1970 by the same couple who own the Portobello Hotel, this was the hangout favoured by Notting Hill's original hip bohemians and still has its charm.

Just past Julie's, facing south towards Holland Park, the road forks on either side of the Cowshed spa. Portland Road, on the left, leads directly to Holland Park Avenue, as does the more interesting Princedale Road, soon reached via the right-hand fork, Penzance Place.

Turning left from Penzance Place into Princedale Road, the first junction you pass is with Penzance Street, the last home of the fashion designer Ossie Clark, who was murdered here by his lover on 7 August 1996. Ossie had a long association with Notting Hill, starting in Linden Gardens, where he lived during his marriage to Celia Birtwell, followed by a long spell in Cambridge Gardens and brief stays in Powis Terrace, better known for its association with David Hockney. The two men were once close friends and though they eventually fell out, Ossie Clark was immortalised in Hockney's celebrated painting *Mr and Mrs Clark and Percy,* in which he and Celia are depicted with their beloved white cat (actually called Blanche).

Gazing along the neat terraces of pastel-coloured Victorian houses that make up Princedale Road, it's odd trying to associate this peaceful,  mainly residential street with its past political connections – first as home of Colin Jordan's Fascist British National Socialist Movement (BNSM), then as the birthplace of Release, a help and advice centre for people in trouble with the law over drugs, and later for the offices of *OZ*, one of the most innovative and unruly publications to come out of the 1960s underground press.

The film director and film historian Kevin Brownlow recalls the hazards of shooting not far from the BSNM's headquarters in the early 1960s. His film *It Happened Here* (1963) was a drama about what might have happened if Britain hadn't won the Second World War and included a sequence picturing the Notting Hill riots:

The main prop in the riot sequence was a magnificent REO bus which Andrew [Mollo] and I had helped the owner restore. We painted it field grey, with Mosley's lightning flash on the side, and used it as a riot bus. It held 36 black-shirts. Early on the morning of the session, it passed by the headquarters of Colin Jordan's British National Socialist Movement in Princedale Road. Three members, one in breeches and jackboots, stood chatting on the pavement. Suddenly they spotted the riot bus and stared as though at an apparition. As soon as they had recovered from their surprise, they leaped on motorcycles and gave chase. But the bus doubled back into a parallel street and threw them off. Our location was uncomfortably close to the Nazi headquarters, but they never located it, even when the bus roared down Holland Park with its bell clanging. Local residents, however, decided that the worst had happened and telephoned the Special Branch: 'Colin Jordan has mobilised!'

Less than ten years later, in 1967, Caroline Coon and Rufus Jones set up Release at No. 70 Princedale Road. Typical of the time, Release helped everyone from teenage runaways to rock stars and, according to a relatively recent interview with Caroline Coon, 'At one point, the organisation was handling one-third of all drug busts in Britain.' Coon stayed with Release until 1971 but it was a hard struggle, as Richard Neville, former editor of *OZ*, recalls in *Hippie Hippie Shake* (1995):

Caroline Coon turned up at Release to find the door knocked down, the furniture burnt, phones ripped out and the files stolen. A message was scrawled on the wall,

'Give Release to the people.' At least fifteen 'people' were in court that morning, expecting Release to help. A solicitor offered the Release team a basement as emergency headquarters. Meanwhile, the invaders wanted Caroline Coon to face 'the people'.

At a meeting in Princedale Road, I was hauled in to mediate. Despite her fabulous Forties' filmstar look from the Chelsea Antique Market, Caroline stood alone, blue-eyeshadowed and grim: an exotic outcast. Having fled home at sixteen, she never discussed her family background.

Mick Farren, on behalf of the White Panthers, accused her of "poncing around King's Road while the kids are being busted in the streets".

'If it wasn't for Caroline,' I said, 'most of you would be in jail.'

Mick said Release was politically flabby: 'Why don't you bomb the police stations?'

'You can bomb them if you want,' said Caroline. 'My work's in the courts.'

A deal was hammered out. Caroline agreed that Release could be 'given to the people', if the files were brought back. 'See Caroline, that's the way it works,' commented Farren, 'continuous revolution.' His hands shook as he spoke, the legacy of a teenage splurge with amphetamines. I stood in the doorway, an arm around Caroline's waist, as Mick muttered to his mates, 'She doesn't even smoke pot.'

A painter, Coon has been trying to raise funding for an archivist to work on the Release papers, and still lives in what she describes as 'the heaven of Ladbroke Grove'.

When Release moved to larger premises in around 1968, *OZ* took over the offices. The brainchild of Australian Richard Neville, this was one of the most influential underground magazines of the 1960s, famous as much for its psychedelic graphics as for the radicalism of its politics. It lasted only three years, culminating in the celebrated *OZ* trial in 1971, which, though successful for its defendants, dissipated their energy. The magazine folded, Neville returned to Australia and everyone involved went their separate ways.

THE RISE AND FALL OF OZ

By the time Richard Neville established **OZ** in London he had already been tried in Sydney for the Australian edition. The British version was originally conceived as a satirical magazine along the lines of a more outrageous **Private Eye** (still going strong). In Neville's own words on the publication of the first issue of the magazine in 1967, '**OZ** has it all – satire, sex, sharp and ideological perversity'. But it soon evolved into something even more adventurous. Driven by the increasingly psychedelic graphics of Martin Sharp, it embraced the drug culture that so influenced the Sixties, led by people's growing experimentation with LSD. But it was the magazine's dedication to non-censorship and sexual liberation that caused its downfall. It wasn't long before **OZ** was attracting accusations of pornography from the establishment,

Mick Farren

and the attention of the police. Things came to a head in the spring of 1970 with the Schoolkids' issue, inspired by the following advertisement, placed in **OZ** 26 (quoted in Jonathon Green, **Days in the Life**, 1988):

Some of us at *OZ* are feeling old and boring. So we invite any of our readers under 18 to come and edit the April issue. Apply at the *OZ* office in Princedale Road W11 any time from 10am to 7pm on Friday March 13. We will choose one person, or several, or accept collective applications from a group of friends. You will receive no money except expenses and you will enjoy almost complete editorial freedom.

Around 30 responded, many of them pupils from nearby Holland Park Comprehensive. The resulting fusion of sex, drugs, rock'n'roll and school kids turned out to be the most outrageous edition that Neville and co-workers Jim Anderson and Felix Dennis had ever produced. The police pounced and the threesome were charged with 'conspiring to corrupt public morals'. The Old Bailey trial that ensued became one of the **causes célèbres** associated with the 1960s. (The counsel for the defence was writer John Mortimer.) In the end, the conspiracy charge was rejected by the jury but the magazine never revived.

A NOTE FOR DRIVERS

The layout of this area is confusing, especially for drivers. The combination of one-way systems and streets blocked off for pedestrians can easily send you round in circles. For example, Pottery Lane and the Church of St Francis of Assisi are only accessible from Hippodrome Place on foot – drivers need to approach from the south side of Pottery Lane. Generally speaking, anyone visiting the church and Clarendon Cross by car is advised to park in one of the surrounding streets, such as Portland or Clarendon Road, and walk.

Holland Park Avenue and the Park

Grand houses guarded by lines of statuesque plane trees give Holland Park Avenue the appearance of a European boulevard, an impression enhanced by the scattering of French patisseries and other specialist food shops that border the near side. The southern border is almost entirely residential. Turning immediately left from Princedale Road into this long, straight thoroughfare takes you past a variety of small businesses. Daunt Books is a relatively new and exceedingly popular addition. Several of the food shops, most notably Lidgate's the butchers, Jeroboams cheese and wine shop (owner of Mr Christian's on Elgin Crescent) and the Maison Blanc patisserie, are renowned for the high quality of their produce.

The Ice House, Holland Park

After passing Lidgate's and Clarendon Road, the next turning left, by the tube station, is Lansdowne Road, leading almost immediately to the tall brick edifice of Lansdowne House. Nowadays it is a recording studio, used by both rock and classical musicians, the most notorious being the Sex Pistols, who recorded *Anarchy in the UK* here in 1976. Lansdowne House also has an interesting history through its association with art collectors Edmund

ARTISTS AND LANSDOWNE HOUSE

In 1889 Sir Edmund Davis, who was born in Australia in 1862 and made a great deal of money from mining in South Africa, Australia and China, moved into No. 9 Lansdowne Road. He and his wife Mary had the house enlarged and decorated by Charles Conder and Frank Brangwyn. They started a collection of old masters and patronised several contemporary artists, among them Auguste Rodin. In 1900, they began the building of Lansdowne House. It was designed by William Flockhart to have six flats for artists, each with a two-storey studio with good north light, communal bathrooms in the basement and a Real Tennis court. The first occupants were the sculptor Charles Ricketts (1866–1931) and the painter Charles Shannon (1863–1937), who moved in here in 1902. Although not hugely successful as artists, they had a mass of successful friends including Diaghilev, Nijinsky, Leon Bakst, Isadora Duncan, WB Yeats and George Bernard Shaw. Other artists lived in Lansdowne House: Glyn Philpot (1863–1937), Vivian Forbes (1891–1937), James Pryde (1866–1941) and F Cayley Robinson (1862–1927). Edmund Dulac (1882–1953) lived close by at Studio House in Ladbroke Grove. Aston Webb, the architect of the Victoria and Albert museum in South Kensington, also lived in Ladbroke Grove. Edmund and Mary Davis died in 1939 and 1942 respectively, leaving most of their collection to galleries in Paris and South Africa.

and Mary Davis, who in 1900 commissioned its construction as a place where artists could enjoy the luxury of working and living under one roof.

Not far after the junction with Lansdowne Road, the wide road on the other side of the Avenue is marked by the corner statue of St Volodymyr, ruler of Ukraine from 980 to 1015. As its plaque specifies, the statue was erected in 1988 by Ukrainians living in the UK, 'to celebrate the establishment of Christianity in Ukraine by St Volodymyr in 988'. The road is called Holland Park and soon traces the boundaries of the park itself.

One of London's most beautiful and secluded public spaces, Holland Park's long list of attractions include the Japanese Kyoto Garden, a wildlife reserve, excellent children's play facilities, tennis courts, opera and exhibition spaces in the Ice House and the Orangery of Holland House and an upmarket restaurant. The east wing of what remains of this Jacobean mansion serves as a youth hostel. You can enter Holland Park from the road of the same name through a door in the wall by the Greek embassy.

Aubrey Road, Campden Hill Square and Aubrey Walk

Both Aubrey Road and Campden Hill Square, to the east of Holland Park, were once part of the gardens of Aubrey House. It was built in 1698 for use as a spa – hence its original name of Wells House – but soon became a private residence occupied by, among others, Lady Mary Coke. A wealthy divorcee, Lady Mary combined a love of court gossip with a passion for gardening, both of which are recorded in great detail in her four volumes of *Letters and Journals* (see Writings, p 256).

HOLLAND HOUSE

Holland House was built circa 1607 for Sir Walter Cope, who lent it the original name of 'Cope's Castle'. Cope died in 1614 without a male heir, and the estate eventually came to his daughter Isabel. With the support of her husband, Sir Henry Rich (made the first Earl of Holland in 1624), Isabel initiated a number of improvements to the house, both inside and out, as did the succession of noblemen who lived here over the centuries following her death. Isabel died in 1673, after which the family residence became known as Holland House. The house was inherited by her eldest son, Robert, who became the second Earl of Holland, but it later passed out of the hands of the immediate family to be leased by several tenants, one of whom, Henry Fox, bought Holland House in 1768. During this time, right up to its virtual destruction by fire in 1940, the building was a lively centre of social, literary and political life, entertaining such visitors as Byron, Macaulay, Disraeli, Dickens and Sir Walter Scott. The original Jacobean mansion was subjected to almost continuous renovation, including the addition of a garden ballroom in the former stables in around 1845. The last great social occasion here took place on 6 July 1939, when King George VI and Queen Elizabeth came to a grand ball attended by the cream of society. Just over a year later, Holland House was struck by incendiary bombs during enemy action, never fully to rise again. There was much debate as to what to do with the building and its extensive grounds, until it was eventually bought by the London County Council in 1952. The grounds were transformed into a public park and the east wing reconstructed for use as a youth hostel, augmented by new buildings designed by architects Hugh Casson and Neville Conder. The Ice House, which once stored ice and later became a dairy, is now used for small art exhibitions, as is the surviving Orangery. For information on the park's many activities, see Listings, p 193.

Among some of the many inconveniences noted by her pen was the occasion, in 1774, when her usually peaceful garden overlooking Holland Park Avenue was invaded by a foxhunt in full cry:

I have had another vexation that never happen'd to me before, the having of a pack of hounds in my garden, & several men on Horseback broke into my

grounds, leap'd into my North Walk, & from thence into Lord Holland's lane.
These things are disagreeable, and so near London was not to be expected.

In the years following Lady Mary Coke's departure in 1788, Aubrey House eventually came into the hands of the Alexander family, with whom it remained for nearly two centuries. It is not known who lives there now and, hidden behind high walls, it retains an air of mystery.

The residents of Campden Hill Square are less elusive. Evelyn Underhill (1875–1941), the Christian philosopher and teacher lived at No. 50. Today's inhabitants includes three eminent literary figures: playwright Harold Pinter, historian and novelist Antonia Fraser, and the crime writer PD James – the last of whom has set at least one of her novels in and around Notting Hill. The following is an extract from *A Taste for Death* (1986), in which Detective Kate Miskin contemplates the world outside her mansion flat in Holland Park:

She poured herself an inch of whisky, mixed it with water, then unlocked the security lock of the narrow door which led from the sitting room to the iron balcony. The air rushed in, fresh and clean. She closed the door then stood, glass in hand, leaning back against the brickwork and staring out eastward over London. A low bank of heavy cloud had absorbed the glare of the city's lights and lay, palely crimson, like a colour-wash carefully laid against the richer blue-black of night. There was a light breeze just strong enough to stir the branches of the great limes lining Holland Park Avenue, and to twitch the television aerials which sprouted like frail exotic fetishes from the patterned roofs fifty feet below. To the south the trees of Holland Park were a black curdle against the sky, and ahead the spire of St John's church gleamed like some distant mirage. It was one of the pleasures of these moments, seeing how the spire appeared to move, sometimes so close that she felt that she would only have to stretch out a hand to feel its harshly textured stones, sometimes, like tonight, as distant and insubstantial as a vision.

Aubrey Walk, with Aubrey House at one end and the Gothic-Italianate Church of St George at the other, can be reached via Campden Hill Square or else directly via Aubrey Road. Running between Holland Park and Campden Hill Road, it's a quaint, narrow street of old brick houses. The novelist John Galsworthy lived here around 1903–05.

THE CHURCH OF ST GEORGE

This small church, nestled among the houses of Aubrey Walk, has an interesting and some-times beleaguered history. Consecrated in 1864, the building was funded by John Bennett of Westbourne Park Villas, whose son George was its first incumbent. It originally served a con-gregation from the poorest part of the parish – the area surrounding the Kensington Gravel Pits – and became the local driving force of the Temperance Society. The church was also a key distributor of charity, opening a soup kitchen, a workingman's club and organising holi-days to the country and the seaside. Essential to the funding and help with this were the wealthy residents living nearby (Campden Hill was nicknamed 'The Dukeries').

Over time, the congregation changed, as did the nature of worship, towards high church Anglo-Catholic liturgy. The local population was decimated by World War I and congregations began to decline, but the worst period for St George's was in the years following Second World War. The building suffered war damage, and although repairs were made, the congregation dwindled. In 1948, the parish was forced into bankruptcy and fell under the wing of St Mary Abbots. In subsequent decades there were sporadic threats that the church would close alto-gether. More recently St George's fortunes have turned around, not least due to the energy of the Reverend Michael Fuller, who began his ministry here in 1994. The demographic has changed radically since the church's early popularity and the old slum dwellings near the gravel pits have been replaced by elegant homes. But St George's again has a thriving con-gregation and has finally returned to being an independent parish.

The fabric of the building bears the marks of the changes in fortune. Designed by Enoch Bassett Keeling, it is one of the few examples of the eclectic Gothic style, characterised by the use of variegated colours of stone and brickwork. **The Building News** described the exte-rior as 'continental Gothic, freely treated', understating the impact of the building's glorious-ly unrestrained style, which would have been even more striking when the original striped blue-slate and red-tile roof was in place, along with original spire. It was a remarkably tall spire, and featured in the illustrations of early editions of **Peter Pan,** as the one over which Peter Pan and Wendy flew (JM Barrie lived nearby).

The interior was by all accounts bold and adventurous, incorporating fine and very mod-ern materials. The stonework included blue, red and black bricks, yellow stocks, Bath and red Mansfield stone. The columns supporting the structure were of the highest quality and grade of cast ironwork with elegant dog-tooth cut capitals made of concrete. The architectural his-torian, William Pepperell, found it 'exceedingly beautiful and original', particularly admiring the iron columns and the nave roof.

During the 20th century drastic changes took place. Deemed unsafe after war damage, the spire was replaced by a pyramid copper cap. Changing fashion (Pesvner condemned the interior as 'excessively patterned') and the need for repair led to the obliteration of the inte-rior. The brickwork was whitewashed, the apse demolished and the concrete capitals cased in to make them resemble stone piers. Of Basset Keeling's interior, only the nave arcades, the jagged saw tooth nave principals (rafters), and the west-gallery front remained untouched. A few other details survived, including two exquisite commemorative windows in the (liturgical) north wall (one by Henry Thomas Bosdet, made in 1905, depicting the sacrifice of Isaac), and a magnificent organ, now restored. Music has always played an important part in the life of the church.

A twelve-year restoration project was completed in 2007, with the congregation raising £170,000 towards the costs. Among many changes, some of the whitewash has been painstakingly removed, revealing the coloured brickwork of the arches; the concrete capitals have been freed from their casings and the chancel has been fitted out with a floor made in Purbeck marble. A new altar has been made using slate, Purbeck marble and Bath stone, the detail on which echoes the dog-tooth carving found throughout the body of the church. The narthex has been made into an inviting community area, and the overall result is welcoming and spiritually uplifting. For information, telephone 020 7221 6546.

The top of Campden Hill Road brings us full circle to the favourite haunt of GK Chesterton featured in Chapter 1. Many artists and writers have lived in this neighbourhood, especially on the south side of the hill, where you'll find quite a few houses dotted with blue plaques. One of the most renowned addresses is No. 77 Bedford Gardens, where the Scottish painters Robert Colquhoun and Robert MacBryde shared a studio. In 1943, *The Listener* dubbed Colquhoun the 'most promising young painter to have appeared in Britain for some time', while writer Wyndham Lewis had already called MacBryde 'the wittiest man in the area'. John Minton joined the household of the Roberts (as they were known), and the studio's welcoming atmosphere drew a string of visitors. Sundays would often begin in the Windsor Castle in Campden Hill Road, where they were joined by Lucian Freud, Dylan Thomas and the poet WS Graham, and the smallest bar became their private domain. The merry group would then return to Bedford Gardens and embark on readings from Gogol, Cervantes and Burns, with Dylan Thomas playing the ham actor. Another resident of No. 77 was Ronald Searle, who moved in 1946 into one of the top studios while recovering from three-and-a-half years in Changi Gaol in Singapore. All the studios were looked after by Mrs Carrie Reynolds, who had moved into the porter's flat at the turn of the century with her eight children, and would cook the artists their breakfasts, clean their shoes and lend them money.

Finally, returning north to Holland Park Avenue on the fringes of Notting Hill Gate, another Scottish artist, the gifted etcher James McBey, lived at No. 1 with his American wife Marguerite. At the beginning of the 20th century they added a wonderful north-facing studio to the top of the building. After McBey died in the 1960s, Marguerite went on living there until her death at the age of 95 in 1999.

PLACES TO STAY

YHA Holland House
Holland Walk W8
0870 770 5866/hollandpark@yha.org.uk
Open 24 hours, all year round

This youth hostel in the grounds of Holland Park has to be one of the most peaceful places to stay anywhere in London. The accommodation comprises 200 beds in single-sex dormitories. Facilities include a garden-terrace cafeteria, games and TV rooms, bike hire, a self-catering kitchen and a luggage store. Prices per night start at £21.50 for adults and £19.30 for under-18s; bedlinen is included. Full English breakfasts, packed lunches and three-course dinners are also available from around £3.50.

EATING & DRINKING

CAFÉS & TAKEAWAYS

Armadillo Café
11 Bramley Road W10
020 7727 9799/www.armadillocafe.co.uk
Mon–Fri 8am–4.30pm; Sat 10am–3pm

Good coffee, soups and sandwiches, ready-made with fresh ingredients, can be eaten in but are best enjoyed outside, where there are plenty of tables on the pavement. The next door Armadeli has sadly closed but it is hoped that owner Edward Berry's award-winning ice cream will now be sold here.

Cyrano
108 Holland Park Avenue W11
020 7221 3598/www.cyranobrasserie.co.uk
Mon–Sat 7.30am–10.30pm;
Sun 8am–10.30pm

Describing itself as a 'hip new French-fusion brasserie', Cyrano is good for all-day breakfasts, including very strong coffee and excellent Spanish omelettes, and morning detox drinks for the more healthy-minded. Cocktails and dinner also served.

Chelsea Spice & Grill
126 Bramley Road W10
020 8969 0992/www.eats.co.uk
Sun–Thurs 5.30pm–11.30pm; Fri & Sat
5.30pm–midnight
No credit cards

Situated under the Westway, a few minutes' walk from Latimer Road tube station, it would be hard to find a grimmer location for this award-winning Indian takeaway, but for good food at very fair prices it's worth making the journey. Set meals are unbeatable value, especially with free local home delivery.

Paul

82a Holland Park Avenue W11
020 7727 3797
www.paul-uk.com
Mon–Fri 7am–8pm; Sat 8am–8pm;
Sun 8am–7pm

Hand-made traditionally baked bread, sandwiches, salads and mouthwatering patisseries ensure that this new branch of the French bakery chain does a brisk trade. A few tables outside.

St Helen's Foodstore

55 St Helen's Gardens W10
020 8960 2225
Mon–Fri 8am–8pm; Sat 8am–6pm;
Sun 9am–4pm

Lunch-time crowds eating out on the pavement are testimony to the delicious salads and hot dishes served in this deli-café, also available to take away. Typical options on the menu are salade niçoise with fresh tuna, lemon chicken, couscous with cherry tomatoes and courgettes and a salad of three green beans. Less healthy but equally good are the all-day fry-

ups featuring Gloucester Old Spot sausages – the tastiest around. Cheeses, charcuteries, chocolate, organic fruit juices and wine are among the high-quality groceries for sale. Chef Sarah Rowden also makes spectacular birthday cakes to order and runs a catering service with business partner Ruth Day.

Thai River

308 Latimer Road W10
020 8960 5988
Mon–Fri 12 noon–3.30pm & 6pm–10.30pm;
Sat & Sun 6pm–10.30pm

A delightful setting, tasty food and charming service make this one of the best budget café-restaurants around. Duck and seafood dominate the menu. *Tod Mun Pla*, Thai fishcakes served with a spicy sweet and sour peanut cucumber sauce, are especially recommended, and there is plenty of choice for vegetarians. The cottage-like interior holds only a few tables but, thanks to patio heating, you can eat out in the small front garden all year round. Also does takeaways and home delivery. Bring your own drink.

FOOD SHOPS

Handford

12 Portland Road W11
020 7221 9614
www.handford.net
Mon–Sat 10am–8.30pm

Owner James Handford is a Master of Wine and personally selects his fine bottles from all over the world but with the emphasis on France and Spain. Much of the wine is kept in bond, but the shop has an interesting selection and provides wine for many launches and parties. Handford also runs a wine school that welcomes beginners and arranges a series of tastings throughout the year.

Jeroboams

196 Holland Park Avenue W11
020 7727 9359
www.jeroboams.co.uk
Mon–Fri 9am–7.30pm;
Sat 8.30am–7pm;
Sun 10am–4pm

Cheese is the mainstay of this lavish shop, and the selection, including several unpasteurised varieties, is impressive. Connoisseurs will love to ruminate over which particular parmesan, stilton, manchego or camembert to eat with delicious breads. Jeroboams also stocks a few dried foodstuffs, preserves, puddings and a range of high-quality wines.

Lidgate

110 Holland Park Avenue W11
020 7727 8243
Mon–Fri 7am–6pm;
Sat 7am–5pm

David Lidgate is the fourth generation of his family to run this 150-year-old business, possibly the oldest in the area. What makes this butcher's unique is not just the excellence of the meat but the quality of the service and advice. Lidgate deals direct with farmers and personally selects organic and grass-fed beef, lamb and pork from, among others, Highgrove, Gatcombe Park and the Buccleuch estate. By only selecting the best, he aims to improve what he sells every year. Homemade sausages and pies vie for space with meat, game, cheese, jams and chutneys. An order received before 11am ensures same-day delivery. Although Lidgate's is busy throughout the year, the queues at Christmas for the famous bronze turkeys are almost a tourist attraction in themselves.

Maison Blanc
102 Holland Park Avenue W11
020 7221 2494
www.maisonblanc.co.uk
Mon–Thurs & Sat 8am–7pm;
Fri 8am–7.30pm; Sun 8.30am–6pm

One of the best patisserie chains, Maison Blanc blends in perfectly with the other specialist food-shops along this stretch. Succulent chocolate mousse gateaux, creamy *millefeuilles* and wonderful *tartes aux fruits* (cassis is particularly recommended) are displayed alongside Belgian chocolates and other continental confectionery. All the breads on the back shelves are painstakingly baked in stone ovens, using authentic French ingredients. Everything tastes as good as it looks, with prices to match.

Speck
2 Holland Park Terrace, Portland Road W11
020 7229 7005
Mon–Fri 8.30am–8.30pm;
Sat 8am–7pm

This Italian delicatessen, with its low ceiling and white-tiled floor, is filled with a wide range of dry pasta, Italian wines, liqueurs and panettone as well as a selection of homemade pasta sauces, soups and ready-made dishes. A good standby if your cupboards are suddenly bare.

Also see **St Helen's Foodstore,** p 188

PUBS & BARS

The Castle
100 Holland Park Avenue W11
Mon–Sat 11am–11pm; food served 12 noon–3pm & 6.30pm–10pm

Modern, very spacious pub with a relaxed and comfortable atmosphere that hots up considerably at weekends with the addition of a DJ. Other days, the music is constant but not intrusive. The crowd, aged around 25–30, tends towards the trendy, and the food, untried but looking good, is quite expensive and fancier than average pub fare.

The Prince of Wales
14a Princedale Road W11
Mon–Sat 12 noon–11.30pm;
Sun till 10.30pm

More of an old-fashioned pub, the Prince of Wales attracts a range of locals of all ages. Facilities include a pool table, jukebox and a quaint beer garden that is a great summer retreat from the traffic and expensive trappings of Holland Park Avenue. Unless you're into football, avoid on match days, when an excited crowd gathers around Sky TV.

The Station House
41 Bramley Road W10
020 7229 1111/www.station-house.net
Mon–Sat 12 noon–11pm;
Sun till 10.30pm

Across from Latimer Road tube station, the Station House is a laid-back, comfortable pub that draws people from all around. Good-quality Mediterranean food is served all day and the large garden is lit by hundreds of fairy lights, making it a perfect place to eat and drink in summer.

RESTAURANTS

The Belvedere
Holland House
Holland Park W11
020 7602 1238/www.whitestarlineorg.uk
Mon–Sat 12 noon–2.30pm, 6pm–10pm;
Sun 12 noon–3pm

Situated in the Jacobean splendour of Holland Park, with terrace seating on the first floor overlooking the landscape, this is a perfect location for lunch on a good summer's day. Parties of up to 60 can be accommodated on the balcony floor. The atmosphere is cool but relaxed, with attentive staff. Worth a visit, but bear in mind that food is only part of the experience. Expensive. Booking essential.

The Bombay Bicycle Club
128 Holland Park Avenue W11
020 7727 7335
www.thebombaybicycleclub.co.uk
Mon–Sat 6pm–11pm; Sun 6pm–10.30pm

Named after a popular meeting place for colonial officers and soldiers during the Raj, The Bombay Bicycle Club focuses on dishes designed to suit European tastes, ie spicy and aromatic but not too hot. It's a successful formula: this is the company's third restaurant and it also runs an extensive home-delivery and catering service, with kitchens all over London. Reasonably priced.

Cool Monkey
6 Clarendon Road W11
020 7727 3330
Daily 12 noon–3pm & 6pm–11pm

This friendly, unpretentious Thai is another welcome addition to the otherwise pricey restaurants that tend to dominate Holland

Park. Eat in or take away, plus free delivery on orders over £20.

Julie's Wine Bar & Restaurant

135 Portland Road W11
0207 727 7985/Restaurant 020 7229 8331/www.juliesrestaurant.com
Bar: daily 9am–10.30pm.
Restaurant: Mon–Fri & Sun 12.30pm–2.30pm; daily 7pm–11pm

Julie's has been in the area for over 35 years and still has a loyal following. The restaurant is a collection of small atmospheric rooms; we dined in the 'Garden of Love', with mirrors, plants and soft music. The food was disappointingly bland, although the steak was good. In other parts of the warren-like building there are bars and rooms where you can sink into cushions in a private nook and drink tea. Popular for illicit liaisons.

Notting Grill

123A Clarendon Road W11
020 7229 1500
www.awtonline.co.uk
Bar: Mon–Thurs 6.30pm–11pm; Fri & Sat 6.30pm–midnight; Sun 12 noon–10pm.
Restaurant: brunch Sat & Sun 12 noon–4pm;
lunch Tues–Fri 12 noon–2.30pm;
dinner Mon–Thurs 6.30pm–10.30pm;
Fri & Sat 6.30pm–11.30pm;
Sun meals 12 noon–10pm

Excellent steak and chips are the mainstay of this particular corner of Antony Worrall Thompson's empire, but there are plenty of fish and vegetarian options on offer for starters. Seating is comfortable, the atmosphere relaxed and there's a terrace for eating outside. Pricey.

ENTERTAINMENT

CHILDREN

Bramley's Big Adventure

136 Bramley Road W10
020 8960 1515
enquiries@bramleysbig.co.uk
Mon–Fri 10am–6pm;
weekends and holidays daily 10am–6.30pm

This indoor activity playground can be something of a godsend to parents, especially on a rainy winter's day. Play areas are divided in two, for the over- and under-fives, with a good choice of equipment, from slides, balance beams and ball pools to the more unusual – monkey swings, an aerial runway and a 'spooky den'. Accompanying adults have to stay on the premises but there's a café where you can relax while your charges tire themselves out. Prices start at £3 for under-fives during school days; £3.50 weekends and holidays. Bramley's is also a popular place for parties, costing from £8 per child for 75 minutes' play, a party meal and a goody bag and balloon. Or you can simply hire the whole place, including experienced staff.

Holland Park
020 7602 9483
Open from sunrise to sunset all year round
Adventure Playground
020 7603 6956
Daily 10am–6pm
One O'Clock Club
020 7603 2838
Mon–Fri 1.30–4pm

Holland Park has something for everyone and children are especially well catered for. There are seven entrances but the main one (with car park) is on Abbotsbury Road, which runs directly off Holland Park Avenue, opposite Norland Square. The Adventure Playground offers a range of activities for 5- to 16-year-olds, including arts and crafts and a network of outdoor structures such as rope swings, poles and runways between the trees. However, it's currently under threat from council budget cuts, so phone for the

latest developments. Next door, the One O'Clock Club is for under-fives, with an indoor area for dressing up and construction games, while other toddlers play in the sand-pit or scoot around on trucks outside. Both places are supervised by experienced play leaders. The park has an **Ecology Centre**, established in the refurbished stable block of Holland House, which holds displays and exhibitions based on the local and natural history of the park. It's also a starting point for nature trails, guided walks and pond exploration, usually organised for schools. For more information contact the main park telephone number above.

Westway Stables
20 Stable Way (off Latimer Road) W10
020 8964 2140
Daily 9am–6pm

Stable Way is a narrow lane at the far south end of Latimer Road. It's a bit of a dumping ground for rubbish, but don't be put off – the stables are just around the corner. It's a friendly place, if a bit chaotic, and ponies come in all sizes and temperaments, so you're almost sure to find one to suit you or your child. Novices can start with a 15-minute pony ride and there are half-hour group lessons, while more experienced riders can do an hour's hack on Wormwood Scrubs Common. It's a far cry from riding in the country but the sand-pit ring is a good size and, for those with some experience, the common offers a surprisingly picturesque open space.

MUSIC

Holland Park Opera
Box office: 0845 230 9769
www.operahollandpark.com

Holland Park's highly regarded three-month opera season (June–August) is something of a jewel in the royal borough's crown. The open-air theatre's setting among tall trees in the heart of the park is due to be enhanced in 2007 with the unveiling of a spectacular new canopy designed by architects Landrell Associates, together with new comfortable seating, a decked picnic area, two bars and much improved visibility. See website for forthcoming productions.

HEALTH, BEAUTY & FITNESS

The Cowshed
119 Portland Road W11
020 7078 1944
www.cowshedclarendoncross.com
Treatments: Mon–Fri 9am–8pm;
Sat 9am–7pm; Sun 10am–5pm.
Café: Mon–Fri 8.30am–8pm;
Sat 9am–7pm;
Sun 10am–5pm

This new spa on the site of what used to be Orsino's restaurant offers a variety of (rather expensive) treatments as well as selling a range of its own products. The café has a large round table that can also be hired for dinners for up to 12 people, with or without treatments.

Hair & Tanning Rooms
53 St Helen's Gardens W10
020 8969 7582/8960 0344
Mon & Thurs 9am–6pm;
Tues & Wed 8.30am–6pm;
Fri 8.30am–7pm; Sat 8am–5pm;
Sun 10am–2pm

Tony and Sandra Tahir have been running this neighbourhood salon since 1979, and their team of friendly and experienced cutters are hard to beat. In addition to sunbeds, the salon offers nail care and drinks from the downstairs bar; you can also relax in the garden while waiting for your colour to cook.

Westway Sports Centre
1 Crowthorne Road W10
020 8969 0992
www.westway.org
Mon–Fri 8am–10pm;
Sat 8am–8pm;
Sun 10am–10pm

Established to encourage local children and young people to take up sport, this impressive centre incorporates indoor tennis courts, four Astroturf pitches for football and hockey, as well as outside courts and a network of all-weather climbing walls. Despite being situated in the unwelcoming shadow of the A40 (near Westway Stables), the facilities are more than adequate, and prices are very much geared to encouraging as many participants as possible.

SHOPPING

BOOKS

Daunt Books
112–14 Holland Park Avenue W11
020 7727 7022
www.dauntbooks.co.uk
Mon–Sat 9am–8pm;
Sun 11am–6pm

With its oak floors and comfortable seating, this branch of Daunt's is a welcome addition to the neighbourhood. Although there is no particular specialisation, the shop has strong art, children's and travel sections, and the enthusiastic staff are impressively well informed. Books displayed on tables also make for good browsing. On Wednesdays at 4pm, the talented Zoe Greaves reads stories to children. The shop also organises occasional conversations with notable authors at nearby Leighton House.

CHILDREN'S CLOTHES, TOYS & ACCESSORIES

Dotty Dot
67a St Helen's Gardens W10
020 7460 3405
Mon–Sat 10am–6pm

Local resident Fiona Joffey sells high-quality children's clothes (up to age 10), quirky accessories and toys, wooden bikes and furniture, and the much sought-after Dr Robby skincare range for children. The opening of this attractive shop in 2006 is yet another reflection of the changing population of Notting Dale.

FASHION & VINTAGE

The Cross
141 Portland Road W11
020 7727 6760
www.thecrossshop.co.uk
Mon–Sat 11am–5.30pm

Few serious shoppers come to Notting Hill without visiting this quintessential girlie boutique for the home and wardrobe. Nothing is cheap but much is quirky and desirable, especially if you go for the bohemian look. Cashmere, silk, velvet and brocade garments, throws and cushions come in a blinding selection of colours, while delicate pieces of jewellery and hair accessories glitter from the shelves. Other items include shoes, bags, ceramics, T-shirts and a few children's toys at the back. The shop's clientele reads like an A-list of models and movie stars,

so don't be surprised if you bump into Kate Moss or Madonna. Also see **Cross the Road.**

Mary Moore
5 Clarendon Cross W11
020 7229 5678
www.marymoorevintage.com
Tues–Sat 11am–6pm

Mary Moore's long-held passion for vintage fashion is reflected in this lovely shop, where many of the dresses and skirts on display originate in her own personal collection. The daughter of sculptor Henry Moore, she has a wonderful eye and is for ever adding items picked up on her travels.

Virginia
98 Portland Road W11
020 7727 9908
Mon–Fri 11am–6pm;
Sat by appointment only

Established long ago, this magical shop is filled with exquisite vintage clothes: upstairs has evening dresses and coats covered with beads and lamé, while in the downstairs boudoir everything is pale grey or white. There is a feeling of decadence and temptation, and, as the stock changes constantly, it is worth going regularly – and increasing the chance of encountering celebs Nicole Kidman, Angelica Huston, Naomi Campbell or Liv Tyler, all of whom are customers.

FLOWERS

Orlando Hamilton Floral Design
59 St Helen's Gardens W10
020 8962 8944/www.orlando-hamilton.com
Mon–Fri 9.30am–5.30pm; Sat 10am–3pm

With clients like Madonna, Jade Jagger and Bono, Orlando Hamilton has a strong reputation as a celebrity florist, with prices to match. Beautiful displays adorn the pavement, with more afford-able bouquets available at Sainsburys.

Toms
73 Clarendon Road W11
020 7792 8510
Mon–Fri 9am–6pm

This tiny narrow space with its equally small basement is where Tom creates his wonderful floral arrangements for parties and other functions, as well as individ-ual bouquets. The shop has regular customers but most of the cut flowers are sold from his stall at the corner of Elgin Crescent and Kensington Park Road (see p 84).

Outside is a mini-nursery selling pots, garden furniture and a small selection of outdoor plants.

GALLERIES

The Kiln Gallery & St Francis
Community Centre
Pottery Lane W11
020 7792 8259

The centre is hired out to various groups including the NCT (National Childbirth Trust), the Princes Trust (for drawing), ballet classes, Al-anon and various parish groups.

Louise T Blouin Institute
3 Olaf Street W11
020 7985 9600/www.ltbfoundation.org
Mon–Fri 10am–6pm;
Sat & Sun 12 noon–5pm

Billed as 'one of the largest non-government funded, not-for-profit cultural spaces in London', the institute opened in October 2006 with an exhibition of the lightworks of Californian artist James Turrell, plus a permanent installation that at night beautiful-ly illuminates the building's façade. The institute has trumpeted its educational role and commit-ment to collaborating with the local community (entry is free for schoolchildren and concessions, otherwise £10), but it's hard to imagine how the vast and elegant interior, with its white walls and concrete floors, can ever be brought to life.

Pruskin
96 Portland Road W11
020 7243 1568
www.pruskin96@pruskingallery.org
Mon–Fri 10am–6pm;
Sat 11am–5pm

Pruskin deal in all kinds of decorative art from 1880 to 1960, including paintings, mirrors and sculptures. They will find specific objects on request and have a large private clientele as well as being popular with interior designers.

Redfern's Music Picture Gallery
3 Bramley Road W10
020 7792 9914/www.redferns.com
Tues–Fri 10am–6pm; Sat 11am–6pm;
other times by appointment

David Redfern has photographed many of the greatest stars of rock, pop, folk and jazz, from the Beatles, the Rolling Stones, Jimi Hendrix and Frank Zappa to Duke Ellington, Ella Fitzgerald, Miles Davis and other key figures

in American jazz. The gallery puts on several exhibitions a year – recent themes include 'Pink Floyd: Shine on you Crazy Diamond' and 'Jazz, Giants and Journeys' – but Redferns' main resource is the extensive picture library, accessible online.

Temple Gallery
6 Clarendon Cross W11
020 7727 3809
www.templegallery.com
Mon–Fri 10am–6pm (Sats during exhibitions)

For more than 45 years the Temple Gallery has specialised in icons dating from the Middle Ages to the 19th-century revival period. Prices vary enormously but everything sold comes with a guarantee of authenticity. The gallery gives valuations, provides a conservation and restoration service and produces splendid catalogues.

GIFTS & HOME

Arch 18
Kingsdown Close W10
020 7229 5391/www.arch18.co.uk

Under the name of Arch 18 (but located in Arch 12), Michael Reed has been designing and manufacturing unique pieces of contemporary furniture for 30 years. His style is best described as 'high-tech William Morris', combining fine craftsmanship, using wood from sustainable sources, with imaginative, elegant and sometimes quirky ideas. The arch is a friendly place and Michael, who exports his one-off furniture designs worldwide, is usually happy to take on a new challenge.

Big Tomato

75 St Helen's Gardens W10
020 8968 1815
www.bigtomatocompany.com
Mon–Fri 10am–5.30pm

Starting from her love of old advertising signs and packaging, Gloria Daniel-Washington has built up a business by adorning traditionally made creamware in the form of mugs, bowls, etc. with witty slogans, images and letters. Big Tomato is a local family affair (Gloria was born in Notting Hill and spent years as an antique dealer on Portobello), with this tiny space starting out as an office and becoming a shop through popular demand.

Cath Kidston

8 Clarendon Cross W11
020 7221 4000
www.cathkidston.co.uk
Mon–Sat 10am–6pm;
Sun 12 noon–5pm

Kidston's distinctive style pervades this pretty shop, perfectly suited to the picturesque Cross. Her ultra-feminine, old-fashioned designs are transferred onto various materials to make a whole range of items, from floral trays, shower caps, furnishing fabrics, paisley quilts, pastoral wallpapers and cushions to handbags and T-shirts in crisp cotton for women and children. She also sells vintage items, sometimes hard to distinguish from the new, and runs an efficient mail-order service.

Cross the Road

139 Portland Road W11
020 7727 6886
www.thecrossshop.co.uk
Mon–Sat 11am–5.30pm

With a similar feel to its sister shop across the way, the emphasis here is on interiors – embroidered cushions, hand-painted lampshades, scented candles and other items for the fashionable home.

Last Place on Earth
37 Bramley Road W10
No phone
Mon–Sat 10am–6pm

Allied to the shop of the same name on Portobello Road (p 77), this intriguing outlet sells a combination of painted distressed furniture and vintage clothes and accessories, the latter dating sometimes as far back as the 19th century up to the inexplicably popular Eighties. The back room is stacked with an ever-changing display of bags, belts, hats, clothes, boots, shoes and textiles, not to mention picture frames, mirrors, lamps and the odd book. Simon and TJ, who rent the shop, are old hands from the market and it shows. A delightful find.

Myriad Antiques
131 Portland Road W11
020 7229 1709
Tues–Sat 11am–6pm

Sara Nickerson has a particular eye and fills her shop with an eclectic mix of decorative antique objects and furniture for the house and garden. Generations of customers return again and again to buy her latest acquisitions. Among the many objects crowding the two floors are 'shabby château-style' French painted furniture, rustic chandeliers, Victorian and Edwardian calico chairs and a mass of delightfully quirky objects.

Summerill & Bishop
100 Portland Road W11
020 7221 4566
www.summerillandbishop.com
Mon–Sat 10am–6pm

'We love our shop,' say the owners, and this is evident from the impeccably chosen mixture of old and new kitchenware on sale. Old French cafetières, linen and glasses are ranged side by side with new pottery, wooden chopping boards, ostrich-feather dusters, and storage baskets. This kind of elegance and quality does not come cheap, but everything in the shop is chosen because Summerill and Bishop would have it in their own houses, and there's not a plastic item in sight.

DIRECTORY

CASH MACHINES

Abbey, 174 Portobello
Road W11
Abbey, 88 Notting Hill
Gate W11
Barclays, 35 Notting
Hill Gate W11
Barclays, 137 Ladbroke
Grove W11
HSBC, 25–27 Notting
Hill Gate W11
HSBC, 152 Portobello
Road W11
Lloyds TSB, 50 Notting
Hill Gate W11
NatWest, 46 Notting
Hill Gate W11
**Royal Bank of
Scotland,**78 Notting
Hill Gate W11
Woolwich, 83–85
Notting Hill Gate W11

BANKS/CHANGING MONEY

**Thomas Cook Exchange
HSBC Bank**
152 Portobello Road W11
Mon–Fri 9.30am–3.30pm

BICYCLE REPAIRS & SALES

EJ Barnes
285 Westbourne Grove W11

020 7727 5147
Mon–Wed & Fri 11am 7pm;
Thurs 11am–6.30pm;
Sat 11am–6pm

Bicycle Workshop
27 All Saints Road W11
020 7229 4850
Tues–Sat 10am–6pm
(closed 2–3pm)

CAR RENTAL

Portobello Rental
44 Lockton St,
Bramley Road W10
020 7792 1133
Mon–Fri 8am–7.00pm;
Sat 8.30am–5.30pm

CAR SHARE

City Car Club
0845 301234
www.citycarclub.co.uk

Streetcar
0845 644 8475
www.streetcar.co.uk

Zipcar
020 7960 6421
www.zipcar.com

CHILDCARE

Playgroups information
Childminders
(Council-approved)

Services for under-8's
020 7361 2503

DENTAL EMERGENCY SERVICE (CENTRAL LONDON)

020 8748 9365 or
07074 455 999

DISABLED SERVICES

General
020 7361 2137

DRUGS ADVICE

The Blenheim Project
321 Portobello Road W10
020 8960 5599
Mon–Fri 1pm–4pm;
Tues 6pm–9pm

EMERGENCIES ACCIDENT & EMERGENCY DEPARTMENTS

St Charles's Hospital
(minor injuries only)
Exmoor Street W10
020 8962 4262
Daily 9am–9pm
X-ray Mon–Fri 9am–8pm;
Sat & Sun 10am–8pm

St Mary's Hospital
(24-hour) Praed Street W2
020 7886 6666

FAMILY PLANNING

Raymede Clinic
Exmoor Street W10
020 8962 4450
Ring for appts 9am–5pm

FURTHER EDUCATION

Kensington & Chelsea College
020 7573 5333

GAY & LESBIAN INFORMATION

Gay and Lesbian Switchboard
020 7837 7324

GLASS, GLAZING & MIRRORS

Lister Glass
485 Latimer Road W10
020 8969 5682
Mon-Fri 7.30am–6pm;
Sat 9am–1pm

HOUSING

Housingline
020 7361 3008
www.rbkc.gov.uk/housing

Noise & nuisance service
020 7361 3002/3484

LEGAL HELP

Citizens Advice Bureau
Westway Information Centre
1 Thorpe Close W10
0870 122 2313
Mon, Tues, Wed & Fri
10am–12.30pm

North Kensington Law Centre
74 Golborne Road W10
020 8969
7473/www.nklc.co.uk
Mon–Fri 10am–1pm,
2pm–5pm (closed Wed am)

LIBRARIES

Kensington Central
Phillimore Walk W8
020 7361 3010/(24-hour renewal) 020 7361 3610)
services@rbkc.gov.uk
Mon, Tues & Thurs
9.30am–8pm;
Wed 9.30am–5pm;
Fri & Sat 9.30am–5pm

Kensal Library
20 Golborne Road W10
020 8969 7736
Mon, Tues & Thurs 1pm–6pm;
Fri 9.30am–5pm;
Sat 9.30am–1pm &
2pm–5pm

North Kensington
108 Ladbroke Grove W11
020 7727 6583
(24-hour renewal)

020 7361 3610
Mon, Tues & Thurs
9.30am–8pm; Wed,
Fri & Sat 9.30am–5pm

Notting Hill Gate
1 Pembridge Square W2
020 7229 8574
Mon 1pm–8pm; Tues
1pm–7pm;Thurs
9.30am–1pm; Fri & Sat
9.30am–1pm & 2pm–5pm

Mobile Library
020 8968 6012

OPTICIANS

Shannon & Carton
102 LadbrokeGroveW11
020 7229 2218
Tues–Fri 9am–5.30pm;
Sat 9am–4.30pm

PEST CONTROL

Environmental Healthline
020 7361 3002

PHARMACIES

Bliss
5–6 Marble Arch W1
020 7723 6116
Mon–Sun 9am–midnight,
365 days a year

Zafash
117–119

Old Brompton Road SW7
U20 7373 2798
Open 24 hours, 365 days

PLANNING & CONSERVATION

For applications, enforcement
and planning appeals
020 7361 3012

POLICE

Notting Hill Police Station
101 Ladbroke Road W11
020 7221 1212

POST OFFICES

Z.Pujani
2 Ladbroke Grove W11
Mon–Fri 9am–5.30pm; Sat
9am–4pm

Ladbroke Grove Post Office
116 Ladbroke Grove W10
Mon–Fri 9am-5.30pm; Sat
9am–1pm

Main Post Office
190 Kensington Church Street
W8
020 7229 2009
Mon–Fri 9am–5.30pm; Sat
9am–12.30pm

St Ann's Road Post Office
25 St Ann's Road W11

Mon-Fri 9am–5.30pm; Sat
9am 1pm

Portobello Post Office
corner of Chesterton Road &
Portobello Road W10
Mon-Fri 8am–5.30pm; Sat
9am–1pm

PUBLIC LAVATORIES

Notting Hill Gate,
outside Tescos
Portobello Road,
junction with Lonsdale Road
Portobello Road,
junction with Tavistock Road
Turquoise Island,
Westbourne Grove W11

PUBLIC TRANSPORT

UNDERGROUND
Notting Hill Gate:
Central, District and Circle
lines

Ladbroke Grove, Latimer Road and **Westbourne Park:** Hammersmith & City
line

Holland Park: Central line

BUSES
Notting Hill Gate:
12, 27, 28, 31, 52, 70, 94,
148, 328, 452, 452,N12,
N28, N31, N52, N94, N207

Westbourne Grove:
7, 23, 27, 28, 31,70, 328,
N7, N23, N28, N31

Westbourne Park Road:
7, 28, 31, 70, 328

Ladbroke Grove:
7, 23, 52, 70, 295, 452,
N23, N52

Bramley Road:
295

Holland Park Avenue:
94, N94, N207

Further information from
Transport for London
www.tfl.gov.uk

Disabled Transport
020 7361 2546

Dial-a-ride www.tfl.gov.uk
(registration necessary)

National railway information
0871 200 4950
www.nationalrail.co.uk

RECYCLING CENTRES

Golborne Road
Elkstone Street W10
Kensington Sports Centre
Walmer Road W11
Sainsbury
Ladbroke Grove W10

Car park
St Mark's Road W10
Under the Westway
Tavistock sub-depot
Portobello Road W11
West Row/Southern Row W10

Orange bags for recycling
and green bags for garden
waste can be obtained from:

The Council Offices
37 Pembroke Road W8
Market Office
72 Tavistock Road W11
**North Kensington
Library**
108 Ladbroke Grove W11
**North Kensington
Sports Centre**
Walmer Road W11
Notting Hill Library
1 Pembridge Square W2
Reception Office
Stable Yard,
Holland Park W8
**Town Hall reception
desk**
Hornton Street W8

For other refuse enquiries
Streetline: 020 7341 3001
streetline@rbkc.gov.uk

RESIDENTS PARKING

Parking Shop
19-27 Young Street W8
020 7361 3004
parking@rbkc.gov.uk
Mon, Tues & Thurs

8.30am—4pm;
Wed & Fri 8.30am—4pm

Parking appeals
If you wish to challenge a
parking ticket, write to the
Council at: RBK &C
PO Box 4294
Worthing BN13 1WW

SCHOOLS ADMISSIONS

Schools Services
020 7361 2210
education@rbkc.gov.uk

SECURITY

**Mario's Security
Services &
Locksmiths**
132 Talbot Road W11
020 7727 5429
Mon—Sat 9am—5.30pm

TAXIS

Just Airports
0800 096 8096

Karma Kars
020 8964 0700
Tobias: 07770 693979
karmakabs@aol.com
www.karmakars.net

Black cabs
020 7272 0272

MINICABS

Z Cars
020 8968 3363
Chepstow Cars
020 7229 7576/3361

VETERINARY CLINICS
Andrew Carmichael
7 Addison Avenue W11
020 7603 4407
Mon, Tues & Thurs 9—11am &
5—7pm; Wed & Fri 9—11am &
4—6pm; Sat 9—11am

WINDOW CLEANERS

**R Walsh Cleaning
Services**
020 8958 7808
07956 379 666

YOUTH CENTRES

Community Learning
125 Freston Road W10
020 7938 8000
www.rbkc.gov.uk

PART 2

MUSIC & FILM

GETTING IT STRAIGHT IN NOTTING HILL GATE

Tom Vague

Tom Vague has been getting it straight in Notting Hill Gate since 1978 as a music journalist, film critic and local historian. After covering the punk scene in the fanzine **Vague** and the music mag **Zigzag**, he has published the acclaimed Notting Hill history booklets **Entrance to Hipp** and **London Psychogeography**, written the liner notes for the Clash's **London Calling** CD/DVD, and edited the Kensington & Chelsea community history newsletter. The following speed history of Pink Floyd, Hawkwind, Bob Marley and the Wailers, and the Clash is extracted from his **Portobello pop market guide** (**Vague** 40) www.historytalk.org

Pink Floyd: In Interstellar Overdrive at All Saints Church Hall

After the Albert Hall beat poetry happening in 1965, the next key event in the history of British counterculture was the London Free School. This proto-community action group has been described as an 'anarchic temporary coalition' of post-Rachman housing activists and the new beatnik/hippy generation. To varying degrees of involvement, the Free School class of '66 numbered John Hopkins, Michael X, Pete Jenner, Andrew King, Michael Horovitz, John Michell, Julie Felix, RD Laing and Pink Floyd.

In the Free School building, 26 Powis Terrace (a former brothel opposite David Hockney's studio), by all accounts not much happened apart from band practices in Dave Tomlin's psychedelic basement. Michael X, posing Puff Daddy-style with a silver-topped cane, is said to have scared off any actual local people. Yet the Free School received its best publicity through Michael when Rhaune Laslett's playgroup at 34 Tavistock Crescent was visited by Muhammad Ali. The social worker Rhaune Laslett is widely credited for organising the 1966 Notting Hill Fayre and Pageant which became Notting Hill Carnival. She told *Time Out* in the Nineties that the idea came to her in a vision, after she had dealt with a landlord-tenant dispute, 'that we should take to the streets in song and dance to ventilate all the pent-up frustrations born out of the slum conditions'. The outcome was a weeklong series of events following the traditional English carnival format. The procession along Portobello Road consisted of the London Irish girl pipers, a New Orleans-style marching band, an Afro-Cuban band and Russell

Henderson's Trinidadian steel band. Throughout the week All Saints church hall on Powis Gardens hosted 'social nights' including 'international song and dance', jazz and folk, and 'old tyme music hall'.

After the Fayre, John 'Hoppy' Hopkins, photographer, publisher, promoter and leading light of the hippy underground, presented an All Saints hall 'pop dance featuring London's farthest out group The Pink Floyd in interstellar overdrive'. Encouraged by the liberal vicar and promoted by Timothy Leary's 'turn on, tune in, drop out' slogan, this turned into a 12-gig residency through October and November. Pink Floyd's 'Sound/Light Workshops' have been variously described as initially ill attended, or elite 'social nights', educational events with questions from the audience afterwards, and auditions for EMI. As they developed their whimsical folk pop further out there into the progressive-rock freakouts 'Interstellar Overdrive' and 'Astronomy Domini', the legendary original singer, Syd Barrett, was inspired to write 'See Emily Play' by the 'looning about' of early Floyd fan Emily Young.

It was also here that the British psychedelic lightshow was developed, after the Leary associates Joel and Toni Brown turned up, tuned in and projected slides on the group at the first All Saints gig. Hoppy's main counterculture cohort, Pete Jenner, duly gave up his day job as an LSE lecturer to become Pink Floyd's manager and set up Blackhill Enterprises with Andrew King (now of Mute Records) on Alexander Street, off Westbourne Grove.

During the '67 'summer of love' Courtney Tulloch wrote in *International Times* of worsening relations between the police and the black community and looked back to the '66 Fayre, incorporating steel pans and jazz enthusiast police, as hippy heaven W11. Paradoxically Emily Young has recalled the Free School adventure playground, on the cleared strip where the Westway was about to be built, as a vision of Notting Hell or 'the dark side of the moon'.

As well as Pink Floyd, psychedelic lightshows and adventure playgrounds, the Free School launched the British underground press and the rave concept of clubbing on the world, from All Saints hall. *International Times,* or *IT*, the first UK hippy underground paper, was a continuation of the Free School newsletter *The Gate/The Grove* published by Hoppy and Barry Miles's Lovebooks. After *IT* was inaugurated with an 'all night rave' at the Roundhouse, Hoppy and Joe Boyd opened the UFO psychedelic nightclub on Tottenham Court Road, as a larger venue for Pink Floyd to expand into from All Saints hall.

Hawkwind: Hawklords of the Manor in the 'Hall of the Mountain Grill'

As Hawkwind came into existence as Group X at All Saints church hall in 1969, some of the band were living on Talbot Road. With the endorsement of John Peel, they turned into Hawkwind under the management of Doug Smith's Clearwater Productions, whose premises on Great Western Road became their practice studio/crashpad. The Dutch music paper *Ear* cited the compositions of founder Dave Brock as capturing 'the wind-blown and semi-estranged character of Ladbroke Grove and probably as a result, Hawkwind quickly grew from an idea to reality'. The name is said to come from a nickname acquired by the singer/saxophonist Nik Turner, on account of his ability to synchronise bodily functions, rather than from a Tolkien character as you might have expected.

At the 1970 Isle of Wight festival Hawkwind recall Hendrix being too depressed to jam at the alternative festival, but they claim he agreed to play Stonehenge with them. The week before Hawkwind had headlined a space-rock skinhead moonstomp on Wormwood Scrubs. After rain and accompanying technical problems (ie electrocution) held up proceedings, they won over the local skinheads as well as the *Kensington Post* reporter who applauded the 'brilliant young men from Notting Hill' for eschewing commercialism, in favour of doing 'their own proverbial multi-echo booming explosive thing'. On the gatefold sleeve of their 1971 album *X in Search of Space* Hawkwind are pictured playing a free gig under the Westway, which they did on several occasions, often merging with the Pink Fairies as Pinkwind.

In 1974, Hawkwind's fifth album, *Hall of the Mountain Grill*, was named in honour of the legendary greasy spoon café at 275 Portobello Road, which acted as the backstage and provided the power supply for the Westway gigs. It was also a spoof of King Crimson's *In the Court of the Crimson King* album. In Pete Frame's *Rock Family Trees*, the Hawkwind singer/sci-fi writer Bob Calvert describes the Mountain Grill as 'a kind of left-bank café-meeting place for the Notting Hill longhairs, a true artists' hangout, but it never became chic, even though Marc Bolan, David Bowie and people like that often went there'.

Thirty years on, it seemed that any pop appeal the premises once possessed had gone with the Wind. Then Mike Skinner, aka The Streets, posed there with a fry-up for some street cred in a photo shoot for the *Observer*. Overnight the rock landmark was gentrified into the takeaway Babes'n'Burgers and the quest for the holy Mountain Grill was lost.

In this mid-Seventies strata of acid-rock geology, the 'Psychedelic Warlords' of the Wind numbered Dave 'Baron' Brock, Nik Turner, aka 'the Thunder Rider', and Lemmy 'Count Motörhead'. After making his debut with Hawkwind in Powis Square, the former Hendrix roadie Lemmy was quoted as saying, 'Hawkwind fits exactly into my philosophy. They're weird – that suits me.' Yet, after their sixth album, *Warrior on the Edge of Time,* and the single, 'Motörhead/Kings of Speed', he was

sacked for the occupational hazard of being busted with speed at Canadian customs. Of all Hawkwind's many *Spinal Tap*-style line-up changes, this is regarded by many as the biggest mistake in rock history.

On Lemmy's dismissal from Hawkwind, he promptly formed Motörhead. After their regular Hammersmith Odeon gigs, he occasionally slept in St Luke's Mews. But usually, when off the road, Lemmy could be found on the fruit machine of the Princess Alexandra pub at 95 Portobello Road, then more commonly known as the Alex, the bikers', speed dealers' and National Front pub. After some pool hall aggro, in which Lemmy sided with a non-Caucasian, the Alex became the first Notting Hill pub to be gentrified – back in the mid-Eighties – into the Portobello Gold bar-restaurant.

In the sci-fantasy novel *The Time of the Hawklords* by the Hawkwind member Michael Moorcock, their post-apocalypse HQ was 'the yellow van commune' at 271 Portobello Road (now the Portobello Hot Food takeaway). In the book the post-apocalypse kids gather outside to remind Hawkwind to play for their sonic healing. In rock reality, when the book came out in 1976, the kids were telling them to stop. Nevertheless, they carried on prog-rocking regardless. As Hawkwind performed space rituals at Stonehenge and Glastonbury, they took punk and acidhouse on board. Three decades later, in 2006, they reappeared under the Westway as Space Ritual (without Dave Brock) at the Inn on the Green.

Bob Marley and the Rise of Reggae: Notting Hill Babylon by 31 Bus

The most important rock and pop route of Notting Hill isn't Portobello Road, it's Basing Street. From the late Sixties, this side street between Portobello and All Saints Road has been twinned with New Orleans jazz label Basin Street as the site of the Island recording studios (currently Sarm West).

The history of Island Records can be traced back to Chris Blackwell's first jazz release in Jamaica in the late Fifties. After his first hit with Laurel Aitken's ska single 'Little Sheila', Blackwell founded the Island label and moved to London in 1962. As he became the UK's premier ska importer, he had his first production company hit in 1964 with Millie Small's 'My Boy Lollipop'. On tour with Millie, he discovered the Birmingham r'n'b outfit, the Spencer Davis Group, out of which came Stevie Winwood and Traffic. As Island became the first big independent label in Notting Hill, their roster went through folk, prog and glam rock, and the Basing Street studios were frequented by Nick Drake, Fairport Convention, Free, Mott the Hoople, Quintessence, Roxy Music, Sparks, Cat Stevens and Jethro Tull. The premises were also used by such non-Island acts as The Eagles, the Rolling Stones and Led Zeppelin.

Chris Blackwell's introduction to reggae came about when he was rescued from a reef by a group of Rastafarians in 1958 and the Wailers rescued him from prog rock. In 1968 he co-founded Trojan Records (which was based at the Saga Centre on Kensal Road) with Lee Gopthal, and set up the Blue Beat distribution network. Having released the first Wailers single in 1966, Blackwell resumed his association with the group six years later. As Jimmy Cliff left Island in the wake of *The Harder They Come*, Bob Marley reappeared and Blackwell perfected the rock-reggae crossover on the Wailers' 1972 album *Catch a Fire*.

After Bob Marley was shot in the run-up to the December 1976 'Smile Jamaica' concert (probably by a supporter of the Jamaican Labour Party, as the gig was promoted by the rival People's National Party), the Wailers came to England for the punky reggae party. During their Babylondon exile they recorded their most commercial album, *Exodus*, on Basing Street.

By all accounts, Bob Marley was initially sceptical of punk rock, and more inclined towards prog. As Chris Salewicz puts it in *Songs of Freedom*, in exile on King's Road, 'at first Bob strongly resisted what he perceived to be simply another manifestation of Babylon'. Don Letts recalls being chastised for wearing bondage trousers when he was managing the King's Road punk shop Boy, with Bob asking him, 'What yuh wan' look like all them nasty punk people feh?' But in Notting Hill, during the *Exodus* sessions, he was won over to the cause. Don says he assured him the Clash were reggae fans, not 'crazy baldheads', and the Island press officer Viv Goldman lent him the album *The Clash* featuring their version of Junior Murvin's 'Police and Thieves' produced by Lee Perry. As a result, Bob, Lee Perry and Aswad came up with 'Punky Reggae Party' as the flipside of the Wailers' first top-ten single 'Jamming'.

One night Bob and the bass player Aston 'Family Man' Barrett were heading back to Chelsea after a 'Jamming' session, when they found themselves held up in traffic on Ladbroke Grove outside 101 Ladbroke Road – Notting Hill police station. Bob and Family Man were inevitably found to be in possession of cannabis and interviewed for the Notting Hill Babylon files. Other Bob Marley-associated sites in the area include: numbers 8 and 18 All Saints Road on the old reggae Frontline, the Mangrove (now Ruby & Sequoia) and the Apollo pub (now studios); the Globe bar and the house of Trevor Bow of Sons of Jah on Talbot Road; Portobello Green, which he visited during the '77 Carnival; the House of Dread Rasta centre on Lancaster Road; and his wife Rita (of the I-Threes)'s Island flat on Basing Street. In the early Eighties the reggae scene revolved around the Upfront record shop on All Saints Road, where today Daddy VGo's People's Sounds shop maintains the tradition while Dub Vendor has become the reggae CD shop at 150 Ladbroke Grove.

In what is widely regarded as the classic Portobello pop pose – even

outdoing the Clash – home-grown reggae band Aswad were photographed by Adrian Boot outside the Golden Cross pub (now the
Market Bar), around a young-ish Sledge the Rasta. Aswad's local history can be traced back to the late Sixties, when the guitarist Brinsley
Forde appeared in the film *Leo the Last*, and continues into the 21st century, making them the top local band, as well as the number one British
reggae act. Carnival kings from the militant days of 'Three Babylon
(tried to make I and I run)', after headlining the first Carnival stage on
Portobello Green in 1979, Aswad made the second stage in Meanwhile
Gardens their own as they were recorded there 'Live and Direct' in
1983.

After the death of Bob Marley in 1981 his spirit lived on in the area
via the Dread Broadcasting Corporation. The Portobello pirate radio
station, launched by Bob's brother-in-law Leroy Lepke Anderson and
featuring his sister-in-law Rankin' Miss P, had a market stall outside 303
(then the Black People's Information Centre), and 286 as its mailing
address. As DBC went 'dread outta control' from a Neasden garden
shed, you could 'tune in if you rankin' to their militant insurgency.

The Clash: The Sound of the Westway

*There's a brick wall in Notting Hill near Portobello market that I would rather
look at for hours than go to Madame Tussaud's and it's totally free and full of
history.* ('My Kinda Town', *The Source* magazine, *The Sun* 6–12 August
1999)

The Westway to the world story of the Clash can be traced back to
1973, when Mick Jones and his gran moved to a flat on the 18th floor
of Wilmcote House, overlooking the flyover north of Royal Oak. As
Mick was forming his first glam rock group up in his tower block, just
along the Harrow Road, Joe Strummer was squatting 101 Walterton
Road. Before long, Joe (then known as 'Woody') had organised his
housemates into El Huaso and the 101 All Stars, for a shebeen-style residency at the nearby Chippenham pub, during which they abbreviated
to the 101'ers.

Their next musical residency, in the Elgin at 96 Ladbroke Grove, put
them and Notting Hill on the pub rock map. They also played the first
gig at Acklam Hall under the Westway (on the site of Neighbourhood

nightclub), a benefit for the North Kensington Law Centre. The 101'ers' last residency was at the Nashville Rooms in West Kensington, with Ted Carroll's Rock On Disco and the Sex Pistols. The first punk rock site in North Kensington is 93 Golborne Road, where from the early Seventies, Ted Carroll's Rock On record stall boasted a 'huge and rocking selection' of rare/imported rock'n'roll.

In punk psychogeography, if not in reality, the Clash formed in Portobello market when Mick Jones and Paul Simonon bumped into Joe Strummer and told him they didn't like the 101'ers but thought he had punk potential. As well as embodying their original post-skinhead image, Paul Simonon came up with the name, by flicking through the *Evening Standard* and finding the word 'clash' cropping up repeatedly in headlines. The bass player also has the best local street cred of the group: having attended Oxford Gardens infants school when the Westway was under construction, he went to Isaac Newton School on Lancaster Road/Wornington Road as Trellick Tower was being built, and also had a job on the market.

In the summer of 1976, Joe wrote the Clash Westway tribute 'London's Burning' at the punk squat 42 Orsett Terrace (near Royal Oak) after watching the traffic from Mick's tower block. The day after the Clash played their first major gig with the Pistols at the Screen on the Green in Islington, Joe and Paul were on Ladbroke Grove for the start of the '76 Carnival riot. As the police charged up Westbourne

Park Road, Joe found sanctuary in the Elgin. Meanwhile, on Portobello, Don Letts was walking into pop history towards Acklam Road, as Rocco Macaulay began taking his famous series of pictures of the next police charge. In due course, Macaulay's shot of policemen reaching the Westway became the back cover of *The Clash* album, and the 'White Riot' tour backdrop; Don Letts's Wild West 10 walk first appeared on the sleeve of the *Black Market Clash* mini-LP.

Inspired by black anarchy in the UK, as much as by the Pistols, Joe wrote the lyrics of the first Clash single 'White Riot' ('I wanna riot, white riot, a riot of my own'), quite clearly meaning that he felt excluded from the black riot but, at the same time, empathy with the cause. Nevertheless, the song was misinterpreted as a call for whites to riot against blacks – 1958 style – by a student's union. On the whole, white hooligan youths got the intended meaning.

Although the Clash already existed, it can be argued that they were a pop culture echo of the 1976 riot. Not least they got into reggae, feeding dub effects, 'heavy manners' stencil graffiti and the apocalyptic rhetoric into the mix. At the end of the Seventies, they previewed their third album *London Calling* under the Westway at Acklam Hall. On the fourth, 'Sandinista', they covered such staple Ladbroke Grove themes as police ('The Crooked Beat'), towerblocks ('Up in Heaven') and the Carnival ('Let's Go Crazy', 'The Street Parade').

In the early Eighties the Clash posed on Freston Road, in front of the squatted Apocalypse Hotel (on the site of the 'Frestonia' Chrysalis office building), Mick Jones already with a hip-hop ghettoblaster. For the rest of the decade Futura 2000 graffiti marked the spot of the punky hip-hop party. In 1983 Mick and Paul starred in Joe's *Hell W10* home movie, as the gangster boss and *The Harder They Come*-style rebel respectively. When Mick first resurfaced in 1985, for Big Audio Dynamite's 'Bottom Line' debut, it was posing Wild West 10-style on Golborne Road in front of Trellick Tower. Mick's post-Clash outfit, originally called Real Westway and featuring the Clash associate film director Don Letts, has recently reappeared at the Inn on the Green.

After Joe's death in 2002 local tributes were paid under the Westway at Westbourne Studios, on Ladbroke Grove in the Elgin, and by the surviving 101'ers at the Tabernacle in Powis Square. In 2006, as Julien Temple filmed *The Future is Unwritten*, about Joe Strummer, under the

Westway, Paul Simonon joined forces with Damon Albarn (of Blur and Gorillaz), Simon Tong (formerly of The Verve) and Fela Kuti collaborator Tony Allen for their local pop history project *The Good, the Bad and the Queen,* showcased at the Electric Proms.

GROWING UP WITH CARNIVAL

Polly Thomas

Polly Thomas was born and raised in West London, where she attended Holland Park School for much of the 1980s. It was during this period that she developed her love of Caribbean culture and first started to attend Carnival. She made her first trip to the Caribbean aged 17, and has since travelled to Jamaica, Trinidad and Tobago more times than she can remember, often as a researcher and writer of **Rough Guides** to the islands. Here she describes why she loves Carnival.

Ask me the best thing about summer in London, and without a moment's hesitation, I'll say Carnival. Growing up on the periphery of Notting Hill, and attending secondary school at Holland Park, just steps away from the heart of the event, I've never been able to understand those joyless souls who don't love Carnival, who refuse to get impossibly excited about the prospect of sharing their streets with some two million revellers intent on sticking two fingers up to the norm for a couple of days and letting it all hang out in public.

Carnival in 1965

Come Carnival Saturday, when the railway bridges and lamp-posts have been transformed into advertising hoardings and an army of entrepreneurs are constructing temporary emporiums along what will be the busiest junctions, there's already a palpable air of anticipation throughout the area. Bars and pre-Carnival parties are packed to the gills, while dedicated Carnivalists are starting early by attending Panorama, the steel band competition held in a local park on Saturday night. By Sunday morning, the music stages are fully functional, the crowd-control barriers and banks of Portaloos are in place and the sound-system operators, having claimed their hotly contested street-corner positions, are warming up their sets, testing the equipment so that the bass bounces and echoes through the high, narrow terraces that spread back from

Portobello Road. Huge articulated lorries laden with yet more speakers ease their way through the back streets to the Carnival route, trailing bands of costumed paraders in their wake and passing the swanky, prominently deserted homes of those who prefer to set the alarms and flee for the duration. By early afternoon, the streets are heaving, and Europe's biggest and best street party is in full, inexorable swing.

Territorial, cliquey and occasionally arrogant about our precious home, West Londoners can seem a strange lot, but in Carnival we've always had something to really feel smug about. Because though it's Caribbean in essence, the substance of today's Carnival is a uniquely W11/W10 affair, a phenomenon that stems directly from the evolving tastes and experiences of the local human hotchpotch. It's a hybrid carnival, in which the reggae, garage, blues and salsa played by the sound systems sit happily alongside the steel-band trucks, where buying a suitably glamorous designer outfit to model on the streets is more common than playing mas with a costume band.

Although the mas bands remain the stock image of Carnival, alongside the inevitable black grandmother dancing with a beet-faced policeman, when I started attending as a teenager in the 1980s, the costumes and other Carnival disciplines always felt like a somewhat peripheral part of the event. For me they were more a gorgeous interlude glimpsed as we weaved our way between what really got us excited: the sound systems.

Steel-band trucks held mild appeal in that we could watch our pan-playing schoolmates in action, and the soca floats offered the opportunity to keep on partying after everything else had been shut down (they always keep the music playing as they wind their way home, mostly as a way of getting people out of the area), but those huge columns of speaker boxes were the real face of Carnival for us. Stacked up on the same street corners where we hung out when bunking off school, the sound systems were the place to be – very public arenas in which to show off our carefully planned outfits and dance in the open air to the most popular tunes of the year. There was a lovely feeling of unity, of somehow getting away with something just by being there.

My fondest Carnival memories – jumping up with thousands of others under the Westway where Rapattack and Mastermind systems held sway, or watching an entire streetful of heads bounce to the same beat during the acid-house summer of 1997 – have little in common with the carnivals of the Caribbean, but they do illustrate what makes Notting Hill such a special affair. Some traditionalists feel that London's Carnival, with its emphasis on sound systems and music stages, is a far cry from 'real' Carnival in the Caribbean. It has little connection with the celebration of freedom that was created by white planters but usurped by newly free Africans after the abolition of slavery, and which, in Trinidad, where it is based around tightly-fought competitions for the best masquerade costume, calypsonian, soca performer or steel band, has become the biggest event of the year. But for most people of my generation, these 'failings' are precisely what keeps us coming back year after year. Rather than sticking to the traditional disciplines of West Indian carnivals, our event has grown and evolved alongside wider society. It reflects the changing passions of Carnival-goers over the decades and accepts almost anything that wants to be a part of it. Brazilian samba bands and traditional Indian drummers fill the streets alongside pumping soca floats and costume paraders, while Glastonbury-style music-stages host everything from World Music crooners to international hip-hop acts which compete for attention with raw ragga. (Only the Royal Navy float, hauled out every year complete with submarine but no music, hasn't really got into the spirit of things.) Carnival has moved with the times, and while the event wouldn't be the same without mas and steel pan, it's vital that it's able to embrace the new as well as the old.

From the beginning, Notting Hill Carnival has been a creation of the area's diverse population, in terms of both race and class, and an offshoot of an underlying bacchanalian spirit set in place by West Indians who settled in Notting Hill during the late 1940s. They set up the clubs and shebeens that first attracted the white middle classes here, eager to prove that they didn't share the xenophobic sentiments of much of the rest of the population. In doing so, they paved the way for the multicultural Notting Hill of today (becoming less diverse as gentrification reaches every last corner), and laid the foundations both of the area's party spirit and of its unending creativity – an ethos that said, if you want something, get up and create it and be part of it rather than watch from the sidelines.

There's always been plenty of contention as to how Carnival began

GROWING UP WITH CARNIVAL **219**

and it's difficult – and perhaps rather pointless – to try and pin down the exact origins of an event that has developed so organically. However, it is generally agreed that the idea of a festival in Notting Hill came about as a means to unify the community in the aftermath of the 1958 race riots. In the early 1960s, Rhaune Laslett, a dedicated community worker who ran a local play group, began organising an annual procession in the tradition of an English summer fête, with children of all races parading the streets dressed up as folk heroes. This has little to do with Caribbean carnivals, but given the local demographics it wasn't long before the West Indian community became more directly involved. Claudia Jones, a political activist and founder and editor of the seminal *West Indian Gazette*, had staged the first of several pre-Lenten 'Caribbean Carnivals' in 1959. An indoor, cabaret-type evening featuring well-known steel bands and calypsonians, Jones's carnival had many of the elements of the event back home, and by the mid-1960s, when Laslett asked local residents to introduce some more Caribbean elements into the summer street parade, they were able to draw on the network of carnival artists who had performed at Jones's event. In 1965, with just three players on foot, the first mobile steel pan band hit the road and the roots of today's Carnival were planted.

Under the guidance of individuals such as Leslie Palmer, who had grown up in Trinidad, the event continued to grow each summer, and a Carnival Development Committee was formed in 1972. By the early 1970s, it was a decidedly Caribbean affair, with all the Trinidadian carnival traditions firmly in place. However, calypso had never really carried the swing in London; the mixed bunch of party-goers at local black clubs had been dancing to Jamaican rocksteady and ska for years. Jamaican reggae had by now become the music of choice in both the Caribbean and Notting Hill, and Carnival got its first taste of the very Jamaican institution of the sound system in 1974. The event was never quite the same again.

The carnivals of the early 1970s also reflected the wider militancy that set the tone for the era. As the Black Power movement took hold in the Caribbean and the USA, and black people in the UK faced ongoing racism from the police, who made full and brutal use of the Sus laws (see p 246), carnival became a focus of black resentment towards the police and vice versa. Disputes were inevitable, and what had become

one of the largest outdoor events in the country became marred by the violence which peaked in 1976. Carnival remained a symbol of defiance, described by local restaurant owner Frank Critchlow as a 'victory' rather than a party. By the time I started attending in the 1980s, the problems of the 1970s were on the wane, and though the fun was marred by crowds of opportunist 'steamers', who pushed through the crowds relieving the revellers of their valuables, the party spirit was firmly to the fore again. Notting Hill's bohemian flavour had become decidedly fashionable, and Carnival became everyone's party.

The Notting Hill Carnival Trust, which has organised the event since the late 1980s, brought in the inevitable corporate touch, generating the sponsorship that allowed Carnival to continue, and seeing off annual calls for it to be moved to the more manageable surrounds of Hyde Park. There have been murders over the years and demands are regularly raised, but it's impossible to imagine how the event could survive enclosure without sacrificing its spirit.

Even though many former Carnival die-hards now prefer to spend their August bank holiday elsewhere, bemoaning the fact that 'Carnival isn't what it used to be since they imposed the 7pm curfew/changed the route/commercialised the whole thing', the event is still as exciting as it ever was for me. And judging from the fact that the crowds continue to grow, I'm not alone.

STEEL BANDS

Steel pans originated in Trinidad and it was Trinis who first brought the pans to Notting Hill. From the very early days when Russ Henderson hit the road with just two other players, 'pans round necks', to the development of fully-fledged bands like Ebony, the Metronomes and the Mangrove, steel pans were integral to the sound and spirit of Carnival. By the 1980s huge mobile sound systems had supplanted them as the event's 'musical heartbeat' but the bands continued to develop, the most successful regularly gaining places in the annual Panorama competition.

Panorama takes place on Carnival Saturday at Horniman's Pleasance Park off Kensal Road. From around 7pm up to ten bands battle it out for the title of the UK's national competition: Notting Hill Carnival Champions of Steel. It's a prestigious event. There are no prizes but winning first or second place means going on to compete in European competitions, culminating in the world championships in Trinidad. The Metronomes, Stardust Steel Band, London All Stars, Southside Harmonics, Eclipse Steel Orchestra and Glissando Steel Orchestra are names to look out for but it's Ebony (led by Pepe Francis) and the Mangrove (led by Matthew Phillip) who tend to steal the show. Both have been winners many times over (the score in 2006 was Ebony 15/Mangrove 7) and rehearse and perform all year round, for weddings, parties and big corporate events, at home and abroad. They also play a significant role in the community, teaching and training

Matthew and Clive Phillip outside the
Tabernacle in Powis Square

A steel pan player, 1960s

young people from as young as eight years old. The last few years have been especially difficult, with Mangrove tenuously based at the Tabernacle and Ebony having no secure home. As this book goes to press, the bands are waiting to hear if their bid for a shared base at the Tabernacle has been successful. For more information see www.ebony.org.uk and www.mangrovesteelband.com

NOTTING HILL IN FILM

Adam Moon and Harry Fogg

Adam Moon is a former resident of Notting Hill. He works as a court reporter and freelance writer in London. Harry Fogg lives in Notting Hill but he is currently based in Paris with the British Council, working in the antique art market and as a film critic.

With the possible exception of Soho, no other part of London has attracted such full and frank treatment on film as Notting Hill. Though criticism of Richard Curtis's 1999 blockbuster *Notting Hill* centred on its 'whitewashed' portrait, the area – in the wider context of a prolific screen career – has largely been typecast as depraved and deprived, trading on a reputation for social, spiritual and structural contrast. Notting Hill's history and transitions have been extensively documented on celluloid.

With its proximity to the studios at the Gaumont, Ealing and subsequently the BBC, Notting Hill has always been a natural choice for location filming. It was here in 1948 that Powell and Pressburger shot *The Red Shoes*. Since then the area has been cast as the backdrop for films by some of the world's most ambitious and reputed directors. Most recently Woody Allen, substituting London for his beloved Manhattan, described the district as 'the perfect location'.

The Westway, a controversially iconic Notting Hill landmark since its erection in the late Sixties, trampled many cinematic locations in its path. One such victim was the old Paddington Green police station, from which the local bobbies in *The Blue Lamp* (1949) embark on an atmospheric car chase, taking in the sights of Ladbroke Grove and Latimer Road.

The streets of Notting Hill proved more difficult for police cars to negotiate in *The Lavender Hill Mob,* the Ealing comedy of 1951. In hot pursuit of Alec Guinness, his gang and their stolen gold bullion, four police cars converge on 'Junction Road', forming a pile-up outside the Bramley Arms at the corner of Bramley and Freston Roads.

This marked the pub's screen debut. After a break from the limelight of some 30 years, its next appearance came in *Leo the Last* (1969), teeming with the community of pimps and prostitutes of what was Testerton

Road. It would go on to win roles in *The Squeeze* (1977), *Quadrophenia* (1979) and *Sid and Nancy* (1986).

The Bramley achieved further international notoriety when it was adopted as a surname by residents of Frestonia to thwart GLC eviction plans. By law the authorities would have been forced to rehouse the squatters with one common name under one roof. The Frestonians, having been hospitable to film-makers over the years, now felt free to borrow back. When they declared independence from Britain, much was made of the influence of film on these developments, particularly the Ealing comedy *Passport to Pimlico* (1949) and the Marx Brothers' *Duck Soup* (1933) (featuring the nation of Freedonia). Now an office block, the Bramley Arms' film and public house career ended in the late 1980s.

By the Sixties, Notting Hill was landing parts in an ever-increasing number of pictures, acquiring the world renown of a film star. The area's crumbling façades and the diversity of its residents made it the setting of choice for directors seeking to reflect the social upheaval and injustices of the period. Of course, this was not always to the liking of the local authorities, who tried to stop the filming of Michael Relph and Basil Dearden's racial whodunnit, *Sapphire* (1959). Shot in the streets around Ladbroke Grove, *The Monthly Film Bulletin* summarised the film as addressing 'the problem of the negro's position in contemporary society'.

The L-Shaped Room (1962) formed part of the New Wave of British cinema. It offered an affectionate, though not uncritical, snapshot of Notting Hill's rich cultural mix. More traditionally episodic in structure and less innovative than the films of the French Nouvelle Vague, Bryan Forbes's adaptation of the Lynne Reid Banks novel of the same name opened with an expansive shot of the London skyline, eventually settling on Notting Hill. Leslie Caron's innocent French protagonist gets off the 52 bus in search of a room in this dilapidated area populated with unsavoury loiterers and mischievous youths. She takes a dank, L-shaped room, at 42 shillings a week in a house on St Luke's Road, sharing with a struggling writer, a black musician, a lesbian and several prostitutes. An obvious model for the Leonard Rossiter sitcom *Rising Damp*, the film drew on Notting Hill's reputation as the centre of Rachman's slum empire. In Michael Winner's 1963 film *West 11*, Joe

Beckett (Alfred Lynch) also lives in a squalid Notting Hill bedsit.

As the area's screen persona became increasingly typecast, the quirky cameo roles flooded in. Portobello Road was by now competing with the King's Road for the accolade 'centre of swinging London', and fast became the place to name-check in films. St Stephen's Gardens off Chepstow Road was the site of Michael Caine's seedy bedsit in *Alfie* (1966); Ringo Starr was chased down Lancaster Road in The Beatles' *A Hard Day's Night* (1964), and Charlie Croker's flat cluttered with bric-à-brac in *The Italian Job* (1969) was filmed on Denbigh Close, off Portobello Road. Tom Courtenay and Leonard Rossiter starred in the spy-thriller *Otley* (1968) at Notting Hill Gate Tube and on Portobello Road, while the same location drew an Oscar-nominated performance from Vanessa Redgrave in *Morgan: A Suitable Case for Treatment*. *The Knack ... and How to Get It* (1965) was also set against the backdrop of Portobello Road, director Richard Lester returning to the area just a year after completing *A Hard Day's Night*. The Orangery in Holland Park and Norland Square were used in Kevin Billington's love story *Interlude* (1968).

The archetypal 'swinging London' film of the Sixties was Antonioni's *Blow Up* (1966). David Hemmings's photographic studio in the film was on Princedale Road; it is now a design consultancy. Princedale Road had only previously won one film part: as the headquarters of the British National Socialist Party in Kevin Brownlow's 'what-if' docudrama *It Happened Here* (1966). In Nazi-occupied Britain the resistance are also based in Notting Hill. Their attack on the occupying forces is launched from the beer-garden of the Prince of Wales on Pottery Lane. Again the area is described as a place where 'anything can happen and usually does'.

Notting Hill's frequent film appearances had by now attracted the curiosity of Hollywood. Although Richard Burton had starred in the bleak *Look Back in Anger* (1958) some ten years previously in and around St Mary's Cemetery, Kensal Green, it was in Joseph Losey's Polanski-esque *Secret Ceremony* (1968) that Notting Hill shared the screen with some of the most celebrated names in film. Robert Mitchum, Elizabeth Taylor and Mia Farrow all starred in this psycho-drama which featured the curiously photogenic Debenham House at 8 Addison Rd, between Holland Park Avenue and Kensington High Street. One of Notting

Hill's most willing landmarks, the house made appearances in *Trottie True* (1949), *Richard III* (1995) and *The Wings of the Dove* (1997).

And so it was that Warner Brothers executives commissioned a London-based film starring Mick Jagger towards the end of the decade, naively assuming that Nicolas Roeg and Donald Cammell would produce an equivalent to *A Hard Day's Night*. The resulting gangster-psychedelia was not what they had bargained for. An experimental film, *Performance* featured scenes of graphic violence, sex and drug abuse. Warner Brothers were said to have wanted the negative destroyed. Their attempts failed and, after the acclaim for *Easy Rider*, they were persuaded to release the film belatedly in 1970.

James Fox's gangster-on-the-run goes into hiding with a washed-up, washed-out, rubber-lipped rock star and his groupies – Anita Pallenberg among them – in the basement of 81 Powis Square (in fact No. 25 was used). During his first phone call on arrival at the address, Fox describes the area as 'a freak-show … a right piss-hole – long hair, beatniks, druggers, free love, foreigners'. The directors chose Powis Square for its 'kaleidoscopic moods in a strange and faded area of London'. Although the then owner of 25 Powis Square refused permission to film the interior of the house, the desolation of the square is unmistakably authentic. Only months earlier, after a concerted effort by locals, the perimeter fencing had been torn down to allow public access. In the spirit of revolution, it is not altogether unthinkable that the children seen playing on the wasteland in *Performance* may have been responsible for the creation of the playground that occupies the square today.

Marcello Mastroianni added clout to Notting Hill's widening film CV when he appeared in the title role of John Boorman's *Leo the Last* (1969), a surreal vision of a Notting Hill of social deprivation and cultural clashes. The neighbourhood, viewed through a telescope from Leo's window, has the look of Hitchcock's *Rear Window* (1954) set – but was in fact Testerton Road pre-Westway. Demolition of the area was in progress during filming, and Boorman took the opportunity to paint the houses an ominous black. Cast members were said to have mixed freely in the community and locals enjoyed free electricity at the time thanks to the immense generators of the film crew.

Italian ties were strengthened when Michelangelo Antonioni

returned to film in Notting Hill in the 1970s. Foreign directors were now increasingly conscious of the area's cinematic potential – none more so than Antonioni, who reportedly created scripts to suit locations. After *Blow Up* in 1966, his 1975 masterpiece, *The Passenger*, starring Jack Nicholson and Maria Schneider, was filmed on location in Spain, Germany, Algeria and Lansdowne Crescent.

Richard Attenborough starred in Richard Fleischer's 1971 dramatisation of the infamous John Christie murders of the mid-1940s and early 1950s. *10 Rillington Place* was filmed entirely on location just before the street was renamed, demolished and redeveloped. Rillington Place, it seems, had become too notorious, even some 30 years after Christie began his ten-year killing spree at the address. The exact site of the original 10 Rillington Place can be traced today to between 26 and 29 St Andrew's Square.

Stephen Frears and Hanif Kureishi were among the few film-makers who sought to address the Notting Hill of the 1980s. Their 1987 collaboration *Sammy and Rosie Get Laid,* led to Kureishi's solo directorial debut, *London Kills Me* (1991), with Notting Hill landmarks featured throughout. More often than not, directors in the 1980s ignored the present day and sought to re-create the Notting Hill of the Sixties. *Absolute Beginners* (1986), a musical adaptation of Colin McInnes's 1959 novel, shot entirely in a studio, made reference to 'cash to the landlord once a week' and to the place being 'a disaster area' and no one's idea of a 'desirable address'. In *Scandal*, a 1989 dramatisation of the Profumo affair, Notting Hill was the obvious place for Christine Keeler to buy drugs and let her hair down with Jimmy Cliff and the Minister of War.

The cult classic *Withnail and I* (1987) looked back to the end of the Sixties and passed off a squalid flat in Notting Hill as Camden. When Withnail ordered 'two large gins, two pints of cider – ice in the cider', in the fictitious Mother Black Cap, he set in motion a chain of events that saw the site used for filming on Tavistock Crescent eventually converted into a pub – and ceremoniously christened 'The Mother Black Cap'.

In 1990, Finnish director Aki Kaurismäki's downbeat, deadpan comedy *I Hired a Contract Killer* (1990) presented a more original, almost noirish view of the area. With its focus on the criminal nderworld, however, it also conformed to the now predictable 30-year-old Notting Hill stereotype.

Whether or not Richard Curtis's *Notting Hill* amounted to a denial of the area's past or not, it did, for the first time, present Notting Hill as an idyllic, if rather quaint, London village. For all its former representations as slum-central, a freak-show or a disaster area, it was now being recognised as one of London's prettiest areas and presented with something of a lifetime achievement award – the title role in a blockbuster. The blue doorway was Curtis's own and the bookshop was modelled on that owned by this book's editor, in Blenheim Crescent. The film has renewed international interest in the area, and, rather less happily, spawned a wave of forgettable British comedies set in and around the district.

Since then, only *Kidulthood* (2005) has sought to redress the affluent perception of the area *Notting Hill* helped create. Director Menhaj Huda introduced its grimier side, reminding viewers once more of its contrasts. This is the Notting Hill of a younger generation – given a day off school after the suicide of a pupil, local teenagers go on the rampage. They steal beer from a newsagent on Ladbroke Grove, suffer morning sickness at Royal Oak station, and perform sexual favours for businessmen in Holland Park in exchange for hard drugs. As in Horace Ove's 1975 feature *Pressure*, which used local young squatters, there is a strong sense of authenticity about the cast. It rescues the film from its overambitious, sensationalised plotline. Huda used his old bedroom at his mother's house for filming.

However, the relative success of *Kidulthood* has by no means influenced other directors' use of the area. Woody Allen's unimaginative use of London as a city and the clunky 'English' dialogue in *Match Point* (2005) made audiences wince. Notting Hill landed the role of playground for the rich, with many of the outdoor scenes being shot around Holland Park. However, the veteran director is famed for churning out films and, as his love affair with London looks set to continue, we can assume Notting Hill's film career still has exciting prospects.

PORTOBELLO FILM FESTIVAL

Since starting as a relatively small event in 1996, the Portobello Film Festival has developed into an internationally recognised forum for independent film-makers to show their work. The main festival takes place over three weeks in July and August, with occasional screenings arranged at other times. Typical venues are the Tabernacle, Inn on the Green, Westbourne Grove Church, Horniman's Pleasance Park and a circus tent under the Westway. And it's free.

The technical quality of films has improved progressively over the years as the number of submissions has risen – from less than 200 in the beginning to 600 in 2006. Last year's festival ran from 31 July to 22 August, with something happening in at least two separate venues every night. Highlights included presentations from other London Film Festivals – **Halloween**, **Soho Super Shorts** and **Something from Brasil** – a Human Rights Watch evening with **Conversations on a Sunday Afternoon** from South Africa and a talk on HRW activities, a special evening of work from Ireland, Holland and Spain, and the Portobello Film Festival Video Café, where film-makers and audience can select movies from a menu and bring their own on the night.

More than half the films shown in 2006 came from abroad yet the festival still has a strong local flavour. That year featured performances by bands Gaz Mayall's Trojans, The Members and Hawkwind, with a screening of Michael Moorcock's cult film **The Final Programme**; comedy from Ladbroke Grover Tony Allen; programme text by Tom Vague; and photographic exhibitions by John Hopkins and Charlie Phillips, co-author of **Notting Hill in the Sixties**. Charlie was also one of the main subjects of Nike Hatzidimou's documentary **Rootical**, winner of the Agnès B Award/ Medal & 500GBP for best first film. For more information on past and future events and how to subscribe go to www.portobellofilmfestival.com.

PART 3

HISTORY

A BRIEF HISTORY OF NOTTING HILL

Annabel Hendry

Annabel Hendry studied social anthropology in London and specialised in the cultural effects of tourism. She has also worked and lived in Malta, Ireland and Brussels.

Notting Hill today still retains strong reminders of its history as one of the most grandiosely conceived suburbs in the country. The mansions and villas so characteristic of the area were mainly built during the middle of the 19th century to house the growing population of London, and they reflect the fanciful imaginations of enthusiastic Victorian speculators and architects. But the beauty of these façades sits uneasily in a rather dislocated urban geography, reflecting the area's sometimes troubled social history. Notting Hill was both a beneficiary and a victim of the mid-Victorian spirit of entrepreneurship: by the end of the 19th century it had some very grand suburban houses, cheek by jowl with areas of the most squalid living conditions in the country. During the 20th, the area suffered some of the most brutal examples of urban

Notting Hill in 1750

redevelopment, and became a focal point for events in the period of turbulence and social upheaval in the 1950s and 60s, but emerged with new hope from the 1970s into the present. Into the 1990s, people spoke of how the area resisted gentrification. Historically, it seems that this was always so.

Early history

The name Notting Hill probably derives from the Saxon 'sons of Cnotta (or Cnotingas)', who settled here around AD 700, near to the 'sons of Cynesige', who founded Kensington. The area's location, on a hill bounded by two streams, with a commanding position at the crossroads between London and the West, has always been significant, and throughout history has attracted the rich and the roguish in equal measure.

Notting Hill was originally part of the huge Kensington Estate given by William the Conqueror to Geoffrey, Bishop of Coutances, then held by the De Vere family until the reign of James I. In the 12th century it was divided into four manorial estates: Abbot's Manor Kensington, Earl's Court, West Town (the fields west of Addison Road stretching between Kensington High Street and Holland Park Avenue) and Notting Barns (north-west of Notting Hill Gate). In about 1100 the Abbot's Manor portion of the estate (between the present Church Street and Addison Road) was given by Aubrey de Vere to the Abbot of Abingdon in reward for curing his sick son. During the 14th and 15th centuries, other portions of land were gradually leased off to a series of large estate-holders, most of whom held on to their property until the end of the 18th century.

One of the most significant of these landowners was Walter Cope, a politician with influence at court who was knighted by James I in 1603. In eight years he acquired almost the whole area: West Town in 1591 and the Manors of Abbot's Kensington and Notting Barns in 1599. It was at Notting Barns that in 1607 he began building his Cope's Castle, later to become known as Holland House. This magnificent mansion was to become a social centre for the great and the good for centuries.

A second mansion was built in this period by another of James I's courtiers, Sir George Coppin. Originally called Sheffield House, this was to become Kensington Palace when William III bought it in 1689.

Kensington had become a 'royal suburb of London' and a highly fashionable centre for aristocratic social life. Several more substantial mansions were built in this early period, including Aubrey House on Campden Hill.

With only a small cluster of houses, Notting Hill at this time was little more than a hamlet and remained so until the middle of the 19th century, when Portobello Lane (as Portobello Road was then called) was still described as 'one of the most rural and pleasant walks in the summer in the vicinity of London'. However, there was some early industry in the form of the Kensington Gravel Pits which, for centuries, were worked on either side of what is now Bayswater Road and Notting Hill Gate. At one time, the desirability of the area was enhanced by the belief that emanations from the carts carrying the newly turned gravel from the pits to London were beneficial to health, and for a brief period the region was even extolled as a spa, when purgative springs were discovered on what is now Campden Hill.

From hamlet to suburb: the 19th-century building boom

In the first part of the 19th century, a series of building and development projects began to alter the rural character of the area. The earliest of these schemes were the cutting of the Paddington branch of the Grand Junction (now Grand Union) Canal, opened in 1801, and the allocation of land at Kensal Green in 1831 for the first custom-built cemetery in London (see p 143). But these developments were only foretastes of what was to come. Waterways were soon to be superseded in importance by railways, and the dead outnumbered by the living. By the end of the 1820s the area was witnessing the beginning of one of the greatest, most ambitious and certainly most uneven building booms in the history of England.

The story of this boom begins in the early 1820s, when two of the largest local landowners, the third Lord Holland and James Ladbroke, began to develop their estates, building the first houses on Campden Hill and around the area now known as Ladbroke Square. Such speculations were a little premature, for the swell of population was yet to arrive, and both developers were severely hit by the financial crash of 1825. However, the enthusiasm of their original enterprises set the tone for a costly, fanciful and, for some, financially disastrous boom which lasted until the 1870s.

The original plans (there were many, but those for the Ladbroke Estate were the most impressive and extensive) amounted to a kind of collective Victorian dream, and employed some of the best architects of the time. Complex and ambitious, they incorporated every possible style, from Tudor Gothic (see St George's Church, Aubrey Walk) to classical-Italianate (the villas around St Peter's Church). They also boasted the latest plumbing – not easy to achieve given all the clay and gravel in the area. The idea was to develop a series of estates providing spacious and stylish housing for the rising middle-class and professional population of London. Notting Hill was believed to be an ideal location, on the margins of fashionable Kensington and close to the flourishing West End. In spite of Lord Holland's and Ladbroke's hastiness, their planning soon proved fairly well-timed: as a result of decreasing mortality rates, in the first two decades of the 19th century the population of London had increased by 20 per cent. People wanted somewhere to move out to, and the most attractive magnets were the suburban areas close to the main highways.

A fair number of these newcomers included the extremely well-heeled. Campden Hill was nicknamed 'The Dukeries', and Kensington Palace Gardens was known as 'Millionaires' Row'. Others, of the

The north-west corner of Kensington Church Street in 1879

recently monied middle class, moved into the areas around Ladbroke Grove in the 1850s and 60s. As the century progressed, a growing working-class population began to settle here too, drawn by work opportunities offered by the construction of the railways. In 1863 the Metropolitan Railway, connecting Paddington and Farringdon Street, was inaugurated as the first underground railway in the world. A year later, the first feeder line was opened, extending from its western terminus at Hammersmith, through Shepherds Bush and Notting Dale (with a station at Ladbroke Grove) to Westbourne Park. The building of this line gave new life to the defunct Western London Railway, which was linked to the underground by a branch line from Latimer Road.

However, the realisation of the original dream for the estates was thwarted from the start, and things did not turn out as the speculators

Construction of the railway at Ladbroke Grove c. 1863

had hoped. The two problems were uncertain finance and uncertain takers for all the grandly conceived houses, which included plans by the architect Thomas Allason to build a spectacular circus in the style of John Nash's work at Regent's Park.

More building and 'graveyards of buried hopes'

Following a failed venture to establish a racecourse on the slopes of Notting Hill during the slow-down in building after the crash of 1825, the land reverted to Ladbroke and was re-leased for the construction of the estate of villas with spacious gardens which, instead of Allason's circus, now occupy the area around Ladbroke Grove, Kensington Park Gardens and Stanley Crescent. Further financial crises afflicted the project, leaving several developers bankrupt and countless legacies of half-finished shells along the way. As late as 1861, Ladbroke Gardens was described by *Building News* as 'a graveyard of buried hopes ... naked carcasses, crumbling decorations, fractured walls, slimy cement. Courageous builders have occasionally touched them and lost heart and money by the venture.'

Among the courageous builders who lost heart and a great deal of money was the Reverend Dr Stanley Walker. Described as a pious and very amicable man, he began building on both the Ladbroke and Portobello Estates, but sadly went bankrupt before he was able to finish what is now All Saints Church, intended as a monument to honour his parents. About the only survivor of all this activity was Charles Henry Blake, a retired Calcutta merchant and one of Walker's partners. Blake became responsible for the construction on the Portobello Estate of much smaller, more modest houses for the growing working-class population – each now worth a cool few million pounds. He also bought up many of the leases elsewhere and completed the half-finished houses. By the time the building craze ended in 1880, 13,000 buildings, most of them houses, had been erected in 60 years.

Along with the problem of shaky finances, there was the growing difficulty of supply outstripping demand. The simple fact overlooked by the developers was that some of the land occupied by the estates was either too far from the West End or fashionable Kensington or too close to the working-class districts around the Potteries (described below) and the railways to attract the clients they were hoping for.

Thus, houses built in the remoter areas, designed for single families and their servants, very soon became tenement blocks, leased off piecemeal at low rents. Others became overcrowded boarding houses. By the late 1860s, whole streets on the Norland Estate were crammed full of tenants very different from those for whom they had been designed, and squalor soon set in.

By the end of the 19th century, the area was marked by pockets of tremendous wealth, a good proportion of middle-class inhabitants, plus a massively growing working-class population hemmed into declining housing in areas away from the fashionable centres. A not dissimilar situation exists in several pockets of Notting Hill today.

Notting Dale

Just to the west of Notting Hill, on land which formed part of the Norland Estate (originally part of Abbot's Manor Kensington), was an area known in the1800s as the Kensington Potteries, later absorbed by Notting Dale. From early days it was a place where gypsies settled on a seasonal basis, arriving in late spring. The yellow clay soil of the area was ideal for making bricks to supply the rapidly expanding buildings of London. A large brick-field was established, as well as a pottery which made tiles, drains and pots, and the industry thrived until the clay was worked out by the 1860s. Over this period, labourers flooded in, many driven from Ireland during the years of the potato famine, and by the middle of the century the area was already overcrowded with unregulated housing.

Alongside the brick-makers grew a population of pig-keepers. The colony was started in 1818 when Samuel Lake, scavenger, chimney

sweep and pig-keeper, was forced to move from his previous premises in Tottenham Court Road. He leased land near to the brick-fields, with the idea that this isolated rural spot would cause less distress to the neighbours. Quite a colony developed – by the 1840s the settlement comprised 'a small village, where no less than 3,000 pigs shared 260 hovels with 1,000 inhabitants'. In an

A kiln in Walmer Road

area of very poor natural drainage, there were no proper roads, let alone proper sewerage, and the need to boil down the fat and offal of the animals as part of the industry led to a horribly fetid and unhealthy atmosphere. Life expectancy was very low: in the years 1846–48 the average age of death was 11 years and 7 months, compared to 37 years for the rest of London – and this was before the cholera epidemic of 1849.

Conditions continued to worsen. Cholera struck again in 1854, and in the next decade the population rapidly increased as people moved in from other parts of Kensington and from Paddington, driven out by slum clearances and the building of the railways.

The plight of the inhabitants of Notting Dale finally came to national attention when *The Morning Post* published a shocking report, declaring it to be a 'West-End Avernus' (Avernus was the Roman mouth of hell).

Amid all this squalor, given the uncertain employment of the men as work in the brick-fields dried up, the women turned to laundering and ironing, taking in washing from well-to-do households. By the end of the 19th century there were so many businesses that the area became known as 'Laundry Land'. Some of this work was extremely skilled, and a local saying went that 'to marry an ironer is as good as a fortune'.

Poverty, social problems and the birth of the housing trusts

Until the establishment of the London County Council (LCC) in 1898, local government, such as it was, was in the hands of the Kensington Vestry, which cared little about the growing social problems in the area. Following the famous 'Avernus' article in *The Morning Post*, on the urging of the parish priest of the church of St Francis of Assisi, the Vestry Works Committee undertook an inspection, only to report that any problems were merely 'brought about by the vicious proclivities and evil habits of the people themselves'.

The Vestry was a tight-fisted body. It delayed in allowing a public wash-house in Notting Dale on the grounds that, since so many families made their living from laundering, it might well be used for commercial purposes. It also did nothing to alleviate threats to public health from the particularly putrid expanse of clay sludge and pigswill known as 'the ocean'. Eventually, it was the parish priest of St Clement's who initiated a project to fill it in; he managed to raise £637 by publishing a letter of appeal in *The Times*, and the area was eventually covered over in 1892 to become what is still Avondale Park.

This initiative by a parish priest was, in many ways, typical of the plethora of philanthropic activities carried out by churches, private individuals, associations, trusts and clubs that filled the vacuum left by local government. It was part of the tradition of community self-help and direct action that has characterised the area for so long.

In spite of charitable efforts, the fundamental problem of inadequate housing remained unresolved, particularly in the region of Notting Dale. In 1898, the newly formed LCC instructed a medical officer to investigate the area, and accepted his recommendations that it should buy and renovate lodging-houses and build more itself. By this time, Notting Dale had been nicknamed 'the Guilt Garden' and certain streets had been designated as a 'Special Area'. The then mayor of Kensington made a large interest-free loan, and by 1906 had built 120 new tenements housing 490 people.

Here again, the efforts of private individuals played an important part. Two pioneers in improving housing conditions for the poor, Octavia Hill and Amy Hayne, joined forces with like-minded people, such as Octavia's cousin Sir Reginald Rowe, to buy houses, renovate them and encourage the tenants to take an interest in maintenance and upkeep. They put a tremendous amount of energy into improving conditions, working alongside the 'shiftless, the pauperised, the unemployed and the almost unemployable', as they described them, and formed the first housing trust in the area: the Improved Tenements Association. In 1920, this trust amalgamated with the Wilsham Trust (which had been formed by ladies-in-waiting at Kensington Palace) to form the Rowe Housing Trust.

The Kensington Housing Trust followed in 1926, along with the Sutton Dwellings and the Peabody Trusts. By the 1930s, these three trusts had built almost twice as many new dwellings as the borough council. At last tenements actually designed for multiple occupation were erected. Something was being done, but it was never enough.

War and the roots of immigration from the Caribbean

As in the rest of the country, the First World War caused many casualties among young men. Left at home, women became involved in the war effort, working in munitions factories and making canvas field tents for the front. Although bombing in the Second World War did not devastate the area, the local population was dislocated and suffered its fair share of damage. In addition, one particular development at this time was to have an unprecedented impact on Notting Hill's history: the recruitment of people from the Caribbean into the armed forces.

The first group was made up of sons of professionals and administrators who came over as volunteers to join the RAF as officers at the start of the war. A second group was later actively enlisted to provide supply staff for maintenance of frontline fighters in the invasion of Europe. These ground crews came from a wide social spectrum, including farmers and agricultural labourers. As Mike and Trevor Phillips write in *Windrush* (1998), 'this was an unprecedented opportunity for them to travel abroad and to change the entire course of their lives. This time recruitment was by invitation and, instead of in hundreds, they came in their thousands'. In spite of the grim circumstances, these recruits were welcomed with warmth. Many wanted to stay on at the end of the war but were encouraged to repatriate.

Following repatriation, there was a general eagerness to return to the UK. Conditions in the Caribbean were very poor, the war having totally disrupted the sugar trade on which many of the islands' economies depended. Also, the war had opened West Indian eyes to the fact that people did actually work in England – they weren't all of the 'governor' class to which they had previously been exposed; and in a UK busy trying to reconstruct itself after the war, there were clearly plenty of opportunities for work.

Word soon got around that passages to England were available on a troop carrier, the *SS Empire Windrush*. A Jamaican newspaper, *The Gleaner*, announced the fare to be £28 and 10 shillings, and many got together to find the funds for the journey; others boarded the ship as stowaways. On 24 May 1948, the *Windrush* left Jamaica with between 450 and 490 West Indians on board, most of them young men. They had a perfect right to go to the 'mother country' and as much right as any other citizen to live here. The 1948 British Nationality Act confirmed this. Stories of life on board during the journey reveal an exuberant group of people buoyed up by hope, fully expecting work, roofs over their heads and a proper welcome as total citizens. By many accounts, these young men were not wanting to spend a lifetime in the UK; most hoped to earn some good money and return home after a few years.

Late 1940s and early 1950s England was drab, recovering from the war and still enduring rationing. Men returned from battle hoping for heroic futures to reflect their wartime experiences, and found instead depression, restriction and little space to live in. Although Notting Hill and Notting Dale had not been as badly bombed as the East End, housing conditions had worsened during the war as even further decay set in. Overcrowded dwellings were, as ever, infested with bugs and rats; basements were frequently flooded. Piecemeal attempts to improve the situation over the previous decades had been insufficient, and most of the poor in Notting Hill and Dale were crammed into three-storey terraced houses each designed for one family.

This depressed area with its cheap housing received a steady flow of Caribbean arrivals from 1948 onwards. The immigrants did not receive the welcome they had expected. In fact, the future looked grim for the unsuspecting passengers on the *Windrush*, who were already perceived as a problem before even setting foot on British soil. As the boat steamed towards England, anxious letters were being passed between Government ministries questioning who had instigated this regrettable move. Inevitably, the press took up the story, with the *Daily Express* announcing the arrival of '500 unwanted passengers'.

On landing at Tilbury Docks, those classified as having 'no contacts in the UK' were placed in shelters. As soon as they found work, they moved out to join those already searching for somewhere to live. This proved difficult. Notting Hill was not the only place in England to begin displaying signs that read 'No Irish, No Blacks, No Dogs' in the windows of properties to let, but it was one of them. It was also an area where countless willing West Indian workers applied for posts (often below their qualifications) to be told that, for various spurious reasons (other workers wouldn't like it, the union would object etc), they couldn't be taken on.

In some ways, the decade from 1948 was one of the ugliest periods in the area's history, in that it exposed a previously unmined vein of racism, culminating in the vicious riots of 1958 and the murder of an innocent man nine months later.

The 1950s and 60s: shame, scandal and sleaze

Shame: riots and the killing of Kelso Cochrane

A spate of attacks on black immigrants by gangs of white youths throughout the summer led up to the riots of 1958. It was not an organised movement, but racist sentiments were already being whipped up by the neo-fascist Union Movement of Oswald Mosley, who was to stand as a parliamentary candidate for North Kensington in 1959 on a platform of 'Keep Britain White'. At the end of August, full-scale rioting broke out in Nottingham, to be followed a week later by three days of mayhem in Notting Hill. Large groups of youths stampeded through the streets, trashing any commercial premises known to be 'friendly' to blacks, and attacking any Caribbean immigrants they encountered. Although this was regarded as the worst race riot the country had ever seen, nobody was killed.

The wider circumstances of these events were, undoubtedly, far more significant than given credit for by the judge who condemned nine white youths after the disturbances as being 'a minute and insignificant section of the population'. One of the most shocking aspects of the riots is the way people, apparently, just stood by and let them happen.

It was not a simple case of xenophobia. The community was long used to absorbing immigrant populations. There was already a well-established Polish and Eastern European community in the area, along with many Spanish who had come here during and after the Spanish Civil War. There were also quite a few Portuguese. But with the West Indians, as with the Irish who had arrived so much earlier, the reaction was different. The lack of a welcome was certainly connected with muddled ideas about Empire: people in the colonies were considered as inferior and belonging 'over there'. The fact that the West Indians were not foreign immigrants but newcomers taking up their rightful place as citizens was a cause for panic; they were feared as a threat to jobs and housing – a fear that intensified with the Rent Act of 1957 (see Rachman, p 243) and the economic downturn of 1958.

An element of perverse moral panic and collective sexual jealousy were also involved. Again, the prejudice ran deep and was widespread; there were plenty of examples of employers forbidding West Indian men from working alongside white female workers on the grounds that the former amounted to some kind of threat. In addition, Notting Hill represented a particular case: its proximity to the West End had resulted in the neighbourhood becoming an offshoot of the Soho vice empires and an overspill area for the prostitutes who lined up along the Bayswater Road. As Mike Phillips remarks in *Notting Hill in the Sixties* (1991), 'whilst many immigrants deeply resented the propinquity with what they saw as vice and immorality, others plunged enthusiastically into the life they found here'. Some of the young men were determined to have a good time, which they organised with a style, glamour and openness quite new to Notting Hill. A network of clubs, 'blues' and shebeens was established – places to hang out and party.

The disaffected white youths who terrorised the streets for those three days of riots resented this gregarious, exotic scene that attracted a mixture of white people, including young women. It is no accident that accounts of both the Nottingham and Notting Hill riots record that they were sparked off by attacks on white women with black partners.

The following spring, a quiet-living carpenter from Antigua called Kelso Cochrane was stabbed to death in the street by six white youths. The killers were never identified. This murder sent a wave of shame and shock throughout the community. Cochrane's funeral at Kensal Green Cemetery was one of the biggest ever held in the area: the procession was joined by more than 1,200 people in a dignified public display of mourning. The event marked a turning point. Influenced by the Civil Rights and Black Power movements in the United States, with leaders such as Darcus Howe, Ben Bousquet, Stokely Carmichael, and Michael de Freitas (later known as Michael X, see p 277), from this time onwards the black community became determined to assert itself.

Scandal: the Profumo Affair

Notting Hill again came to public notice in the early 1960s during the Profumo Affair, one of the most sensational scandals in recent political history. At the core of the affair was beautiful call girl Christine Keeler, who divided her time between various flats in the West End and Notting Hill, and Spring Cottage on the luxurious Cliveden Estate owned by Lord Astor. She also frequented cafés such as the Rio and Fiesta One in Notting Hill.

As well as her West Indian boyfriend, Johnny Edgecombe, Keeler's consorts included Lucky Gordon (another West Indian), Stephen Ward (society osteopath and friend to the rich), Jack Profumo (Secretary of State for War) and Captain Eugene Ivanov (Russian military attaché). The national security risk, and hence the national scandal, centred on the Keeler-Profumo-Ivanov triangle. Rumours were already circulating in 1962, but the events leading up to the disclosures involved a series of violent misunderstandings between Keeler, Gordon and Edgecombe. At one point, Edgecombe needed to talk to Keeler, who was holed up with her friend and colleague Mandy Rice-Davies (mistress to Peter Rachman) in Stephen Ward's West End flat. When she refused to let him in, he tried to gain entry by firing gunshots at the door to break the lock. Edgecombe ended up being charged with attempted assault and possession of a firearm, and Gordon with assault.

The press had a field day and the copy made riveting reading, but the implications for Notting Hill were darker. Again the area was in the headlines, but associated with notoriety rather than fame, and the affair disclosed yet another unsavoury aspect of Notting Hill's history: the activities of Peter Rachman.

Sleaze: Peter Rachman's shady empire

Rachman died in 1962, a year before the Profumo scandal broke. His role in it was marginal, but his activities came under the public gaze because of his close association with Mandy Rice-Davies and Christine Keeler. The range of his slum empire and shady activities were well known locally and the local press had long been on his case, but it was the Profumo Affair that raised his reputation to that of a national villain.

Born in Poland, the son of a Jewish dentist, Rachman fled to England after the war, in 1946. He soon fell in with property tycoons and began controlling a few flats in Bayswater, let out mainly to prostitutes. Before long he became a property owner and, by 1955, owned houses in and around Powis Square and Colville Terrace, the most notorious of the Notting Hill slums. At its height, his empire included more than 100 buildings in West London. His method was to buy run-down properties at extremely low prices, divide them up into multiple tenements, then let and sub-let them at extortionate rents. He had a network of agents, middlemen and rent-collectors running his empire,

Gypsy in Blenheim Crescent, 1970

which extended to gambling and night-clubs, and was a very difficult man to pin down.

In 1957, a new Rent Act was passed, removing the upper limit on rents that could be charged on furnished proper-ties once any sitting tenants had moved out. The idea was to increase the hous-ing stock available. Instead, it led to landlords such as Rachman forcibly evicting sitting tenants and re-letting properties at vastly inflated prices. In Notting Hill, many of those threatened or forced out of their flats were poor working-class white tenants, who were replaced by homeless West Indians desperate for somewhere to live. A deeply ambiguous character, Rachman championed himself as a 'friend of the coloureds', and it was true that he was one of the few landlords who did not operate a 'No blacks' policy. Also, several who knew him speak of his kindness to old ladies. The whole truth of Rachman's activities was never established, but the word 'Rachmanism' entered the vernacular as a term for the exploitation of slum tenants by unscrupulous landlords.

The rest of the 1960s and 1970s: community action, redevelopment and Carnival

After the infamies of the previous years, the rest of the 1960s and 70s brought further new twists in the area's history. Changes during these decades laid the basis for much of what attracts contemporary visitors to the area: it became truly multicultural, the Carnival injected a large dose of excitement and joy, and Notting Hill began to be fashionable in an offbeat kind of way, as new waves of people moved in.

Community action

After you have finished beating each other up, you still have to live in the same area. People found eventually that they had to live together and love each other. It is a process that people knew should happen. (Ben Bousquet, quoted in Sharon Whetlor, *The Story of Notting Dale*, 1998)

Following the riots there was a considerable amount of rethinking and regrouping in the community. The Methodist Church in Lancaster Road took one of the first initiatives (see p 163). The church already had strong links with the Caribbean and brought in young priests to help organise a truly mixed congregation, welcoming all. It was one of the main instigators of the Notting Hill Social Council, an informal forum involving a wide spectrum of community and social workers, who met to discuss and find solutions to the problems of poor housing, race conflicts and disaffected youth. These developments were part of a wider anti-racist movement that was sweeping the whole country.

Other voluntary organisations that began in the 1960s included the Notting Hill Housing Trust, set up in 1963 by Bruce Kenrick (1920–2007), a Presbyterian minister who went on to start Shelter, a national campaign for the homeless. The Notting Hill Community Workshop developed in the mid-1960s into the Notting Hill Summer Project. Again involving a coalition of churches, local groups and volunteers, the project organised a housing survey. Its findings produced depressing echoes of those a century earlier: in some areas 70 per cent of households had only shared, or no access at all, to a bath or shower. The Project also set up three neighbourhood centres and organised adventure playgrounds for children. Although it made a start at tackling social problems, it could not prevent some of the ugliest redevelopments taking place, such as the Lancaster West Estate – buildings epitomising poor planning and design. One of the longest and most successful campaigns to counter the devastation caused by redevelopment was the achievement of low-cost housing for the former squatters of Frestonia (see p 291).

Part and parcel of all this community action was the diversifying population. The spirit of defiance and anarchic optimism that suffused most of these movements was catching and, throughout this time, students, writers, musicians, artists, hippies, social workers and political activists began to move in, further attracted by the cosmopolitan atmosphere. Notting Hill was finally becoming fashionable again.

Carnival: pageant, symbol, ritual of resistance?

The 1960s was the heyday of Caribbean street and night life, centred on local clubs and bars, such as Frank Critchlow's Rio Café, and on the many informal meeting places in the Hill, the Dale and the Grove. From the early Sixties onwards, the August bank holiday Carnival came to symbolise the joie de vivre embodied in West Indian culture. From small beginnings as far back as the late Fifties, the Carnival had developed by the end of the Sixties into one of the largest outdoor celebrations on the calendar, attracting participants from far beyond the immediate community. Outsiders were largely made welcome and joined in the dance. (One of this writer's finest memories is of sheltering under the Westway during Carnival in 1972 and joining in an impromptu calypso, 'Rain Won't Stop the Carnival!')

But at the same time that outsiders were being attracted to all the fun of the Carnival, storm clouds were again beginning to gather round the community that gave it life. During the late Sixties, many of the areas where the Caribbean population had been concentrated were being pulled down and rebuilt, and the people were dispersing to more distant suburbs. Meanwhile, the sprawling street life began to shrink to a few islands. In this context, as Mike Phillips and Trevor Phillips point out in *Windrush*, for those who flocked in from the suburbs to take part in the processions, the Carnival became 'a symbol of the West Indians' continuing presence in the spot haunted by so many memories; and from all over West London they came to stage a re-creation of the legends of the Hill, the Dale and the Grove'.

Carnival had also become a symbol for the police, one of urban exuberance and disorder: something they did not control. Throughout the 1970s relations between the black community and the police went from bad to worse. In an example of policing gone mad, they launched a massive attack on inner-city crime, for which special units (the Special Patrol Groups) were deployed and equipped with a particular power – to charge 'a suspected person loitering with intent to commit an offence'. This application of the Vagrancy Act of 1824 became known as the Sus laws, under which black people and especially black youths were targeted in what amounted to a witch-hunt.

The Carnival provided the most dramatic example of over-policing. Until 1976, despite ever-growing crowds, it was a peaceful occasion, but the police wanted it banned. When this failed, they mobilised 1500 to police the event, fighting broke out and 500 were injured. By the following August, the Carnival had become a 'Public Order' issue listed under the category 'Demonstrations' in the Police Commissioner's report. Ensuing years saw the Carnival become a focus for provocation, counter-provocation and violence, until 1981, when the number of police officers deployed had risen to 13,000. That year marked a watershed, as riots in protest at police discrimination against black people erupted throughout the country. A wholesale reassessment of police practices was put into motion and, although it was never quite the same again, the Carnival was re-established as an occasion for fun.

The 1990s

By the late 1990s much had changed since the heady days of the 1960s and 70s. In All Saints Road and Westbourne Grove, 'blues' gave way to boutiques and upmarket restaurants, shebeens were replaced by chi-chi cafés and delicatessens and a halfway house for the homeless was turned into a fashionable hotel. Large, impersonal chains were beginning to take over quirky old shops and public houses, and mansion blocks in places like Powis Square were finally being occupied by the kind of people for which they were originally designed: the rich, the fashionable, professionals.

Although the ghosts of Reverend Walker and his colleagues might well have welcomed some of these changes, many locals felt the sense of foreboding expressed by Rosalind Da Costa below. Yet the market was thriving and community action was still a key element of the area. Long-established secular and church organisations continued to flourish, joined by others to meet changing needs, and most of the local facilities were still in place.

The new millennium

Now it's THE place to live in I dread the future! Two tiny words that are worth millions:West Eleven … We have nothing against new residents and the natural progress of evolution but if people do not like to live among the working-class folk then please leave. We will not change for you nor alter our beloved Portobello. (Rosalind Da Costa, 2000)

Lost Office: For Notting Hill P O, Westbourne Grove, London W11 (1908–2004)

Dear Government Postal System: —
          Why paint your mouth that pillarbox red
          If you don't want our letters popped in?

Time was, all post could be addressed
          With some degree of confidence
          Royal Mail would deliver it to its haven.

But now in the Whizzdom of its wilful degradation
It's Post Office Limited's own bum administration
That sinks the heart, head and lifeblood of our nation
          By ponceing on the cancer of commercialisation

— For this flower'd Grove's Crown jewel since 1908
Is one of hundreds being axed, for the routine dross-market fate
Of yet another multisquillion scoop for real-estate
Sharks
          (though wiser humans might, like dolphins, rather wait
          and count the ways to save such friendly arks, than wreck them
          with such indigestible and eco-fruitless force):

— Here's barking at you, for dumping thus our prime community resource
          With such base grovelling to Mammon's ruthless course
— Unless — post haste, you heal the waste, reopen —Yea! restore
Good public service as of yore, switch on again those lights — our mainstay
          In the fight — to feed real need, stamp out greed — to redeem
          And transact again your — and our — most essential daily rights.

Michael Horovitz
(pp countless long-suffering Post Office Losers)

Michael Horovitz is not alone in mourning the loss of Westbourne Grove's main post office, situated opposite the Turquoise Island (p 102). Since over 8000 residents campaigned unsuccessfully to retain it, this once busy resource has remained empty and unused for the best

Michael Horovitz outside the closed post office in Westbourne Grove

part of three years. And it's not only the post offices that are closing. Other disappearing amenities include three public toilets, including one of the most visited, in Talbot Road.

So was Rosalind Da Costa right to dread the future? Probably yes. Things have moved on rapidly over the last six years, and, as far as the local population are concerned, not for the better. In preparing this new edition, the most disheartening task has been updating the listings.

Independent shops, services, businesses and restaurants are falling like dominoes throughout the area, unable to keep up with rising rents. Most of the antique shops and galleries around Westbourne Grove have given way to the

CLONE TOWN SYNDROME

Richly reflected in this book are Notting Hill's flexibility, diversity and sense of community. All are now challenged by their antithesis: the clone town syndrome. This term was adopted by the New Economics Foundation, an independent 'think-and-do' tank founded in 1986 as an alternative to the G8 summit. In a 2005 report it describes how throughout the country high streets are becoming monochrome strips of global and national chains, easily mistaken for each other.

Forty-eight per cent of London 'villages' have been thus affected and Notting Hill is under threat. The cycle is simple: rapid and dramatic rent rises force established local small traders out, in favour of the usual suspects (Starbucks, McDonald's, Next, Gap and Pret a Manger, to name a few) and estate agents multiply. Rents rise further, making it almost impossible for new small traders to establish a foothold, further clones claim the space and the income they generate flows back to their headquarters instead of into the community.

likes of Joseph, Whistles and LK Bennett, the once famous 192 has become a pizzeria and the building that housed Culture Shack and the Grove Café on Portobello is set to become luxury flats. Eagerness to hike rents is not restricted to commercial landlords. A small art gallery was forced to close when its rent was raised from £45,000 to £110,000 a year. The landlord was the Octavia Hill housing association, whose directors explained that they were only seeking to maximise market value (Octavia Hill will be rolling in her grave).

Location, location, location

This phrase must make the heart sink of anyone wanting to establish a foothold in the area. It was first coined by Harold Samuel (later Lord Samuel of Wych Cross), founder of Land Securities, the leading property development company in the UK and champion of the retail park. The company has now set its sights on Notting Hill Gate. In a joint venture with Delancey and in the guise of the Metro Shopping Fund, Land Securities has recently acquired 98,000 sq ft in the cluster of buildings near to Notting Hill Gate station, an area that includes 52 shops and restaurants, three office premises, an educational institution and the Coronet cinema. The company prides itself on its policies of property consolidation and estate rationalisation, and in order to make 'a positive impact on whole areas' it always looks to 'develop blocks of retail premises, rather than scattered individual properties'. For this, one can read that its mission is to rip out old shop fronts and interiors to replace them with shopping malls and spaces affording a rationalised retail experience. For those who like variety, the future for this already beleaguered stretch of high street looks bleak.

A similar fate is looming over Portobello Road, in this case led by a company called UK Investments. The market has already been badly affected by competition from supermarkets and convenience stores. If more clones move in, with their uniform façades, demanding a de-cluttering of the pavements outside, the market is likely to diminish further. Markets are all about clutter: individual traders might fiercely resist being 'rationalised', but they have little power.

The role of the Royal Borough of Kensington & Chelsea

In a BBC interview the councillor in charge of development and regeneration commented:

One of the problems is that virtually all of the businesses are privately owned and we have no power to stop anyone selling to whomever they want. Of course we want shops for local people and to keep the character of the market. But there's a misconception that the council can just stop development, and that's not true.

FRIENDS OF PORTOBELLO

In 2005 a group of traders and locals set up Friends of Portobello. United by a commitment to preserve Portobello's distinctive and dynamic atmosphere, the group aims to have the road redesignated as Britain's first Business Conservation Zone. If building and nature conservation zones make sense, why not zones for protecting sole traders and helping to maintain local community and culture? This has been done in Paris. Specifically, Friends of Portobello would like each shop on the road to keep its unique frontage, to prevent shops being knocked together into one, for shops to be primarily for sole-trader retail and for the stalls to remain the prime focus of the market. They constantly battle against rent reviews. In short they aim to halt the march of the clone town syndrome.

One tactic is to talk to property developers and the Council. The group is consulted under the Local Development Framework, a consultation forum where a wide range of people are able to suggest what they want to include in the planning guidelines over the next 10 years. Also important is lobbying local support and, above all, getting people involved. As Tim Burke of the group puts it, 'The key to successful activism is to make a boring issue interesting by using imagination.' The Friends have already had results: it was partly thanks to their pressure that a plan to transform the site of Woolworth's into an extensive retail development was blocked, and they were instrumental in getting the **Evening Standard's** Small Shops campaign under way. There's also a campaign to reopen the public toilet in Talbot Road. For more information see www.friendsofportobello.com.

The council only owns 107 retail outlets in the borough, and most of its property is in North Kensington and Chelsea. On its own land it practices a fair rent policy, and tries to ensure that properties are let out to independent retailers providing for local needs, ie butchers, bakers, fishmongers, grocers, etc. This policy does not always work. One shop was let out to a fishmonger but lack of local support for fresh fish led to the enterprise failing.

A recent development has been the setting up by the council of an independent Commission on Retail Conservation Areas headed by Sir Terence Conran. The commission's brief is to advise and engage others in debate as to how to get the retail balance right. At a national level, as this is being written, Conservative MP Nick Hurd is presenting a Sustainable Communities Bill to Parliament, which, if it goes through, will urge the Government to give more real power to local councils.

The new giant on the doorstep: Westfield

Visitors studying their map will see a white area beside the Westway in White City with the word 'depot' at its centre. This white section signifies what is called a brownfield site (sinisterly defined as 'land which may or may not be contaminated'); it covers 40 acres and has been derelict for over 20 years. The depot marks the site of a long-disused railway depot. Abutting this large plot is a huge council estate that ranks among England's most deprived neighbourhoods; at another margin it is little more than a stone's throw from the stuccoed mansions of Holland Park.

The cranes have now moved in and all is poised to change. After a great deal of skulduggery, Westfield, the Australian retail giant, won the contract to develop what is promised to be a vast airport-like space containing myriad shops, a food court with 40 restaurants, a 14-screen cinema and valet car parking with space for 45,000 cars. The site is conveniently placed just outside the boundary of the extended London Congestion Charge zone, which came into operation in February 2007.

Speculation (in every sense of the word) is rife, with property prices rising in anticipation. High-class shops are promised, an upmarket retail utopia, but will it turn out to be yet another dystopic mega-mall? Some say it will just cause gridlock in an already congested area and spell disaster for local shops. Others welcome this promised injection of glamour and hope that it will bring new life into a depressed area.

Effects of the Congestion Charge

This charge of £5 on vehicles entering the London Congestion Charge zone (with some exemptions) was introduced in 2003 and covered eight square miles of central London. In 2005 the charge was raised to £8, and in 2007 the zone was extended westwards to include most of the Royal Borough of Kensington & Chelsea. It has encouraged cyclists and is said to have reduced the load of traffic by up to 30 per cent in the areas involved. We are told that public transport has been upped and improved as part of this change.

Visitors may disagree. Moving around London remains a hellish experience. The Congestion Charge is largely hated in the area, mainly for the costs it adds to small businesses, and the western extension is predicted to cause the loss of 6,000 jobs and £236 million in annual revenue. Many see the charge as an infringement of human rights and in true Notting Hill style, a dramatic 'funeral procession' was organised to try and stop the extension. It had no effect. We shall see. It did, after all, take a little time to get the Turnpike Act of 1769 revoked.

End note

The history of Notting Hill has always been a bumpy ride. Writing this in early 2007, the outlook seems gloomy. Crucial now is how the very glamour and trendiness that attract so many visitors threaten to smudge out the area's individuality – those rough, often tough and sometimes ridiculous edges that make it unique.

PART 4

WRITINGS

DAYS IN THE LIFE OF LADY MARY COKE 1767–69

Lady Mary Coke was born on 2 February 1726, the youngest daughter of John, Duke of Argyll and Greenwich. In 1747 she married Edward, Viscount Coke, only son of Thomas, Earl of Leicester. After two years of constant disagreement they separated, after which he died in 1753. A wealthy widow, Lady Mary moved to Notting Hill in 1767, where she took up residence at Aubrey House, close to Holland Park. Nicknamed the 'White Cat' on account of her albino colouring and passion for gossip – the cattier the better – she remained here for 22 years. Apart from court gossip and politics, Lady Mary dearly loved her garden, which in those days extended almost as far as Holland Park Avenue. These interests, together with such familiar topics as disputes with neighbours, vandalism, the ill health of royals, flooding and the inconveniences of having builders in the house, are reflected in these extracts from her letters and journals. Lady Mary remained in Aubrey House until 1788 and died, still a widow, in the Manor House at Chiswick in 1811. She is buried in Henry VII's chapel in Westminster Abbey. The four volumes of her writings from which these extracts are taken were edited by the Hon JA Home and published in 1889–96.

1767

Saturday

The wind continues very high & there has been several showers of rain. I went at ten o'clock to my House. I had appointed a Gentleman that lives in the Neighbourhood, one Mr Phillimore, to come & speak to me. He has a field that comes close up to my garden, which wou'd be very convenient for me to have, & I offer'd him anything he pleased to ask, either to buy it or rent it. His answer was he had let it a long time ago, & he supposed all his estate that lies about here was worth the double what he let it for, but that he never raised his rents, that he was now old, & that everything shou'd go on in the way it had during his time, & that he cou'd not sell it as it was intailed upon his Son, who was under age. I then ask'd if he had any objection to my taking it of his tenant. To this he did not care to make me an answer, but in conclusion said he wou'd think of it & write me word, for he was going farther into the Country for a Month. I then told him I had another favour to beg, that he might Observe there was a tree in his ground that very much interrupted my view, & that I shou'd be much obliged to him if he wou'd cut it down. To this he agreed & said he wou'd order it to be done, & I am not out of hopes of getting the field. His Son that he mentioned had this year a fortune of a hundred thousand pounds left to him. I cou'd not help liking the Old Man, he seemed so disinterested.

1768
Friday

'Tis a very fine day, which makes me impatient to get back to my small retreat, & having no curiosity to learn the news of the Birthday, I am leaving Town without seeing a human being. No losses among my animals, but of one duck. This place looks in greater beauty than you have seen it, notwithstanding the malice of some unknown enemy, who has cut down all the roses & honeysuckles that were planted in my North Walk near the benches even with the ground, & done the same to all the flowers that were in bloom. I wonder they think I have too many pleasures, as they seem desirous of depriving me of all that is in their power. The Plasterers are still in my new rooms, & have fixt their Scaffolds in such a manner that I can't get in to see the situation they are in. I found employment in my garden till it was dark, & then writt & read. It wou'd seem as if I had been amused, for I set up till after one o'clock, not thinking it so late by above an hour. The Gentleman Dove is setting upon one egg, the perverseness of the Lady having occasion'd the breaking of the other; but She is now so ill treated, I forgive & pity her. She seem'd to desire (& I thought very reasonably) to hatch her own egg, but whenever She shew'd that inclination, her Husband used her so ruffly that he has not left her one feather in her tail, & has deprived her of several in her head. She has now very wisely given up the attempt, & I expect the Gentleman to hatch on Sunday or Monday.

1768
Wednesday

'Tis a very fine day. I have all sorts of Workmen about, & am very impatient for the fence in the North Walk being finished; the sheep have broke in again last night & done me more mischief. I hope for you I shall see somebody from Town before the week is ended, otherwise it will be a terrible dull journal. I've heard nothing from Lady Betty Mackenzie since She left Town, & as She did not tell me how to direct to her, I fancy She does not mean I shou'd write. In the Evening we walked on the outside of my grounds into some very pretty fields, which leads us to the back part of Kensington; 'twas warm & pleasant.

Have you ever read Mademoiselle's *Memoires*? You must remember I recommended them to you before you went to Yorkshire, as I'm persuaded they will entertain you better than any other that was wrote at the same period of time. She mentions a circumstance relating to the death of the Queen Mother of England, her Aunt, that I don't recollect having met with anywhere else. She says She was always unhealthy, & that, after her last return to France, She was advised to take pills to make her sleep which succeeded so well that She never waked again. I suppose they put too great a quantity of opium by mistake, for there does not seem the least reason to believe it was intended. Tell Lord Strafford my Servants are very busy making sweetmeats that he may not be without a dessert when he is so good to dine with me, for I despair of ever seeing him at this time of the Year, when, if my garden had not been robbed, I cou'd have given him excellent plumbs of three different kinds; the poor remains are now making into sweetmeats, as they tell me they do mighty well. I have great plenty of apples, & some good pears, but as they are now ripe, I dread a second visit.

Thursday (Sept. 1)
At twelve o'clock it began raining, which continued one hour; 'tis now fair … It did not hold fair above a quarter of an hour, & after the rain began again it never ceased, & about eight o'clock it was with a violence I almost never heard. I don't suppose there cou'd ever fall a greater quantity of rain in the time. My Workmen, when they return'd to Town, could not go by Knightsbridge, the water lay too deep. It continued raining all night.

Friday
When I got up this morning I saw two Rivers, the grounds two or three miles off being all under water, & the Thames made a fine appearance. My Servants tell me two Houses at Knightsbridge have been washed away, & one of the Bridges on the King's road. It has almost carried away all my gravel walks, and my garden is the Picture of desolation.

1769
Friday
'Tis a very pleasant day: I did not pass it in Town. I was here very *early*

& have worked very hard in my garden and have given up Lady Holland's Assembly to finish my Journal, as you was so good to wish to hear from me before you left Boughton. I propose going to Sudbrook on Sunday & I shall call at Kew, tho' I think it is not probable I shall find Lady Charlotte, as I imagine the young Princes will go to Town that day. My best wishes attend Lord Strafford. Pray tell M' Hull, as Soon as it is convenient, I shall be glad to have my Cow.

Saturday

I sow'd a great many flowers before eleven o'clock. 'Till then it was a pleasant day: soon after it rain'd, & has continued ever since. 'Tis now one o'clock. My prospect is much enliven'd by a dozen Women gathering peas in the field joining to my garden: they are so merry, & laugh so excessively that it gave me spirits to hear them, but this abominable rain has drove them out of the field & me out of my garden … The rain is over, & I must go out. The evening made up for the rainy morning; it was quite clear, & I think I never saw the prospect in greater beauty.

CLARENDON ROAD CIRCA 1883

Arthur Machen

Arthur Machen was a writer and specialist in the occult. In 1880, aged 17, he left his native Wales for London, where he lodged for some 18 months in Clarendon Road, near Holland Park. When he wasn't writing, much of his time was spent cataloguing diabolistic and occult books, through which he discovered various secret sects and societies, and joined the Order of the Golden Dawn. Machen is best remembered for his mystical, supernatural tales of evil and horror, among them **The Great God Pan** (1894), **The Three Imposters** (1895) and **The Hill of Dreams** (1907). The extracts below are taken from his autobiography, **Far Off Things**, published in 1922. He died in 1947.

At this time and for the next year and a half I was living in Clarendon Road, Notting Hill Gate – or Holland Park, to give the politer sub-direction. I am sorry to say that I had not a garret, since the houses of that quarter, being comparatively modern, do not possess the sloping roofs which have seen the miseries of so many lettered men. Still, my room had its merits. It was, of course, at the top of the house, and it was much smaller than any monastic 'cell' that I have ever seen. From recollection I should estimate its dimensions as ten feet by five. It held a bed, a washstand, a small table, and one chair; and so it was very fortunate that I had few visitors. Outside, on the landing, I kept my big wooden box with all my possessions – and these not many – in it. And there was a very notable circumstance about this landing. On the wall was suspended, lengthwise, a step-ladder by which one could climb through a trap door to the roof in case of fire, and so between the rungs or steps of this ladder I disposed my library. For anything I know, the books tasted as well thus housed as they did at a later period when I kept them in an eighteenth-century bookcase of noble dark mahogany, behind glass doors. There was no fireplace in my room, and I was often very cold. I would sit in my shabby old great-coat, reading or writing, and if I were writing I would every now and then stand up and warm my hands over the gas-jet, to prevent my fingers getting numb. I remember envying a man very much indeed on a certain night in late winter or early spring. It was a very cold night; there was a bitter north-easter blowing, and the wind seemed to pierce right through my old coat and to set my very bones shivering and aching. I had gone abroad, because I was weary of my den, because I was sick with reading and in no humour for writing, because I felt I must have some change, however slight. But it was an evil and a bitter blast, so I turned back after a little while, coming down one of the steep streets that lead from Notting Hill Gate Station to Clarendon Road. And half-way home I came upon a man encamped on the road by the pavement. He was watching over some barrows and tools and other instruments of street repair, and he sat in a sort of canvas wigwam, well sheltered from the wind that was chilling me to the heart. His coat, too, looked thick and heavy, and he had a warm comforter round his neck, and before him was a glowing, ardent brazier of red-hot coals. He held his hands and his nose over the radiant heat, and smoked a black clay pipe; and I think he had a can of beer beside him. I envied that man with all my heart; I don't think I have ever envied any man so much.

Occasionally I had applications for the loan of a book from my step-ladder library. These came from the lodgers on the ground floor, an

Armenian and his wife, who annoyed the landlady by sleeping in cushions piled about the carpet and hanging their blankets in front of the doors and windows. It was the Armenian lady who had literary tastes, and her desire was always for 'a story-book'. I never saw her or her husband, but I often heard him calling Mary, the servant. He would stand at the top of the kitchen stairs and shout 'Marry! Marry!' and then, reflectively, and after a short interval, 'Damn that girl.' He gave a fine, oriental force to the common English 'damn'. Other lodgers that I remember were a young Greek and a chorus girl, mates for a single summer. They occupied the first floor and were succeeded by a family from Ireland. I have a confused notion that there was something a little queer about the head of this household. He was, I think, a major and I know he was Evangelical. As I went down the stairs I heard him more than once muttering in loud, earnest tones the words 'Let us pray.' This was startling; and one of his daughters would always shut the door of their room with a bang on these occasions, and that was startling, too.

The little table in my little room turned out to be a very useful piece of furniture. I not only read at it and wrote on it, but I used it as a larder. In the corner nearest the angle of the wall by the window I kept my provisions, that is to say, a loaf of bread and a canister of green tea. Morning and evening the landlady or 'Marry' would bring me up a tray on which were a plate, a knife, a teapot and a spirit lamp, which came, I think, from under that serviceable table – one may fairly say from the cellar – I made the hot water to boil and brewed a great pot of strong green tea …

As the spring of 1883 advanced, and the weather improved and the evenings lengthened, I began the habit of rambling abroad in the hope of finding something that could be called country. I would sometimes pursue Clarendon Road northward and get into all sorts of regions of which I never had any clear notion. They are obscure to me now, and a sort of nightmare. I see myself getting terribly entangled with a canal which seemed to cross my path in a manner contrary to the laws of reason. I turn a corner and am confronted with an awful cemetery, a terrible city of white gravestones and shattered marble pillars and granite urns, and every sort of horrid heathenry. This, I suppose, must have been Kensal Green: it added new terror to death. I think I came upon Kensal Green again and again; it was like the Malay, an enemy for months. I would break off by way of Portobello Road and entangle myself in Notting Hill, and presently I would come upon the goblin city; I might wander into the Harrow Road, but at last the ghost-stones would appal me. Maida Vale was treacherous, Paddington false – inevitably, it seemed, my path led me to the detested habitation of the dead.

THE NAPOLEON OF NOTTING HILL

GK Chesterton

Gilbert Keith Chesterton became a professional writer in his twenties when he made his name in journalism, 'the easiest of all professions'. He was principally a reviewer and essayist. Among the newspapers he regularly contributed to was the **Daily News**, founded by Charles Dickens. **The Napoleon of Notting Hill** (1904), a bizarre fantasy set at the end of the twentieth century, was his first novel. The main protagonists are Auberon Quin (the King) and Adam Wayne, Provost of Notting Hill and the Napoleon of the title. Inspired by the waterworks tower that once dominated Campden Hill, it is a comic, bellicose and somewhat confusing tale of a small community resisting destruction by the march of progress and modernity. Chesterton went on to write many other novels, as well as verse, literary criticism and his **Autobiography** (1936), from which the first of these two passages is taken. He became a Roman Catholic in 1922 and died 12 years later at the age of 62.

I was one day wandering about the streets in part of North Kensington, telling myself stories of feudal sallies and sieges, in the manner of Walter Scott, and vaguely trying to apply them to the wilderness of bricks and mortar around me. I felt that London was already too large and loose a thing to be a city in the sense of a citadel. It seemed to me even larger and looser than the British Empire. And something irrationally arrested and pleased my eye about the look of one small block of little lighted shops, and I amused myself with the supposition that these alone were to be preserved and defended, like a hamlet in a desert. I found it quite exciting to count them and perceive that they contained the essentials of a civilisation, a chemist's shop, a bookshop, a provision merchant for food and a public house for drink. Lastly, to my great delight, there was also an old curiosity shop bristling with swords and halberds; manifestly intended to arm the guard that was to fight for the sacred street. I wondered vaguely what they would attack or whither they would advance. And looking up, I saw grey with distance, but still seemingly immense in altitude, the tower of the Waterworks close to the street where I was born. It suddenly occurred to me that capturing the Waterworks might really mean the military stroke of flooding the valley; and with that torrent and cataract of visionary waters, the first fantastic notion of a tale called *The Napoleon of Notting Hill* rushed over my mind.

Extract from *The Napoleon of Notting Hill*

'My God in Heaven!' he said; 'is it possible that there is within the four seas of Britain a man who takes Notting Hill seriously?'

'And my God in Heaven!' said Wayne passionately; 'is it possible that there is within the four seas of Britain a man who does not take it seriously?'

The King said nothing, but merely went back up the steps of the dais, like a man dazed. He fell back in his chair again and kicked his heels.

'If this sort of thing is to go on', he said weakly, 'I shall begin to doubt the superiority of art to life. In Heaven's name, do not play with me. Do you really mean that you are – God help me! – a Notting Hill patriot – that you are ...'

Wayne made a violent gesture, and the King soothed him wildly.

'All right – all right – I see you are; but let me take it in. You do really propose to fight these modern improvers with their boards and inspectors and surveyors and all the rest of it –'

'Are they so terrible?' asked Wayne, scornfully.

The King continued to stare at him as if he were a human curiosity.

'And I suppose', he said, 'that you think that the dentists and small tradesmen and maiden ladies who inhabit Notting Hill, will rally with war-hymns to your standard?'

'If they have blood they will,' said the Provost.

'And I suppose,' said the King, with his head back among the cushions, 'that it never crossed your mind that' – his voice seemed to lose itself luxuriantly – 'never crossed your mind that anyone ever thought that the idea of a Notting Hill idealism was – er – slightly – slightly ridiculous.'

'Of course they think so,' said Wayne. 'What was the meaning of mocking the prophets?'

'Where?' asked the King, leaning forward. 'Where in Heaven's name did you get this miraculously inane idea?'

'You have been my tutor, Sire,' said the Provost, 'in all that is high and honourable.'

'Eh?' said the King.

ALL DONE FROM MEMORY

Osbert Lancaster

Sir Osbert Lancaster (1908–1986), artist and writer, was best known as a cartoonist on the **Daily Express** from 1939. He also designed stage sets for several theatrical productions and wrote many books, including two volumes of autobiography, **All Done from Memory** (1963) and **With an Eye to the Future** (1967). The following extract from the first volume tells of his childhood around Notting Hill.

In my subconscious eagerness to prolong my evening stroll, I must have walked right through the haunted district I had set out to explore and emerged into the once familiar playground of my childhood on the slopes of Notting Hill. The fact that I had done so all unawares, that I had passed the formerly so firmly established boundary line without for a moment realising it, spoke far more clearly of what had happened here in the last thirty years than could many volumes of social history. As I walked on up the hill, regardless for once of a flying-bomb now following the course of Ladbroke Grove seemingly only just above the chimney-pots, I noticed with a certain proprietary satisfaction that the progress of decay had not been halted at Elgin Crescent; that the squares and terraces that had once formed the very Acropolis of Edwardian propriety grouped round the church had suffered a hardly less severe decline. Some of the most obvious signs of degradation were certainly the result of five years of war and common to all parts of London, but here this enforced neglect was clearly but a temporary acceleration of a continuous process. The vast stucco palaces of Kensington Park Road and the adjoining streets had long ago been converted into self-contained flats where an ever-increasing stream of refugees from every part of the once civilised world had found improvised homes, like the dark-age troglodytes who sheltered in the galleries and boxes of the Colosseum. Long, long before the outbreak of war these classical façades had already ceased to bear any relevance to the life that was lived behind them; the eminent K.C.s and the Masters of City Companies had already given place to Viennese professors and Indian students and bed-sitter business girls years before the first siren sounded. And yet I who was only on the threshold of middle-age could clearly remember the days when they flourished in all their intended glory. At that house on the corner I used to go to dancing classes; outside that imposing front-door I had watched the carriages setting down for a reception; and in that now denuded garden I had once played hide and seek.

'Take me back to dear old Shepherd's Bush'

I was born in the eighth year of the reign of King Edward the Seventh in the parish of St John's, Notting Hill. At that time Elgin Crescent, the actual scene of this event, was situated on the Marches of respectability. Up the hill to the south, tree-shaded and freshly stuccoed, stretched the squares and terraces of the last great stronghold of Victorian propriety: below to the north lay the courts and alleys of Notting Dale, through which, so my nurse terrifyingly assured me, policemen could only proceed in pairs.

The Crescent, like all border districts, was distinguished by a certain colourful mixture in its inhabitants, lacking in the more securely sheltered central area, grouped in this case round the church. While residence there was socially approved and no traces of 'slumminess' were as yet apparent, there did cling to it a slight whiff of Bohemianism from which Kensington Park Road, for instance, was quite free. Of the residents several were connected with the Stage, and some were foreign, but neither group carried these eccentricities to excessive lengths. Among the former were numbered a Mr Maskelyne (or was it a Mr Devant?) who lived on the corner, and, right next door to us, the talented authoress of *Where the Rainbow Ends*, whose daughter, a dashing hobble-skirted croquet-player, remains a vivid memory. The foreigners included some Japanese diplomats and a German family connected with the Embassy, whose son, a fair, chinless youth, was always at great pains to model his appearance on that of the Crown Prince Wilhelm, much to the delight of my father whom a long residence in Berlin had rendered expert in detecting the subtlest nuances of this elaborate masquerade. Fortunately my parents' arrival at Number 79 had done much to erase the principal blot on the fair name of the street, as our house had previously been the home of no less equivocal a figure than Madame Blavatsky.

Number 79 was a semi-detached stucco residence on three floors and a basement with a pillared porch, not differing stylistically in any way from the prevailing classicism of the neighbourhood. At the back was a small private garden opening into the large garden common to all the occupants of the south side of Elgin Crescent and the north side of Lansdowne Road. Such communal gardens, which are among the most attractive features of Victorian town-planning, are not uncommon in the residential districts of West London, but are carried to the highest point of their development in the Ladbroke estate. This area, which was laid out after the closure of the race-course that for a brief period encircled the summit of the hill, represents the last rational, unselfconscious piece of urban development in London. It was unfortunately dogged by misfortune, and the socially ambitious intention of Allom, the architect, and the promoters was largely defeated by the proximity of an existing pottery slum in Notting Dale, which received, just at the time the scheme was being launched, an enormous and deplorable influx of Irish labourers working on the Great Western Railway.

How different it all was in the years before 1914! Then the stucco, creamy and bright, gleamed softly beneath what seems in reminiscence to have been a perpetually cloudless sky. Geraniums in urns flanked each brass-enriched front door, while over the area railings moustachioed policemen made love to buxom cooks. And in every street there hung, all summer long, the heavy scent of limes.

NOTTING HILL IN WARTIME

Vere Hodgson

Winifred Vere Hodgson was born in 1901 and lived in Notting Hill – first at No. 56, then 79 Ladbroke Road – during the Second World War, when she kept a daily record of events, primarily for her cousin Lucy in Rhodesia. She described herself as a diarist of 'ordinary rather than extraordinary people' and was a keen philanthropist, attached to a community known as the Sanctuary, at 3 Lansdowne Road. Before the welfare state, many Notting Hill families came here with their troubles. The following extracts are taken from **Few Eggs and No Oranges** (1971, reprinted 2003). She died in 1979.

Thursday 26th September 1940
On investigation in the morning, we discovered a house in Lansdowne Rd., nine doors from us, was gone inside. The walls were standing, but it was burnt-out inside. Walked to Clarendon Cross. Every pane of glass had gone, and several houses down. A pretty bad night! It does not bear enquiring into too much! There seems no end to it. Our incendiary had put itself out against the Rockery.

Wednesday 9th October 1940
Quiet for the rest of the night. All clear at 6.45. But I heard the news of last night round here. Five houses were struck at the far end of Lansdowne Road. No wonder we felt it. Some people saved – others buried. All round Oxford and Cambridge Gardens, and Ladbroke Grove Station – houses and shops were down. Also Pembridge Place and Chepstow Villas. Mr Booker [owner of the Mercury café] told us the story of two men who were told by a policeman to take cover. They walked on – and were terribly injured. First Aid Parties had to turn out and face the bomb through their foolhardiness.

Thursday 10th October 1940
Went to see the houses in Lansdowne Road that caught it. Just heaps of rubble … several people killed. It is nearer Auntie Nell's flat than this house … right on the corner of Ladbroke Grove – a stone throw from Stanley Gardens. It is 9 o'clock. A nasty sound is getting nearer …

Tuesday 11th March 1941

Out early in Notting Hill this morning a little girl stopped me. She asked me to take her across the road, which I did. I enquired where she was going. It appeared to school – but had never been alone before. She did not know if it was this way – or, pointing in the opposite direction, the other. Here was a conundrum. She was about seven, the dearest little thing. It was her birthday, she said, and she was to have a party, and she had received five picture postcards. The School was called The Fox School, she explained. We went hand in hand to the ironmonger and consulted him. Yes, it was in Kensington Place and was probably bombed. With this information we set off for Church St. There we met a policeman and told him the story. He looked at me and I at him … we both had the same thoughts. She cheerfully set off hand in hand with him, doubtless explaining in fuller detail her birthday and why Mother was not able to take her to school as usual. I have never forgotten her. At the Mercury arrived the Doctor's secretary whom Mr Booker had helped to dig out. We were amazed to see her. She said she still felt awful, but described to us her sensations as the first two bombs came down and knew in her bones that the third would strike her home. She had the presence of mind to turn off the gas. She was in a basement and it dropped in the garden. When she came to she found herself a prisoner. She could see a window, but both doors were jammed. She shouted for help, and a woman came out of the Mews near, and called all right. Then the wardens broke the windows and dragged her out. The others were buried deeper and it took some hours to release them. This woman was cold and I brought her down to the Sanctuary, found her a nice coat, suit and dress. We had no suitable underclothing, but I know others would help. She had a talk with Miss M and went away much cheered. It is considered a landmine exploded in the air over Holland Park on that awful night. That is why I thought the roof was off, and accounts for the terrible roaring. It is the only theory that accounts for the blast breaking so many windows in Shepherds Bush. Indeed we had a lucky escape.

Wednesday 12th

Miss Linde has taken refuge here with her two dogs! There were 38 bombs on Kensington last Saturday night, she says, during two hours

… in addition to the landmine. No wonder we were kept diving under the table. Mr Major, head Warden on Campden Hill, is very badly injured. He fell into a bomb crater, broke his arm and is paralysed from the waist. Saw the secretary again. She has worked twenty years for the same doctor, and mercifully had put all his records in the refrigerator. Hopes they are safe. She looked as if shock was beginning to tell.

Walked along to Kensington Place. It is a mess. All the little houses have been struck in one way or another. Kit Sauvary had lunch at the Mercury with me. They are nursing a casualty from Church St. They had terrible cases from Hendon. One man lay there for five days before he was claimed – he died eventually.

Thursday 25th June 1942
There was a bomb at 72 Ladbroke Road. I knew just the house. Mrs Beck had to find the bomb – which was said to be at the back. A very large house – eventually it was found in basement. We got the pump going quickly, the Warden said. I was first on the nozzle, then went to fill buckets. I had seen a notice on a door: 'Baths full on first floor'. So I rushed there, but a pond had been found in the garden. Bomb extinguished and we reported back to Lansdowne House. A further fire was reported at 181 Ladbroke Road.

Sunday 5th September 1943
Walked back with a lady and daughter. The mother was a Florentine! Daughter on industrial welfare work but began the canteen at Holland Park Tube station during the blitz. Was there every night, and well remembers the occasion in October 1940, when the bomb skimmed our roof and nearly fell on the hundreds in the Tube station. Lots rushed into the street.

Sunday 6th February 1944
Oranges in N. Hill Gate, but so far have not achieved any. Long queues at the Old Pole's. He never knows when they are coming.

Wednesday 17th January 1945
Oranges in Notting Hill today. Not unpacked, but I could return. I spread the good news. We have a Disagreeable Greengrocer round

SUNNY NAPOLI

Colin MacInnes

Colin MacInnes was born in 1914. He spent some of his childhood in Australia and on his return to England went to art school for a time before embarking on a career as a writer and journalist. He is best remembered for his novels of teenage and black immigrant culture, **City of Spades** (1957) and **Absolute Beginners** (1959), which ends with a vivid description of the Notting Hill riots of 1958. For many years MacInnes lived in the area he affectionately described as 'Napoli', and was a familiar figure in the club and coffee-bar life of the 1950s and 60s. He died in 1976. The following extract has been selected from **Absolute Beginners**.

I'd like to explain this district where I live, because it's quite a curiosity, being one of the few that's got left behind by the Welfare era and the Property-owning whatsit, both of them, and is, in fact, nothing more than a stagnating slum. It's dying, this bit of London, and that's the most important thing to remember about what goes on there. To the north of it, there run, in parallel, the Harrow road I've mentioned, which you'd hurry through even if you were in a car, and a canal, called the Grand Union, that nothing floats on except cats and contraceptives, and the main railway track that takes you from London to the swede counties of the West of England. These three escape routes, which are all at different heights and levels, cut across one another at different points, making crazy little islands of slum habitation shut off from the world by concrete precipices, and linked by metal bridges. I need hardly mention that on this north side there's a hospital, a gas-works with enough juice for the whole population of the kingdom to commit suicide, and a very ancient cemetery with the pretty country name of Kensal Green.

On the east side, still in the w.10 bit, there's another railway, and a park with a name only Satan in all his splendour could have thought up, namely Wormwood Scrubs, which has a prison near it, and another hospital, and a sports arena, and the new telly barracks of the BBC, and with a long, lean road called Latimer road which I particularly want you to remember, because out of this road, like horrible tits dangling from a lean old sow, there hang a whole festoon of what I think must really be the sinisterest highways in our city, well, just listen to their names: 'Blechynden, Silchester, Walmer, Testerton and Bramley – can't you just smell them, as you hurry to get through the cats-cradle of these blocks? In this part, the houses are old Victorian lower-middle tumble-down, built I dare say for grocers and bank clerks and horse-omnibus inspectors who've died and gone and their descendants evacuated to the outer suburbs, but these houses live on like shells, and there's only one thing to do with them, absolutely one, which is to pull them down till not a one's left standing up.

On the south side of this area, down by the w.ll, things are a little different, but in a way that somehow makes them worse, and that is, owing to a freak of fortune, and some smart work by the estate agents too, I shouldn't be surprised, there are one or two sections that are positively posh: not *fashionable*, mind you, but quite graded, with their big back gardens and that absolute silence which in London is the top sign of a respectable location. You walk about in these bits, adjusting your tie and looking down to see if your shoes are shining, when – wham! suddenly you're back in the slum area again – honest, it's really startling, like where the river joins on to the shore, two quite different creations of dame nature, cheek by thing.

Over towards the west, the frontiers aren't quite as definite, and the whole area merges into a drab and shady and semi-respectable part called Bayswater, which I would rather lie in my coffin, please believe me, than spend a night in, were it not for Suze, who's shacked up there. No! Give me our London Napoli I've been describing, with its railway scenery, and crescents that were meant to twist elegantly but now look as if they're lurching high, and huge houses too tall for their width cut up into twenty flatlets, and front facades that it never pays anyone to paint, and broken milk bottles *everywhere* scattering the cracked asphalt roads like snow, and cars parked in the streets looking as if they're stolen or abandoned, and a strange number of male urinals tucked away such as you find nowhere else in London, and red curtains, somehow, in all the windows, and diarrhoea-coloured street lighting – man, I tell you, you've only got to be there for a minute to know there's something radically wrong.

Across this whole mess there cuts, diagonally, yet another railway, that rides high above this slum property like a scenic railway at a fair. Boy, if you want to admire our wonderful old capital city, you should take a ride on this track some time! And just where this railway is slung over the big central road that cuts across the area north to south, there's a hole, a dip, a pocket, a really unhappy valley which, according to my learned Dad, was formerly at one time a great non-agricultural marsh. A place of evil, mister. I bet witches lived around it, and a lot still do.

And what about the human population? The answer is, this is the residential doss-house of our city. In plain words, you'd not live in our Napoli if you could live anywhere else. And that is why there are, to the square yard, more boys fresh from the nick, and national refugee minorities, and out-of-business whores, than anywhere else, I should expect, in London town. The kids live in the streets – I mean they have *charge* of them, you have to ask permission to get along them even in a car – the teenage lot are mostly of the Ted variety, the chicks mature so quick there's scarcely such a thing there as a little girl, the men don't talk, glance at you hard, keep moving, and don't stand with their backs to anyone, their women are mostly out of sight, with dishcloths I expect for yashmaks, and there are piles and piles of these dreadful, wasted, negative, shop-soiled kind of *old people* that make you feel it really is a tragedy to grow grey.

You're probably saying well, if you're so cute, kiddo, why do you live in such an area? So now, as a certain evening paper writes it, 'I will tell you.'

One reason is that it's so cheap. I mean, I have a rooted objection to paying rent at all, it should be free like air, and parks, and water. I don't think I'm mean, in fact I know I'm not, but I just can't bear paying more than a bob or two to landlords. But the real reason, as I expect you'll have already guessed, is that, however horrible the area is, you're free there! No one, I repeat it, no one, has ever asked me there what I am, or what I do, or where I came from, or what my social group is, or whether I'm educated or not, and if there's one thing I cannot tolerate in this world, it's nosey questions. And what is more, once the local bandits see you're making out, can earn your living and so forth, they don't swing it on you in the slightest you're a teenage creation – if you have loot, and can look after yourself, they treat you as a man, which is what you are. For instance, *nobody* in the area would ever have treated me like that bank clerk tried to in Belgravia. If you go in anywhere, they take it for granted that you know the scene. If you don't, it's true, they throw you out in pieces, but if you do, they treat you just as one of them.

The room I inhabit in sunny Napoli, which overlooks *both* railways (*and* the foulest row of backyards to be found outside the municipal compost heaps), belongs to an Asian character called Omar, Pakistani, I believe, who's regular as clockwork – in fact, even more so, because clocks are known to stop – and turns up on Saturday mornings, accompanied by two countrymen who act as bodyguards, to collect the rents, and you'd better have yours ready. Because if you haven't, he simply grins his teeth and tells his *fellahin* to pile everything you possess neatly on the outside pavement, be it rain, or snow, or mulligatawny fog. And if you've locked the door, it means absolutely nothing to him to smash it down, and even if you're in bed, all injured innocence and indignation, he still comes in with his sickly don't mean-a-thing kind of smile. So if you're going to be away, it's best to leave the money with a friend, or better still, pay him, as I do, monthly in advance. And when you do, he takes out a plastic bag on a long chain from a very inner pocket, a tucks the notes away, and says you must have a drink with him some time, but even when I've once or twice met him in a pub, he's never offered it, of course. Also, if you make any complaint *whatever* – I mean, even that the roofs falling in, and the Water cut off – he smiles that same smile and does positively Sweet bugger-all about it. On the other hand, you could invite every whore and cut-throat in the city in for a pail of gin, or give a corpse accommodation for the night on the spare bed, or even set the bloody place on fire, and he wouldn't turn a hair – or turn one if anybody complained to him about you. Not if you paid your rent, that is. In fact, the perfect landlord.

ANNA KAVAN

Virginia Ironside

Virginia Ironside has been a writer and journalist all her life and now has a weekly column on **The Independent** newspaper. She was born in the Royal Borough of Kensington and Chelsea and lived in Notting Hill until the Seventies, when prices forced her into neighbouring Shepherd's Bush, a move from which she has never recovered. As further reading she recommends two books about Anna Kavan: **The Case of Anna Kavan** by David Callard (1992) and **A Stranger on Earth: The Life and Work of Anna Kavan** by Jeremy Reed (2006).

When I was 15 years old, in the late 1950s, I'd go up with my class to play tennis at the Campden Hill courts, just off Church Street in Notting Hill Gate. None of us were any good and I'd always return home to our house in South Kensington with a gloomy headache that used to be cured, oddly, with a spoonful of vinegar.

I hoped I had put those dreadful hot days behind me, until recently I became obsessed with the work of a then little-known writer called Anna Kavan. She wrote of lunatic asylums, feelings of alienation, addiction … her internal loneliness was tangible. Desperate for more information about this fascinating woman who seemed to be describing a place of suffering I knew only too well, I tracked down her biography and was amazed to find that not only had she spent the last half of her life in Notting Hill, just down the road from where I used to live, but that she actually described, in a letter to a friend, the sound of the balls on Campden Hill tennis courts. Had she, I wondered, heard me angrily banging my racket, trying to get the ball over the net so that I could take time off 'looking for it' in the wild undergrowth beyond? Had I perhaps passed her on the pavement as I stomped back home, my satchel bumping furiously on my bottom? I felt even more personally involved with this enigmatic writer, wishing that I'd had a chance to meet her.

Who was this doomed creature, one of only 753 heroin addicts recorded in England in 1964?

Anna Kavan was born in Cannes, on the French Riviera in 1901. Her mother, with whom she had an extremely difficult relationship, was an avid socialite who frequently abandoned her strange only child, first to a wet-nurse, then to nannies and finally to boarding schools in America, France and eventually Malvern Girls' College in England, which she hated. When Anna was 14, her father jumped overboard to his death from a liner bound for South America, leaving her mother in relative poverty. Although, at 19, Anna begged to be allowed to go to Oxford, her mother refused and encouraged her to marry one of her own cast-off lovers, Donald Ferguson, an engineer on the Burmese railways. The couple set off for Mandalay, via Rangoon, and in order to pass the time and relieve the stress of a miserable liaison, she started writing.

After a while, Anna left her young son with her increasingly boorish husband and got divorced. She fell into the company of racing drivers in the south of France and it was they who introduced her to what was to become a life-long addiction to heroin.

It was in the early 1950s that Kavan settled in Notting Hill Gate, first at 8 Kensington Court, then Nos. 27 and 99 Peel Street, until she ended up at 19 Hillsleigh Road, off Holland Park Avenue, in the house where she died. It was a perfect place for her to live: to the south was genteel Kensington, with the department stores and retired upper-class couples taking their walks in Kensington Gardens; to the north was Notting Hill, a run-down area, where recent immigrants from the West Indies struggled to survive in overcrowded, dilapidated housing.

Kavan spotted that this was an up-and-coming part of London, and, with an architect friend, soon formed Kavan Properties, the object of which was to buy, refurbish and sell houses. Topped up by a small allowance, this made enough for her to live as a writer.

Anna Kavan's design sense was remarkably modern. A friend describes how the Notting Hill house was like a Chinese puzzle box, with white walls, polished parquet floors covered with off-white Indian rugs, and electric underfloor heating. Her bed had a canopy over it, and a leopard skin lay draped over the sofa. A portrait of her mother by Vladimir Trechikoff (known for his painting of the green Chinese girl which is reproduced all over the world) hung above the fireplace, alongside a Graham Sutherland and various pictures she had executed herself – hideous pseudo-Picassos featuring raving women with huge, mad eyes.

During her time in Notting Hill, Kavan worked for Cyril Connolly at *Horizon*, the literary magazine; she was described by Anaïs Nin as 'an equal to Kafka'; Doris Lessing admired her, as did JG Ballard and Brian Aldiss, who declared: 'She is de Quincey's heir and Kafka's sister.' Even *The New Yorker* raved over one of her books. She was 'a writer of such chillingly matter-of-fact, unselfpitying vigour that her vision transcends itself', pronounced the reviewer. But despite being one of the most original English women writers of her generation, Anna Kavan never became a household name. True, her writing is not for the faint-heart-ed. Her stories tell of mysterious sanatoriums in which deranged heroes and heroines are incarcerated, of friends who are really spies, of tigers and birds who come to comfort her, of sinister fortresses in which the guards play table-tennis with rats, of a terrifying inner landscape of evil and threat, a landscape that she seemed to inhabit for most of her life. All is arid and destitute, every minute is spent waiting for a reprieve that never comes, or, worse, a punishment. And yet, for anyone who has experienced the merest whisper of true depression or mental illness, her books – with titles like *Let Me Alone, A Scarcity of Love* and *I am Lazarus* – are strangely reassuring. Reading them is like coming across a guide to a country that you thought only you had ever visited. Kavan writes of it with fear, with respect, with elegance, with art and style – and often with black humour. But she writes as a true citizen of that strange interface between reality and hell.

Every day at Hillsleigh Road Kavan wrote for three hours. It was here that she penned *Ice*, the book raved about by science-fiction fans, Brian Aldiss included. Sometimes she would go out to buy books at a now defunct bookshop, Bodkin Books in Notting Hill Gate, or go into town to buy mille-feuilles at Peter Maranca's patisserie in New Compton Street. She was not, of course, your typical heroin addict. She was genteel and never 'let herself go', always dressed immaculately, her platinum hair beautifully set. Even in summer she would often wear a fur coat, being, as addicts so often are, permanently cold.

After the First World War, although illegal, heroin was easily available in London on the black market. Members of fashionable society bought their supplies from a Chinaman, Mr 'Brilliant' Chang, or Lady Frankau, a GP of who it was said 500 heroin addicts depended on, although they often sold her prescriptions on. But Anna Kavan had another person to rely on for her supplies: Dr Theodore Bluth, a psychiatrist who lived around the corner in Campden Street.

Much older than Anna, Dr Bluth was a maverick psychiatrist who had escaped from Germany before the war. He wrote poetry and hammered away on a white piano in his Notting Hill surgery before injecting his patients with a mixture of ox blood and methadone. He persuaded her to register as a heroin addict with the Home Office so that he could supply her, legally, until his death.

They met on one of her many detoxes, though her heart was never in getting off heroin. She saw it as a normalising, cathartic experience, not one to give you a great high – but it could make her behaviour erratic. Once, during dinner at Hillsleigh Road, she hurled a roast pheasant across the table at one of her guests, retiring to her 'bazooka' (her name for her needle) and was found later on her bed reading a novel and eating chocolates.

Dr Bluth's death not only caused Anna intense grief, but it also triggered a huge drug problem. In 1961, the Brain Committee recommended that heroin addicts should attend outpatient clinics to get their fixes. Terrified that she might be forced to undergo compulsory withdrawal, she frantically stockpiled her supplies in her bathroom.

Anna Kavan died of a heart attack in the winter of 1968, on the very evening she was due to attend a Notting Hill party given by her publisher, Peter Owen, to meet her greatest admirer, Anaïs Nin. She was found lying on her bed, her head on the Chinese box in which she kept her drugs. Later, the police admitted that they found in her house enough heroin to 'kill the whole street'.

The garden at Hillsleigh Road was like a Rousseau painting, densely foliated and guarded by such high walls (built by Anna) that the neighbours complained. Kavan's ashes are buried here, at the base of a small tree.

MICHAEL X: VIEWS FROM THE GROVE

John Michell

John Michell was born in 1933 and, taking refuge from various failures and fiascos, in 1965 retreated to his imagination and to live in Notting Hill, where he is still. He has had writing published in **International Times**, 'underground' and small presses and has written more than 20 books, as well as endless pamphlets and pieces of journalism, all in reaction against the narrow outlook of modern education and towards a more complete and satisfying world view. Here Michell writes about Michael X as he remembers him in the 1960s.

There are still many of us around who remember Michael. He was called Michael de Freitas, then took the name Michael Abdul Malik, and in between he became known as Michael X. His heyday in Notting

278 INSIDE NOTTING HILL

Hill was the 1960s, after which his life took a downward turn and in 1975 he was hanged for murder in Trinidad.

When you talk to his old friends around here, you hear very different accounts of Michael. Some of his fellow West Indians despise him as a fraud and a bully, who played the part of black man's champion simply for his own gain and glory. To others he was a great man and a great loss. Terry Radix, for example, who was once Michael's lieutenant (Terry X), speaks admiringly of what he did and tried to do. Another of his closest companions, Capitan, claims that Michael was totally non-violent: 'He was actually a coward; when faced with trouble he would back down.'

My own impression, and that of other friends I have spoken to, is similar to Capitan's. We liked Michael and were made easy by his mild, sympathetic manner. His admirers included William Burroughs, Alex Trocchi, Colin MacInnes, William Levy and other prominent writers of the time. In 1966 he discovered LSD and did his first acid trip. This exposed him to the hippy idealism of the period. Images of peaceful, loving communities entered his mind, competing with the fierce, radical doctrines that his militant followers expected of him.

Michael's life began in 1933 in Trinidad. His absentee father was Portuguese and his mother was a black witch in the voodoo tradition, though officially Roman Catholic. She wanted her son to be like a white boy and discouraged his black playmates. As soon as he could, aged 14, he ran away to sea and spent the next ten years or so voyaging on merchant ships to all parts of the world. He then came to Britain, first to the Tiger Bay area of Cardiff and then into our part of London. In 1959 he married Desiree de Souza, a beautiful young Guyanese woman who remained loyal to him through thick and thin, right up to the end. Their best man at their wedding was Roy Stewart, owner to this day of The Globe, Talbot Road.

The Grove, as it was then called, stretching from Ladbroke Grove eastwards towards Paddington, had never been a fashionable district, and by the end of the war it was partly derelict. Rooms and flats in its crumbling houses were among the cheapest in London. This made it attractive to West Indian immigrants, many of whom have made it their home ever since. In Michael's partly ghost-written autobiography, *From Michael de Freitas to Michael X* (1968), he describes how he settled among them and helped them in their troubles with racist thugs and grasping landlords. It is a fantastical book, full of good anecdotes, but as a record of Michael's career in the Grove it is somewhat unreliable.

In *False Messiah: The Story of Michael X*, Derek Humphry and David Tindall tell a different story – of Michael's mean crimes and vicious cruelties, his deceptions and treacheries, his vain pretensions and ruthless exploitations. They expose the nature of his property dealings in the Grove; while posing as a protector of tenants' rights he betrayed his own people to the notorious landlord Peter Rachman, for whom he extorted rents. Michael's innate depravity, say the authors, was apparent in his childhood when a neighbour prophesied to his mother, 'That boy will end up on the gallows.'

A *Sunday Times* article in 1965 dubbed him Michael X and hailed him as the British successor to the American Black Muslim leader, Malcolm X. Michael accepted the set-up and the duties it imposed upon him, making himself host to black celebrities visiting England, including Martin Luther King, Muhammad Ali, Dick Gregory and Sammy Davis Junior. Fame and respect settled upon him. 'He is a writer of considerable distinction,' claimed William Burroughs. Literary journals published his thoughts and verses, he lectured to the Cambridge Union,

Michael X (left) and friends c. 1970

and he represented Trinidad at a Commonwealth Poetry Conference in Cardiff.

Trouble came when, at a London symposium called Dialectics of Liberation, he shared the platform with Stokely Carmichael, the American Black Power agitator. Always impressionable, Michael was struck by Carmichael's violent, anti-white rhetoric, and he imitated it in a speech to a West Indian group in Reading. Arrested by the police, he became the first person to be convicted under the newly enacted Race Relations laws. After nine months in prison, he turned to community projects, setting up black people's libraries and social centres. This attracted the support of idealistic white people. An eccentric young millionaire, Nigel Samuel, contributed a large property in north London, which Michael named the Black House, and the Lennons, John and Yoko, donated their shorn hair to be auctioned for Michael's benefit.

From the time of his partnership with Nigel Samuel, I saw less of Michael. Exploits I heard of were his trips with Nigel, Trocchi and others to Africa and Asia for talks with third-world leaders. Much of this seemed crazy and there were signs that Michael was cracking up. On his last night in England he came to see me in Powis Terrace, worried and in a dark mood. Charges had been brought against him which compelled him to leave the country and go back to Trinidad. That was the last I saw of him, though we often corresponded, up to and throughout his agonising last months on Death Row. Michael wrote that he was living on a smallholding with Desiree, her four children and a few followers. Dick Gregory and Muhammed Ali both visited this rural commune, and John Lennon arrived with Yoko, staying two days with the Maliks and presenting their children with a piano.

Then came the murders. There is a detailed account of the whole thing in *False Messiah*, and it is gruesome, involving blood-drinking rites and the dark gods of voodoo. The horrors began with a visit from Hakim Jamal, a Black Muslim from Boston, and his doting girlfriend, Gale Benson, daughter of a Conservative MP. Jamal, a weak, excitable character, fell under Michael's spell. Even when Michael determined to sacrifice Gale (his assassins dug a pit in the garden, threw her into it, slashed her with knives and buried her half-alive) he made no move to save her.

The next person to be killed was a young Trinidadian who disobeyed one of Michael's commands. This time, according to the account, Michael himself carried out the execution, slicing up his victim with a cutlass. A few days later another of his followers died in what looked like a drowning accident. Michael disappeared to Guyana where, after seeking refuge in the jungle, he was arrested.

During his 32 months on Death Row in Trinidad's Royal Gaol, Michael always insisted that he was innocent. John and Yoko, faithful to the last, promoted a petition on his behalf, signed by many great names in entertainment, the arts and radical or sexual politics. All was in vain, and when his long wait was over, Michael walked quietly to the gallows. God rest his soul.

John Michell

NOTTING HILL CARNIVAL POEM

Michael Horovitz

Michael Horovitz is a jazz poet, torchbearer-coordinator of Poetry Olympics festivals, and editor-publisher of **New Departures** publications (www.poetryolympics.com). His latest volume of verse, prose and pictures is **A New Waste Land: Timeship Earth at Nillennium** (Bluechrome/New Departures 2007). A long-term resident of Notting Hill, he wrote this poem at the first Carnival, in 1966, which was essentially a summer festival street-party and revival of the pre-war Notting Hill Fayre.

> *A pageant of floating foliage*
> *beating conga drums and dustbin lids*
> *with clarion pipes and wild smoke paint*
> *and fancy dress stirs joy*
> *enough to get*

> policemen even dancing
> up the Grove – O rittum, the rhythm
> joins peace-loving light-
> and dark-skinned hands
> and hearts and heads and bands
> in jumping jubilee –
> grabbing great branches, a shuffling swaying
> triumphal march in glad hurrah – every-
> body do dis t'ing
> – children – all ages
> chorusing – 'We all live
> in a yellow submarine'
> – trumpeting tin bam good-time stomp –
> a sun-smiling wide-open steelpan-chromatic
> neighbourhood party making love not war
> – and the televisions all around
> have closed their electronic eyes
> knocked out by spontaneous reality
> now autumn welcomes you to spring
> in Notting Hill
> where universe collides
> with universe, and still
> nothing gets broken

THE MAGICAL CITY

Jonathan Raban

Jonathan Raban's most recent novel is **Surveillance** (2006). He lives in Seattle with his daughter. He wrote **Soft City** (1974) while living in Earl's Court, from which Notting Hill was a nearby but distinctly foreign land. He lived in North Kensington from 1980 to 1985. The following extracts are taken from 'The Magical City' chapter of **Soft City**.

In Notting Hill Gate in London, or it might be Greenwich Village in New York, the unreasonable city has come to the point where it cannot be ignored by even the civic authorities. The streets around Ladbroke

Grove, with their architecture of white candy stucco, are warrens of eccentric privateness; they are occupied by people who have taken no part in the hypothetical consensus of urban life – the poor, the blacks, the more feckless young living on National Assistance or casual jobs on building sites or bedsitter industries like stringing beads or making candles. The district is notoriously difficult to police: it has a long, twenty-five-year-old record of race-riots, drug arrests, vicious disputes between slum landlords and their tenants, complaints about neighbours, and petty litigation. Like many impoverished areas in big cities, it is picturesque in the sun, and Americans walk the length of the street market in the Portobello Road snapping it with Kodaks; but on dull days one notices the litter, the scabby paint, the stretches of torn wire netting, and the faint smell of joss-sticks competing with the sickly sweet odour of rising damp and rotting plaster. Where the area shows signs of wealth, it is in the typically urban non-productive entrepreneurism of antique shops and stalls. Various hard-up community action groups have left their marks: a locked shack with FREE SHOP spray-gunned on it, and old shoes and sofas piled in heaps around it; a makeshift playground under the arches of the motorway with huge crayon faces drawn on the concrete pillars; slogans in whitewash, from SMASH THE PIGS to KEEP BRITAIN WHITE. The streets are crowded with evident isolates: a pair of nuns in starched habits, a Sikh in a grubby turban, a gang of West Indian youths, all teeth and jawbones, a man in a fedora, greasy Jesus Christs in shiny green suede coats with Red Indian fringes at their hems, limp girls in flaky Moroccan fleeces, macrobiotic devotees with transparent parchment faces, mongrel dogs, bejeaned delivery men, young mothers in cardigans with second-hand prams. These are the urban spacemen, floating alone in capsules of privacy, defying the gravity of the city.

… Notting Hill Gate incorporates a central paradox of city life, in that its nature is as prolific and untameable as anywhere in London, yet for some at least of its inhabitants it has been accommodated to an order so benign as to be cosy.

The messy prolixity of the place makes it a perfect territory for the exercise of natural magic. Its unpredictability, its violent transitions from extreme wealth to extreme poverty, its atmosphere of being crowded out with disconnected loners, its physical characteristics as a maze of narrow streets and irregular crescents, combine to force the individual into a superstitious, speculative relationship with his environment. He cannot, merely by studying the arrangements and amenities of the district, deduce from them who he is, for the answers he would get would be impossibly various. Society in Notting Hill Gate reveals no rationale, no comprehensible structure. The sets of values embodied in it are almost as diverse as the number of people on the streets. If untutored man were to be set down on a tropical island and told to construct a pattern of beliefs and morals from what he saw around him, he could hardly have more difficulty than a newcomer to Notting Hill Gate. It is a place where anything is possible, a nightmare – or paradise, perhaps, for some – of chance and choice.

... Notting Hill Gate is a superstitious place because it seems to exceed rational prescriptions and explanations. On the Portobello Road, one feels oneself growing more insubstantial, less and less able to keep a sense of personal proportion in the crowd of people who all look so much poorer, or richer, or wilder, or more conventional than one is oneself. It is certainly hard to keep in touch with other people in the city; it may sometimes be almost as difficult to keep in touch with one's own self – that diminishing pink blob which rolls and slides like a lost coin in a gutter. The people who float on the tide of metaphysical junk – freaks of all kinds ... into macrobiotics, yoga, astrology, illiterate mysticism, acid, terrible poetry by Leonard Cohen and tiny novels by Richard Brautigan – have managed, at a price. The new folk magic of the streets promises to have some unhappy political consequences but as a way of responding to the city it does reflect a truth about the nature of the place which we had better learn to confront.

The truth is one of an ultimate privacy, in which the self, cosseted and intensified, internalises the world outside and sees the city as a shadow-show of its own impulses and movements. Privacy and reality are profoundly equated, so that what is most real is located in the deepest recesses of the self. The external world turns into an epic movie, supplying details on which to feed one's fantasies; like Disney's *Fantasia* which, when shown in London three years ago, drew crowds of hippies who dosed themselves with acid at selected points in the film. Like

Notting Hill Gate itself, it was perfect trip material and Disney's original intentions were as irrelevant as those of the civic architects who first laid out those streets and crescents.

In this search for the disappearing self, the physical body becomes a central symbol; the stomach, intestines, and organs of reproduction are solemnly attended to, as vessels in which the precious self is contained. In Ceres, the macrobiotic shop on Portobello Road, I bought *Macrobiotics: An Invitation to Health and Happiness* by George Ohsawa:

The kitchen is the studio where life is created ... Knowing that no absolute rules exist, or can be followed forever, we start with principles that are as adaptable to the constantly changing world we inhabit as possible. Only you are the artist who draws the painting of your life... Strictly speaking, no one eats the same food and the same amount even from the same cooking pot. Such recognition of individuality leads us to the fact that we are living by ourselves and we are creating our life by ourselves.

The girls who drift about the store, filling wire baskets with soya beans, miso and wakame seaweed have the dim inwardness of gaze of Elizabeth Siddall in Rossetti's 'Jenny'. In bedsitters in Ladbroke Grove, they create themselves over gas rings, feeding their immaculate insides on harmoniously balanced amounts of yin and yang foods. It is hard to tell whether their beatific expressions come from their convictions of inner virtue or from undernourishment. When they speak, their voices are misty, as if their words had to travel a long way from their inscrutable souls to the naughty outer world. Serious, narcissistic, terrifyingly provident, like all fanatics they brim with latent violence; when they exclude and condemn, they do so with a ringing stridency that smacks more of mothers in Romford and Hornchurch than of Oriental sages preaching doctrines of universal gentleness. 'Oh, man ...' withers its recipient as skilfully as any mean current of suburban disapproval. Their city is a pure and narrow one: they are miniaturists in their talented cultivation of themselves. In her scented room, Annette feeds herself on honey and grape juice and brown rice; she reads haiku by Basho. 'I think that's really beautiful,' she said ... a vague poem, with a horseman and some bullrushes in it, a long way from the things you see at the Gate.

… Playing at being a Red Indian in a bandanna, or an Asian peasant in a tie-dyed sari, or a workman in a boiler suit, is a carefully stage-managed announcement. It trumpets a commonplace city freedom – the freedom to be who you want to be, without bonds of class, nationality, education, occupation, or even sex. It further expresses an allegiance to the irrational, mystical or magical values which the Red Indian, the peasant or the labourer are presumed to possess. The Mohawks and Cherokees of Notting Hill Gate belong among the lofty savages of Fenimore Cooper, not in the downtrodden reservations of the real USA. It is also a homage to 'dressing up'. Grown-ups don't dress up and indulge in make-believe; children do, and the boutique is the industrial equivalent to the Edwardian dressing-up box, that grotto of old wedding dresses, turbans, yashmaks collected by a grandfather on furlough, and clumpy shoes all buckles and straps. There is something of the same coy, schmaltzily 'fetching' little-girlishness in the way the young rig themselves out in their incongruous costumes on the Portobello Road – elderly children smirking complacently under broad-brimmed hats. But they take childhood seriously, more seriously than politics, at least. The tradition of childhood represents their only real foray into history; they see themselves as terrible Blakean infants, or as Wordsworth's boy evading the growing shades of the prison house, or as Alice, wise in her naiveté. To be a child is to be in touch with dark, para-rational, para-urban forces, and to see the equivocations, arrangements and compromises of adulthood as a lunatic charade.

… These people at the Gate have clearly embraced the idea of a magical city. Their clothes, their language, their religious beliefs, their folk art belong to a synthetically reconstructed tribal culture ruled by superstition, totems and taboos. Most of what they have is borrowed, affected and contrived; it reflects a sturdy unoriginality. But perhaps its very tawdriness is a measure of the urgency of the need which has created it. We live in a society in which magic is supposed to have been outlawed or outgrown, in which secular rationalism is presumed to be the standard by which everyone lives. Yet at the same time we have created an environment in which it is exceedingly hard to be rational, in which people are turning to magic as a natural first resort. Television clergymen fondly interpret the evidence of Notting Hill Gate or the box-office returns of *Jesus Christ Superstar* as the first twitches of a spiritual reawakening. That seems, to put it mildly, doubtful. The kind of magic I have been examining is profoundly solipsistic, self-bound, inward. Its very ignorance of plan or creation is its most obvious strength. One would not deduce the existence of God from the Portobello Road; but one might register from it the force of the amoral, the relative, the anarchistic. One might also discover, with shock, one's own isolation, the space-suit of privacy and its attendant rituals, in which one travels in a state of continuous locomotion through the city. Leaning against the spiked railings of the Salvation Army Hall next door to a Woolworths and a Wimpy bar, one could hardly be further away from Plato's city state and its supremely intelligible contractual relationships. The Gate opens not on to the gentle pot-smoking whimsy of Gandalf's Garden, but on a ruined Eden, tangled, exotic and overgrown, where people see signs in scraps of junk and motley. It may look like affectation, a boasting juvenile pretence, but perhaps it is real – a state of natural magic to which the fragmented industrial city unconsciously aspires.

ROCKING UNDER THE WESTWAY

Michael Moorcock

Michael Moorcock was one of the key figures of the so-called counter- culture that flourished in Notting Hill during the 1960s and 70s. A prolific writer, he started producing work about the area in 1965 in the first volume of **The Cornelius Quartet**. Since then he has written more than 70 works of fiction and non-fiction on various subjects. During his many years in Notting Hill Moorcock edited the seminal imaginative fiction magazine **New Worlds**, which was based in Portobello Road, home of much of the underground press. As well as novels, he wrote lyrics and performed as a guitarist with several bands, including Hawkwind and the Blue Oyster Cult. The passage below, reprinted from his rollercoaster tale, **King of the City** (2000), is based on an actual gig that took place under the Westway in 1972. Moorcock lives with his wife Linda in the USA.

As it happened, I didn't meet Julie through Jack. She didn't know I was a relative. She just thought I was cool. I was performing under the motorway, doing a free Saturday lunchtime gig with Nick Lowe, Brinsley Schwarz and a scratch band made up of anyone we could find who could stand up before noon. Basing Street was only round the corner. Half the people we knew did session work there. Some hadn't gone to bed yet. Martin Stone hadn't been to bed for three years. His black beret was twitching on his scalp. He was beyond gaunt. His black little eyes were somewhere in the region of his cortex. He was so skinny you could use him to chop his own lines. He mumbled in a guarded, abstracted monotone. His guitar was getting edgier and edgier. He said warningly that it was all right, he was still warming up.

It was a benefit for Erin Pizzey's Women's Shelter. She was there with her journo husband. She'd only recently started it. Nice dope. Good vibes. Happy audience: youf, rastas, oldsters, hippies, proto-punks, all together. Naturally there were prune-faced ex-colonial protesters with lifted telephones at a couple of distant back windows. The first chord we played, they called the police and complained about the noise. The jollies were only too happy to respond. Call them out on a rape and see how long they took. We opened with a nice fast selection of Nick's best rock-and-roll songs and some ragged Chuck Berry stuff. Then we had to stop and sort ourselves out. As we tuned up, I looked into the audience. I'd never seen so many good-looking women. No-contest stunners. Swedish flower children. American yippies. French ippies. And Julie May, a Saxon virgin, with daisies in her yellow hair, serene and tall in her tie-dyes and a perfect image of the perfect day.

I should also mention the lust. I longed to have my camera with me. To record the moment. It was frustrating. Then Nick's disciplined, insistent rocking guitar put my mind back where it should be. But I played every note for her. Normally I never looked at the audience when I was on stage. My eyes were usually on the middle distance, listening to the others. It was the way I worked. And that day I was, needless to say, also whacked out on the nastiest speed money could find. Wired for sound. I was all over the stage in those days. It's a wonder I didn't spin myself up in the cables and vanish. There's a lot to be said for that really raw yellow Iranian whiz. While it lasted, it was our muse. Our inspiration. Don't say the Ayatollah's all bad. You could say he tried to silence one man, but actually he got an entire generation talking their heads off. The crowd had packed itself into the tiny theatre, made from a motorway bay, and spilled out over the whole of Portobello Green saturated in sunshine. Any time I looked forward I stared directly into her huge blue eyes. And got a godzilla power jolt. She was a Russian Earth Goddess.

Epic Hero v. the Beast! I turned into a spastic maniac. I was helpless. In the grip of a rock-and-roll orgasm, a holistic fit, I was flung back and forth like a Jack Russell's rat. And the way she kept moving closer in to the stage told me she was definitely there for the best reasons. Crouched over my instrument, I must have looked like I was being buggered by the Invisible Man.

If I'd been a pigeon I'd have had my chest puffed and my tail feathers flared. As it was, my hair seemed to be standing upright from my head. Which was blazing with copper fire. My eyebrows itched like scabs. There were suddenly thin red scars all over my fingers. I can remember the riffs, each one a rippling wall of colour, the way the set built and built. Every bone in my body was jumping to a different beat. I was hurting. Solid unrelenting pain. I found chords I never knew existed. My teeth screamed. But I couldn't and wouldn't stop. I never once lost control. My guitar was beginning to make Martin's seem mellow. I was electrocuted by love. Jazzed with the joo-joo juice. People still remember that gig.

The set lasted for over an hour. Then the jolly peelers muscled up with a dog in tow, armed with some garbled by-law to prove we shouldn't be irritating them by having fun for nothing. We dealt with the dogs in the usual way and they were soon running about whining to themselves, but finally the jollies turned off our power and we finished with the traditional chanting and drumming until we all got tired of it and the poor dogs sat down, their eyes and tongues lolling. They never could work out how we sorted their dogs. Always nice to leave a baffled bobby behind you.

Julie came over while we were packing up our gear. I felt her warmth against my cold sweaty back as I turned, pulling off my T-shirt. I winked at her. Friendly. Already intimate. She smiled uncertainly but had that familiar determined stance. This was her day for getting laid. She wasn't going home until it happened. I don't seek out female company just for the sake of it. I like being on my own. So I wasn't seeing anyone else.

I was still technically married to Germaine and living in Colville Terrace, but it was well over. I didn't yet have a drum of my own and Germaine's living room didn't seem the right place for the occasion. So I took Julie with us when we went up to the Princess Louise in Portobello Road. I thought she was foreign at first. The usual score. I thought she was a tourist. Her wide, pink face looked more Slavic than Surrey. Her father must have been that Polish Count she'd sometimes mentioned, who was a friend of her family's in Shepperton. I said she looked like some epic Northern heroine. She laughed and showed me the little bit of coke she'd bought at school. We did it all in the ladies' toilet before going on. It was getting cool and neither of us had much in the way of clothes.

After a while we went down to the Prince of Wales off Portland Road. I had a desperate idea. I was lucky. I scored a couple of half-an'-halfs off Little Ronny and an ounce off Geronimo and caught sight of Germaine who'd just come in with one of her friends. No need to tell her anything. She gave me the keys to the Pink Panther, her van. I didn't like to ask if the mattress was still in it.

The van was parked in a lock-up behind St James's School. A few minutes' hasty walk from the pub. And the mattress was still there, if a bit damp. Julie seemed perfectly happy with it all and took everything for granted. She told me later she'd no idea what was normal.

I apologized. I thought maybe she expected more from a rock-and-roll hero. But she was in heaven. She thought it was romantic. About as far from Shepperton as she could get without a spaceship. It made her gently randy.

It wasn't too much longer before I was engulfed in her slowly relished appetites. She enjoyed it from the first moment. And so did I. I was never a breast man, but those tits and buttocks were primeval. They took me back to the dawn of time, to the long slow pleasures of genesis, spending like mercury. At one point we did a bit of speed and then obsessively rolled enough joints to stone an army. We set the controls on cruise and didn't get up till Tuesday. You're dead right. We were having a better time than you.

Check it out. 10 October 1972. I was almost twenty. Maybe you weren't even here then. A golden age.

THE FREE AND INDEPENDENT REPUBLIC OF FRESTONIA

Nicholas Albery

As Frestonia's erstwhile Minister of State for the Environment, Nicholas Albery (1948–2001) was a key figure in the community protest that followed the initial devastation caused by the building of the Westway. A writer, activist and remarkable social inventor, he edited and co-edited many books, among them: **Poem for the Day** (1994), an anthology of poems worth learning by heart; **Seize the Day** (2001), 366 tips for living; **The Time Out Book of Country Walks** (1997); **The New Natural Death Handbook** (2000); **Alternative Gomera** (1998), a walking guide for La Gomera island near Tenerife; and **The Book of Visions** (1992). He founded several charities including the Natural Death Centre, the Institute for Social Inventions and the Befriending Network. The following account of how Frestonia came to be a free and independent republic is an edited version of the original Frestonia document. Tragically Nicholas died in a car crash only a few days after the publication of the first edition of **Inside Notting Hill**.

The Free and Independent Republic of Frestonia was founded on 27 October 1977.

The residents in Freston Road, Notting Dale, London Wl0, threatened with eviction to make way for a giant factory estate, held a referendum. There was a 95 per cent majority in favour of independence from Great Britain and a 73 per cent majority in favour of joining the Common Market. The following application for membership, complete with coat of arms, was sent to the United Nations, along with its warning that a peace-keeping force might be required.

APPLICATION

Tribal Unity

Our national newspaper is called *The Tribal Messenger* and the motto of our country is 'Nos sumus omnes una familia' ('We are all one family'). In celebration of this desire for unity, every citizen has been granted the honorary surname of 'Bramley'.

Geography of Frestonia

Frestonia is a very small nation, following the precedent of

Luxembourg and Monaco, and the precept of the late Dr Schumacher that 'Small is Beautiful'.

Frestonia is an area of approximately eight acres [later found to be one acre], a distinctly isolated island of near-dereliction surrounded by the West 10 and 11 sectors of London, England.

History

The first residents of the area were pig-keepers who settled here early in the nineteenth century. Later on, when the railways were built, they were joined by Irish brick-makers. The area also developed into a centre of laundry work.

The area was more recently acquired by the Greater London Council (GLC), an organ of the British Government, and by their own confession, the area was allowed by them to deteriorate over the years into a derelict site, with tenants moved out of their homes, the well-established community destroyed, and empty sites of demolished buildings fenced off with corrugated iron and used for dumping rubbish, with half-demolished houses next to people's homes.

The GLC and the British Government thereby demonstrated their lack of concern for the area and their unfitness to remain as its rulers and to plan for its future.

Over the last four years, the present inhabitants of Frestonia moved in and took over the empty houses as caretakers and pioneer home-steaders, and have renovated their homes to a remarkable extent, including putting roofs on houses which lacked roofs. Our architect's report confirms that, if the present period of uncertainty could be ended, it would be possible for the residents to give their buildings a long lease of life – and eventually of course to rebuild.

Two large areas of building rubble have been cleared for open space and horticulture. Greenhouses have been erected and a waterfall created.

Population

Presently the population of permanent residents has climbed to approximately 120, involved mainly in light industrial work within the Frestonian boundaries, although some work abroad. Examples of established and developing light industries in Frestonia include lute-making, weaving, sign-writing and pottery. With industries blossoming all the time, and with more derelict houses yet to renovate, the population will no doubt expand in the future.

Our population and land-mass are both relatively small. There is no international law which requires nations to be of a certain minimum size.

British and GLC imperialism

The GLC announced in 1977, without prior public participation and consultation, that they had put out tenders to lease off the whole area for industrial development. It was left to the Hammersmith Council to produce a belated newsletter explaining these proposals, which was circulated to all residents in Frestonia and to other local residents in the Wll and W10 areas abroad, inviting everyone to a public meeting to discuss these proposals.

At this public meeting on 26 October 1977, at which over 100 local people were present, the unanimous vote was against the GLC's proposals.

Our case is that the GLC and the

Nick Albery and friends at Frestonia

British Government, through a long history of neglect and mismanagement of Frestonia, have forfeited the right to determine the future of the area.

We appeal to the United Nations and ask for our application to be debated by the General Assembly at the earliest possible opportunity; and for the United Nations to recognise the will of the inhabitants of Frestonia and our free decision for independence from Great Britain. We ask that our evident and expressed desire for self-determination, as a tribe and as a people, be respected, and that our existence as a nation state be officially recognised.

294 INSIDE NOTTING HILL

Frestonian Government

Our Frestonian Government is egalitarian and democratic. We have adopted as our National Bill of Rights the United Nations' own Declaration of Human Rights. All major proposals for action are submitted to referenda. All citizens have freedom to do whatever they wish, as long as it does not injuriously conflict with the freedom of another. There will be no conscription or involuntary service.

Government is by a large cabinet of Ministers – a list of the present Ministers of State and their portfolios is appended, as are the names of other government officers and the ambassadors to Frestonia.

Ministers will surrender their portfolios every three months, and roles will be rotated, to allow maximum experience of government to all inhabitants of Frestonia. At any time, ministers can be dismissed by a referendum's majority decision – any citizen is entitled to issue such a referendum.

Frestonia's resources

We realise that for many years still Frestonia will be unable to attain self-sufficiency in food and other requirements – the same is however true of many existing small nations. We shall over the years concentrate on developing our own resources, and we hope that tourism will prove to be a major growth industry. We shall also endeavour to generate our own power supply.

Radio station

We shall also develop our own national radio station, which will in no way interfere with the broadcasts of neighbouring nations.

UN peace-keeping force

We appeal to the United Nations, in particular to other small, emerging and non-aligned nations, to treat our application with the utmost seriousness and urgency. If delay in processing our application occurs, an invasion into Frestonia and eviction by the Greater London Council and other organs of the British Government may occur, in which case there will exist a crisis with international ramifications, and the necessity may arise for Frestonia to require the UN to send a token peace-keeping force. These are developments which we must at all costs avoid.

Referendum

If necessary, we would of course co-operate with a repeat referendum of Frestonian citizens, supervised by the United Nations, which would again reveal the desire of the overwhelming majority of inhabitants for self-determination and independence from Great Britain.

We await your swift reply

Yours faithfully,

David Rappaport-Bramley
Minister of State for Foreign Affairs, on behalf of the Free Independent Republic of Frestonia, 113 St Ann's Road, Frestonia (via London W11, England)

There were 120 residents in Frestonia living in about 30 houses on one acre of land.

Everyone who wanted to take part became a minister; there was no prime minister. The Minister of State for Education was a two-year-old, Francesco Bogina-Bramley, and the Minister of State for Foreign Affairs was a dwarf, the actor David Rappaport Bramley (who wore a T-shirt saying 'Small is Beautiful').

The media descended on Frestonia from around the world. The *Daily Mail* printed a leader column and a report 'from our Foreign Correspondent in Frestonia'. Japanese television filmed New Zealand TV filming nothing much going on in our uneventful communal garden. Coach loads of young tourists, mainly from Denmark, arrived, and were shown round the borders in ten minutes or so, receiving their Frestonian passport stamps and leaving, rather dissatisfied.

A National Film Theatre of Frestonia opened in the People's Hall, with the first showing being *Passport to Pimlico* and films by the Sex Pistols. The theatre opened with the international première of *The Immortalist* by Heathcote Williams, preceded by no less than three national anthems. (The London *Evening Standard* had urged their readers to submit suitable anthems to us.) Frestonia applied to join the International Postal Union and printed its own postage stamps, with replies to our letters coming in from around the world.

It all worked like a dream. The Greater London Council (GLC), who previously had refused to deal with us, now told the media that they would negotiate with us 'in New York or wherever' and their Tory leader, Sir Horace Cutler, sent us a letter saying 'If you did not exist it would be necessary to invent you.' We replied: 'Since we do exist, why is it necessary to destroy us?' Sir Geoffrey Howe MP wrote to us that as one who has 'a childhood enthusiasm for *The Napoleon of Notting Hill* he could hardly fail to be moved by our plight.

We were suddenly transformed in the GLC's eyes from a bunch of squatters, hobos and drug addicts into an international incident that was providing them with an opportunity to show how enlightened they were and threatening them with the prospect of negative media coverage if they carried on with their plans to evict us.

A public enquiry was ordered. The GLC had their QC, and I represented Frestonia as the Minister of State for the Environment. We proposed that Frestonia become a mixed-use site for houses and craft workshops. We won the enquiry.

Frestonia was eventually rebuilt to our design with several millions of pounds of foreign aid from Great Britain, channelled via the Notting Hill Housing Trust to our own co-operative. We used the superb *Pattern Language* book by Christopher Alexander (published by OUP) on timeless architecture, which is as simple as painting by numbers, to vote as a co-op on the various architectural patterns we wanted incorporated in our new development.

Today, I am immensely proud of the development that was built, complete with its overhanging roofs, enclosed communal gardens and decorated brickwork. Recently, there was a great party in a marquee in the communal garden to mark the twenty-first anniversary of independence. The spirit is still strong. Frestonia goes to show that with imagination and humour you can run rings round the establishment.

Apocalypse Hotel, Frestonia

WORKING AT THE NORTH KENSINGTON LAW CENTRE

Elisa Segrave

Elisa Segrave first used to visit Notting Hill and the Portobello Road as a teenager in 1966. In the early Seventies she worked at the North Kensington Law Centre in Golborne Road. She has lived in Notting Hill since 1978. Segrave has had two books published by Faber & Faber: **The Diary of a Breas**t (1995), an autobiographical account of her successful fight against breast cancer, and **Ten Men** (1997). She is currently working on a book on her mother and writes a daily diary, which she has done for years, much of it centred on Notting Hill. The names of clients and their circumstances have been changed in order to protect their identities.

In 1972 I became a volunteer at the North Kensington Law Centre, the first organisation of its kind in Britain. The Centre was at 74 Golborne Road, W10, in an old butcher's shop, and had been started in July 1970 by Peter Kandler, a solicitor, and Lord Gifford, a barrister. It was intended to help the local community and encourage poorer people to seek legal help informally and without prohibitive costs. City and Parochial Foundation provided a grant of £2,500 and the Pilgrim Trust gave £1,500. The Royal Borough of Kensington and Chelsea agreed to make available, on a short-life basis, at low rent, the butcher's shop, where the Law Centre, in the year 2000, is still based.

I had no legal training. At first I sat at Reception, where I operated a small telephone switchboard. Our clients had to put their heads through a cubby-hole to talk to me.

'Good afternoon, I'm Miss Franks.'

She had a very pale face and spots and was wheeling a pram. 'I've come for me dad. I've got a letter. Got to see the little bloke with the moustache.'

I took her letter. It was to do with car insurance. I buzzed the switchboard to James.

'Who?'

'Miss Franks. Her father's called Mr Harley.'

'Not my client,' said James, and banged down the phone.

'Will you wait here please with the pram,' I said.

James Saunders, slight, with a spiky beard like a goat's and horn-rimmed glasses, had started when the Law Centre opened, as Peter Kandler's articled clerk after only three months' training. During the first three weeks, two hundred people had come. James had coped. I knew that he, Peter and the other solicitors could have been earning higher salaries in conventional law firms. There were other volunteers but the regulars in the office with me in 1972 were Jim Peevey, an American solicitor, Paddy, in love with Jim, who'd been a journalist on a women's magazine, solicitor Pam Ditton, fresh-faced and cheerful, Walter, blond with big blue eyes, from a law centre in Canada, and Peter Kandler, the Director. Everyone was a bit frightened of Peter, who had a gruff manner and was overworked. A lovely older woman called Liz came to do the accounts. She had just left Woolworths. 'I thought, well, I'm taking home a measly fourteen pounds and the rest goes into Barbara Whats'ername's pocket. Much better do a job here and try to help.' Liz was motherly and was always offering us coffee and biscuits. She had a teenage son, Hubert, whom she was bringing up on her own.

After I'd been there about a week, I attended court, in South

London. I had to escort one of our clients. A Mrs Griswold and her husband had been accused of stealing Coronation mugs from a Notting Hill neighbour. Mrs Griswold had grey skin and a mouth that was not like a mouth at all – just a slit in her face. Her hair was greasy and her right wrist was covered with a dirty bandage. She had just tried to kill herself. 'I'm all of a tremble,' she told me outside the courtroom. 'I'll ring the psychiatric hospital to see if they'll take you back,' I told her. Mrs Griswold explained that she had left the hospital early of her own accord because she was so nervous about the court case. Also, her husband needed her support. He had just been bashed up by a crowbar in their basement flat. I watched him join her outside the courtroom. Both his eyes were nearly closed. He didn't want to talk. Mrs Griswold spoke for him. 'He wants to go to the toilet.'

In court, she was surprisingly smooth. Although the neighbour, an elderly man, had made a list of his stolen mugs – 'Mrs Griswold told me she collected Coronation mugs' – and the couple had been in his flat the whole afternoon of the theft, there was not enough evidence to convict them.

Mrs Griswold was often in and out of the Law Centre for immoral earnings and petty thieving. A few weeks later, while I was at Reception, I saw her across the street. She was skipping and wearing light blue sandals, inappropriate for the time of year. She had dyed her dull hair the colour of a gold coin. I watched her stop at one of the stalls in the Golborne Road, by a shop called Pramwear, examine an old teapot, then skip across towards the Law Centre, where she pushed the door open and put her face up to the cubby-hole. She had painted a smoky star on her forehead.

'It's like a family, the Law Centre, isn't it? I've got my nightdress on under this!' she cried gaily.

I buzzed upstairs. 'Send her up!' said Peter Kandler.

That morning an old lady had come in about being rehoused. 'I never buy the food round here. Too many blacks. I'm used to a better area. I used to work in Derry & Toms. My son served in the Army. I think Mr Heath's a wonderful man. I sent him a letter the other day. I think it's a shame that hussy threw a bottle of ink over him. The young today don't know where they're at.'

She had a very white, thickly powdered face, a little rouge on her cheeks and she wore a pepper and salt tweed coat.

'You might think I'm well dressed. Well, I can tell you, I've had this coat twenty years. I bought it with the money they gave me when I retired from Derry & Toms. It's scandalous how they treat old people today. Seven pounds ten a week I pay for my council flat and I've got bronchitis with the damp. Some boys threw a stone through the window and killed my budgie.'

I tried to be sympathetic in between operating the flashing lights on the switchboard. The old lady leaned forward: 'Excuse me, dear, but I can see you're a country girl. I used to live in Surrey. It's so nice to talk to you young ladies. Especially living in an area full of blacks. I used to work in Kensington.'

In those first few years the majority of the Law Centre's cases involved tenant *v* landlord and 'loitering with intent'. There was a crisis between the police and the young males of the area, mostly black. You could be brought into a police station for 'being a suspicious person loitering with intent', charged and put in prison without a solicitor to represent you. Beatings in the local police station were common. Only in the Eighties were these infamous Sus laws abolished.

The housing situation was bad. In the Sixties Rachman had used Alsatian dogs to terrorise his tenants. Stephen Sedley, a barrister (now a judge) who often worked for us, once drove a judge to North Kensington to show him some of the conditions in which people lived. The judge was so horrified that Sedley won his case.

Mr Giles, one of our clients, had trouble with his landlord. It was raining. Mr Giles nearly fell. The Centre's windows were steamy. Mr Giles had a grey film over his eyes. Mr Giles was nearly blind. He came and sat by our electric fire, nodding his head.

'I have to take my pills. Otherwise I get blackouts. They all know me; the grocer knows me, the butcher knows me. They've had to pick me up off the street. Sometimes I think to myself, "I won't take my pill today". But if I don't, I get another blackout.'

Outside, a hearse went by. The man in charge of the fruit stall crossed himself. Mr Giles didn't see the hearse. His head was bent very low. He couldn't see me at Reception either. He was waiting to talk to a solicitor.

'My brother, he's paralysed. The landlord knows this. He's not a civilised man. He bothers us all the time. We pay the rent. But he's not just.'

'Why do you get blackouts?'

'I was pushed off a bridge in Jamaica.'

In July 2000, invited by Brian Nicholls, a long-time adviser at the Law Centre, I went to its thirtieth birthday party, where Peter Kandler made a speech. He said he was a socialist, 'which means a commitment to the poor and deprived'. He now runs a criminal law office a few yards away from the old butcher's shop. Jim Peevey left. He married Paddy and they had three children, then divorced. James Saunders practises criminal law and left North Kensington a few years ago. Pam Ditton champions the rights of aborigines in Alice Springs. Liz, the book-keeper, died. The Law Centre continues but now it focuses on immigration, welfare benefits, mental health advocacy, discrimination, employment and education. I'm proud to have worked there.

METROPOLITAN MYTH

Glenys Roberts

Glenys Roberts is well known as a newspaper and magazine writer. She also writes books — fiction and non–fiction and her work has been collected in comic anthologies. She has lived in many different parts of London and in Paris, New York and Los Angeles, where she was recruited into screenwriting by US action director John Sturges. This extract is taken from her first book, **Metropolitan Myths** (1982), a wry look at the differing characters of London's villages. Originally appearing as a series of essays in London's **Evening Standard**, it became the longest-running newspaper series ever and was turned into four short films for the BBC. It marked Roberts, in the words of **The New Yorker** magazine, as 'an original and often very funny writer'.

The saying goes that if you tilted the United States on its side, all the odds and ends would finish up in California. If you tilted London on its side all the odds and ends would finish up in Notting Hill.

Notting Hill is an extremely seductive part of London, although its wide avenues and high façades boast mostly faded glory. Those who can afford to do so, do up their homes; those who cannot, board them up. This may happen in the same street – or even in the same building – which is why Notting Hill is not a safe place for those solely interested in investment. Notting Hill has never gone all the way down, but neither has it come all the way up. Sociologists, teachers and students of life marvel at the colourful fluidity of the neighbourhood. Art students live off it. Yet few people other than Rachman have dared to become heavily involved as landlords. Brave pioneers have bought houses in it and then fled its vicissitudes.

Notting Hill is unpredictable. Creeping graffiti take over the peeling whitewash and Victorian slums make way for council ones. Grand colonial mansions co-exist with corrugated iron, white liberals with black liberals. Notting Hill is very liberal indeed. Notting Hill is liberal to the point of lunacy. If pottery is the major art form in Fulham and placemats the major art form in Richmond, lunacy is the art indigenous to Notting Hill. There is no one form of lunacy in the area – indeed that is the whole point of lunacy. There may be as many forms of lunacy as there are people. The main thing is to be out on a limb, but if everyone is out on the same limb this is known as suburban. If everyone is out on a different limb, this is known as Notting Hill.

Notting Hill people would be very uncomfortable in the suburbs, just as suburban people would be very uncomfortable in Notting Hill. The suburbs do not openly encourage green hair and glue-sniffing, art movies and dissident rock. They take exception to fringe politics, tricky intellectuals, witchcraft, vandalism and fun. They do not like to see people in fancy dress in broad daylight, hanging out on street corners in all weathers, eating malodorous takeaway foreign food, wearing more hair than clothes and bopping to a few thousand decibels to which the rest of the neighbourhood is forced to listen. Suburbanites are not keen on mixed marriages and second-hand wardrobes, too much make-up and too few undergarments. They do not like to see purple worn with pink nor red worn with orange. They don't care for art on the walls (never mind on the streets) but prefer it safely tucked away in safely supervised galleries. They do not like to see droves of nymphets in tennis shoes unless they are on the way to the local tennis club. Slim chance in Notting Hill.

Such things make suburban people nervous. They like to be able to leave their two-year-old cars outside their houses without their neighbours scratching things like EAT THE RICH into the paintwork on the bonnet. They like to be able to walk through the streets without being bottled by yobbos, mugged by minors and robbed by anyone who stops to ask them the time. They like to be able to drop into the local for a pick-me-up without someone breaking down the bar around them. Notting Hill people take a risk on this sort of thing every time they leave the house. Some Notting Hill people don't even have to leave the house to live dangerously. They do not necessarily expect to see the fathers of their children ever again, or, for that matter, the children themselves. They do not expect to see their cars in the morning if they leave them on the streets at night. They dare not for a moment let go of a dog or a bike or a pram, or flaunt a shopping basket or a pound note. Every year there are more than five thousand burglaries, deceptions, assaults and thefts in Notting Hill. Every year there are nearly three thousand cases of petty damage and bicycle theft. More than two thousand cars disappear, or their contents. Notting Hill creditors settle matters with broken arms and busted noses. Notting Hill police burst in first and ask questions later. So popular are assaults on other people in this part of the world that one pub is universally nicknamed the GBH.

When Notting Hill people are not in the GBH looking forward to a knee-capping, they are scoring some other sort of dubious activity in another pub, where middle-aged, unnatural blondes hang out with black eyes and black escorts. When they are not drinking rum and Red Stripe these people are likely to appear as bit-part actors in television about real life like *The Sweeney*. Notting Hill is where life and art meet and neither triumphs. That is why Notting Hill people live there. But, unlike Earl's Court – where things are so unsavoury that people boast that they live in the Royal Borough of Kensington and Chelsea – Notting Hill people never disown Notting Hill or rename it deceptively. They are proud of the Gate, as they call it, as in gate-crash, gate-money, gate-fold and Newgate.

People who live in much grander adjacent places, in Holland Park, in Campden Hill, in Bayswater, are all apt to say that they live in Notting Hill. People who live in Belgravia are apt to visit it to pursue at least some of their vices. Instability and possibility is the whole point of living in the area and addiction or predilection to thrills or even spills, Few people, after all, move away from Los Angeles just because they know they can get shot going out to dinner. Notting Hill people are a lot like Los Angeles people. They are fringe people first and foremost, crazy for all the fads they fancy. They enjoy brinkmanship and they enjoy provocation. They are not rich and it is not entirely certain whether they would really like to be, even if they do make the odd attempt at someone else's expense. They live by their wits, by their eccentricities and by their unpredictabilities.

Whereas Hampstead thinkers always agree with other Hampstead thinkers, Notting Hill thinkers do not even agree with what they themselves thought yesterday. Notting Hill is open to new ideas. Notting Hill is a market-place, and not just on Saturday down the Portobello Road. What you can see is for tourists: the locals buy what you can't. Notting Hill markets the most meagre talent. If you are a drag queen you have no intention of becoming Danny La Rue. If you are a housewife you recycle what you have in your closet – possibly to a drag queen. Closet knitters open stalls of baby clothes. Landladies boil down slivers of soiled soap and sell them as marbled toiletries. Amateur gardeners open 'head' shops, amateur cooks sell cups of lentil soup. Yesterday's ethnic frocks become tomorrow's fashion points.

Notting Hill people are much more avant-garde than Chelsea people think they are. Chelsea people never know what to buy until Notting Hill has given up buying it long ago. By the time fashions reach Chelsea they have been cleaned up, toned down and packaged ready for the consumer classes. Notting Hill people are meanwhile already on to something else. If Notting Hill discovers Victorian water closets, Chelsea people will discover them two years later. Two years after that they will be heralded in Camden Passage. Five years on Clapham will be delighted by them, and Clapham people will be faking them. Ten years on Sotheby's will charge the earth and the fake will be part of history.

Notting Hill discovered the Pill, hippies, the Sixties, communes and squatting. Notting Hill discovered cruising when Earl's Court was full of brigadiers. Many of the gays in Notting Hill make most of the gays in Earl's Court look like amateur theatricals. Notting Hill gays would never wear anything as butch as leather. They go about their business wearing 'his and his' sweaters and matching 'taches. Notting Hill was first with reggae, first with punk and first with New Wave. Hampstead people still think New Wave refers to a French film made in the Fifties. Notting Hill people know that New Wave is already Old Hat. They have forgotten all about the Fifties, they have forgotten all about the Sixties, and the Seventies, and they don't have much time for the Eighties, Notting Hill people, like Los Angeles people, are living in another century and they are not sure whether it is all coming or whether it has been.

LONDONERS

Nicholas Shakespeare

Nicholas Shakespeare's books include **The Dancer Upstairs** (1995), which was chosen by the American Libraries Association as the Best Novel of 1997, and **Bruce Chatwin: A Life** (1999). He is a former literary editor of the **Daily** and **Sunday Telegraph**, and a Fellow of the Royal Society of Literature. Shakespeare has had a base in Ladbroke Grove since 1984, and it was here that he wrote **Londoners** (1986), described by Michael Moorcock as 'one of the best books on London'. The following is an extract.

Emma Tennant's latest novel, *The Adventures of Robina*, carries as its subtitle 'The Memoirs of a Debutante at the Court of Queen Elizabeth II'.

Tall, blonde, her nails full of the pheasant she has just plucked, Emma Tennant stands at her Elgin Crescent window in North Kensington and remembers the day she was presented at Court. A Lenare portrait taken at the time, in 1956, shows her in an afternoon dress, dark gloves, and a choker of pearls. 'Artificial', she says triumphantly.

'That green dress looked like a crushed lettuce leaf by the time we reached the Palace. Everyone had hired Daimlers, and we sat in this queue which edged slowly, slowly forward. It must have taken twenty minutes to get down The Mall, and it was terribly embarrassing because, of course, you felt a twit.'

Bobbing a flustered curtsey before the Queen, who sat 'drumming her fingers like a waxwork' – had she lost an innocence by being shown to the sovereign in this way? Emma Tennant thinks possibly she had.

She replaces the portrait in its brown paper bundle under a drinks table, and goes on to talk about moving house. In Kensington, more people – sixty-eight per cent – own their homes than in any other part of London. (Tower Hamlets, not surprisingly, comes at the bottom of the league with less than three per cent.) Emma Tennant is moving round the corner because she needs the money she will make from buying a smaller house. And because, ironically, the area has become too smart.

'This area used to have the highest density of writers in London. Now it's like the smart Paris suburb of Passy. Full of French and Belgian bankers and heads of BBC departments. Last year, I watched two compete in the parents' egg-and-spoon race. They both held their eggs with their thumbs, which made me suspect that was how they'd got to the top.' She gestures through the window at the communal gardens. 'I'm the bane of the Garden Committee. Twice a year the bell rings, and everyone rushes out to plant crocuses and sweep leaves. It's just like a village, they say. We've got a squirrel and two owls here now,' she adds with mock pride, in mimicry of this inner-city rural fantasy. 'One male that goes too-wit-to-woo. One female that goes goo-wit, goo-wit.'

She turns back into the shambolic, crumbling room and continues excitedly.

'Actually, there's a really bad taste story about the owls. I overheard a neighbour saying, 'Isn't it wonderful, we've got the owls back.' I told Hilary Bailey, who's lived here for ages in a flat that costs her five pounds a week or something. She said, apparently it isn't the owls at all. It's the call the Notting Hill Gate rapist makes every time he plunges into an au pair's basement.'

Comic, grotesque, outrageous, it is the kind of story that appeals to the author of fantasies like *The Crack* – an apocalyptic tale of what happens when the Thames splits open. 'But I'd never have written my books here had it not been for the communal gardens, and the fact my children could run out and play without me worrying they were wandering into the road. Sadly, you no longer hear the shriek of children. It's complete silence because they're all at Eton.'

Emma Tennant's mid-Victorian Italianate home, like the home she is buying, lies on the Ladbroke Estate. Conceived as a great circus, with villas rising from the fields and quarries west of Notting Hill, it was a speculative development that signally failed. The collapse of the estate in the 1850s made the word 'Ladbroke' synonymous with the risks attached to property – 'a graveyard of buried hopes', according to an 1861 edition of *Building News.*

The houses built for the gentry became rookeries. Whole families lived in a single room, dividing where they slept from where they ate with a curtain down the middle. Then the gentry began moving into the mews houses previously occupied by their servants.

Recently, albeit over a century later than intended, they have started to inhabit the villas in the way originally planned by developers like Cith Blake, Samuel Walker and Thomas Allom. Today, many of the houses around Elgin Crescent have been restored to the status of single homes, and their honeycomb conversions removed.

'The money about,' said one estate agent, 'never ceases to amaze me'.

It takes some doing to amaze an estate agent.

In 1985 the value of property in London went up nineteen per cent. Andy, who is a partner in Emma Tennant's local estate agent, Faron Sutaria, reckons the telephone rings, on average, every ten seconds. Last year he only went out to lunch twice: once with a cousin who had come back from abroad, and once with another estate agent. They went next door for half an hour and had a pizza. That, says Andy, is how hard he works.

Andy is an unlikely young man to find in property. A graduate in Russian studies, he decided that the only way to secure himself a job was to advertise. Offering £1,000 for the most interesting job opportunity, and with the catchline *I Want To Move With The Times,* he placed an advertisement in that paper. He could not have foreseen the result. The newspaper stole his phrase. More importantly, other newspapers reported the ad.

The London *Evening Standard* ran their story the following day. The headline changed with each edition. 'There were two reasons why it was taken up,' Andy says. 'My offer coincided with the latest record unemployment figures. And no one till then had accepted the idea that a graduate would find it difficult to get a job. After the first few phone calls, I realised I wouldn't have to pay a thing.'

He spent three days at the BBC, being interviewed on various radio programmes as to what had prompted him. Offers of job interviews came in their hundreds. 'I'll give you five grand in cash,' said one insurance executive, 'if you say you are going to join my company. Because of the publicity I'll get.'

Totting it all up, Capital Radio reckoned Andy had earned himself £700,000 worth of international publicity. He had calls from Australia, Vancouver and Switzerland. The most persistent was from a man who said urgently he had to meet him at the Skyline Hotel. 'He wouldn't give a name, just said that he had to meet me. He would be wearing such and such. It was so bizarre, I felt I had to go through with it. Not even then did he tell me what he wanted. Then he called from Canada to arrange lunch. We met in Mayfair. It turned out he wanted me to sell gas stoves to north-east England.'

In the midst of this, Andy met Faron Sutaria, an Indian Parsee who, calling himself the 'Real Estate Agent', had started up his business in a basement flat off Baker Street. Andy was impressed. 'Most estate agents are complete nurds. They don't need any qualifications. Often they are as thick as the bricks they are selling. And they spend most of the time with the purchasers, when they should be acting for the vendors. In America, you pay for both services. You use an agent to both buy and find.'

Each day, Andy shows four or five people round the properties on his books. *Immaculate* is not an adjective he eschews to describe a lavatorially bricked terraced house. Nor is *superb*. But then, what he is offering for £150,000 is the fantasy to make it so.

Most people coming to Andy want to live in the Notting Hill Gate area because of the Central line. It is therefore an ideal location for, say, the bankers and broadcasters so disliked by Emma Tennant. Andy finds it easy to divide the city like this. Mention Bayswater, and to him the word conjures up the first-time flat buyer and Arabs overlooking the park. Mention Barnes, and out come epithets like snob, arty-farty, minor television actors. Mention Richmond, and he tells you, with a dreamy, faraway look in his eye, of wealthy, liberal middle classes with the highest educational standards of any borough in the country.

'As in jobs, everyone upgrades themselves.'… People don't live in

W8 or W2. They live in Kensington or Bayswater. They mention the area because of the connotations that go with it. Also, because some postal codes cover a multitude of sins. W11 includes parts of both Westbourne Grove and Holland Park – overlaying a gulf wider than any you can imagine.

MY LONDON

Mustafa Matura

Playwright Mustafa Matura left the Caribbean in 1961 to live and work in London. He is now an established theatre figure in Britain: **The Times** called him 'our finest dramatist of West Indian origin'. His latest play is **Rum an' Coca Cola**. In 1981 he moved to Notting Hill, where his greatest source of inspiration is the Portobello Road.

I first discovered the West London area of Ladbroke Grove during the 'Swinging Sixties'. At that time it was a vibrant cosmopolitan community attracting those in search of its liberating lifestyles. It was the home of young long-haired hippies parading in their colourful clothes and new-found freedom; a large Caribbean community, adding a spicy flavour to the proceedings; and the annual street Carnival. Others, drawn to its slightly soiled, roguish atmosphere, added to it the hustle and bustle of the antiques and fruit and vegetable market stalls on the Portobello Road, which on Saturdays competed with the visitors' exotic fashions for attention. The whole area was bursting with life.

Coming from and writing about the Caribbean, it is not surprising that the area became (as we say) my *lime*, my watering hole. Why not? Hemingway found his Spain, Joyce his Dublin, Runyon his Bowery. I had found my London.

I have seen Ladbroke Grove pass through many phases since then, some good, some bad: hippy, punk, radical chic, rasta, bourgeois respectability. Like most areas of London, 'the Grove' has had its fair share of notoriety. There were famous murderers, who caused the council to change the name of the place where their crimes were committed; there were shady landlords who knew certain call girls, who knew certain cabinet ministers, who resigned in disgrace in the Sixties, who all went on to have Hollywood movies made about them. As they might say in the Grove, 'I should be so lucky.'

Nowadays, on a good day, having written my fill, I can begin a stroll, walking south along the still hustling and bustling (even more so) Portobello Road market. Fancy surreal hairdressing salons, *objet de* kitchen shops, new New-Age religious shops stocked with mandalas, crystals and Brazilian witches, rub shoulders with honest record shops, all pumping out the latest in-music, next to travel and cookery shops. I could see Jo Kenyatta in his red, gold and green knitted hat and his shiny, third-hand suit, who will shadow-box me while telling me tales of his wayward nephew Brandy, 'who if he doesn't look out, he go' get in bad trouble', as if I am to deliver that message. Or I could decide between Malaysian or Italian for lunch. These days the Italian pizzeria is in the ascendency, with delicious melted cheeses that are a joy to behold. Then a black mini-skirted silhouette will pass by; following her progress, I will see the latest pictures and pieces being hung at one of the many art and ceramic galleries, containing mostly large daubs for large reception areas, or huge alien-like figures looming in the carefully trained spotlights. I swear, a recent exhibition is of all black painted canvases of different sizes.

On the next corner, I could see Red Reg in his sharp black leather hat and wind-proofed coat, arranging incense, hats, socks and pictures of Martin Luther King, Malcolm X, Pope John, Caribbean childhood scenes and soft-focus, semi-erotic couples coupling, all of which he sells. I could walk past him and go to Rose, sitting behind her glass-fronted show-case which reflects the glittering baubles inside, and the shimmering party frocks hung above her; and Rose might tell me of her last exotic trip abroad, or one she is planning. How she does it I do not know … I just don't go to the right parties, that's all.

Or I could cross Lancaster Road and browse at a shop containing the most beautiful stone, metal and wooden works of art from India, from everyday utilitarian objects to the most intricately carved windows and doors; or similar stuff, in a shop opposite, from Africa. I walk past the betting shop quickly, having once been hooked on numbers; I have a 'there but for the grace of God' attitude to the dazed men I glimpse inside, and move on to the Warwick Castle, a pub that has been pre-

served in time by the thick layers of nicotine and grime that occasionally peel off, further concussing its unfortunate customers. But it has
the distinctive attraction of having two green baize pool tables that
attract the finest players from miles around.

Through the smoky haze, I could glimpse Classical in his long over-
coat, nursing a half of Guinness, watching the action, checking who to
play (meaning, who he can beat) before putting down his token coin. I
could see Manny, Indian Tony and Lindsay arguing over whose coin is
next while moving their own to the front; then Prang with his booming voice, with the authority of his flowing dreadlocks, would settle
matters by shouting, 'Nobody en' playing next, me playing next, dat's
my ten pence dere. I put my mark on it an' it's mine. You Manny an'
Lindsay an' Tony, too cheat.' And while the shamed trio withdraw in
disarray, blaming each other for their own bad reputations, I would
slide my coin next to Prang's.

And to prepare for the mammoth battle of skills, wills an' wiles to
come, I could wash down the fine lasagne with a pint of lager, not by
any means the best, but better bad beer than no pool, I tell myself.

I sometimes win, and sometimes lose, as the wise man said. But during those one (or two or three, or four, five, six) hour periods that I
spend trying to play next, liming, gossiping, marvelling at others' skills,
luck, misfortune, blunders, observing the karmatic dimension of the
games, I am in a writer's paradise.

People don't just give me ideas for stories; in the Grove they give
you their life stories also, and they come in every shape and size, from
the acted-out telling to the perfectly timed punch lines; what more
could one ask for? It's like being in a real-life, long-running soap opera,
which I tell myself I'm only researching in order to write about.

Not true. I became a character in it some time ago, 'de writer
feller', the one who prays that the gentrification process that is taking
place in the area now does not totally destroy its unique character and
characters, and who hopes that somehow, by writing about it, he is pre-
serving it, but now with the added knowledge that the Grove's own
vibrant, resilient sense of life will continue to replenish itself, and those
that lime there.

Why, yesterday, I swear I saw a young hippy girl, wearing a bright,
new afghan coat, with a mirrored bag hanging from her bony shoulders

and yellow, flared, velvet trousers flapping at her ankles, striding up the 'Bello. It's that kind of area.

Hanging out in the 'Grove', with Mustapha Matura

A TASTE OF THE ACTION

Duncan Fallowell

Duncan Fallowell was born in London in 1948 and moved to Notting Hill Gate in 1970, though he has lived in many other parts of the world. He is the author of travel books and novels, the latest being **A History of Facelifting** (2003). These diary extracts were originally published in the London **Evening Standard** in 1998.

To the Cobden Club for a drink with Vasko, a Serbian. Now that sweet Iris Palmer has taken the fashion victims into the basement, the upstairs room has become one of the dreamiest resorts in town. Something about its theatricality reminds me of St Petersburg: huge, grand, with a dash of barbarism.

Vasko asks if he can tell the Home Office he's my long-term boyfriend in order to obtain asylum, residency, work permit, whatever, in the UK. Actually he lives with an Italian girl on Denmark Hill – where do they find these places? Whenever I've landed on

Denmark Hill it's because I'm totally lost. I tell him he'd have better
luck in Denmark. 'No – Denmark Hill,' he reiterates. He doesn't get
the joke. His English isn't good.
Why not marry the Italian? 'She married already.' Unfortunately, I have
to say no too, because I may wish to use the option one day for a genuine love and if I've already shot my bolt an' stuff ... 'Boltons?' Vasko
picks up, 'you know someone in Boltons?' No, no, no. He's overheat-
ing. It must be the red wine – normally he drinks only vodka. He looks
downcast. To mollify him, I say I'll ask the barman.

   Kymon is thinking of joining the Royal Navy, which is an attractive
thing to do but it would be a loss – he's the nicest barman in London,
with wonderful eyes and a wicked laugh. I ask, 'Do you know any girls
who might marry a charming Serbian? They don't have to be ethnical-
ly clean.'

   Kymon tilts his head and clicks his tongue: 'Sorry, but the only girl I
know who wants to get married is a Bosnian. And she wants to get married for the same reason.' 'Perhaps they could marry each other?' 'What
would be the point of that?' wonders Kymon. What indeed.

The Champion pub in Notting Hill Gate was the first gay bar I ever visited – that was in 1967 and I've been popping in occasionally ever
since, though it's not my scene and has had an odd series of landlords,
some of them homophobic. In Gay Liberation Front days a couple of
mates of mine were thrown out of it for wearing crinolines. The bar-
men, with rare exceptions, were morose and the customers generally
resentful of the most innocent attempts at communication.

   More recently it has become stranded between the traditional gay
pub and the new style bar, with neither the mixed chumminess of the
former nor the youthful buzz of the latter. In fact it has a sullen ghast-
liness all its own, laced with a strong dose of self-disgust. So why go in
at all? Because it's there, conveniently sited on the Gate for a quick
drink and a look, hope pathetically springing eternal.

   But now it's overstepped the mark. A blackboard was hung in the
Gents several landlords ago for playful graffiti. Chalked on the blackboard these days is a large message: 'No loitering – anyone found

loitering will be asked to leave.' Occasional naughtiness has occurred in there but it was never hopping and surely a certain informality is understandable in the Gents of a gay bar.

I asked the lunchtime barman the reason for this horrid message. Had there been complaints from the public or interference from the police? 'No,' he replied tautly, without looking at me and continuing to stack glasses, 'we put it up ourselves. People were loitering in there and it's against the law and we uphold the law.'

Well, this is the first time I've ever seen such a sign in such a place and if they really had to, could it not have been phrased more sweetly or prefaced with 'Sorry, lads, but'? Oh no. They have chosen to reproduce exactly that nasty, life-hating puritan tone we've been fighting all our lives. So after more than thirty years, it's good-bye, Champion.

The Ground Floor Bar has been trying to gayify itself by advertising in the gay press. If it succeeds it might do something to soften the brutal atmosphere of Portobello Road at night. So I checked it out with Chris, my Polish Bristolian friend who prefers women.

'The music's too loud,' he said, 'and everyone is too far apart.' 'Everyone's too far apart, Chris, because it's not very full, but I like that. Can you see anyone gay?' 'What about that bald chap in the corner?' 'He's about as gay as a baboon's arse.' 'I thought so.' 'No, Chris, that means not very gay at all. There's someone reading over there.' 'Is that gay?' 'Depends what the book is.'

We crane. 'A.S. Byatt, he says. 'Oh gawd, about as gay as a soggy banana. What, Chris, are you reading these days?' '*In With the Euro, Out With the Pound*. And you?' '*Memories and Portraits* by Ivan Bunin.' 'Is he gay?' 'No. He was a Russian of the ancien régime who wrote incredibly modern short stories on the subject of love. Ah, I spy two pretty Cockney boys watching football on the telly. I hope they're gay.'

We crane again. 'Don't think so. Oh look!' says Chris. His eyes light up as a young man flaps by in Oxford bags and a very tight shirt. 'Is that one?' he asks. 'Could be.' Tight shirt leans over an occupied table and says something in a fey voice. Chris gives me a knowing glance. 'I believe I've spotted one too,' I confide, 'the butch one down there drinking incognito with a girl. Doesn't fool me.'

Oh – it's closing time. When are the authorities going to kill this absurd 11pm guillotine? It makes a mockery of London's claim to be the world's most happening city, and killing it would do more than anything to humanise the streets at night. As for the Portobello Road, I don't think we really need a gay bar. Round here everyone mucks in.

THE REAL NOTTING HILL

Tim Lott

Tim Lott was born in 1956 in Southall, Middlesex and studied Politics and History at the London School of Economics. He first came to Notting Hill in the seventies when he helped in his father's greengrocer's shop. As well as journalism, he has worked in publishing and broadcasting, and was editor of the London listings magazine **City Limits**. **The Scent of Dried Roses** (1996), an account of his mother's depression and suicide, won the JR Ackerley Prize. His first novel, **White City Blue** (1999), a portrait of a group of young male friends, won the Whitbread First Novel Award. It was followed by **Rumours of a Hurricane** (2002), the story of a couple living in Britain at the beginning of the 1980s. His latest novel is **The Seymour Tapes** (2005). Tim Lott no longer lives in Notting Hill but returns to the area to work.

My first memory of Notting Hill was fundamentally unhappy. My father's entire working life was spent in a greengrocer's shop in Notting Hill Gate called Cornelius O'London (now, inevitably, a mobile phone shop), 50 yards west of the Coronet Cinema. I used to work there on Saturdays, as a teenager in the early 1970s.

I was a terrible greengrocer. I couldn't remember the names of the different produce (not that there was much variety in those days), I would invariably dish out the wrong change, and I would always drop the produce all over the street when I was delivering it, carpeting Camden Hill Road with mushrooms.

But I was aware – particularly when making deliveries to the elderly Ladies and upmarket bohemians that even then flourished in the area – that Notting Hill was a very different kind of place to the West London suburb, Southall, from where I commuted. The walls of their flats and houses were often painted bright colours instead of off-white, and the furniture was sometimes designed like the set of *A Clockwork Orange* or *Space Odyssey*. People wore strange clothes, and seemed much better-looking than anyone in Ealing or Greenford. 'There's quite a few weirdoes round here,' my determinedly suburban father (all the same a true Notting Hill 'character') would tell me.

Occasionally, I would deliver to the north of the borough, in the environs of Portobello. It scared me. It seemed poor and desperate. 'This place is becoming very trendy nowadays, you know,' my father said confidently. I didn't believe him. It was a slum.

Fast-forward to the mid-1980s. My father was still in his shop, and I was a mature student studying at the LSE. I had a partner who was considerably more fashionable than me. She was intent on moving to Notting Hill. She thought it was very cool. I still thought it was a slum.

I was presented in 1987 with a choice between buying a two-bed flat in Hampstead, and one just off the Portobello Road, in one of the decaying terraces in Colville Houses. My partner convinced me to buy the latter, for the sum of £49,000. I immediately regretted it.

The flat turned against me as soon as I moved in. Foul cooking smells came from below. Cacophonic noises came from above. Cracks appeared in the ceiling. I found myself desperately regretting my ill-advised attempt to be more bohemian than I actually was. Outside, in what is now the Portobello central village punctuated with designer boutiques and delicatessens, there was only the restaurant 192, and its neighbour, Monsieur Thompson's, as a sign that things might one day become more prosperous. The Electric Cinema was long closed down and decaying. Notting Hill riots were still a tradition. The All Saints Road was a no-go area. The market, on weekdays, was strictly fruit and veg – no Spanish soaps and cheeses, no interesting food and clothes stalls. My error appeared more and more grave with each passing month.

But gradually, as my father and girlfriend had prophesied, Notting Hill began to change. Older residents mourned the 'yuppification' of the area. However, I could not see any immense downside to crummy old dilapidated shops being turned into pleasant restaurants (like Osteria Basilico and First Floor), bars (the Market Bar, I think, was one of the first), and interesting shops. I liked Graham & Green. I liked Mr

Christian's. I absolutely loved Books for Cooks, where I now eat almost every day.

The area eventually captured my imagination – so much so, that I actually bought a three-storey house there, at the north end of Portobello, in the early 1990s (for the remarkable sum, even then, of £140,000). It was like central Portobello in the early days – alkies and crazies on the streets, the blasting vibrations from the nightclub under the Westway and a threatening after-dark vibe. Ross and Scotty's junk shop on the corner furnished most of our house. Patchy was putting it mildly.

But I believed in change now and sure enough it continued. Portobello Green filled with interesting shops (I particularly love Adam the suit-maker, the grumpy old watch repair man and Steve the tailor), and the Portobello Café became the (now defunct) Japanese Café. By now I had fallen in love with Portobello, and began with my wife raising a family there. My two daughters went to Fox School, a wonderful place with a fairytale head teacher which to my mind still represents the model of what an inner-city state school should be.

Notting Hill as a family area represented a big step from what it seemed as someone single. But by now the Tabernacle had a good programme of kids' events, and the Westway tennis centre had been built. We went horse-riding under the Westway, enjoyed the Kids Club at the newly opened Electric, painted ceramics in Art 4 Fun, hung out on Tavistock Square on a long summer's evening at the wonderfully 1970s vegetarian café and the Italian pizza shop. Some people talk about raising children in the inner city as an aberration. I can only think of living in some ghastly picture-postcard sleeper suburb as being the aberration. Sure my children were confronted with drug dealers, the homeless, dirt on the streets, dog shit and chaos. They saw life. They were among it. That's what being alive is for.

Things kept changing. I got divorced. My wife moved into Arundel Gardens, and I temporarily moved back into my once-cursed flat in Colville Houses. I celebrated the millennium on the roof, four storeys up, as I watched the fireworks in the distance over the Thames. In the evenings, I would watch the enormous sunsets to the west from my balcony, drunk on the romance of city life and *cerveza* from Garcia's.

More change and more change. I realised that some of the complaints about the character of the area disappearing were not entirely unfounded. On one occasion I cycled with my life partner on a rainy New Year's Eve for a meal at Bali Sugar, the Sugar Club's equally superb successor. We were scruffy and wet from rain. We walked in to be confronted almost entirely by disapproving gazes from designer-clad 'young people' who were drifting in from the far more foreign reaches of Westbourne Grove, which was now turning into a version not of Notting Hill but of South Molton Street. This was a place I truly did not have an affinity for. The Westbourne Grovers (or, as I think of them, the East Villagers) are a different breed, mainly trustafarians and fashion wonks. Meanwhile, in my block of flats, the writers, painters and musicians were being replaced by doctors, lawyers and city brokers.

But the real Notting Hill endured – at Mario's locksmiths, at the East West Gallery, at Mike's Café, at Rough Trade Records, at Woolworths and Brilliant Buys, at Barnes Cycles, at the Lisboa, at the Travel Bookshop and of course on the market itself, with fat Barry still lustily yelling his lungs out every day, counterpointed by the unremitting melancholia of the girl selling the pastries at the bread stall outside the Tea & Coffee Plant. Yes, Barnett's dodgy toy-shop has gone, and Combined Harvest, and 192 itself, but much of what was worthwhile has survived with remarkable tenacity.

Thus it was with a deep and genuine sense of grief that I found myself destined to move out of the area after my divorce. I could no longer afford what was once very affordable. Like many of the old Notting Hillers, I found myself shunted north, by economic necessity, to the new territories of Kensal Green and Kensal Rise – which I also have grown to love as a true neighbourhood, which is taking on the character of Notting Hill in the late 1980s, a new frontier. But the idea that I would be in exile from what I thought of as my hard-won homeland hurt me.

But as luck – or, as I prefer to think of it, destiny – would have it, I managed to secure myself a small, cupboard-sized office in the building in Colville Houses where I used to live. So every day, I come back here again, and watch Notting Hill ebb and flow, a place both conserving itself and transforming itself. And it's still wonderful. I like the new Japanese restaurant in Tavistock Square, I like Cheeky Monkeys toyshop, and the new Garcia Café, and even the horribly expensive Grocer on Elgin which does the best bread I've ever tasted. This place is still frothing with life, and to walk among the tourists, friends and acquaintances every day is a perpetual refreshment for me.

Now I have become what I suppose I always fantasised, as a suburban teenager, I would one day be, a Notting Hill veteran, and, if not quite a bohemian, then at least an artist of sorts, writing novels in my tiny office every day. My world is very strictly circumscribed – Geales fish shop is as far as I tend to go south, the Turquoise Island as far as I go east, Kensington Sports Centre as far as I go west, and Golborne Road as far as I go north. This is the real Notting Hill, and it still is real, and I don't only love it – it is me now, it is built into the fibre of who I am.

The Congestion Charge Extension may do much damage. I hear talk of Golborne Road being 'cleaned up' and redeveloped. Will they really shut down Woolworths? Is a Macdonalds really going to put and end to the German Burger and Bratwurst stall? But as long as the market survives, which is the lifeblood of the artery that is Portobello Road, I believe that the spirit of Notting Hill will survive. You can mock it, envy it, and wish you were in tarted-up slums like Brick Lane or Stoke Newington, or old-money places like Kensington Proper instead, but the reality is that Notting Hill remains the ultimate model of a successful, mixed, vibrant, creative urban community. It is the place I always dreamed of being, and it has in fact now dreamed itself into being what I imagined. It is mine and it is me. And I will never leave it.

A PASHMINA INCIDENT

Justine Hardy

Justine Hardy was born in England, trained as a journalist in Australia and now works between India and London, writing books and making documentaries. She lives in New Delhi and Notting Hill. The following pashmina incident was recorded in her book **Goat** (2000).

… Then the idea came if I sold shawls it would be a way of making some of the money that Gautam needed. It would be so simple. I knew I could do it. I had already made my first sale without even trying a few weeks earlier, on a brief trip to London.

It had been cold too in Notting Hill. People on the street had surprised expressions, caught out by the first frost. They scuttled along, looking up at the sky just to check that it really was as bleak as it felt. The beautiful but weary were making their way to a popular café to while away the long hours until another evening's entertainment began.

I was not looking my best. The back of my grey tracksuit resembled the sagging folds of an elephant's bottom. My gym shoes were a memento of an inter-school netball tournament circa 1982. The one redeeming feature of my ensemble was a pashmina shawl. It was the colour of flame-tree flowers and it had been given to me by a houseboat owner in Kashmir with whom I had stayed years before. I had become immediately attached to it without really knowing anything about pashmina.

As the Notting Hill rain started, I retreated into the folds of my shawl and took refuge in the doorway of a post office. Inside, a woman in a tight white jersey was shrieking at a man behind one of the glass serving screens, telling him that he had absolutely no idea about service. He didn't seem to mind, happy, perhaps, just to admire the sharp nipples that the tight white jersey showed off so nicely. Its wearer abandoned her tirade and came towards me.

'Can you believe how rude some people are?' she said in Manhattan Islandese.

I smiled back at her.

'That shawl, I want it. Where did you get it?'

'From Kashmir.'

'Belief.' She pulled one end of the shawl towards her.

'I must have one.'

I looked at her.

'Oh, forget my manners. It's a New York thing. Let me buy it from you.'

I couldn't think of anything to say.

'Come on, how much is it? I have cash, I'll pay you right now.'

'£200.'

The shawl was four years old – £50 a year seemed reasonable.

'Great.'

She tugged more forcefully at the dangling end of the shawl. It fell free, aflame at her feet. She picked it up, twined it around her neck and grabbed my hand, pulling me down the street. We stopped in the rain outside an antique shop with a French mirror in the window (one of those ones that have reflected the image of a thousand courtesans). The American twirled in front of the glass.

'1 love it, I love it.' She opened her bag. 'Now, what about a discount?'

'Please, may I have my shawl back?'

I remember holding out my hand.

'Come on,' she wheedled.

'If you would like it I have told you how much it is, otherwise please may I have it back?'

She pushed four £50 notes into my hand and walked away.

BUT THEN, NOTTING HILL

Nikki Gemmell

Nikki Gemmell has written four novels, **Shiver, Cleave, Lovesong** and **The Bride Stripped Bare,** as well as a work of non-fiction, **Pleasure: An Almanac for the Heart.** Her work has been internationally acclaimed and translated into many languages. She was born in Wollongong, Australia and now lives in Notting Hill with her family. Here she describes living in England and moving to W11.

Although he enjoyed his time in London, he admits that he "felt like someone from another planet". A naturally shy man, by 1970 he had decided to return home. "One day I looked at the man in my local service station and I suddenly realised that if I lived here ten years I wouldn't know that man any better."(Peter Carey The Book Collector).

Arrival

I moved to London because of a man, at the age of 30, and I didn't know what to expect. About the man, or the place. I'd heard that the region of greater London had a population the size of the country I'd left. That Britain's average density was 632 people per square mile, compared to six in Australia, where I was from.

The man had a flat on Fleet Street. One room. It figured.

In those first, glazed days of arrival I began the search for green, and space, and sky.

I found pocket parks and squares tucked within the city but they were reluctant, they wouldn't let me in. I walked around and around those squares' empty green but the gates were locked and the fence iron was spiked and couldn't be scaled and I didn't understand. My new home was a tough nut to crack. It had stone that was harder and sharper and smoother than the honey-grainy sandstone I had left far behind; the new stone was fine and cold to the touch and stained the tips of my fingers black. It had a sky that was low, so low that it hung like the water-bowed ceiling of an old house. And its rain was soft, there was no weight in it, and I wanted wind and push and wet, I wanted rain like at home that drenched clothes in three seconds.

I began dreaming of home too much, of ready smiles and tall skies and flinging sun into my lungs, of *warmth.*

The man said to hang in there, that one day we'd be rich enough to move out, to walk in one of those reluctant parks, imagine that. But I'd read in one of this country's newspapers that this was the land that looked askance at ambition, and boldness, and striving, that took refuge in denigration and sneer.

For 18 months I hung in there, in our one room on Fleet Street. Because of the man, not the city. It refused to enchant me. I walked cobbles and pavements that whispered of old smoke and grit and blood and spit and I wondered, often, at what I'd done. My man, another expat, did not understand this attitude: he'd read the *Spectator* since he was eight, belonged to the PG Wodehouse Society, loved his Scotch and his Savile Row suits and was from Melbourne, a wintry city. This was his life's goal, to be in this land. Whereas I was from Sydney, a warmer place, and the English cold felt as if it had curled up in my bones like mould. Like so many Australians in the UK, I hadn't yet learnt how to dress warmly, hadn't learnt the secret of layers.

We had no proper kitchen, no oven, no washing machine and my grandmother couldn't understand the life choice I'd made, the dramatic drop in my standard of living. But the man wouldn't allow me to give up. He taught me to lean far out of the window and twist my neck to catch the sky. To warm my fingers on the hot water bottle before I touched his skin. To look, really look at the history around us. He showed me the Roman walls by the Barbican, and the plaques in Postman's Park, and St Bride's, the writers' church with its ancient crypts, and we managed to brew a happiness in our dark, little bedsit.

But still I had that nagging gravitational pull south, it was like the smudge of a storm cloud between us. Home filled my heart. I couldn't find a new home in London. I constantly tasted air that was stained by cars, the cram of exhausts. My lungs had been coddled for most of my life and in this new place my breathing shallowed and my walking slowed and my sleeping ballooned in the tenacious cold. I slept a lot. And my life shrank.

What I was told

'You'll never be invited into an English person's house.'

'They have plastic tubs in the kitchen sink.'

'It's impossible to get a decent shower.'

'They'll only invite you into their homes as you're leaving.'

'Every kitchen has Fairy washing-up liquid. Isn't that hysterical? Fairy.'

'They sunbake on grass. On the one day of sunshine a year.'

'If ever you DO get invited into one of their houses, just remember the magic words *would you like another cup of tea*?'

'Why?'

'Because they actually mean "Would you go now, please." They never say what they mean.'

The colour of the city

I'd read that London was a red city, sanguine. From the Great Fire to the bombs of the Blitz to the phone boxes and mail boxes and buses, red was the colour of the energy of the place. But to me it was a cold, steely grey, an energy that was uptight, unwelcoming, hard. I only saw red when the smartly dressed woman on Regent Street poked me in the head with the spoke of her umbrella, and drew blood, and didn't stop, didn't look at the damage she'd inflicted. The English were meant to have invented manners, weren't they, so why were they so impolite? Why wouldn't they meet my eyes? Or tell me their name when I thrust out my hand and gave them mine.

I wrote to my grandmother that sometimes I didn't understand what I'd done, I didn't know why I was here.

'You're in love', she replied, and left it at that.

What happened at the laundromat

One Monday evening, during the weekly laundromat ritual, the man steered me into a jewellery shop in Covent Garden and bought a ring in the middle of the washing cycle. He later proposed, formally, over the ironing board. *He* was doing the ironing. I was soaring.

He signed a three-year work contract. He was wedded to this place, I was not. But I was wedded to him. And so I stayed.

Go west, young woman

I must have been just about the only person who moved to Notting Hill in the late 1990s without knowing what Notting Hill was. The man's new job was out west and we needed somewhere closer to his office. I favoured Kensington or Chelsea. I'd read about those glossy places as I slavishly pored over English *Vogue* as a teenager in the sticks, dreaming of being a Sloane. But the man liked a flat in some suburb with a Hill in it. He said a film was coming out soon and I would see what he meant. I'd heard of a film about a murderer who put acid in a bath. He said not that one. This one was about a different Notting Hill.

I twigged when the person looking at the flat ahead of us was one of the girls from the All Saints, wanting to buy a gift for her mother. I began to think that maybe I could like this place, suddenly I wanted that flat and this suburb, I wanted to beat the girl from All Saints. We were told we would have to be quick.

The colour of Notting Hill

White, and green.

White, from those lovely rows of stately terraces – the London of Henry James and prams wheeled by nannies in parks, the London, at last, of my imagination. White, from the cherry blossoms in the early spring that floated down to the roads like tissue paper snow. Green, from the awning of the deli on Elgin Crescent that's crammed with goodies (at last, proper food!). Green, from the coolness of the beautiful communal gardens, empty, languid and dank in the heat.

We didn't live in one of those terraces, and we didn't have access to any communal gardens, but we had a little garden of our own, a handkerchief one at the back of our flat. The All Saints girl wasn't interested in the end. Things were looking up. Especially when I began telling people about where we had bought and they began filling me in about this Hill place.

'But it's only a basement flat, and it's tiny, and it's just hanging on by its fingernails to W11. The street's really ugly, it's all bare, with council flats down one side.'

'It doesn't matter. You just wait.'

First impressions

It wasn't the best beginning.

What was all the fuss about Portobello Road? It was meant to be glamorous and chic, but to me it just seemed dirty, messy, scruffy. And then there was the nightmare ride into town during rush hour on the 23 bus. (Why did people in England cough so much, and why didn't they cover their mouths?) And don't get me started on the cram that is Tesco on Portobello Road. Or the post office near Ladbroke Grove tube. I hadn't yet learnt how to meekly queue. I was too jittery and impatient for all that.

Home wasn't much better. People used the entrance to our flat as a communal rubbish bin; they just tossed their refuse over the rail. In our back garden, lolly wrappers and empty cigarette packets and a sanitary pad were all thrown over the back fence. Cigarette butts were flicked from a window above us onto our terrace. What was it about the

English, and respecting someone's personal space? Maybe it had to do with that ratio of 632 people per square mile compared to six. Maybe that's why they coughed so much. And the post office was always packed. I had a lot to learn.

The husband said we should try to prettify the front area, to dissuade people from using it as their rubbish bin. I bought a plant from the market – it was stolen. I bought a shiny silver rubbish bin – it was stolen. One day we came home and one of our front windows was smashed – the stereo was gone too. And all my favourite CDs, none of the husband's, they didn't want his. We managed to laugh at that.

They didn't steal the damp. It had begun sprouting its insidious spores the week we moved in. We realised the sellers had been canny, scraping the flaking back and painting over it and urging a quick sale before they had to scrape again. Someone told me that Notting Hill was built on mudflats, that there was often dampness and subsidence here. We would have to live with it. We did. We were newly married, and euphoric with it. We could cope.

I much preferred the story of Notting Hill being built on the piggeries. That we lived where they slaughtered the livestock last century and a terrible smell used to emanate from the area. A century later the smell was bliss after the dirty, steely, black-lung taste of Fleet Street. Something was happening to me in Notting Hill, I was uncurling, relaxing, walking taller.

I was loving playing in history in this land.

I was loving the fractious energy of London, the dynamism of being in such a vast metropolis now that I had my sanctuary to return to each night. I felt like I was finally living *in* the world, rather than on the edge of it.

And after two long years of living in England, I was making friends.

The key
'To be fair to the English,' said a Kiwi who'd been in the UK about the same time as me, 'maybe they don't befriend us because they don't think it's worth it. Maybe they think we're just here for six months, or a year at the most, so they can't be bothered. It's only perhaps when they sense that we're making an effort to stay, and like it, that they extend themselves. Maybe that's the key for us – sticking it out.'

'The English will keep you at a distance,' said an American film director, 'until you speak up and give it back to them. Then they know they can't intimidate you and they respect you for it. And after that they're rock solid, loyal friends.'

Rock solid, loyal friends. Suddenly we were making them around Notting Hill. When our flat was flooded because of a dodgy plumber renovating the bathroom above us, we had a daisy chain of neighbours helping us rescue our books. I was bumping into people I knew, again and again, as I walked up the street. I was talking to English people. We were getting invitations to dinners and readings and parties. And we didn't have to take the bus to them or the tube, we could walk.

'It just takes time,' said the husband.

'And Notting Hill. I feel like I'm back in a community again.'

'Yeah, maybe that. And maybe it's just you. Maybe your attitude has changed.'

'Yeah, perhaps.'

What I love about Notting Hill

That I walk up the road to post a letter, and come back with a chair.

That I know the lady at the fruit stall on Portobello Road who sells me mangoes and peaches from all over the road, and calls me darlin', no matter how wet and cold the day has been or how long she's been standing out in it.

That our postman is called Terry, and always stops for a chat, and people back in Australia say incredulously: *you know your postman?*

The cherry blossoms in spring, that walking through them as they fall still makes me smile out loud.

That there used to be a racecourse called the Hippodrome around the rim of the hill, and there's a plaque that tells me that.

That there *is* a hill. I love the dynamism of places that aren't flat.

That I once saw a squirrel in our garden.

That the rubbish in our front entrance doesn't get to me any more.

That the Nu-Line hardware stores are just up the road, and they always have what I need, and suggest canny things that I didn't even know I need, but do.

That there's a cool cinema within walking distance, right near a great second-hand bookstore, right by a good coffee place.

That the smoothie shop opened.

That pastries on a Saturday morning, from the green-awninged deli, have become a garden ritual.

That the silvery eucalyptus in our backyard, with its startling colour against the English greens, is thriving.

That one of my favourite pastimes is sunbaking on a warm weekend, with the ten national newspapers of this land, on a rug in our backyard, *on the grass*.

That I don't know the service station man, but I do know the people in the deli, and the woman in the plate-painting shop, and the vintage clothing store.

That I've started being invited into English people's houses.

And no, I'm not about to leave.

FRESH & WILD RENDEZVOUS

Rachel Johnson

Rachel Johnson was born in 1965 and has lived in Notting Hill since 1979. **Notting Hell**, from which the following extract is taken, is her first novel.

And now I've got to dash to Fresh & Wild to meet poor Marguerite for lunch. She says she's got some interesting gossip for me, so I must peel off my tracksuit bottoms and put on something more Westbourne Grovey, i.e. something feminine yet edgy that will not make me feel too middle-aged and frowsy when I inevitably bump into Stella McCartney buying vegan baby food at the chill cabinet.

I decide on Converse sneakers, no socks, skinny Superfine white jeans that aren't so skinny on me and a Gharani Strok top that floats serenely over my lumps and bumps, and hope that if I do see Stella, she will see that I am channelling Liz Hurley. I've often noticed that any shop that purveys peace and gastro-enteric well being at premium prices has many more bad-tempered customers in it than a famously harmonious shop like, say, Ikea.

The staff, a wholemealier-than-thou bunch handpicked for their inability to speak English, work slower and slower the more people they have to serve. Somehow the combination of the slowness of service, the purity of the produce and the beautiful people treating their bodies as temples is less calming than you would imagine. Fresh & Wild is not merely a wholefood supermarket, butchery, fishmonger and café. It's a warzone.

Last month, a woman exited the store after a light, gluten-free lunch and found a traffic warden in the process of writing her a ticket and affixing it to the windscreen of her Mercedes jeep. She picked up a brick off a skip and hit him over the head with it, knocking him out. She ripped off the ticket, laid it on his prone body, then she hopped into her car, reversed into the car behind, and drove off at speed, almost killing Ruby Wax on the pedestrian crossing. Presumably, the woman felt that braining a hard-working Ghanaian immigrant after spending his entire annual salary on a morning's groceries was a very appropriate climax to her ethical retail experience.

I enter into the fruit and vegetable produce side of the store, which wafts conceit in the same way that supermarkets pipe the smell of fresh-baked bread at their customers. Every so often hidden jets spritz the fruit with mineral water with a sound like a Russian babuschka sighing – *paah!* – over the loss of her family dacha in the steppes.

Today, there are so many young women with off-road, all-terrain 4x4 buggies on the stairs gazing intently at tomatoes on the vine that I have to thread my way past them to reach the cafeteria-juice-bar-baked-goods section. *En route*, past the kelp, I stop to have a quick look at the customer noticeboard. Someone has pinned up a note complaining that the store still doesn't have the special olive oil from the Kazakhstani collective she asked for *at least* a month ago – even though she left the telephone number and email of the one stockist with the resident homeopathist.

While I'm sitting at a high table trying to decide whether to have a juice or a smoothie, a catfight breaks out behind me. It is between two women who were both reaching at the same time to grab the last packet of Sproutpeople pea shoots at the chill cabinet.

'I'm sorry, but I had it first,' one snaps.

'No, you didn't, you only grabbed it because you saw me reaching for it,' the other screeches back.

A shop assistant summons the assistance of not one but two security guards but, by the time they arrive, the two women have established they both took Lolly Stirk's Pregnancy For Yoga classes together as *primigravidae* and are already exchanging hugs and birth stories.

Which only reminds me – as if I need any reminding, that is – that just as all Notting Hill children are either special needs or gifted, no Notting Hill mummy can ever admit to having had a normal, painful seven-hour labour. Parturition is either over in five seconds thanks to whale music and breathing, or is, of course, a life-threatening blue-light-flashing thirty-six-hour hospital drama ending in emergency C-section, performed, of course, by London's top ob-gyn consultant.

After they're both done with birthing, they move on to the perenni-ally fascinating subject of what they put in their children's mouths.

I hear one say to the other that she's so into this place because they have all the best stuff, and when something sprouts, 'It's, like, at the peak of its life force and energy'. I make a mental note that people talk about wholefood these days in just the same reverential and boring way they used to talk about Ecstasy in the 1980s.

I cannot bear this for much longer (the converted do so love to preach to each other), so I go up to wait in line to order a root juice of beetroot, apple, ginger and carrot when I see Marguerite arrive, look-ing almost translucent in her whiteness. She is wearing tailored city shorts, heels, a wonderful, puffy and delicate Victorian blouse and a Belstaff biker jacket and, I have to say, she totally rocks, despite her pal-lor.

She usually looks very grown-up in Prada and Lanvin and so on and, seeing her today, I suddenly wonder whether this all might be the mak-ing of Marguerite.

She spots me at the counter and I point to our table, so she sits down and glances at a leaflet trumpeting the credentials of all Fresh & Wild's marvellous, caring, communitarian organic suppliers.

After my mandatory twenty-minute wait, I carry my tiny carton of juice (ounce for fluid ounce, more expensive than Cristal) back to our table and kiss Marguerite's cool white cheek.

'Shall we just get the food ordeal out of the way and then concen-trate?' I suggest. I know this can take some time. Marguerite doesn't do tea, coffee, alcohol, dairy, red meat, wheat or toxins. No one can understand how she and Patrick, a burger-chomping, red-blooded male, ever got it together.

We go up to the food counter.

'How about some sesame and ginger tofu teriyaki?' I say, as we study the smorsgasbord of dishes, 'with a spelt wrap? That must be fine, surely?'

Marguerite finally asks for two rolls of pink sushi made with avocado, cucumber and beetroot paté rolled up in sheets of nori, and another small portion of courgette 'pasta' with cashew mint cream, reminding me that she always serves her boys 'spaghetti' sauce atop a depressing tangle of no-carb cabbage rather than spaghetti.

We wait what seems like an age to pay while the staff chat among themselves and ignore us, so I combine our trays and Marguerite waits at the juice bar for her smoothie. Then I finally go back to our table, me with my little bottle of Fiji water. While waiting, I read the label.

'One of the purest waters in the world issuing from a virgin ecosystem of aquifers deep beneath the volcanic highlands and pristine tropical forests of Viti Levu,' it says.

Sometimes I think that if Fresh & Wild sold little bottles of fresh Swiss mountain air, we'd buy that, too.

SOURCES AND FURTHER READING

Ackroyd, Peter, *London: The Biography*, Chatto & Windus 2000

Adams, Eddie (ed.), *Westbourne Grove in Wealth, Work and Welfare*, Gloucester Court Reminiscence Group 2000

Amis, Martin, *The Information*, HarperCollins 1995; *Money*, Cape 1984

Athill, Diana, *Stet,* Granta 2000

Ballard, JG, *Concrete Island*, Cape 1974

Banksy, *Wall and Piece*, Century 2005

Barlay, Nick, *Crumple Zone*, Sceptre 2000

Barrie, JM, *Peter Pan* 1902

Begbie, Harold, *Broken Earthenware*, Hodder & Stoughton 1909

Chesterton, GK, *The Napoleon of Notting Hill*, John Lane, The Bodley Head 1904; *Autobiography*, Hutchinson 1936

Coke, Lady Mary, *Lady Mary Coke Letters and Journals 1756–1774*, Kingsmead Reprints, Bath 1970

Curtis, Richard, *Notting Hill*, Hodder & Stoughton 1999

Da Costa, Rosalind, *Growing Up in Notting Hill, Notting Hill Revealed,* mynottinghill.co.uk 2000

Denny, Barbara, *Notting Hill and Holland Park Past*, Historical Publications 1993

Dickens, Charles, *Household Words* 1849

Monica Dickens, *An Open Book*, Heinemann 1938

Dirsztay, Patricia, *Church Furnishings: A NADFAS guide*, Routledge & Kegan Paul 1978

Donald, Anabel, *The Glass Ceiling*, Macmillan 1994

Duncan, Andrew, *Taking on the Motorway: North Kensington Amenity Trust 21 Years,* Kensington & Chelsea Community History Group 1992; *Walking London*, New Holland 1997

Ellen, Barbara, 'Still fighting the bad guys', Interview with Caroline Coon, *Observer Review*, 30 July 2000

Gladstone, Florence and Barker, Ashley, *Notting Hill in Bygone Days*, Anne Bingley 1969 (1924)

Gordon, P, *White Law: Racism in the Police, Courts and Prisons*, Pluto Press 1983

Green, Jonathon, *Days in the Life: Voices from the English Underground 1961–1971*, Heinemann 1988/Pimlico 1998

Hardy, Justine, *Goat*, John Murray 2000

Alethea Hayter, *A Sultry Month*, Faber 1965

Heath-Stubbs, John, *Collected Poems 1943–1987*, Carcanet 1988

The Historic Buildings Board of The Greater London Council, *Survey of London XXXVII: Northern Kensington*, University of London, The Athlone Press 1973

Hodgson, Vere, *Few Eggs and No Oranges*, Persephone Books 2003

Hollinghurst, Alan, *The Line of Beauty*, Picador 2004

Holmes, Chris, *The Other Notting Hill*, Brewin Books 2005

Horovitz, Michael, 'Notting Hill Carnival Poem' from *Wordsounds and Sightlines: New and Selected Poems,* Sinclair-Stevenson 1994

James, Henry, *The Wings of the Dove*, 1902

James, PD, *A Taste for Death,* Faber 1986

Jephcott, Pearl, *Notting Hill: A Troubled Area*, Faber 1964

Johnson, Rachel, *Notting Hell,* Fig Tree 2006

Jones, Richard, *Walking Haunted London*, New Holland 1999

Keeler, Christine and Thompson, Douglas, *The Truth at Last: My Story*, Sidgwick 2001

Kennedy, Ludovic, *10 Rillington Place*, Gollancz 1961

Kensington and Chelsea Talking Newspaper, *Voices* (double cassette), KCTN, 1999

Kindersley, Tania, *Goodbye Johnny Thunders*, Hodder Headline 1996

Kureishi, Hanif, *Sammy and Rosie Get Laid*, Faber & Faber 1988

Kurtz, Irma, *Dear London: Notes from the Big City*, Fourth Estate 1997

Lambton, Lucinda, *Temples of Convenience*, Gordon Fraser 1978

Lancaster, Osbert, *All Done from Memory*, John Murray 1953

Letts, Don, with Nobakht, David, *Culture Clash: Dread Meets Punk Rockers,* SAF
    Publishing 2007

Lewis, Wyndham, *Rotting Hill*, Black Sparrow 1951

Logue, Christopher, *Prince Charming*, Faber & Faber 1999

Low, Crail and Minto, Lucy (compilers and editors), *Rock & Pop London: The Handbook
    Guide*, Handbook Publishing 1997

Machen, Arthur, *Things Near and Far*, 1923; *Far Off Things*, Secker 1922

MacInnes, Colin, *Absolute Beginners*, Allison & Busby 1959

Mayne, Roger, *Photographs*, Jonathan Cape 2001

Mitchell, Leslie, *Holland House*, Duckworth 1980

Moorcock, Michael, *King of the City*, Scribner 2000

Neville, Richard, *Hippie, Hippie Shake*, Bloomsbury 1995

Oliver, Paul (ed.), *Black Music in Britain*, Open University Press 1990

Phillips, Charlie and Phillips, Trevor, *Notting Hill in the Sixties*, Lawrence & Wishart
    1991

Phillips, Mike and Phillips, Trevor, *Windrush: The Irresistible Rise of Multi-racial Britain*,
    HarperCollins 1998

Raban, Jonathan, *Soft City*, Hamish Hamilton 1974

Read, Piers Paul, *A Season in the West*, Secker 1988

Rendell, Ruth, *Thirteen Steps Down*, Hutchinson 2004

Richardson, Anthony, *Nick of Notting Hill – The Bearded Policeman*, Harrap 1965

Roberts, Glenys, *Metropolitan Myths*, Victor Gollancz 1982

Rous, Henrietta (ed.), *The Ossie Clark Diaries*, Bloomsbury 1998

Salewicz, Chris, *Redemption Song*, HarperCollins 2006

Selvon, Samuel, *The Lonely Londoners*, Alan Wingate 1956 / Longman 1985

Seth, Vikram, *An Equal Music*, Orion 1999

Shakespeare, Nicholas, *Londoners*, Sidgwick & Jackson 1986

Shaw, Henry, *Notting Hill Synagogue 1900–1960*

Sherriff, RC, *The Hopkins Manuscript*, Victor Gollancz 1939

Sinclair, Iain, *Lights Out for the Territory*, Granta 1997

Soremekun, Sarah, in Whetlor and Bartlett *Portobello: Its People, its Past, its Present* 1996

Tennant, Emma, *Burnt Diaries*, Canongate 1999

Vague, Tom, *Entrance to Hipp: An Historical and Psychogeographical Report on Notting Hill*, Vague 29, 1997; *London Psychogeography*, Vague 30, 1998; *The Grove*, unpub lished manuscript (ongoing)

Waugh, Teresa, *The Gossips*, Sinclair-Stevenson 1995

Wells, HG, *Love and Mr Lewisham,* London 1900

Whetlor, Sharon, *The Story of Notting Dale: From Potteries and Piggeries to present times*, Kensington & Chelsea Community History Group 1998

Whetlor, Sharon and Bartlett, Liz, *Portobello: Its People, its Past, its Present,* Kensington & Chelsea Community History Group 1996

COPYRIGHT ACKNOWLEDGEMENTS

Extract from *Burnt Diaries* by Emma Tennant reprinted with permission from Canongate Books Ltd. 14 High Street, Edinburgh EH1 1TE. Copyright © Emma Tennant 1999

Tom Vague *Entrance to Hipp: An historical and psychogeographical report on Notting Hill,* Vague 29, 1997; *London Psychogeography,* Vague 30, 1998; *The Grove,* unpublished manuscript (ongoing) Copyright © Tom Vague

Extract from *The Gossips* by Teresa Waugh reprinted with permission of the author. Copyright © Teresa Waugh 1995

Extract from *Love and Mr Lewisham* reprinted with permission of AP Watt Ltd on behalf of the Literary Executors of HG Wells

Extract from *Portobello: Its people, its past, its present* by Sharon Whetlor and Liz Bartlett © 1996 Kensington & Chelsea Community History Group

Index

Absolute Beginners 270
Acklam Road 133, 214
Ackroyd, Peter 98
Adams, Eddie 108
Albery, Nicholas 291–6
Aldridge Road Villas 94
Ali, Muhammad 99
All Done from Memory 264
All Saints Road 93,94, 95
Amenity Trust 56
Amis, Martin 55, 136
Anderson, Jim 180
Antique Shops
Alice's 44, 76
Arbon Interiors 155
Bazar 142, 155
Eighty-eight Antiques 142, 156
Katrina Phillips 77
Les Couilles du Chien 142, 156
Mac's 156
Myriad Antiques 176, 200
Ollies 142, 157
Sheila Cook Textiles 78
Apocalypse Hotel 167, 214
Archer Street 103
Architects & designers
George Alexander 23,
Thomas Allason 16, 234–5,
Thomas Allom 24, John
Francis Bentley 58, 107, 174,
William Burges 174, Sir

Hugh Casson 182, Henry
Clutton 57, 174, Neville
Conder, 182, Theo Crosby
106, William Flockhart 181,
Ernö Goldfinger 141, Piers
Gough 102, John Griffith
145, Enoch Bassett Keeling
184, Henry Edward Kendall
145, Thomas Meyer 107,
Alex Michaelis 165, AWN
Pugin 174, JP St Aubyn 170,
John Hargrave Stevens 23,
Lewis Vulliamy 169, Aston
Webb 181, Will White 101,
124, Henry Wilson 132,
Robert Jewell Withers 169
Art material shops
Lyndon's 78
Lyndon's Stitch & Beads 78
Print Gallery, The 36
Arthurs Stores 108
Artiste Assoiffé 21
Artists & writers
Diana Athill 20, Asher Balin
48, JG Ballard 55, 56, JM
Barrie 21, Ben Uri Gallery
26, Lazar Berson 26 , Frank
Brangwyn 181, Lord Byron
146, 182, Angela Carter 49,
Bruce Chatwin 49, Robert
Colquhoun 185, Charles
Conder 181, L. Credito 48,

Thomas Creswick 16,
Charles Dickens 105, 182 ,
Jim Dine 42, Ashley Dukes
17, Edmund Dulac 181, TS
Eliot 17, Vivian Forbes 181,
Ford Madox Ford 16, Antonia
Fraser 183, Lucian Freud
185, William Powell Frith
103, John Galsworthy 183,
Shlomo Goldenberg 48, WS
Graham 185, Thomas Hardy
94, Hans Werner Henze 25,
Damien Hirst 16, David
Hockney 42, 99, WH
Hudson 94, Ted Hughes 49,
AM Kaizer 48, Hanif Kureishi
43, 226, Leo Koenig 48,
Wyndham Lewis 185, James
McBey 186, Robert
MacBryde 185, Thomas
Babbington Macaulay 182,
Katherine Mansfield 26,
Roger McGough 42, Barney
McMahon 14, John
Middleton Murry 26, John
Minton 185 , Henry Moore
42, Alberto Moravia 49,
William Mulready 16,
Alexander Myerovitz 48,
George Orwell 42, Glyn

Philpot 181, Shamai Pinaky
48, Harold Pinter 183, James
Pryde 181, Jean Rhys 20,
Charles Ricketts 181, F.
Cayley Robinson 181, Sir
Walter, Scott 182, Ronald
Searle 185, Will Self 55,132,
Charles Shannon 181, Dylan
Thomas 185, Yevtushenko 49
Ashwell, Lena 105
Aubrey House 232, 256
Aubrey Walk 182–3
Avondale Park 173, 238

Ballet Rambert 18
Bananas 49
banks & money exchange 201
Banksy 55
Barlay, Nick 140
Bedford Gardens 185
Bennett, John 184
Bike shops
  Barnes 104
  Bicycle Workshop 97, 119,
  201
  Halfpipe 157
Birtwell, Celia 176
Black Music in Britain 134
Blake, Charles Henry 235
Blavatsky, Madame 266
Blenheim Crescent 26,
  51–2
Bookshops
  Blenheim Books 51, 79
  Books for Cooks 51, 79
  Daunt Books 180, 195
  Notting Hill Books 36
  Oxfam Bookshop 79
  Travel Bookshop 51–2, 79
Boot, Adrian 212
Borromeo, St Charles &
  Oblates 107, 174
Bousquet, Ben 244
Bramley Road 166
Branson, Richard 44
British National Socialist
  Movement (BNSM) 177
Britten, Benjamin 18
Brownlow, Kevin 171, 177
Burnt Diaries 49

Cabbies' shelter 18
Cafés

202 110
Arancina 28
Armadillo Café 187
Baalbak 149
Babes 'n' Burgers 59
Books for Cooks 79
Bossa Nova Café 60
Caravaggio 60
Chelsea Spice & Grill 187
Cockney's Pie & Mash 58
Costa's Fish Restaurant 28
Cyrano – Brasserie 187
Eve's Market Café 60
Garden Café 149
Grocer on Elgin 63
Hummingbird Bakery 63
Lazy Daisy Café 42
Lisboa 142, 149
Lucky 7 & Crazy Homies 110
Makan 60
Negozio Classica 44
Ottolenghi 111
Paul 188
Progreso 60
Rotisserie Jules 28
St Helen's Foodstore 188
Taste of Punjab 150
Tea & Coffee Plant 51
Tea Palace 111
Tea's Me 150
Thai River 166, 188
Tom's 105
Yum Yum 151
Caine, Nelly 51
Cambridge Gardens 135
Cameron, David 165
Campden Hill 232
Campden Hill Residents
  Association 15
Campden Hill Road 14, 185
Campden Hill Square 182–3
Campden Hill Towers 16
Carnival 216–221, 245
Ebony 221, Russ Henderson
221, Horniman's Pleasance
Park 221, Claudia Jones 219,
Rhaune Laslett 98, 219
Mangrove 95, 221, mas 217,
Metronomes 221, Notting
Hill Carnival Champions of
Steel 221, Notting Hill
Carnival Trust 220, origins
206, Leslie Palmer 219,
Panorama 216, 221, shebeens

218, soca float 217, sound-
systems 217, steel-bands
221, *West Indian Gazette* 219
Charity shops
  Charity Shop, The 37
  Oxfam 37, 106, 19
  Trinity Hospice 37
Chepstow Road 108
Chepstow Villas 21
Chessure, Jesse 163
Chesterton, GK 185, 262–4
Chesterton Road 136
Chevalier, Albert 104, 168
**Children's clothes & toys
& entertainment**
  Bramley's Big Adventure
  192
  Holland Park –
  Adventure Playground,
    One O'Clock Club 193
  Playstation Skatepark 153
  Princess of Wales Memorial
    Playground 33
  Skate Bowl 153
  shops
  Cheeky Monkeys 80
  Dotty Dot 195
  Honeyjam 80
  One Small Step One Giant
    Leap 80
  Sasti 80
  Their Nibs 81
Christie, John 161
**Churches & places of
worship**
  All Saints Church 101, 235
  Kensington Temple 18
  Notting Hill Methodist
    Church 104, 163, 245
  Notting Hill Synagogue 47
  Peniel Chapel 47
  St Clement 170, 238
  St Francis of Assisi 174, 237
  St George's 184
  St James Norlands 168–9
  St John the Evangelist 23
  St Mary of the Angels 57, 107
  St Peter's 24
  St Sava's Serbian Orthodox
    132
  Westbourne Grove Baptist 106
Churchill, Sarah 52
Cinemas and theatres
  Bijou Theatre 105

Electric Cinema 50,68
Gate Cinema 13
Gate Theatre 17, 34
Mercury Theatre 17
Notting Hill Coronet 13, 34
20th Century Theatre 104–5
Clarendon Cross 176
Clark, Ossie 16, 176
Clinton, Bill 65
clone town syndrome 249
Clothes shops
Aimé 119
Beatrice von Tresckow 81
Bill Amberg 120
Celia Birtwell 120
The Cross 176, 196
The Dispensary 81
Duchamp 120
Euforia 81
Ghost 121
J & M Davidson 121
The Jacksons 122
Jane Bourvis 157
Laundry Industry 122
London Beach Store 82
Nancy Pop 82
Paul Smith 38
Paul & Joe 122
Pistol Panties 122
Portobello Road Cashmere
Shop 83
Preen 83
Ray Harris 123
Still 83
Sub Couture 84
Supra for Boys 84
Supra for Girls 84
Sweaty Betty 123
Teaze 39
Wall 123
vintage & second-hand
Antique Clothing Shop 76
Crazy Clothes Connection 157
Dolly Diamond 37
Mary Moore 196
Mensah 77
Rellik 158
Virginia 176, 196
Cnotta, sons of, 231
Cobden Club 140
Cochrane, Kelso 241–2
Cohn-Bendit, Dani 25
Coke, Lady Mary 182, 256
Colegio Español 57

Colville Mews 102
Colville Terrace 50, 101
Comper, Sir Ninian 101
Congestion Charge 252
Conran, Tom 94
Cook, Peter 44
Coon, Caroline 177–8
Cope, Sir Walter 182, 231
Coppin, Sir George 231
Costa, Rosalind Da 247
Critchlow, Frank 96, 220, 245
Crookes, Sir William 21
Crumple Zone 140
Crystal Cleaners 47
Curtis, Richard 53

Davies, Arthur & Sylvia
Llewelyn 21
Davis, Edmund & Mary 181
*Days in the Life: Voices from the
English Underground* 99, 179
Dear London 25
Denbigh Close 44
Denbigh Terrace 44
Dennis, Felix 180
Denny, Barbara 22
Depp, Johnny 20
Devlin, Arabella, Cheryl &
Sonny 50
Dickens, Monica 41, 168
Directory 201–4
Dog Shop 52
Dukeries 184, 234
Duncan, Andrew 18
Dupon, Monsieur 101
Dutschke, Rudi 25

Edgecombe, Johnny 243
Electric House 51
Elgin Crescent 45–47
Evans, Timothy 161

Fallowell, Duncan 312–315
Farren, Mick 178–9
Few Eggs and No Oranges 267
Films 222–228
Absolute Beginners 226, *Alfie*
224, Woody Allen 222, 227,
Michelangelo Antonioni 225,
Kevin Billington 224, *Blow Up*
224 *The Blue Lamp* 222, John
Boorman 225, Donald
Cammell 98, Basil Dearden
223, *Duck Soup* 223, Richard

Fleischer 226, Stephen Frears
226, *The Future is Unwritten*
214, *A Hard Day's Night* 224,
225, Menhaj Huda 227, *I Hired
a Contract Killer* 226, *Interlude*
224, *It Happened Here* 171,
177, 224, *The Italian Job* 224,
Aki Kaurismäki 226, *Kidulthood*
227, *The Knack* 224, *The
Lavender Hill Mob* 222, *Leo the
Last* 222, 225, *London Kills Me*
43, 226, *Look Back in Anger*
224, *The L-Shaped Room* 223,
Match Point 227, *Morgan: a
Suitable Case for Treatment* 224,
Notting Hill (see own entry),
Otley 224, Horace Ove 227,
The Passenger 226, *Passport to
Pimlico* 223, *Performance* 98,
225, Michael Powell 222,
Emeric Pressburger 222,
Pressure 227, *Quadrophenia*
223, *Rear Window* 225, *The Red
Shoes* 222, *Richard 111* 225,
Michael Relph 223, *Rising
Damp* 223, Nicholas Roeg 98,
Sammy and Rosie Get Laid, 226,
Sapphire 223, *Scandal* 226,
Secret Ceremony 224, *Sid and
Nancy* 223, *The Squeeze*, 223,
10 Rillington Place 226, *Trottie
True* 225, *West 11* 223, *Wings of
the Dove* 225, Michael Winner
223, *Withnail and I* 226
Fitzpatrick, Martin 132
Flower shops
Flowered Corner 158
Orlando Hamilton 197
Toms 45, 84, 197
Valerie's Flowers 58, 84
Wild at Heart 123
Fogg, Harry 222–8
Food & wine shops
Breadstall 61
Clarke's Shop & Café 28
Corney & Barrow 61
Farmer's Market 29
Fish Shop at Kensington
Place 29
French Cheese Stall 62
P De La Fuente 62
Gail's 62
R Garcia 54, 63
Golborne Fisheries 151

Grain Shop 54, 63
Grocer on Elgin 63
Handford 189
Hummingbird Bakery 63
Jeroboams 180, 189
Kingsland 64
L'Etoile 151
Le Maroc 152
Lidgates 180, 189
Lisboa Delicatessen 151
Maison Blanc 180, 190
Melt 111
Mr Christian's 45–6, 61
Negozio Classica 44, 111
Oporto Patisserie 142
Ottolenghi 111
Portobello Wholefoods 64
Speck 190
Spice Shop 64
St Helen's Foodstore 188
Tavola 108, 112
Tawana Thai Supermarket 112
Tea & Coffee Plant 64
Tom's 112
Fox School 12
Frestonia 166–7, 245, 291–7
Fresh & Wild 106
Friends of Portobello 251

Gaine, Mary 136
Galleries
Axia 124
East West 85
England & Co 124
Flow 106, 124
Gallery Maya 124
Hanina Fine Art 125
Kiln Gallery 197
Louise T Blouin Institute
  167, 197
Portobello Auctions 85
Portobello Print & Map
  Shop 85
Pruskin 198
Redfern's 198
Richard Morant 125
Sacred Space 23
Stern Art Dealers 125
Temple Gallery 198
Turf Gallery 125
Wolseley Fine Arts 106, 126
Gemmell, Nikki 321–8
Gern, Augustus 169
Gift & home shops

Arch 18 198
B & T Antiques 126
Bellhouse 86
Big Table Furniture 126
Big Tomato 199
Brissi 126
Buyers & Sellers 158
Cath Kidston 199
Ceramica Blue 86
Chloe Alberry 86
Cloth Shop 86
Cross the Road 199
Fez 158
Frontiers 38
Gong 45, 86
Graham & Green 45, 87
Jenny-Lyn 127
John Oliver 38
Jones Lighting 127
Lanna 127
Last Place on Earth 55, 77,
  200
Portfolio 159
Revival Upholstery 127
Sebastiano Barbagallo 38
Summerill & Bishop 176, 200
Temptation Alley 58, 87
Themes & Variations 128
Verandah 87
Vessel 39
Warris Vianni & Co 159
Yaya 88
Gladstone, Florence 97
Golborne Road 136–138
Gordon, Lucky 243
Gossips, The 12
Grand Union Canal 232
Grant, Hugh 13, 52
gravel pits 41, 232
Great Escape, The 139
Green, Jonathon 99, 179
Guilt Gardens 238
gypsies 166, 236

Hairdressers
Base Cuts 69
Bladerunners 35
Children of Vision 69
Kell Skött 154
Halse, Emmeline 23
Hardy, Justine 319–20
Hare, Cecil 101
Hasaniya, Al- 56
Hayne, Amy 238

Health, beauty & fitness
Beauty Works West 117
Bliss 69
Calders Pharmacy 35
Cowshed 176, 194
DR Evans 70
Hair & Tanning Rooms 194
Lambton Place Health
  Club 117
Life Centre, The 36
Miller Harris 118
Nail 2000 118
Portobello Green Fitness
  Club 70
Portobello Green Room 70
Saint's Tattoo Studio 71
Scin 47, 71
Screen Face 118
SPACE.NK 118
Virgin Active 155
Westway Sports Centre 195
Zarvis 71
Heath-Stubbs, John 109
Henry Dickens Court 168
Heseltine, Michael
Hill, Octavia 238, 250
Hillgate Village 12
Hippie, Hippie Shake 178
Hippodrome Place 173, 176
Hippodrome Racecourse 21–22,
  235
History 230–53
Hodgson, Vere 266–9
Holland House 182, 231
Holland, Lord 232
Holland Park 181
Holland Park Avenue 180
Holland Park Opera 194
Hollinghurst, Alan 19
Hollings, Father Michael 107
Hopkins, John 'Hoppy' 206–7
Horovitz, Michael 206, 248, 281
Hotels & b & bs
Abbey Court 27
Astors Leinster Hostel 110
Earl Percy 149
Gate Hotel 59
Guesthouse West 108, 110
Lennox Hotel 27
Portobello Hotel 20, 27
Portobello Gold Hotel 59
YHA Holland House 187

Ice House 182

immigration 137, 239–41,
Improved Tenements
  Association 238
Information, The 55
International Times 207
Ironside, Virginia 273
Ivanov, Eugene 243

James, PD 183
Jenkins, William Henry 103
Jephcott, Pearl 171
Jewellery shops
  Andea Jewellery 88
  Dinny Hall 128
  Horace 88
  Isis 88
  Jessie Western 89
  Sarah Bunting 89
  Solange Azagury-Partridge
    108, 128
Johnson, Rachel 328–31
Jones, Nick 51
Jones, Richard 14
Jones, Rufus 177
Jordan, Colin 177

Karma Kars 105, 204
Kavan, Anna 273–7
Keeler, Christine 242
Kempe, Charles Eamer 23
Kennedy, Ludovic 161
Kenrick, Bruce 245
**Kensal Green Cemetery
  143–8, 232**
Kensal Green Cemetery,
  Friends of 144
  Thomas Allom 147
  Augustus Frederick 145
  James Barry 147
  George Birkbeck 147
  Emile Blondin 147
  Isambard Kingdom Brunel 147
  William Burges 148
  Lord Byron 146
  George Frederick Carden
    144
  Ossie Clark 147
  Wilkie Collins 146
  Dissenters Chapel 145–6, 148
  Andrew Ducrow 147
  John Elliotson 147
  Thomas Hood 146
  John Henry Leigh Hunt 147
  Augusta Leigh 147

Freddy Mercury 147
John Samuel Murray 147
Duke of Portland 148
Terence Rattigan 146
Charles Spencer Ricketts 148
William Henry Smith 147
Princess Sophia 148
Harriet Stephen 146
Leslie Stephen 146
William Makepeace
  Thackeray 146
Anthony Trollope 146
William Whiteley 147
Kensington Church Street 13
Kensington & Chelsea
  Community History Group 163
Kensington Housing Trust 238
Kensington Park Gardens 21
Kensington Park Road 11,
  17–21, 47–9
King of the City 46, 56, 287
Kossuth, Louis 103
Kurtz, Irma 25

Ladbroke Association 19
Ladbroke Gardens 235
Ladbroke Grove 21, 131, 234
Ladbroke, James 103, 232
Ladbroke Square 19, 232
Laing, RD 206
Lake, Samuel 236
Lambton, Lucinda 102
Lancaster, Osbert 26, 264-6
Lancaster Road 53, 161
Land Securities 250
Lansdowne Crescent 25, 26
Lansdowne House 180
Lansdowne Road 180
Laslett, Rhaune 98, 206, 219
Latimer Road 165
laundry protests 237
Leamington Road Villas 94
Ledbury Road 106
*Letters and Journals of Lady Mary
  Coke* 182, 256–9
Libraries 202
Lichfield, Patrick 165
Lights out for the Territory 144
Line of Beauty, The 19
Linden Gardens 16
Little, Alastair 112
Lloyd, Marie 104
Lockhart, Mother Elizabeth
  57, 107

Logue, Christopher 44
London: The Biography 98
London Free School 99, 206
London Lighthouse 132–3
Londoners 305
Lonely Londoners, The 145
Lonsdale Road 101
Lost Office 248
Love and Mr Lewisham 93

Machen, Arthur 259–62
MacInnes, Colin 52, 270–3
Mangrove 94, 96, 211
Manning, Cardinal 57, 107
Matura, Mustafa 309–12
Meanwhile Gardens 141
Metropolitan Myths 301
Metropolitan Railway 132, 234
Michael X (Michael de Freitas)
  98, 206, 277–81
Michell, John 206, 277–81
Millionaires Row 234
Mollo, Andrew 171, 177
Money 136
Monsieur Thompsons 49
Montessori School 48
Moon, Adam 222–8
Moorcock, Michael 45, 55–6,
  209, 287–91
Moorhouse Road 107
Moroccan community 138
Mosley, Sir Oswald 171, 241
Mr & Mrs Clark and Percy 176
Museum of Brands, Packaging
  & Advertising 102, 116
Music – people and places
Acklam Hall 133–4, 212–4,
Damon Albarn 167, 215, All
Saints 96, Leroy Lepke
Anderson 212, Natalie &
Nicole Appleton 96, Aswad
134–5, 211–2, Band Aid 97,
Syd Barrett 207, Basing Street
210, Chris Blackwell 135, 210,
Mel Blatt 96, Blur 97, Mark
Bolan 52, 208, David Bowie
208, Joe Boyd 207, Boyzone
97, Dave Brock 208–9
Chrysalis Music 167, The Clash
211–2, 214, Daddy VGo 95,
211, Sammy Davis 96, Julie
Felix 206, Pete Frame 208,
Carol Grimes 135, *Hall of the*

Mountain Grill 208, Hawkwind 134, 208, 210, Russell Henderson 207, Jimi Hendrix 25, 134, *In the Court of the Crimson King* 208, Island Records 210, The Jacksons 97, Pete Jenner 207, Mick Jones 212–3, Cheb Khaled 142, Lemmy Kilminster 209, Last Poets 134, Annie Lennox 46, Shaznay Lewis 96, M People 97, Madonna 53, 97, Bob Marley 135, 210–2, Pink Members 135, Merger 135, Metamorphosis Studios 96, George Michael 97, Sugar Minnott 135, Motörhead 97, 209, 101'ers 134, 213–4, the Passions 135, Courtney Pine 135, Pink Fairies134, 208, Pink Floyd 99, 206–7, punk 134, Radiohead 97, Rai music 142, The Raincoats 135, reggae 135, 210, Sarm West 97, 135, 210, Sex Pistols 180, Nina Simone 96, Paul Simonon 213, 215, ska 210, Mike Skinner 209, The Slits 135, Heather Small 97, Sons of Jah 135, 211, Space Ritual 210, Joe Strummer 48, 95, 212–3, T Rex 52, Nik Turner 208–9, Virgin, Wailers 210,
Music shops
    Dub Vendor Records 158, 212
    Honest Jons 57, 89
    Intoxica 90
    Minus Zero 51, 90
    People's Sounds Record
        Shop 128, 212
    Portobello Music 129
    Rough Trade 90
    Sounds 91

Napoleon of Notting Hill, The 262
Needham Road 106–7
Nehru, Jawaharlal 26
Neville, Richard 178
Newsagents: Rococo 91
Noble, Matthew 146
Norland Estate 235
North Kensington Law Centre 213, 297

North Kensington Library 132
Notting Dale 161, 236
Notting Hell 328–331
Notting Hill film 45, 53, 222, 227
Notting Hill and Holland Park Past 22
Notting Hill Gate 11–39
    Origins 11
Notting Hill in Bygone Days 97
Notting Hill in the 60s 242
Notting Hill Housing Trust 99, 136, 245
Notting Hill Improvements Group (NHIG) 14, 102
Notting Hill Social Council 245
Notting Hill race riots 98, 171, 241

Octopus Challenge 45
Olivier, Laurence 26, 104
On the Demolition of the Odeon Cinema 109
192 restaurant 48, 250
An Open Book 41, 168
Opie, Robert 102
Orangery 181
Oxford Gardens 57
OZ 177–9

Paul, Sir John Dean 145
Pembridge Gardens 16
Pembridge Road 11, 16, 42
Pentagram 106
Penzance Place 176
Pepperell, William 184
Peter Pan 21, 184
Petersberg Press 42
phantom bus 135
Pharmacy, The 16
Phillips, Charlie 228
Phillips, Mike 239, 242, 246
Phillips, Trevor 239, 246
Philsen's Phil-Inn Station 94
Piggeries 172, 236
Pope-Hennessy, James 24
Portland Road 176
Portobello Farm 42, 57
Portobello Film Festival 228
Portobello Green 56
Portobello: Its People, its Past, its Present 48
Portobello market 43
Portobello Road 41–58
Portobello Antiques

Market 72–76
Battersea Pen Home 73,
Beatles Stall 73, Charles
Vernon-Hunt 73, Delehar 73,
Erna Hiscock 74, Eureka
Antiques 74, Hilary Kashden
74, John Carnie Antiques 75,
John Shepherd 75, Kleanthous
Antiques 75, Lawrence Gould
75, Wynyard RT Wilkinson 76
Portobello Road Antique
    Dealers Association 72
Post offices 203
Potteries (see Notting Dale)
Pottery Lane 22, 173
Powis Gardens 97
Powis Square/Terrace 97, 225, 247
Prince Charming 44
Princedale Road 176
Princess of Wales Memorial
    Playground 33
Profumo affair 242
Pubs, bars & clubbing
    Castle, The 190
    Champion 29
    Churchill Arms 29
    Cow, The 94, 112
    Duke of Wellington 65
    Earl of Lonsdale 44, 113
    Earl Percy 152
    Elgin 152
    Fat Badger 67
    Gate 34
    Golborne Grove 153
    Hillgate 12, 29
    Inn on the Green 69
    Ladbroke Arms 30
    Market Bar 65
    Mau Mau 65
    Neighbourhood 154
    Notting Hill Arts Club 34
    Portobello Gold 65, 209
    Prince of Wales 113, 190
    Ruby & Sequoia 113
    Station House 191
    Subteranea 113
    Sun in Splendour 42
    Trailer Happiness 65
    Uxbridge Arms 12, 30
    Walmer Castle 114
    Westbourne, The 94, 114
    William 1V 153
    Windsor Castle 30, 185

Woody's 117
Pushkin Club 26

Raban, Jonathan 282–7
Rachman, Peter 97, 243
Rambert, Marie 17
Ramsden, Omar 170
Rawes, Rev Henry Augustus 174
Redemption Song 48, 95
refugees 137
Release 177
Rendell, Ruth 162
reservoir 15
Restaurants
 Assagi 114
 Belvedere 191
 Bombay Bicycle Club 191
 Bumpkin 94, 115
 Caravaggio 60
 Centonove 115
 Clarkes 30
 Cool Monkey 191
 Cow, The 94, 112
 Electric Brasserie 51, 66
 E & O 66
 Essenza 66
 Fat Badger 67
 First Floor 67
 Galicia 67
 Geales 31
 Julie's 176, 192
 Kensington Place 31
 Ledbury, The 115
 Lucky 7 & Crazy Homies 110
 Malabar 32
 Moroccan Tagine 150
 New Culture Revolution 32
 Notting Grill 192
 Notting Hill Brasserie 67
 Osteria Basilico 49, 68
 Pizza Express 32
 Portobello Gold
 Progreso 60
 Ripe Tomato 116
 Rosa's Dining Rooms 116
 Taqueria 108, 116
 Taste of Punjab 150
 Tea Palace 111
 The Twelfth House 32
 Walmer Castle 114
 Westbourne 94, 114
Rice-Davies, Mandy 243
Roberts, Glenys 301–5

Roberts, Julia 13, 52
Robinson, Rev Arthur Dalgarno 170
Rothenstein, Julian 49
Rowe Housing Trust 238
Rowe, Sir Reginald 238
RBK & C 251
Royal Crescent 168
Rugby Club 172

St Ann's Villas 168
St Helen's Gardens 165
St James's Gardens 168
St Luke's Mews 94
St Luke's Road 94
St Mark's Road 135
St Quintin's Estate 165
St Volodymyr 181
Salewicz, Chris 48, 95, 211
Samarkand Hotel 25
Segrave, Elisa 297–301
Selvon, Sam 142
Shakespeare, Nicholas 305–9
shebeens 95
Shervington, André 98
optician 202
pharmacies 202
security 204
Shoe shops
 Emma Hope 120
 Issues 121
 Olivia Morris 82
Silchester baths 164
Silchester Road 164–5
Simon, Peter 51
Sinclair, Iain 144
Soft City 282–7
Songs of Freedom 211
Soper, Lord 163
Soremekun, Sarah 48
Spanish Convent & School 57
Spanish mural 55, 137
Stanley Gardens 20
Stet 20
Story of Notting Dale 245
Sus laws 219, 246

Tabernacle 95, 214
Talsi, Souad 138
A Taste for Death 183
Taxis, 204
Ten Rillington Place 161
Tennant, Emma 49
Thirteen Steps Down 162

Thomas, Polly 216–220
Travel Bookshop (see book shops)
Travers, Martin 101
Treadgold Street 166, 169–170
Tree, Henry Beerbohm 105
Trellick Tower 139–41
A Troubled Area: Notes on Notting Hill 171
Tulloch, Courtney 96, 207
Turquoise Island 102
Tuvey, Sarah 166
Twisaday, Father John 101

UK Investments 250
Underhill, Evelyn 183

Vague, Tom 206–15
Velimirovic, Bishop Nikolai 133
Vernon, Admiral Sir Edward 42
Vestry Works Committee 237
Video shops
 Channel Video Films 154
 Video City 35

Wakeling, Alan & Linda 50
Walker, Reverend Dr Stanley 97, 101, 235, 247
Walker, Wilf 134
Walking Haunted London 14
Walking London 18
Walmer Road 172–3
Walrond, Arthur 172
Ward, Stephen 243
Waugh, Teresa 12
Wells, HG 93
Westbourne Grove 93, 102–3
Westbourne Grove in Wealth, Work and Welfare 108
Westbourne Park Road 53, 94
Westbourne Park Villas 94
Westfield 252
Westway 54
Westway Development Trust 166
Westway Project 133
Westway Stables 166, 193
Whetlor, Sharon 245
Whiteley, William 103
Wills, WH 173
Windrush 96, 239–40, 246
Wiseman, Cardinal 107, 175
Wren College 97

Young, Emily 99, 207

Established in Notting Hill since 1987, the gallery has a regularly changing exhibition programme of art from Britain and abroad. It represents a number of emerging and established contemporary artists and holds an extensive stock of 20th century art.

Public collections that have purchased works from England & Co include Tate, The Imperial War Museum, The Victoria & Albert Museum, Birmingham Museum & Art Gallery, The Museum of London, The National Gallery of Australia, The Arts Council of Great Britain and The British Museum.

England & Co Gallery
216 Westbourne Grove, London W11 2RH
T +44 (0)20 7221 0417 F +44 (0)20 7221 4499
www.englandgallery.com

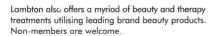
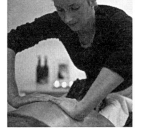

Inside Notting Hill has a personal insight and human touch that guidebooks rarely, if ever, achieve. *The Hill*

Enough instant cognoscenti history to make you feel you've lived there since long before Julia Roberts ever heard of the place. *The Times*

Far from exacerbating the smugness of an area already far too pleased with itself, Davies and Anderson have made a breakthrough in tourist marketing. *Evening Standard*

Wonderful book . . . something I can recommend at last! *Michael Moorcock*

An entertaining read . . . and you won't find a more comprehensive listing of restaurants, shops and bars. *The Observer*

A welcome guide to a glamorous, seedy, funky neighbourhood – the place I love in all her diversity. *Heather Small*

Inside Notting Hill is an illuminating guide to W11 . . . this textual appreciation is the real deal because it was compiled by experts. *The Paddington Times*

There is no better place to live in London and no better guide. *Sebastian Faulks*

In this unique work . . . alongside these short evocative narratives sit the practicalities, the lists of shops, bars, hotels and restaurants. Everything, in fact, both resident and visitor could need. *The Sunday Times*